Sir Walter and Mr. Jones

Walter Hagen, Bobby Jones,
and the
Rise of American Golf

STEPHEN R. LOWE

SLEEPING BEAR PRESS

Sleeping Bear Press
310 North Main Street
P.O. Box 20
Chelsea, MI 48118
www.sleepingbearpress.com

Printed and bound in the United States.

10 9 8 7 6 5 4 3 2

Library of Congress Cataloging-in-Publication Data

Lowe, Stephen R.
Sir Walter and Mr. Jones : Walter Hagen, Bobby Jones,
and the rise of American golf / by Stephen R. Lowe.
p. cm.
ISBN 1-58536-009-0
1. Hagen, Walter, 1892–. 2. Jones, Bobby, 1902–1971.
3. Golfers—United States—Biography. I. Title.
GV964.H3 L69 2000
796.352′0973—dc21
00-009875

For my parents, Stephen R. and Arlene E. Lowe,
and to the memory of my grandmother,
Martha E. Harms (1907–1999)

Preface

Anyone who sets out to write a work of sports history quickly realizes that the literature has been increasingly divided into two groups. The first is scholarly, as well as highly interpretive, sometimes ideological, and ostensibly academic. The second genre is also scholarly but less concerned with academic theory, argument, or analysis than with putting together a well-researched narrative that is detailed, yet still of interest to the lay reader. Put another way, in the first genre, the athlete, event, or sport is often secondary to interpretation, analysis, or theory; in the latter type, the story of the athlete or sporting event is treated as important on its own terms. Each form has its essential audience and purpose, and each its own value and merit. Occasionally, a book transcends the barrier; such works are rare, though, and the majority fall quite neatly into one category or the other.

This book was written from the second approach. My primary purpose was twofold: (1) to produce the first chronological, documented biography of Walter Hagen and Bobby Jones that weaves their stories into one, while (2) highlighting *some* key events that signaled the rise of American golf, especially as a power in international competition.

I confess, then, to possessing no desire to use sports biography as an opportunity to argue class theory; neither is it my purpose to treat Hagen and Jones as reference points for a sweeping history of golf that tracks the sport's evolution as an institution in American life. Nor is it my intent to present my subjects as "symbols for their age." Other historians have made convincing cases for Henry Ford or Charles Lindbergh as symbols for 1920s American society. To offer a precise definition of labels like *modern* and *Victorian*, followed by an effort to fit Hagen into one mold and Jones into the other, would stretch credulity and undermine my purpose.

That said, I have provided some historical context for the lives of Hagen and Jones. Also, a figure does not need to be a "symbol for the age" to provide historical insight. So readers will detect a third, subordinate theme in my work: Hagen and Jones obviously present stark contrasts, and it is necessary to recognize that they represent trends at work in the broader culture, particularly the tension between change and continuity that is omnipresent but that was especially sharp in 1920s America. Hagen, a professional athlete with a northern working-class, immigrant background, was popular because he was unconventional; Jones, an amateur from an old-stock, prominent southern family was adored because he seemed to embody tradition. Yet as knowledgeable readers will quickly point out, it is more complicated than that. Hagen's life also testified to the old-fashioned virtues of hard work, self-confidence, pluck, and the American ideal of success based on ability rather than ancestry. Jones, alongside his manifest respect for tradition, assimilated the rapid change that characterized 1920s America. In those ways, the lives of Hagen and Jones, taken either independently or collectively, offer some view into America's past.

At any rate, Hagen and Jones were golfers, not explorers, business magnates, or political figures. Whether or not their fans wanted to admit it, neither of them would likely have become famous without their extraordinary golf abilities. A discussion of their being representatives of change, continuity, or anything else would be impossible were it not for the place that competitive golf held in their lives. Given that, it seems only right that any biography of Hagen or Jones must be first and last a book about two golfers and the competition in which they engaged.

That raises one other point: a few readers may be put off by the detail of golf tournament coverage or documentation in the form of endnotes. As to the first, I can only admit to considerable pruning that still left tournament material that is, to me at least, necessary. Some golfers may want more, some historians less. Casual readers should feel free to skim over the endnotes; for those who care, I hope that the material therein will be helpful. Endnotes are not particularly common in golf books these days, and I want to thank the folks at Sleeping Bear Press, especially Danny Freels, for understanding the importance of documentation to me and my work.

This book did not originate in a library, archive, or classroom. It began late one afternoon in the summer of 1980, when my father left his study early and took me into the backyard of our Bellefontaine, Ohio, parsonage to give me my first golf lesson. Although the details have faded over the years, I can still recall that the day was sunny and warm, that I learned the difference between the overlapping and interlocking grip, and that the plastic balls were awfully difficult to hit. Mostly, I just remember that my dad set some time aside for me in what was an otherwise ordinary, busy day.

The work started in earnest in the spring of 1995 and since then has been assisted by many generous individuals. Robin R. Moore, Charles C. Alexander, and Sidney L. Matthew deserve special thanks for reading the entire manuscript and making thousands of content and technical improvements. As my sister, Robin had little choice but to help, yet she put in the hours with a smile and always a word of support. Charles Alexander, the country's preeminent baseball biographer, once again proved his friendship by lending his imposing writing skill and knowledge of American history. Sidney L. Matthew—a Jones biographer, collector, filmmaker, all-around expert, and friend—also gave the manuscript a critical examination and provided photographs, clippings, and invaluable encouragement, particularly in the early days of the work. Any remaining shortcomings are, of course, entirely my responsibility.

A number of people helped with the research; some graciously gave me an interview, while others photocopied newspaper coverage, gathered magazine articles, or performed one of another dozen tasks. For interviews, I thank Robert Tyre Jones IV, Lewis Jones Jr., Eugene Branch, Ken Janke, Charles Elliott, Alyce Commisso, Charles Yates, Joseph Peck, Thomas Hancock, and Ernest Fuller. For research assistance, I am grateful to Jerry Harms, Kenneth Moore, Michael Ruhl, Gwynne Chason, Cindy Thompson, Joan Tierney, George Vincent, Professor Mack Moore, Richard Medinis, Peggy Lyons, Mary Barone, and Ross Goodner, who offered encouragement, connected me to Joseph Peck, and permitted me to see his own "Hagen File." I am further indebted to Kay Healey of the Oakland Hills Country Club and Joseph Lee of the Country Club of Rochester, both of whom allowed me access to their clubs' board meeting minutes; to Ruth Ann Williams, who unearthed several key facts of Hagen's genealogy; and to Dennis and Ellen Adams, who shared the property abstract of the old Hagen homestead and took me and my wife on an inspirational walk through Corbett's Glen.

Any significant work of golf literature must rely on the resources of the United States Golf Association's Golf House Library in Far Hills, New Jersey. Its staff, particularly Nancy Stulack and Patty Moran, was a tremendous help. Marge Dewey of the Ralph W. Miller Golf Library provided several dozen photocopied articles on Hagen, and Frances Trimble of the Texas Golf Hall of Fame willingly related her knowledge of the Texas Open. Beverly Bishop Allen, reference archivist at Emory University, also went beyond the call of duty, as did Karen Hewson of the Royal Canadian Golf Association and the staff of the Dwight D. Eisenhower Library in Abilene, Kansas.

I also thank my colleagues and students at Olivet Nazarene University. The team at Benner Library, especially director Kathy Boyens, researcher Mary Jean Johnson, and interlibrary loan tactician Pam Greenlee, tracked down every book and newspaper that I requested. Three of my students, Bjorn Lindren, Elizabeth Smit, and Michael Sczcerba, served as outstanding research assistants. Many of my colleagues displayed enthusiasm for my work, and Kent Olney was a particularly strong encourager. Olivet's dean of academic affairs, Gary Streit, generously dipped into his budget to underwrite much of my travel expense, while my department chair, William Dean, did everything possible in the area of teaching load to facilitate my writing.

Finally, I am most indebted to my family. My parents, Stephen R. and Arlene E. Lowe, taught me the value of sacrifice, education, and Christian faith. It seems that I depend upon them more each passing year. My sister Robin and brother-in-law, Kenneth J. Moore, are always there when I need them.

My wife, Kimberly Kay, once again displayed the quiet strength and patience that make her truly remarkable. In this instance, she listened with interest to my nightly Hagen-Jones updates at the dinner table and spent two summers with me crisscrossing the eastern half of the U.S. by automobile, gathering research and conducting interviews. She forever supports me, and, along with Stephen Robert Jr., and Elizabeth Grace, makes my life happy and complete.

Bobby Jones's grandfather, R.T. Jones, believed that "no man ever accomplishes anything really worthwhile alone. There are always two additional forces at work—other people and Providence." He was right.

Contents

Prologue:

Sarasota, Florida
Winter 1926

Walter Hagen could hear the murmur within the gallery. Several hundred of his fans were nervously whispering to each other, watching his every move, and wondering just how he might reach the sixth green. He crouched low to examine his ball, nestled against the rough. Then he stood up and nonchalantly surveyed the pine tree in front of him; finally, he stepped aside and looked down the fairway to the putting surface. Shielding his eyes from the sun, he said a few words to his caddie and smiled. If his fans were anxious, Hagen seemed calm enough. It was hardly the first time that he had been in a tough spot during a big golf match. He went to his bag, selected and reselected his club, deciding on a midiron, and set up over his shot. The low hum from the gallery faded; all was quiet.

Hagen had indeed been involved in many important events, but this one was different. This time his opponent was the outstanding amateur from Atlanta, Bobby Jones. For years, golf fans and writers had contemplated a head-to-head match between Hagen and Jones. By early 1926 Walter Hagen had collected seven major championship victories: two U.S. Opens, two British Opens, and three match play PGA crowns, most recently in 1924 and 1925. He was considered the nation's top professional and most dangerous match play opponent. Bobby Jones, in a shorter period, had also put together an impressive record in major championships. He had captured the U.S. Open title in 1923 and was runner-up in that event in 1922, 1924, and 1925. He also had won the match play U.S. Amateur title in 1924 and 1925. Many observers regarded him as the finest medal player in the world. In late 1925 the two finally agreed to wage a home-and-home, seventy-two-hole affair that would be contested over consecutive Sundays later that winter. Most sportswriters would call it the

Unofficial World's Championship of Golf; the *Southern Golfer* simply dubbed it "The Battle of the Century."

The fact that it was a test of amateurism against professionalism added excitement to the epic duel. Between 1888 and 1920, amateurs played some of the finest golf in America, winning three out of the four U.S. Opens between 1913 and 1916. Their dominance was easy enough to understand; upper-class amateurs, often of old Anglo-Saxon stock, were the only ones to have access to the nation's finest golf courses, laid out on private clubs. Born into wealth, amateurs had the time to practice and play golf. They were an elite group, and golf authorities recognized them as such, always introducing the amateurs at open events as "Mr. Robert T. Jones" or "Mr. Charles Evans." Professionals, by contrast, were simply announced by their initials and last name, as in "W.C. Hagen." For the pre-World War I generation, golf was an especially exclusive sport. Jones, from a prominent, moderately wealthy family of Welsh descent, was only the latest in a long line of accomplished American amateur golfers.

Hagen, on the other hand, had been reared in an obscure working-class German-immigrant family from Rochester, New York. He was the finest example of the new homebred golf professional who had entered the game through the caddie ranks. Others, most notably Gene Sarazen, had followed Hagen's trail into the sport. So when he competed against Jones in the winter of 1926, it was not just another big event; "Sir Walter" was playing for pride—his own and that of professional athletes everywhere. As Hagen put it, "Winning that challenge match was equally important to both Bobby Jones and to me." Jones confirmed this: "Although this match involved no championship, it did carry a sizable load of prestige, and I wanted badly to win it."[1]

The money seemed almost incidental, but the two camps agreed that gate receipts should be collected and divided between the players, and a businessman friend of Hagen's put up an additional $5,000 prize, which would be given to charity if won by Jones. There was unusual prematch ballyhoo; the *New York World* even reported that in the St. Petersburg area the golf match "eclipsed" the arrival of Babe Ruth's Yankees for baseball spring training. Betting odds had Jones a 3–2 favorite, based on his medal scoring average and on sentimentality. Gould B. Martin of the *Metropolitan Golfer* noted that "the American sporting public is so constituted that its sympathies are always with the amateur—and Bobby

Jones is no mere amateur, he is one of America's best beloved athletes." Hagen took it a bit more personally, feeling that "the public somehow had come to consider the amateurs as the Galahads of golf. While I was a professional—the natural villain of the game."[2]

So it was with much anticipation that approximately 1,200 spectators gathered on Sunday morning, February 28, 1926, at Whitfield Estates, Jones's "home" course in Sarasota, Florida, to witness the first rounds of golf's Battle of the Century. The breeze along the Gulf Coast was balmy and pleasant. The players arrived at the first tee similarly clad in knickers, long ties, and pullover sweaters; Hagen, as he always did to show off his perfectly combed, sleek hair, went hatless, while Jones opted for a rakish fedora. At thirty-three years of age, Hagen was ten years older than his opponent. And at 5' 11" and 180 pounds, Hagen was also considerably bigger than the 5' 8", 165-pound Jones. After an eye-to-eye handshake, Jones lit a cigarette; then Hagen won the honor, and the match got underway.

They seemed nervous in the early holes, but Hagen settled himself more quickly than Jones, particularly on the greens, and grabbed a 3-up lead by the lunch break. Nothing changed through the first five holes of the afternoon. As the pair teed off on the par-4 sixth, Jones planned to build some momentum going into the last nine of the day. Both men hit solid drives, but while Jones's was down the middle, Hagen's bounded toward the rough. Jones hit his approach to within twelve feet of the flag; at that point, with Hagen's ball in a tricky lie behind a pine tree, it looked like a win for the amateur.

Then came the turning point. Jones had watched Hagen crouch low over his ball, examine his lie, the pine tree, and his difficult path to the green. He saw Hagen smile when he went to his bag and talked to his caddie. And, like everyone else, he fixed his gaze on Hagen as he began his backswing. Sir Walter had decided to reach the green by slicing a midiron shot around the tree, but the stroke did not come off as planned. Instead, he completely mishit the ball, topping it so that it took off under the tree branches. To everyone's amazement, the ball carried down the fairway, through a bunker, up a bank that guarded the front of the green, and finally rested about ten feet from the flagstick. Now Jones was under pressure to make his twelve-footer; his putt rimmed the cup but stayed out. Hagen then delicately rolled his ball into the hole for a birdie three, and, rather than trailing by only two, Jones was again 4 down.

Jones later told his biographer O.B. Keeler, "I watched that shot [from the rough], and I said to myself, I'm four down to a man who can miss one like that! When a man misses his drive, and then misses his second shot, and then wins the hole with a birdie— it gets my goat!" It was the kind of performance which caused Leo Diegel to remark, after losing to Hagen in a 1925 PGA match, "I never want to play him again; he's killing me!"[3]

As they made the final turn, Hagen went on the offensive and played for birdies. The strategy paid off, and he started a run that all but finished Jones. The Atlantan played the last nine in a solid 36, but Hagen scorched it in 32 (–4). After the first day, Hagen was 8 up.[4]

Although they were only at the halfway mark, during the intervening week dopesters began writing concluding analyses. Martin believed that the first half of the match had taught so-called golf experts an important lesson: "Professional golfers are far better than amateurs, and especially is Hagen the best of the pros, better than Jones, the best of the amateurs." Most commentators were more restrained, but no one suggested, at least in print, that Jones had a chance to come back the following Sunday at Hagen's Pasadena Golf Club in St. Petersburg.

Apparently, many golf fans refused to give up on Jones; on March 7 a gallery nearly twice the size of the previous Sunday's gathered at Pasadena to witness the last rounds. After halving (or tying) the first hole, Jones must have felt that fate was still against him, because he lost the second in a most demoralizing fashion when Hagen dropped a putt of nearly sixty feet to go 9 up. Despite his lead, Sir Walter kept his "fighting mask" on all day, playing as though he was behind. He finished the third round 12 up, with a medal score of 69 (–3) to Jones's 73. Hagen's total provided the basis for a famous joke that "Walter had gone around in 69 strokes and Bobby in 69 cigarettes."[5]

When they started the fourth and final 18, the only uncertainty was how soon the end would come. They approached the seventh (61st) hole with Hagen dormie 12. In other words, Hagen could not lose in regulation, and in order to win, Jones would now have to take the final twelve holes of the contest—he could not afford to halve even one of them. Both men made the fringe of the par 4 green in two. Jones's fans roared when he sank his chip shot for a

Jones putting in the final rounds of the Battle of the Century. Apparently unconcerned, Hagen looks the other way, quietly conversing on the fringe. Notice also that Hagen's ball remains on the green.
Courtesy: Western Golf Association

birdie, but Hagen quickly silenced them, also chipping in his third for a halve and the victory. Although the two played out the last eleven holes to please the paying spectators, their "Battle of the Century" was over. It had not been the tension-filled wire-to-wire match that many had hoped it would be. Rather, Hagen had over-whelmed Jones, 12 and 11. Hagen later called it "my greatest thrill in golf." To Jones, it represented a "glorious licking . . . far and away the most complete" defeat he ever experienced in match play.

By that point in his career, Jones's behavior in defeat was as endearing as in victory, and in this "severe drubbing" he was at his best. Someone suggested that the gate receipts should be given to a charity, but Jones countered that Hagen should keep all of the money. Hagen did take the Whitfield Estate receipts, about $1,800, as well as the $5,000 prize, but he gave away the Pasadena earnings—more than $5,000—to the St. Petersburg Hospital. The champion still cleared $6,800, the largest purse in the history of golf up to that time. Hagen also gave Jones a handsome pair of cuff links to thank him for the match. He said in the closing ceremony, "Jones realizes that a professional makes his living out of the game . . . . I want the world to know that I appreciate his attitude and that I consider his action the most generous in the history of American sport."

The USGA agreed with Hagen's last point; in fact, it thought Jones too generous and soon after prohibited any more exhibitions involving amateurs, unless all of the money was given to charity. That upset golf fans who wanted a quick rematch. Such an event never materialized, though, and there would be only one Hagen-Jones Battle of the Century.[6]

Golf writers, historians, and fans ever since have debated the meaning of the 1926 Unofficial World's Championship of Golf. Most of the discussion has centered on the lopsided outcome. Jones's supporters have refused to believe that it was anything other than an anomaly and that their man was still the best of his day, if not the best ever. They have argued simply that he had been off his game, while Hagen had overachieved. To Hagen's fans, such observations are little more than excuses. Sir Walter was the best golfer of the period, and he had proved it once again. But the Hagen-Jones Battle of the Century contains rich significance besides the un-resolvable, if enjoyable, debate over each player's competitive greatness; indeed, the contest brought together two of the most popular, yet contrastable athletes of the 1920s.[7]

Although many Americans have heard of Bobby Jones through the Masters tournament he cofounded, not nearly as many recognize the name of Walter Hagen. That is puzzling, because his competitive record is among the best ever. During the period from 1914 to 1932, Hagen won eleven of the currently designated major championships: two U.S. Opens, four British Opens, and five match-play PGA titles (four in a row from 1924 to 1927). In 1922 he became the first American-born golfer to win the British Open. Hagen also won five Western Opens, giving him a total of sixteen contemporary major titles. His record in the majors has been exceeded only by Bobby Jones (unless one counts Hagen's Western titles), and, more recently, by Jack Nicklaus. In addition to his major championships, Hagen recorded some thirty other tournament victories in his career, including three Metropolitan Opens and three North and South Opens. Because he was so tough in match play, Hagen was named the captain of the first United States Ryder Cup teams. Sportswriter Al Laney concluded, "all of us who wrote golf in Hagen's day made too much of his flamboyant showmanship [and] not nearly enough of his golf."[8]

Nonetheless, as Laney suggests, Hagen's importance goes beyond his statistical golf record. Hagen, in many ways fulfilling the popular image of the 1920s, was an original, colorful figure and did much to popularize the game. According to Herbert Warren Wind, Sir Walter was "a born showman," who "loved the big gesture" and attracted thousands of people to tournaments with his knack for the spectacular in behavior and dress. In the spring of 1925, Keeler described him as "the leading showman of sport today," characterizing Hagen's charisma as an "instinctive, natural ebullition," unseen since the days of the great prizefighter John L. Sullivan. Laney remembered that Hagen's "mere arrival on the scene did something, caused something to happen. His every appearance seemed to be accompanied by the figurative blaring of trumpets and a metaphorical waving of banners, and Walter was perfectly conscious at all times of his role as a performer."[9]

In addition, analysts noted that even Hagen's swing was original. It was obvious to golf experts that he had played a lot of baseball in his youth; his stance was wide, his swing plane relatively flat, and he exaggerated his weight shift, creating a "lurching" motion at the point of impact. Hagen was "self-taught and not in the slightest measure a copyist or a patternist," observed H.B. Martin. In a piece entitled "What Makes Hagen a Great Player?" golf writer William Richardson argued that Hagen's greatest asset was not his swing but rather his "head." Others, especially Jones, possessed a more artistic, technically sound swing, but no one surpassed Hagen's mental toughness or tactical skill. Highlighting Sir Walter's ability to win, British golf writer Arthur Croome wrote that Hagen "makes more bad shots in a single season than Harry Vardon [a British golfer who helped pioneer the game in America] did during the whole period 1890–1914. But he beats more immaculate golfers because three of 'those' and one of 'them' count four, and he knows it." On the course, Hagen was a pure utilitarian; he cared far less about what his swing looked like than about whether he won or lost, and he always played to win. Robert

Signature Hagen follow through, complete with wide stance,
weight leaning forward, and hands low at the finish,
the result of a flat swing, circa 1920.
Courtesy: Sidney L. Matthew Collection

Harlow, Hagen's close friend and manager, believed that "if Walter got into a game of tiddledywinks with a couple of kids on the nursery floor, he would try as hard to beat them as he did to win the British Open championship."[10]

Hagen was unconventional off the course as well; anecdotes about his carefree lifestyle are legion. Wind wrote that Hagen drank "what would have been for other people excessive quantities of liquor. . . . [He] broke eleven of the Ten Commandments and kept on going." Hagen could, apparently, party all night, show up at the locker room the following morning to prepare for a tournament, and ask his competitors: "Well, who is going to be second?" Much of this is legend. Actually, Hagen took decent care of himself during his playing days and drank far less than was commonly believed. At a party, Hagen would often ask the bartender for a ginger ale, which he would nurse as if it were a cocktail, or he might merely walk around with a drink, sipping and then discarding it as inconspicuously as possible. "I could make one highball last longer in my own glass than any Scotchman ever born," Hagen remembered. As for staying up all night, he once admitted that he usually had little choice; that is, he could not always sleep before big competitions. So Hagen was not quite as indulgent or cool as everyone assumed.[11]

But if Hagen's drinking has been exaggerated, the stories concerning his womanizing are probably all true. He was certainly popular and undisciplined with female fans, often finding an evening's companionship within his gallery. "I met beautiful and charming women all over the world," bragged Hagen. "A roving eye was my Geiger counter; my claim was staked with a devoted appreciation of their potentials and ability to make my travels and my leisure moments more enjoyable." According to one story, Hagen was introduced to Ernestine Schumann-Heink, famous contralto of the Metropolitan Opera. Although he had never heard of her, he took one look at her "ample bosom," and reputedly said, "My dear, did you ever stop to think what a lovely bunker you would make?" Extended exhibition tours with "roving eyes" as "Geiger counters" did little for Hagen's family life; during a period in which divorce was still relatively uncommon, he was married and divorced twice.[12]

Yet Hagen displayed other notable qualities, besides his unconformable behavior. It seems that early in his career he was a modest, even unassuming individual, but once established, he was rarely humble and often cocky to the point of arrogance. J.H. Taylor believed, however, that Hagen's showmanship was "but a pose designed to impress and to conceal real anxieties." Given his modest roots and limited formal education, Hagen must have occasionally felt out of place, even insecure, in the culture of golf. Whatever the motive, Hagen did exude confidence. Recalling his first experience with Hagen, Croome wrote: "It was at once borne in on me that here was a man who would not fail through excess of modesty." But while sometimes appearing arrogant and materialistic, Hagen also impressed people with his generosity, playing many matches for charity and giving away money to caddies, friends, and hospitals, as in the Jones match. And, according to H.B. Martin, Hagen's two outstanding characteristics were his refusal to court sympathy or self-pity and his utter disregard for making an alibi—whatever the breaks might be. Those rather traditional attitudes endeared him to competitors, who generally admired and respected Hagen, in spite of his showmanship. "I love to play with Walter," Jones declared. "He goes along chin up, smiling away; never grousing about his luck, playing the ball as he finds it. He can come nearer beating the luck itself than anybody I know."[13]

Hagen is also significant because his career signaled a new stage in the evolution of his sport. He is regarded as the country's first professional touring golfer; he was the first golf professional to abandon the traditional role of giving lessons and selling equipment for a country club, showing that one could make a comfortable living by playing in tournaments and exhibition matches. Other working class youths had risen to fame and fortune through baseball or prizefighting, but not in the exclusive sport of golf. During the 1920s, Hagen's annual income ranged from $45,000 to $75,000, depending on his standing. In retirement, he carried the distinction of being the first golfer to earn a million dollars. In an age that idealized amateurism, when "professionals" in sports were often frowned upon as common and crass, Sir Walter offered class (his comments to Ms. Schumann-Heink notwithstanding) and commanded respect. He was suave, debonair, and of course, always impeccably dressed. Grantland Rice concluded that, "Hagen, by his tact, deportment, style, and over-all color, did for the professional golfer what Babe Ruth did for the professional ball player."[14]

Sir Walter also challenged the status quo by leading several "rebellions" at the finest golf courses around the world, helping to gain equal treatment and accommodations at clubhouses for both amateurs and professionals. In 1920, for example, Hagen attempted to break down social barriers at clubhouses in Great Britain, where upper-class amateur prejudices toward professionals remained strongest. Upon arriving in England to play in his first British Open, he learned that professionals were prohibited from entering the clubhouse at Deal. So Hagen ordered his chauffeur to park his long, luxurious Austin-Daimler automobile in front of the clubhouse and proceeded to use it throughout the tournament as a sort of locker room. The club secretary asked Hagen to park the car behind the building, but Hagen politely said no. He repeated similar antics at other prestigious British clubs. Although the barriers to professionals did not collapse immediately, they did eventually, and Hagen is justly credited with assisting the process.

Hagen, therefore, represented a curious character and a significant athletic figure. Golf's leading showman and one of its greatest athletes, he was a confident and feared competitor, who was flamboyant, controversial, and original, as well as gregarious, respected, generous, and, within his sport, egalitarian. Much of his irreverent image and lifestyle reflected the so-called "roaring" side of American society in the 1920s. "In Hagen you have the irresponsible playboy of golf, and at the same time a keen and determined competitor," wrote Rice in 1930. Chick Evans, an outstanding American amateur, said of Hagen, "he is in golf to live, not to make a living." Actually, Hagen was in the game to do both. Jones may have put it best when he reflected on Hagen, "He wasn't called Sir Walter for nothing."[15]

As for Bobby Jones, on and, to a lesser degree, off the course, he represented what Hagen did not—continuity and tradition. "Mr. Jones" was unlike Sir Walter except in his achievements on the course. Jones's record is equally impressive. He won his first competitive tournament at the age of nine when he took the 1911 East Lake Jr. Championship in Atlanta. "A pink-cheeked, round-faced, blue-eyed boy," Little Bob splashed onto the national scene in 1916 with his performance in the U.S. Amateur Championship at the Merion Cricket Club in Philadelphia, where he became an instant star, the game's child prodigy.

Observers admired Jones's fluid swing and the studiousness with which he approached the game. He was often described as a methodical "student of good form." "Golf's Great Stylist," he made the game look easy, "with scarcely a blemish in a swing that appeared to onlookers as absolutely perfect." Whereas Hagen "swayed" or lunged at the ball during his swing, Jones had a "classic" and "flawless" swing, marked by "perfect balance," an "orthodox" narrow stance, and a "rhythm" that finished with a "statuesque" follow through. As one golf writer observed, Jones moved "up and down, instead of to and fro." British amateur E.W.E. Holderness noted that Jones's swing "just flows sweetly and smoothly from start to finish" and concluded that Jones was the natural heir to golf's classicist, Harry Vardon. George Duncan, a prominent British professional, considered him an "artist who is never satisfied with anything less than perfection." Yet in the finest tradition of English amateurism, Jones was not a "fanatic" of the game who hit practice balls for hours on end; rather, to him golf was "a game of character" in which "preparing himself was much more important than preparing his shots." The Atlantan even looked old-fashioned on the course; in place of Hagen's dazzling, pin-striped wardrobe, Jones wore drab or navy blue knickers.[16]

Despite his natural ability, Jones took longer than expected to win a major title, and, during the early years of his career, he developed a reputation as a spoiled hothead. "The one fault that [Jones] had to conquer was the over-eagerness and the fiery impatience of youth," concluded Grantland Rice. Eventually, however, he "curbed his temper" and, like a model Victorian, learned from his shortcomings. But it was never quite as simple as his admirers made it seem. In the spring of 1930 Jones admitted, "I've never gotten rid of my temper. I still get as mad as blazes, but I don't show it; I suppress it."[17]

As age and experience had their influence, Jones finally broke through in 1923 to begin an outstanding run in the majors that included thirteen titles before his retirement in 1930 at the age of twenty-eight. In all, Jones won three British Opens, one British Amateur, four U.S. Opens, and five U.S. Amateur titles, including the Grand Slam (all four of those titles) in 1930. Together with Hagen, he promoted international competition by playing on and captaining Walker Cup teams (the forerunner and amateur counterpart to the Ryder Cup).

But apart from their competitive records and popularity, Jones and Hagen had little in common. Jones was blessed with many, if not all, of the advantages a young man could hope for in 1920s America. The son of an Atlanta lawyer, Jones could afford to play the game as an amateur, a luxury denied Hagen; as the child of a

Classic Jones, circa 1930. Note the relatively narrow stance, long, upright follow through, and, most telling, hands high and pointing the club's head toward the ground.
Courtesy: Dave Clark

club member, Jones took the traditional route into the sport. Jones also had the time and resources to acquire a formal education. While Hagen had dropped out of school in the middle grades, Jones provided an admirable example of how one could blend education and athletics. Commentators highlighted his formal education and interest in literature and classical music. Rice informed fans, "In starting for a championship [Jones] might be found with a Latin book or a calculus treatise, completely engrossed, with all thought of golf eliminated until he reached the scene of battle." Of course it was not all classical literature for Jones; like Hagen, he loved billiards, hunting, and, especially, fishing.

Pastimes aside, Jones also developed a personal life that was very different from Hagen's. A model of decorum off the course, he stated that his priorities were family first, vocation second, and golf third, with the game never being a life unto itself. A careful examination of his life reveals that Jones was capable of mixing those priorities, especially golf and vocation, but he certainly prized and protected his wife and children, a Victorian ideal passed on to him by both his father and grandfather. Generally speaking, he lived a disciplined, humble, and orderly life. Although Jones enjoyed a good joke and a few drinks with friends, he was never accused of being raucous.[18]

Interestingly, while many Americans found Sir Walter an alluring figure, they simply adored Bobby Jones. After winning the 1926 and 1930 British Opens, Jones received two of the largest New York ticker-tape parades bestowed on any person, much less an athlete. Upon his retirement, *Golfers Magazine* declared Jones "the greatest sports idol the world has ever known; more loved and admired than a Cobb, Dempsey, Ruth, or Tilden."

Most looked up to Jones because he was, supposedly, a "simon-pure" amateur. "He is the most popular champion in any sport because he is an amateur to the marrow, a sportsman at all times, a lover of the game for itself and not the profit to be made from it," wrote one commentator. H.B. Martin said of Jones, "never was there an athlete who imbued a truer sense of amateurism . . . who steadfastly refused to listen to tempting offers to join the professional ranks."[19]

Yet no one could be truly "simon-pure," and, inevitably, throughout his life Jones profited from golf. Indeed, the irony is that in the long run Jones may have made more money from golf by remaining an amateur than he ever would have made if he had played as a professional. In the 1920s, though, he entered only a handful of professional tournaments and never accepted prize money, ignoring the "golden glow" of profit. For this, Americans gave Jones their undying loyalty and respect. Even when Jones retired in 1930 and "cashed in" to do a series of golf instructional films, observers thought him "wise" because he "chose the proper moment for quitting," having "won everything there is to win" and having a "growing family" to look after. The fact that the films were "educational" lent an amateur flavor to his first major act of commercialism. In sum, to his legions of admirers, Jones was the embodiment of amateurism; actually, he, like everyone else, wrestled with the definition and role of the amateur athlete in the midst of emerging professionalism in sports. Still, all of this was in stark contrast to Hagen's frankly commercial exploits.[20]

Jones was also adored because he seemed to possess the finest personal characteristics. While Hagen was the "cocky showman," Jones was most often perceived as "modest" and "sportsmanlike." William Richardson succinctly remarked, "Bobby is modesty personified." In his diatribe on modern sports, Paul Gallico admitted that Jones was the "One Hero" who "would stand up in every way as a gentleman as well as a celebrity . . . and who never once . . . has let me down in my estimate of him." When Jones won the 1926 British Open, the *Times* of London declared that "no more modest or generous golfer" had ever won the event. The same newspaper compared Jones's retirement to that of George Washington, saying both left the stage "with the blessings" of their "fellow citizens." In the summer of 1930, the Catholic periodical *Commonweal* noted that, "Bobby is widely loved because he is genuinely modest, because he mingles a boyish intentness with the artist's grim obsession with perfection, [and] because he is a model of sportsmanship." Britain's *Golf Monthly* concluded that "the significance of Mr. Jones" was his "character," which "captured the hearts of the golfers of two hemispheres" through "modesty and the sincerity of a nature as honest as the sunlight."[21]

Though a feared competitor, Jones was considerate and kind to his opponents. No one accused him of gamesmanship as he attacked "Old Man Par" instead of his competition. Gallico believed that "Jones could not even work up a grudge against an opponent. His sole enemies were himself and the landscape." Neither did he pursue victory at any price, and he sincerely believed that there were more important things than winning; Jones became famous for calling rules violations and penalties on himself, even while it cost him a major tournament.[22]

But if Jones's public life was nearly a perfect reflection of the finest traditional values, his private views were not always so admirable and were certainly more complex. For example, although he never identified with the dark, intolerant defense of tradition in the 1920s, Jones was characteristically a traditionalist on social questions. On the individual level he was kind and considerate with everyone, regardless of skin color. Unlike the other great Georgian athlete of the early twentieth century, Ty Cobb, there were no incidents of hatred or violence toward blacks in Jones's life. On the public level, though, he never supported progressive civil rights policies and apparently stood by idly while his Masters tournament became a focal point for charges of racism in golf.[23]

Moreover, during competition he was never as calm and collected on the course as he appeared to be. On one occasion he confessed, "People may get the impression that I find it easy to go on playing golf day after day without breaking down. But actually it is really hard work and . . . I [often] feel a bundle of nerves."[24]

In other ways, Jones simply broke from tradition, manifesting modern traits; for instance, he lacked a strong sense of Protestant religious piety. Although reared a Southern Baptist, he married a devout Roman Catholic, permitted his children to be raised Catholic, and was not much concerned with religious conduct or issues. He also cursed and smoked excessively. The "69 cigarettes" quip was only a slight exaggeration, and he regularly enjoyed a glass of corn whiskey, even if it meant breaking the law in the era of Prohibition, which, despite popular misconception, not everyone did. Finally, Jones lived in Atlanta, the city that most embodied the New South, and that also symbolized his familiarity with change and progress. Nonetheless, sportswriters portrayed Jones as the classic southern gentleman, and for the most part, this popular perception had deep roots in reality.[25]

In sum, during the period 1914–1930 Walter Hagen and Bobby Jones dominated golf. The publicity they generated contributed much to the transformation of American golf from an elite pastime to a popular spectator sport, and together they led the way in establishing the U.S. as an international golf powerhouse. Both were outstanding sports heroes, yet their backgrounds, personalities, and public images were remarkably different—even antithetical. Sir Walter and Mr. Jones are revealing enough as individuals, but taken together they provide comparisons and contrasts that illuminate a pivotal period in the history of golf and American society. Beyond that, their stories are some of the most exciting and enjoyable in all of sports, and are simply worth remembering.[26]

Chapter 1

Beginnings: 1888–1912

John Reid was anxious. Although a middle-aged, successful, wealthy New York executive, in the winter of 1888 he felt like a kid. Northern children of all ages, backgrounds, and varying degrees of coordination experience an annual frustration some time in late January. To put it simply, they want to go outside and play. In that respect, life was no different in the late nineteenth century; hundreds of thousands of American boys, and men, were anticipating the arrival of spring and the chance to once again gather on sandlots for a game of ball. Reid's frustration, however, was a bit more original.

The previous fall his friend Robert Lockhardt had visited their hometown of Dunfermline, Scotland. While across the Atlantic, Lockhardt stopped at the golf shop of the legendary Tom Morris Sr. and ordered a basic set of golf clubs that included three woods, three irons, a putter, and a couple dozen gutta-percha balls. The golf equipment was waiting for him when he returned to his home in New York City. The weather was still mild, so he hit some balls in an open area on what was then Seventy-Second Street. He knew Reid was waiting to try it out too, but by the time he got the equipment to his friend, the weather had turned cold. So Reid waited into 1888 for a chance to slice a golf ball. The opportunity came on February 22, a bit earlier than one might expect in New York. The air was unseasonably warm when Reid took a few of his friends to a nearby cow pasture. They laid out three primitive, short holes and, because they had only one set of clubs, Reid and John Upham played a match while the other half dozen made up an interested gallery. No one recorded the outcome, but the experience was so much fun that Reid's friends sent away to Scotland for their own equipment and reconvened at the cow pasture whenever the weather allowed, which by late March was nearly every day.

In April the informal golf club transplanted its course to a bigger cow pasture at the northeast corner of Broadway and Shonnard Place in the town of Yonkers. They played there for the rest of the summer. By the time the cold and snow returned, Reid and his friends were addicts. In fact, they were so caught up in the sport that they decided to organize a golf club. On November 14, 1888, the men gathered at Reid's house and, following a hearty meal, elected Reid president, John Upham secretary-treasurer, and the other three present—Harry Holbrook, Kingman H. Putnam, and Henry Tallmadge—the board of governors. Robert Lockhardt became the club's first member. Finally, abandoning all pretense at creativity, the group named their club St. Andrew's. Quaintly and efficiently, the sport of golf had come to America to stay.[1]

Of course no American sport's origin, except possibly that of basketball, is quite that simple. Golf has an interesting, complex, and somewhat obscure past. No one is sure where the game originated, but most think that it was either in Holland or Scotland. What is known is that the Scots played a version of the contemporary game as early as 1457 and were going around the old course at St. Andrews by 1552. So, wherever it originated, the sport developed in Scotland.

For several hundred years the game was played little outside of Scotland. Indeed, golf gained prominence in England only around 1870, although it was introduced there about 1603. And there is some controversy as to when and where Americans first played the sport. Robert Lockhardt was certainly not the first to strike a golf ball "over here." There is evidence that colonial New Yorkers played a variation of the game in the middle 1600s. The sport also had a brief, limited life in Georgia and South Carolina in the early national period. But golf did not put down roots and Americans played little of it throughout most of the 1800s. Still, by the late nineteenth century a number of cities would claim to be the birthplace of American golf: Philadelphia, Pennsylvania; White Sulphur Springs, West Virginia; and Burlington, Iowa. Golf was played in these and probably other cities before New York, but in each case the game did not survive, and no lasting clubs were established. Then came Lockhardt, Reid, and St. Andrew's, Yonkers; other permanent clubs soon followed.

Throughout the next decade golf became an established sport in the U.S. In 1891 the members of Shinnecock Hills, the first legally incorporated golf club, financed a twelve-hole course accompanied by the country's first clubhouse. By 1892 the wealthy Four Hundred played on a dozen courses laid out mostly on the periphery of northeastern cities, but also in such places as Baltimore, Maryland and Chicago, Illinois. As of 1895 there were more than fifty golf clubs across the country, and the number increased dramatically. In December 1895 the *New York Times* concluded that, "in the history of American field sports [no] outdoor pastime [had] developed and attained such popularity in a comparatively short period of time as the game of golf." At the turn of the century, the total number of golf courses reached 1,040, and there was at least one in every state of the Union.

It soon became clear that the sport needed an officially organized authority. In late 1894 representatives from the leading clubs formed the United States Golf Association, a national governing body for the sport charged with codifying and enforcing rules, holding national championships for amateurs and professionals, and generally promoting the interests of the game. In 1895, the USGA sponsored the first national open, amateur, and women's amateur events. Powerful regional organizations, such as the Metropolitan Golf Association and the Western Golf Association, formed as well to influence the governing of the game and hold regional amateur and open competitions.

By 1900, the summer schedule included a handful of local, regional, and national competitions for amateurs and professionals who were fortunate enough to have access to the game. Most Americans were not so fortunate. In the summer of 1895, New York City underwrote the first public course, a nine-hole layout in Van Cortland Park. But the vast majority of new golf courses were located on private, exclusive country clubs, which antedated the introduction of golf and for nearly a decade had served as recreational resorts for the nation's elite. For example, at The Country Club in Boston, established in 1882, golf was merely an addition to polo, fox hunting, and horse racing. In 1898, British golf historian Garden Smith observed, "Golf in the United States is the amusement of the well-to-do classes alone. The poor man has no place as yet among American golfers and the sport remains as distinctly exclusive as is polo or yachting." Thus, despite the enthusiasm of the *New York Times*, the game's popularity was limited. Golf equipment was expensive, a round was time-consuming, and courses were mostly inaccessible, except for those with the wherewithal to pay club dues.[2]

On top of that, golf seemed the ultimate European effeminate pastime. In 1900, most people believed that real Americans played baseball or watched the most manly of sports, prizefighting. When William Howard Taft became interested in golf, his friend Theodore Roosevelt warned him of its political dangers: "I myself play tennis, but the game is a little more familiar; besides, you never saw a photograph of me playing tennis. I am careful about that; photographs on horseback, yes; tennis, no. And golf is fatal." For the most part, Roosevelt was correct. Golf was not a game played, watched, or admired by the masses. The fact that the obese and otherwise sedentary Taft played probably reinforced many prejudices concerning golf.[3]

As late as 1912, Grantland Rice failed to get permission from his sports editor, Francis Albertanti, to cover golf for the *New York Evening Mail*. Albertanti was from the lower East Side; his expertise was in writing about boxing. When the paper's managing editor, Theophilus England Niles, asked Albertanti why golf was not receiving any coverage, the sports editor replied, "Golf? What's golf?" "Why it's a game—an important game," Niles answered, "A lot of big businessmen are playing it." "Then put it on the financial page," grumbled the sports editor. Despite such prejudices in the period from 1888 to 1913, golf built a secure foundation in American life, albeit as an exclusive entity which interested only a few thousand Americans. It was in this private period of the sport that Walter Hagen and Bobby Jones were born and reared. Indeed, by just taking up and playing golf, Hagen and Jones were extraordinary.[4]

If Walter Hagen was extraordinary for his choice of sports, he seemed typical in most other ways, including his family background. Census and property records indicate that it was about 1855 when Walter's grandfather, Joseph Hagen, emigrated from Germany to the U.S. He probably entered the country through New York City and followed the most popular path from that point, traveling up the Hudson River to Albany and taking the Erie Canal west to Rochester. Located in Monroe County on the Genesee River, Rochester began as a flour mill town, but with the completion of

the Erie Canal in 1825, the city had become an important commercial and transportation link between the northeast and west.
From 1840 to 1860 thousands of immigrants, mostly from southern Ireland and Germany, poured into the U.S. through New York
City to Albany and into Rochester. For most, Rochester was a
"way station" on the path to the cities and countryside of Ohio,
Michigan, Indiana, Illinois, and Wisconsin. But for a minority, including Joseph Hagen, Monroe County became home.[5]

It is likely no one will ever know just why Joseph Hagen settled
in Monroe County, but it was probably because of the county's
increasingly large German-Presbyterian population and its economic opportunities. In 1855 Rochester was the seventeenth largest city in the U.S. Its foreign-born made up 44% of the total
population, which was more than 43,000. The Irish, numbering a
little more than 7,000, were the largest foreign-born group in Rochester, but Germans were challenging them with 6,554 residents,
and soon they would surpass the Irish to become the largest ethnic group in the city.

The majority of German immigrants found work in the burgeoning shoe and clothing industries. Joseph Hagen may have taken
a job in one of these businesses. He might also have worked for
the Canal, as a farm hand, or at one of the many flour and lumber
mills in the area. It is likely, though, that before too long he made
his way into the railroad industry. By 1860 the railroad was sup-
planting the Erie Canal as the most important mode of transportation to and from Rochester. The completion of a suspension
bridge over the Niagara in 1855 permitted the connection of the
New York Central Railroad with the Great Western Railroad in
Canada, and transformed Rochester into an important railroad
center where freight trains from eastern cities were "reassembled"
before going to Buffalo, Cleveland, Detroit, Chicago, Niagara, or
the Northwest. The Pennsylvania Railroad arrived about the same
time as Joseph Hagen and provided stiff competition for the New
York Central. By the early 1860s an average of sixty trains left
Rochester every day. Of course the major trunk lines gave birth,
or at least new life, to numerous regional and local feeder lines,
and Rochester, like every other northern urban center in the second half of the nineteenth century, developed its economy around
the railroad.

Wherever Joseph Hagen worked, he had settled in Brighton by
1866. Organized in 1814, Brighton was a small town of about

3,000 located along the southeastern border of Rochester. Joseph
and his wife, Mary, also a German immigrant, lived on a few acres
of land along Allen's Creek. Across the creek was a hill that the
trains traveled along and beyond that was a beautiful twenty-acre
glen, owned and used first by William Stoneburner and later by
Patrick Corbett to grow vegetables. The Hagens cultivated a small
garden on their land as well. Obtaining food became increasingly
important after Mary Hagen bore her husband four boys, Henry,
Joseph, George, and William, and two daughters named Emma
and Mary.

William Hagen was born in 1860. No doubt as a youth he fished
in Allen's Creek and played ball, but in the period before "adoles-
cence" developed a culture of its own, William probably worked
more than anything else. Like his father, he worked with his hands
as a manual laborer. He eventually became a millwright and took a
job as a blacksmith in the railroad car shops of East Rochester, a
growing economic satellite of Rochester located just north of
Brighton. Also like his father, William was representative of Monroe County's citizenry. By 1875, when William was fifteen and
planning a life and family of his own, Rochester's foreign-born
population had declined to 33% of the total. Yet, it was young
people such as William, the children of immigrants, who were increasing the number of natives. Moreover, Germans now represented the largest ethnic group in the Rochester area. So, as a
German-Presbyterian son of immigrants from the working class
of a large northern city, William Hagen was about as ordinary as
was possible in 1880.

In 1884 Joseph and Mary Hagen sold a plot of their land to
William for $600. He constructed a small two-story house on the
bank of the creek and next door to his parents' home. William may
have acquired the land and built the house in order to prepare for
his own family, because soon thereafter he married a German immigrant named Louise Balko. By 1891 the couple had a daughter,
Lottie.

Then on December 21, 1892, Louise gave birth to Walter on
the "homestead" along Allen's Creek, probably in one of the two
small upstairs bedrooms. The following April 23, William and Louise
Hagen took their son to the Third Presbyterian Church in Rochester, where Pastor Albert Zeller baptized him Walter Martin Christian Hagen. Walter was followed by three more daughters, Freda,
Cora, and the baby of the family, Mabel. Actually, it is not unrea-

The Hagen homestead in Corbett's Glen, circa 1920, where
Walter Hagen was born and raised. Allen's Creek can be
seen in the foreground. Courtesy: Dennis Adams

sonable to conclude that Walter was the real "baby" of the family,
given that he was the only boy surrounded by four sisters and
undoubtedly received special attention from both parents.[6]

Hagen included precious little about his boyhood and family
life in his autobiography. He described his parents as "thrifty" and
recalled that the family "got along fine on the eighteen dollars a
week" his father earned in the car shops of East Rochester. The
three things that impressed him most about his father were his
stature, the size of his hands, and his stubbornness. William Hagen
was not a tall man, standing about 5' 8", but he did have the large,
powerful hands of a blacksmith. His hair was brown, and he wore
a moustache. Walter did not inherit his father's physique or looks,
but rather those of the men in his mother's family. At 5' 11", Louise
towered over William, at least physically. Walter remembered her
as a loving, even somewhat permissive mother. As a teenager,
Walter secretly spent much of his caddie savings on a dilapidated
bright red Indian motorcycle, seemingly not the sort of thing to
make "thrifty" working class parents smile. Yet when Louise Hagen

found out, Walter recalled that his mother simply said, "I've been wishing you could have one of those things . . . now you can have a lot of fun." In sum, there is no evidence of anything dramatic in Walter Hagen's childhood and rearing. Walter's father did not abuse him, as did the father of the great baseball player and manager John McGraw, nor was he an "incorrigible" raised in a Catholic boys' school, as was Babe Ruth. If they were not as affectionate as most parents are today, it seems that William and Louise Hagen genuinely cared for their children.[7]

Young Walter was like most other boys of his day and socioeconomic background; he loved athletics, especially baseball and basketball, and he spent the long Rochester winters ice skating or sledding with his sisters. Living near Allen's Creek and having access to Corbett's Glen, Walter developed a lifelong passion for fishing and the outdoors. He had little use for the classroom and dropped out of school when he was twelve. He also developed an early interest in golf. In 1924, Hagen wrote that he was introduced to the game in late 1895 when he was not yet four years old. His father had a Scottish friend who used to stop by the house regularly for "an evening's chat." As Hagen remembered, the Scotsman always carried a golf club with him and used it for a cane or, if necessary, protection. When the toddler showed some interest in the club, the man returned the next evening with a sawed-off mashie (five-iron) and gave Hagen his first golf lesson, substituting a baseball for a golf ball so that the little boy would have a better chance of making contact. Hagen remembered the experience vividly, including the "gleam" in the Scotsman's eye as he struggled to swing the club.[8]

Coincidentally, on New Year's Day of that same year, the wealthiest sportsmen of Rochester had organized a country club; in 1896 they laid out a nine-hole golf course along Brighton Avenue. The club was within comfortable walking distance of the Hagen property, but even if he so desired (and there is no evidence that he did), William was in no position to apply for membership. He was a friend, however, of Bill Lambert, the caddie master, and in the summer of 1900, when Walter was seven years old, Lambert gave him a job as a caddie. Had the Country Club of Rochester been located anywhere else, even outside of walking distance from Corbett's Glen, it is unlikely that the persona of "Sir Walter" would ever have been born. As it was, though, Hagen liked sports, and the Country Club was convenient. For a young boy looking to satisfy an appetite for ice cream and baseball equipment, the job was vital. "We had a simple comfortable home and good plain food but there wasn't much left over for extras," Hagen recalled. "That caddie job meant the extras for me."

Every summer after 1900 Hagen spent a lot of time around a golf course, carrying the clubs of wealthy members for a few nickels and hoping for a tip. It could be a pressure-filled task for a young lad, but Hagen soon became proficient. Besides toting clubs, his job entailed keeping a sharp eye on drives, finding balls hit into the rough (an especially weighty responsibility inasmuch as lost balls became stroke penalties which might become lost money bet in friendly matches), and cleaning the member's equipment after the round. Throughout the next few years, he caddied for some of Rochester's most powerful men. They liked the little hard-working kid, and the feeling was mutual. Hagen enjoyed being around the club members and was awestruck by their wealth, social stature, and, generally, the comfort in which they seemed to go through life. He remembered being "tremendously impressed by the conversations and discussions of these men regarding their vacations in Florida. I admired the ease with which they spoke of huge money deals and I certainly eyed wishfully their fancy golfing outfits." If he could not be of the elite, the next best thing was to be near them.

When he was not caddying, Hagen played golf on his own course, a three-hole affair that he laid out in Corbett's Glen, or, less often, at the Country Club. (Because he was a favorite caddie of several influential club members, Hagen was given restricted playing privileges.) He also spent a lot of time working on his game by pitching balls short distances to targets of newspapers spread out on the lawn. All of this practice increased his confidence, and at fourteen he thought himself "capable of taking on anybody within five years" of his age. By his fifteenth birthday, Hagen was regularly breaking 80 over the full-length eighteen-hole course. He believed that by that time he had "played more golf and practiced more shots than most young golfers of twenty-one."[9]

The energy not given to caddying or playing golf usually went to baseball. If Walter held ambitions to excel at golf, most of his peers wanted to be baseball stars. The national pastime had deep roots in Rochester, although the city did not possess a major league franchise. In the period when Hagen came of age, Rochester was a

Young Walter quickly established himself as a
favorite caddie at the Country Club of Rochester.
Courtesy: Sidney L. Matthew Collection

hotbed of minor league and semiprofessional baseball. From 1907
to 1912 Hagen played a lot of ball, particularly on weekends, for
the Ramblers, a team in one of several semipro city leagues. He
was a starting pitcher, who could, reportedly, hurl with either arm.
He also played in the outfield. As the years passed, however, base-

ball was increasingly a weekend distraction and golf a weekday obsession.[10]

By the winter of 1907, the fifteen-year-old Hagen had become a regular at the Country Club. Andrew Christy, the club's professional, noticed Hagen's enthusiasm for the game and early that year promoted him from caddie to assistant professional. Obtaining the assistant pro job was a significant step for Hagen. It not only meant more money, but also that he would now assist Christy in the making and repairing of clubs and overseeing the course. In sum, he would become much more familiar with the sport. Most important, as the assistant professional he gained more access to the course for practice rounds, many of them under Christy's instructive eye.

All of that was unsettling to William Hagen. He did not want his only son to become a professional athlete but rather a skilled tradesman like himself and his father. It seems Walter was a bit uncertain about his professional future as well—at the least, his father's objections forced him to behave in an ambivalent manner. Just prior to his working for Christy, Hagen served as an apprentice in a mechanic's garage and took some night classes to supplement his work. Additionally, he landed a part-time job with a piano company as a wood finisher, which fit nicely with the skills needed to craft fine golf clubs. In keeping with his love of the outdoors, Hagen also took a correspondence course in taxidermy. "It seemed natural that anything I'd learn to do would involve skill with my hands. I came from that kind of family," he concluded.[11]

Ultimately, however, William Hagen was destined to be disappointed by his son's choice of career. There is evidence that the two disagreed on the matter. Alyce Commisso, who grew up in the Corbett's Glen area and whose father was a friend of William Hagen, recalled that the senior Hagen referred to his son as a "bullshead" when he refused to become a skilled tradesman, opting instead for a career in professional golf. That is confirmed by the fact that neither William nor Louise Hagen actively supported Walter in competition. William Hagen did not watch his son play in a golf tournament until 1931, in the twilight of his career, and Louise Hagen never saw Walter compete. Even after he won the U.S. Open in 1914, Hagen remembered, "Only my dad could see no future ahead for me. He considered knocking the little white ball around a pasture a silly way to make a living. Although I always thought the British tough people to convince, my dad was tougher." While he did not disown Walter, it is clear that William Hagen withheld his blessing and that both father and son caused each other significant disappointment.[12]

Indeed, by 1910 Walter Hagen had decided that he would organize his life around professional sports. But according to Hagen, he experienced a real dilemma from about 1911 to 1914 concerning whether to pursue baseball or golf. He later claimed that he finally settled on golf because success in that sport depends on the individual, and one does not have to worry about carrying or being carried by a team. "To be perfectly frank," he once told O.B. Keeler, "I wanted to play my own game, in my own way, and take my drubbings or win my victories all by myself. It was individualism that got me, I suppose."

In 1917, for the first time, Hagen related his experience with organized baseball. He briefly explained about his pitching prowess and then said that a few years earlier he had "received an offer from a certain famous club that would almost have turned any boy's head." Hagen did not give any more details. In 1924, he said that when he was eighteen he was approached by Pat Moran, supposedly a scout for the Philadelphia Phillies. Moran had seen him play and wondered if Hagen would consider an offer to join the team. Hagen remembered that after staying up all night to ponder the pros and cons of baseball and golf, he disappointed his friends by announcing that golf would be his sport.

His memory was a bit different years later when he wrote *The Walter Hagen Story*. There he claimed to have met Pat Moran in 1914 while he was wintering as a professional golfer in Tarpon Springs, Florida, supposed site of the Phillies training camp. As Hagen now remembered it, Moran was the manager of the Phillies. After seeing Hagen work out with the team, Moran concluded that he "had possibilities as a ball player" and invited him to rejoin the Phillies the following spring for another training camp. If Hagen did try out with the team in 1914, his performance was not noted in the *Philadelphia Inquirer*'s daily training camp box scores and commentary. Moreover, the tryout did not occur in Tarpon Springs, Florida, under the eye of Pat Moran; in 1914 Charley "Red" Dooin was the manager of the Phillies, and his team spent the winter training at Wilmington, North Carolina. Aside from all of that, there is no reason to disbelieve Hagen's memory of meeting Moran and receiving *some* kind of encouragement from him.

Since no scouting reports were kept in that day for posterity, and given Hagen's confidence and tendency to self-promotion, it is impossible to know the truth about his baseball skills. Over the years the particulars of Hagen's life in baseball became exaggerated; in 1928 the *Los Angeles Times* declared that "at one time [Hagen] was signed by the New York Giants with prospects of a sensational baseball career." Hagen must have possessed some baseball talent. In 1911, he held his own as a pitcher and outfielder on a highly competitive semipro city league; he certainly possessed extraordinary golf talent, and the two sports require many of the same skills. Still, it seems fair to conclude that if Hagen had been another Babe Ruth, someone in the world of Rochester baseball would have figured it out before he turned nineteen in 1911, and so it is unlikely that the option to pursue major league baseball was as viable as the option to pursue professional golf. Possibly, the options were equally viable in Hagen's young mind; if they were, it was most fortunate for him that he chose a career in golf.[13]

So whether he realized it or not, by 1912 events were pushing Hagen into professional golf. Under the instruction of Andrew Christy, Hagen continued to develop an already exceptionally strong game, strong enough that Christy took him to Buffalo that summer for the U.S. (or National) Open. Although he did not compete in the tournament proper, Hagen did play a practice round with Christy and shot a 73. Christy convinced Hagen that he was not quite ready for such tournament competition but suggested that he might enter the Canadian Open later that season.

Encouraged by his practice round in Buffalo, Hagen competed in the 1912 Canadian Open held near Toronto. It was the farthest he had ever traveled from Brighton, and he enjoyed the trip. He played respectably in his first truly competitive golf outing, finishing twelfth and taking solace in the fact that he came in one stroke ahead of Alex Smith, who had won the U.S. Open in 1906. Yet Hagen now realized that tournament golf was not as easy as it looked.[14]

Circumstances outside of competition also moved Hagen toward a commitment to professional golf. The Owesco Golf Club in Auburn, New York, did not maintain a regular professional, but it needed one in the summer of 1912 to help host a state tournament, and called on Hagen. He served as a temporary professional there for two weeks and was so popular with the members that they asked him to stay on permanently. He was considering their offer when he learned that his boss, Andrew Christy, had taken a position at Equinox Country Club in Vermont. Suddenly the post at Rochester was available, and, as Christy's assistant for five years, Hagen was the logical successor.

When the Country Club offered him the job, Hagen readily accepted. He remembered receiving about $1,200 a year in salary (which is in line with the $1,000 salary Christy received for 1910), plus making extra money on equipment sales and lessons to club members. Hagen had come a long way since he was a seven-year-old caddie. Now he had an assistant and was able to get his father a job as a greenkeeper. He still may have harbored hopes of the major leagues, but if so, there was little time to practice his curve ball. The professional's job kept Hagen busy for the rest of 1912. He did not compete in any tournaments that year after the Canadian Open, although he did make plans to enter the 1913 U.S. Open at Brookline, Massachusetts.[15]

By his twentieth birthday, Hagen had become a golf club professional in his hometown and tasted his first serious tournament competition in Canada. He stood 5' 11" and was a lean 165 pounds; he had dark blue eyes, black hair—which he kept neatly trimmed—and was, all in all, a handsome young athlete. Beyond that, he had gained much more respect and stature around Rochester than he had probably ever dreamed possible, certainly more than his father or grandfather had been able to garner. In so many ways it must have seemed to Hagen that he had arrived. Actually, like the sport in which he competed, Hagen's star was only beginning to rise.

While Walter Hagen pondered such serious matters as baseball, golf, money, social stature, his father's wishes, and how each might affect his life in Rochester, a chubby ten-year-old, known as Little Bob, was just taking up the sport of golf on the outskirts of Atlanta, Georgia. Little Bob was too young to worry about career moves but not too young to be sobered by a sloping, breaking three-foot putt. When he got tired of lining up those three-footers, Little Bob played tennis or fished at the East Lake Country Club.

Caddying was one of the things that he did not do. It just was not necessary; if it were necessary to his playing golf, maybe he would have caddied, but maybe not. In any case, Little Bob spent hours upon hours of his boyhood driving, chipping, and putting golf balls on one of the finest courses in the U.S.

He was known as Little Bob because people called his father Big Bob. But Little Bob's story begins with his paternal grandfather, namesake, and the biggest Bob of them all, Robert Tyre Jones of Canton, Georgia. It was mostly because of the original R.T. Jones that Little Bob did not have to caddie and could spend his boyhood growing up on East Lake. The Jones story does not begin with R.T.; the family line runs well back into colonial Georgia. But the life of R.T. marked a turning point in the family's history that permitted the athletic career of "Mr. Jones" and continues to influence the Jones family today.

Robert Tyre Jones was born in 1849 to William Green Jones and Emily Chafin Jones. He grew up on his father's small farm located about halfway between the towns of Covington and Conyers in northern Georgia. His life was hard, and it became even more difficult after the Civil War. The turmoil of back country Georgia left young R.T. with a tough, stern outlook that was further shaped by his southern Protestant faith. In 1867, while still a teenager, he joined the Presbyterian Church. He later transferred his membership to the Baptist Church, where he was baptized on the second Sunday in August of 1870. His pastor probably needed assistance baptizing R.T., who by then had grown to become a huge, strapping man, reaching a height of 6' 5" and weighing more than 230 pounds. R.T. needed all the vigor he could muster, as he helped manage his father's farm while working in his cousin's general store. Of course, keeping a small farm afloat in the Reconstruction period was a dubious proposition, and, after leaving the farm, R.T. often related how he sometimes sat up until midnight finishing odd jobs for extra cash, such as resoling the shoes of tenants for fifty cents a pair.[16]

In 1879, R.T. and his wife of one year, Susan, left the Covington area and settled in Canton, situated about forty miles north of Atlanta. They chose Canton because of its beautiful countryside, and because R.T. believed that the town could sustain a new general store. He immediately invested his savings of $500 into the founding of the Jones Mercantile Exchange and soon gained the respect of Canton's citizens. R.T. managed the store for the next twenty years, becoming an especially influential businessman after he took part in establishing the Bank of Canton. Then in 1899 he created the Canton Textile Mills, which, after a slow start, began turning a big profit. Before long nearly all of Canton and the surrounding rural population depended upon Jones and his mill. The decision to start the mill proved to be the best financial move in the history of the Jones family. By 1900 R.T. Jones was a wealthy man on his way toward greater wealth. His story epitomized the ideals cherished by proponents of the New South.

Life was not all business for R.T. after coming to Canton, and in his personal affairs he was more representative of many southerners. For example, R.T. always felt a strong obligation to his family; when tragedy struck in December of 1888 and his father, William, was robbed and shot to death near the family farm, R.T. traveled back to Covington for an extended stay to help put the family affairs in order. By the time his father was murdered, R.T. had a growing family of his own. Early in 1879, just before the couple moved to Canton, Susan gave birth to their first child, a boy they named Robert Purmedus. For some reason, R.T. chose not to name the child after himself, a decision which later caused his son much disappointment. Susan bore R.T. six more children, adding four boys and two girls. It was a large family to look after, but fortunately R.T. produced the necessary resources.[17]

Aside from his ever-growing family, R.T. was always active in church. He served for forty years as the Sunday School superintendent of the First Baptist Church in Canton. For much of that time he taught the largest adult Sunday School class at the church. R.T. held what can safely be called a theistic world view; he believed that one's faith needed to influence all areas of life. He often reminded anyone who would listen, "No man ever accomplishes anything really worthwhile alone. There are always two additional forces at work—other people and Providence." In 1920 R.T. wrote an article for the *Cherokee Advance*, a local paper, entitled "Christianity as Related to Business." He declared, "There is no question in my mind but that the scriptures plainly teach that if, when we as Christians enter into any line of commendable business (and we should enter into no other), we do so with a view first of service to our Lord, that He will enter into that business with us." He admitted that "we are naturally selfish," but added: "For a business to succeed as the Lord counts success, Christianity should be the dominating power, and the principles of Christianity should govern its operation." Like the pious Christian he was, R.T. usually rested on Sunday, but on at least one Sabbath, circumstances forced him to the office, and when an associate carelessly teased, "Well, R.T., I guess there's no rest for the wicked," Jones sternly replied, "And the righteous don't need it."[18]

Not surprisingly, his faith directed his personal habits and life as well. He never engaged in any of the traditional vices of womanizing, smoking, cursing, or drinking. His grandson, Louis Jones Jr., recalled that R.T. would not even indulge in a Coca-Cola. R.T. was, generally, a serious-minded man who had no time for sports; yet he occasionally relaxed by playing a game of cards, though it was always Rook and never any game requiring face cards. Duty to family, faithful stewardship of time and money, discipline, hard work, sternness, an absolute moral code based upon the Bible, and a strain of intolerance for those with whom he disagreed— these were the traits that marked the life of R.T. Jones and many other Americans in the late nineteenth century.

In every way, R.T. cast a long shadow in Canton. That is probably the reason his eldest son, Robert, ultimately left for Atlanta. Robert Purmedus Jones was unlike his father. Although he attended the University of Georgia and Mercer University, went on to study law, passed the Georgia bar exam, and became a successful corporate lawyer—all to the delight of R.T.—he also gave long hours to playing baseball, and at one time planned to join the Brooklyn club of the National League. R.T. quickly squashed that notion, however, apparently threatening to "disown" his son if he went into professional baseball. O.B. Keeler recalled that when an authority on the game lauded his son's baseball skills, R.T. responded, "You could not pay him a poorer compliment."[19]

Robert Purmedus was not much like his father in personality, either; his fun-loving, carefree, sanguine outlook collided with the seriousness of R.T. When not around his father, Robert drank, cursed, and related adult jokes. Bobby Jones later declared him an "expert at profanity." In sum, Robert Purmedus was more concerned than his father with enjoying this life and less concerned than his father about preparing for the next one. It might be an overstatement to say that Robert actively rebelled against the formalism of his father, but it is safe to conclude that their relationship was marked by respect more than anything else. So, given R.T.'s dominant presence in the small town of Canton, his inflexibility, the differences between father and son in personality and their lack of closeness, it was inevitable that Robert Purmedus would leave town when he was old enough and the right circumstances presented themselves.[20]

The time arrived in 1901, just after Robert completed his education and was about to begin his professional career. Other concerns, beyond professional opportunities and R.T.'s shadow, influenced his decision to leave Canton. The previous year he had married a petite, attractive woman named Clara Thomas from Auburn, Alabama. At five feet, no inches and about ninety pounds, Clara was physically weak. She possessed, however, a strong will which nicely complemented her husband's more congenial nature. Within a year of their marriage, she gave birth to their first child, a boy named William. Like his mother, William was small and frail— so frail, in fact, that he died after about three months. His death saddened the entire family and devastated Clara. In the late summer of 1901, soon after William's death, she became pregnant again and urged Robert to move to Atlanta where she knew that she and the baby could get the best medical care. It did not take much pleading, and before the year passed, Robert and his pregnant wife moved south to Atlanta.

With a population of almost 90,000, Atlanta was a much better place than Canton for Robert to begin his law career. It was the state capital and there was simply more business there. Destroyed by General Sherman's army in the fall of 1864, the city had rebounded extraordinarily in the last quarter of the century. To an even greater degree than in Rochester, the railroad made the difference for Atlanta, which became the most important transportation hub in the New South. By 1895 fifteen lines, upon which a daily average of 150 trains operated, passed through the city, stimulating trade and development.

The city's commerce tripled in value in the 1890s. One of Atlanta's biggest successes of the period was the Coca-Cola Company, founded in 1892 by Asa Candler. By 1900 it had branch offices in Dallas, Chicago, Los Angeles, and Philadelphia. Robert Purmedus Jones was fortunate enough to do work for the company soon after arriving in Atlanta, beginning a relationship between the Jones family and Coca-Cola that survived long after his death. Other signs of modernization appeared in Atlanta. In 1892, a construction crew finished the city's first skyscraper, and by then electric trolley cars were replacing horse-drawn conveyances. In all, Atlanta was a growing, bustling city—the best environment for a young lawyer to make a name for himself.[21]

The couple moved into a house on Willow Street, and Robert quickly acquired the right business contacts. As for Clara, she spent most of her time in bed anxiously awaiting the birth of their next child. Finally, on St. Patrick's Day, March 17, 1902, her baby arrived in the house on Willow Street. As the *Atlanta Constitution* put it two days later, "A little son has come to brighten the home of Mr. and Mrs. Robert Jones." The proud parents named him Robert Tyre Jones, out of genuine respect for his grandfather, and prayed that he would not suffer the same fate as William. Like his brother, he was not very large, weighing just over five pounds, and quite sickly. He had an especially sensitive digestive system, and would be about five years old before he could retain solid food. Undoubtedly, Clara and Camilla, the black live-in "fat cook and nurse," must have spent what seemed like an eternity of sleepless nights helping Little Bob through fits of colic. O.B. Keeler later described toddler Jones as an "almost shockingly spindling youngster with an oversize head and legs with staring knees. Few youngsters at the romper age have less resembled, without being actually malformed, a future athletic champion." His parents took him to no less than six doctors in an effort to improve his health but were pretty much left to their own best common sense. (The doctors offered little more than a diet of egg whites.) Under the care of Camilla mostly and the hyperprotective eye of Clara, Little Bob made it safely into childhood.[22]

As Keeler noted, it was "not much of a start." For five years it was all egg whites, Mother, Father, and Camilla. Big Bob was doing quite well in his law practice, and in early 1907 the family moved from Willow Street to an apartment on West Peachtree Street in a very affluent section of the city. Jones remembered playing his first baseball that summer on Peachtree Street. But the family lived most of the summer of 1907 in a large house bordering the second fairway of the East Lake Country Club's golf course. Big Bob hoped that some exercise and fresh air might do for his son what the doctors seemingly could not do. Owned by the Atlanta Athletic Club (AAC), East Lake was situated about five miles to the east of the city. The Jones family leased several rooms in a home owned by Mrs. Frank Meador, and spent most of their time out-of-doors playing golf and tennis. Neither the Colonel (as Big Bob was often called) nor Clara had any experience with golf, but they both liked the game. Clara especially enjoyed the links and, despite her slightness, eventually became an above average player.

Other golf enthusiasts also rented rooms that summer at the Meador house. One of them was Fulton Colville, who had the distinction of being the man who introduced the sport to Bobby Jones. While practicing on the lawn one day, Colville noticed Little Bob watching him with obvious curiosity. He decided to let the youngster have a swing. After a dismal effort by Little Bob with a club that was so long it poked his colicky stomach, Colville found an old cleek (one-iron), sawed down the shaft, and presented the homemade junior club to the youngster. Jones well remembered that, "the blade was quite shallow, which made it appear long in relation to its depth." However disproportionate, the club served the purpose and, like Hagen and probably every other youngster who takes up golf, Jones and his friend, Frank Meador, laid out a few primitive short holes in the yard and on the dirt road in front of the house. When not otherwise occupied, Jones chipped an old golf ball around his little course.[23]

His family returned to East Lake the following summer, this time renting a building on the club's property, and by then Little Bob's parents permitted him to play the course with them. East Lake had hired a new professional that year. His name was Stewart Maiden of Carnoustie, Scotland, and Little Bob was simply mesmerized by his long, fluid swing. Although as a youth he did not receive any formal, scheduled lessons from Maiden, he did watch the professional carefully, determined to pattern his own swing on Maiden's.

So there was nothing dramatic about the golf beginnings of Bobby Jones. Recalling his start in golf, Jones later concluded, "It all seems to me to be a pretty natural sequence hardly worthy of too much comment." In *Golf Is My Game*, he wrote, "There was nothing very conscious or contrived about the whole procedure. The game was there, I liked it, and I kept on playing." A successful lawyer by 1908, Big Bob joined the AAC's Board of Directors (a position he held until 1947), and each summer the family continued its annual pilgrimage to East Lake. As George and Perry Adair put it a few years later, Little Bob "virtually 'lived on the links.'"[24]

Jones played in a couple of informal competitions when he was six years old, but his first "big" event came in 1911, when, at age nine, he entered the AAC's junior's championship. He surprised

Little Bob stares down a drive in one of his earliest
competitions. Courtesy: Sidney L. Matthew Collection

everyone by winning, defeating Howard Thorne, a big sixteen-year-
old, in the thirty-six hole final, 5 and 4. That was enough to get his
picture in the *American Golfer* and begin his meteoric rise to fame.
Yet Little Bob was not the only youngster with an exceptional
game playing at the AAC. Two other children of club members,
Perry Adair and Alexa Stirling, became accomplished golfers who
competed and practiced daily with Jones.

By the end of 1912, Little Bob had successfully competed against opponents much older than he in several junior events and consistently shot about 90 strokes per round. Few American boys could say as much, but then few of them had had such opportunities. On the whole, Little Bob's childhood was quite comfortable, filled with swimming, fishing, tennis, and, increasingly, golf. For all of that he could thank his father and, especially, his grandfather. Yet it is unlikely he harbored any serious ambitions to make a name in golf. "I do not recall any time at which I decided I wanted to be a so-called 'great golfer,'" he wrote. If he did hold boyish dreams of athletic stardom in 1912, he was in the wrong sport, because golf was still mostly private and not yet a likely avenue to wide public acclaim.[25]

If still a sport played by a wealthy handful on private country clubs, golf had grown considerably in the twentieth century. The number of courses continued to increase, evidence that every year more people played golf in the U.S. A major development in equipment and a few competitive episodes contributed to the sport's growth in the early years of the century.

Although steel shafts and uniform clubs did not arrive upon the scene until the late '20s, by 1900 manufacturers made tremendous advances in ball construction. The evolution of the golf ball is an interesting story. Up until 1848, golf balls had a feather core and leather cover. In that year, though, the "featherie" was replaced by a solid sphere of gutta-percha, a gum-like substance from the gutta-percha tree. For about fifty years the "guttie" was state-of-the-art. British golf heroes of the late Victorian period, such as John Ball and Tom Morris Jr., compiled their records with gutties. At the turn of the century, the golf ball evolved into its next stage when Coburn Haskell of Cleveland designed a ball with a hard rubber core, tightly wrapped with rubber strands and contained in a thin, flexible gutta-percha cover.

Although at first traditionalists sneered at what they dubbed the "Bounding Billy" because of its dramatically increased liveliness, and did what they could to halt its advance, the golfing public generally welcomed the rubber-cored ball because it gave amateurs what they have always wanted: greater distance. With the Haskell ball a good amateur could drive nearly 200 yards, whereas with the guttie a long drive was typically about 170 yards. Moreover, if not struck squarely or hit in cold temperatures, the guttie felt like a rock, while the rubber-cored ball compressed easily and literally made the game more comfortable to play. After Walter Travis captured the U.S. Amateur in 1901 playing a rubber-cored ball and Sandy Herd used one to win the British Open the following year, golfers everywhere and of all skills attested to its superiority. The new ball meant that individual holes, even entire courses, had to be lengthened or else eliminated; a new premium attached to distance seemed worth it, though, because the rubber-cored ball made the game more fun and popular. "If there was any doubt about the future of the game, all illusions were dispelled when the new rubber-cored ball took the place of the old guttie, one of the most important revolutions the game has ever known on either side of the Atlantic," concluded H.B. Martin.

The rubber-cored ball arrived on the heels of Harry Vardon's famous 1900 golf exhibition tour of the U.S. Possibly the greatest British professional of his era (he eventually set an all-time record by winning six British Opens), Vardon barnstormed the country from February to December, traveling an estimated 20,000 miles, playing at least sixty-five matches at various clubs and compiling a record of 50–13–2. He also entered the U.S. Open in October at the Chicago Golf Club in Wheaton, Illinois, where he was joined by another member of the great professional British triumvirate, J.H. Taylor. (James Braid completed the trio; Taylor and Braid each captured five British Opens.) Vardon won, and Taylor finished in second place. It was the first time that any British professionals had competed in the U.S. Open, and their presence gave the tournament and all of American golf an increased prestige, even if the British dominated the event. The tour was sponsored by A.G. Spalding & Brothers, which wanted to promote its new ball, the Vardon Flyer (a guttie, ironically). Harry Vardon represented a sort of sports missionary, showing Americans how to play golf with an "awesome combination of power and grace." Vardon, Robert Browning has written, "brought converts to the game wherever he went and started a new golf boom in the States." His tour received much publicity, and it is hard to overestimate its importance to the growth of the sport in America.[26]

But beyond equipment advances and foreign invasions, American players enhanced the image of the sport with their own remarkable competitive achievements. The most outstanding accomplishment of the decade occurred in 1904 when American amateur, William J. Travis, captured the British Amateur Championship at Royal St. George's Club in Kent, England. The story of the Grand Old Man (he was forty-two) and his match-play march through the field of British players is no less than a saga. Travis was Australian by birth, but he had learned his golf in the U.S. He was the top American amateur when he crossed the Atlantic, having won the U.S. Amateur in 1900, 1901, and 1903; still, few gave him a serious chance to win golf's most prestigious and challenging amateur event. But he stunned the world as he eliminated some of Great Britain's best en route to becoming the first American to win a British golf title. Travis's success rested primarily on his putter, a center-shafted (or "Schenectady"-style) club. A few years later the Royal and Ancient Golf Association, as if still searching for an explanation or an excuse, outlawed the Schenectady putter in Great Britain. That, coupled with what Travis perceived to be poor treatment by British officials during the tournament—he described the caddie assigned to him as "cross-eyed"—left a bad taste in the mouths of American golf fans.

There were other great individual performances on this side of the Atlantic, such as Jerry Travers winning the 1907, 1908, 1912, and 1913 U.S. Amateur events. Willie Anderson, a transplanted Scotsman, became the first and only man to win three consecutive U.S. Opens in 1903, 1904, and 1905, adding to his 1901 title. Then, in 1911, Johnny McDermott of Atlantic City became the first American homebred professional to win the U.S. Open, further signaling the maturation of the sport in America. McDermott successfully defended his title in 1912 at Buffalo, the tournament in which Walter Hagen played his first U.S. Open practice round, and was the American favorite in the 1913 Open. These "firsts," combined with the Bounding Billy, Harry Vardon, and Walter Travis, helped popularize the sport of golf in America and prompted the *New York Times* to proclaim in the summer of 1910 that "Golf In America Has Made Great Gains." Indeed, whatever Grantland Rice's editor thought of it, the sport *had* made great gains, and the shocking, unprecedented events of the 1913 U.S. Open would solidify them.[27]

Chapter 2

Going Public: 1913–1916

X

Since the 1912 Canadian Open, Walter Hagen had been spending his time acclimating to his new job as the pro at the Country Club of Rochester. Overseeing the course and caddies, stocking and distributing equipment, and giving lessons consumed his energy and precluded his hunger for tournament competition. He found time to practice, however, and sharpened his game so that by the end of the summer he was consistently breaking 70. For a year he had hoped to enter the U.S. Open, but he would need, at the least, permission from the club. He optimistically sent his entry to the USGA in the summer and purchased what he considered the finest golf wear ever: a white silk shirt with multicolored stripes, white flannel trousers, and white buckskin shoes with red rubber soles. He completed the outfit with a bright red bandanna that was to be tied "casually" about his neck. Although he failed to wrangle any expense money, he did convince the club's board to give him a week off in September, and so he made day coach reservations for Boston, site of the 1913 U.S. Open.

The tournament was played in the suburb of Brookline at what has always been known simply as The Country Club. The event was more highly anticipated than usual because of the entry of British professionals Harry Vardon and "Big Ted" Ray; Vardon had already won five British Opens, most recently in 1911, while Ray was the 1912 British Open champion and runner-up in 1913. It was just the second British invasion of the U.S. Open, and for months golf insiders discussed the remote possibilities of an American victory. The British stars appeared to be in top form during their summer exhibition matches. Indeed, the pair finished their American tour with forty wins and one loss in foursome competitions. Americans pinned their hopes on Johnny McDermott, who was eager to prove that his game was on par with the best of Britain. He had won the Shawnee-on-the-Delaware tournament a few weeks earlier, despite the presence of Vardon and Ray in the field. Bubbling with confidence after that victory, he remarked, "We hope our foreign visitors had a good time, but we don't think they did, and we are sure they won't win the National Open." The comment brought an official apology and reprimand from the USGA, which thought it rude and unsportsmanlike. Intoned the USGA, "If golf is to degenerate into the practices of the prize ring, to create feelings unbecoming of gentleman, then it were better that golf should cease to exist." Despite the USGA's feelings, the episode further intensified what had already become a full-blown international rivalry. Hagen could not have selected a better year to begin his U.S. Open record.[1]

After checking into his Boston hotel, Hagen went straight to the course. When he arrived at The Country Club, everyone was talking about Vardon and Ray. Nonetheless, Hagen, who had never seen the British professionals, sounded sure of himself as he entered the locker room. He recognized McDermott from Buffalo, walked up to him, and, possibly thinking of the recent brouhaha, said, "You're Johnny McDermott aren't you? Well, I'm glad to know you. I'm W.C. Hagen from Rochester and I've come over to help you boys take care of Vardon and Ray." Hagen recalled that his brassy introduction brought chuckles from the experienced professionals who overheard him. He soon met Vardon and Ray, and remembered "gawking at [Vardon] like any other greenhorn from the pastures." Some of the locker room discussion centered on a young, tall, lanky Brookline native named Francis Ouimet, a U.S.-born amateur of French-Canadian lineage who had earned a state-wide reputation. The same age as Hagen, Ouimet had grown up caddying at The Club, so he knew the layout and was the sentimental pick. To be sure, those who put down money placed it on either Vardon or Ray, whom the odds had as 2 to 1 favorites. As for Hagen, he was correct in his recollection that "Nobody gave me a tumble." After all, he was an unknown whose only competitive accomplishment was a twelfth-place finish in the Canadian Open.[2]

The field of 170 was the largest ever, and the USGA decided to stage the qualifying competition on the British system; that is, the field was divided into two sections, with half playing two qualifying rounds on Tuesday, September 16, and the rest qualifying on Wednesday. The top thirty-two plus ties would make the tournament proper, comprised of seventy-two holes total, thirty-six each on Thursday and Friday.

Things went as expected on the first day as Vardon led the field. Bostonians were pleased by Ouimet's early showing; he qualified in second. To fatten the gate, the USGA scheduled the 6' 1", 200 pound Ted Ray for Wednesday. Once again, a British professional led the field as Big Ted shot the lowest qualifying rounds, 74–74, which was also a two-round competitive course record. Hagen fired 78–79 and finished tied for fifth in his section and ninth overall.

If a bit nervous, Hagen did not seem awed by his first U.S. Open, sustaining his solid play through Thursday. He had an exceptionally good first round of 73 and followed with a 78. After the morning round, he was tied for third place, and by the evening he had dropped into only a seventh-place tie. Although Rochester's *Democrat and Chronicle* got his name wrong, spelling it "Hagin," as did the *American Golfer*, the local paper wrote glowingly that Hagen's "brilliant form" was "the surprise of the tournament." The paper added that "Hagin" was a "homebred 'pro' in every sense that the word implies" and went on to inform readers of his Brighton roots and history at the Country Club of Rochester.[3]

Ouimet was one of the golfers tied with Hagen. They were just four strokes behind the leaders, including Vardon. Ray was in between, having carded another competitive club record of 70 (–1). So, while Rochesterians in particular and Americans in general who followed golf could take pride in their players' showing, Vardon and Ray were still at the top, seemingly poised to battle each other for the title the next day when the pressure would become greater.

All golf fans know that the third round of a seventy-two hole medal event is often pivotal; leaders may either break away from or fall back to their pursuers. The latter happened at Brookline in 1913, in part because of the weather. Although it had been drizzling off and on all week, at about 2:00 Friday morning it began to rain, continuing throughout the day. The cold, damp conditions made scoring difficult and, to a degree, equalized competition. It became virtually impossible for Ray to card another 70. In fact, both he and Vardon struggled in the morning round. Their stumble opened the door for the Americans. Francis Ouimet took the greatest advantage and had the lowest score of the round, a 74. Hagen also gained, but his 76 left him two strokes behind Vardon, Ray, and Ouimet, who were tied for the lead at lunch.

Hagen began the final round a few holes behind the British stars, with Ouimet a few holes behind him. He pushed his drive off the first tee to the left and later admitted, "Perhaps I was a bit nervous when I drove off in the final round." Starting slowly, he settled down after holing a mashie (five-iron) shot from the fairway for a two on the fourth. Hagen then played steadily the rest of the front nine and was pleasantly surprised at the turn to learn that Vardon and Ray had taken high scores on their inward sides, putting him in a tie with Vardon for the lead as he set out on the last nine holes.

The news of Hagen's play circulated among the gallery, and the number of his followers rapidly increased. Although he had never had this many people following him before, much less in the last round of a U.S. Open, he stood firmly under the pressure through the 13th hole. But still tied for the lead as he began the 14th, Hagen began to waver. He hit a decent drive to the par-5 hole, leaving himself with a chance to reach the green in two for an easy birdie. While sizing up his shot, a dangerous one given the difficulty of hitting a brassie (two-wood) off the wet turf, he heard that Vardon and Ray had each scored four on the hole. Convinced that he had to keep up with them, Hagen pulled out his fairway wood and went for the green. He remembered, "I just gave it all I had. I topped the ball. It did not get off the grass . . . [but] just skidded along throwing water in its wake." Frustrated, disappointed, and probably a bit angry, he swung hard at his next shot, wildly hooking it to the left of the green into the thick, wet rough. When it was over, he had taken a seven, losing three shots to Vardon and Ray. He matched them over the final four holes and finished with an 80, for a total of 307.[4]

Safely in with 304s, Vardon and Ray watched anxiously as the rest of the field finished. The British stars, who both shot 79, were disappointed and pessimistic. "There are three or four still out who will beat us." "I am very sorry, but it is my putting that has let me down again. I feared that it would," said Vardon. Ray added bluntly, "I played rotten, and to make matters worse, Harry went out and did the same thing." Nevertheless, MacDonald Smith, "Long Jim" Barnes, and Frenchman Louis Tellier could do no better than Hagen, and the quartet finished in a fourth-place tie.

After defending champion Johnny McDermott concluded his tournament with a 308, the only player left with a chance to catch the British professionals was the twenty-year-old local favorite,

Francis Ouimet. He began the fourth round in a tie with Vardon and Ray, and his sterling front side left him only one shot behind Vardon and Hagen. Ouimet seemed nerveless throughout his last nine holes. He came to the 15th tee needing two fours and two threes (or three pars and a birdie) to tie the leaders. "The task seemed too much for him or anyone else," thought Henry Leach of the *American Golfer*. Unaffected by the gallery, however, which after the 13th hole included Vardon and Ray, Ouimet scrambled for a four on the 15th and made a comfortable three on the 16th. He dropped a fifteen-foot putt on the 17th for the birdie, prompting Leach to declare, "that was a great putt for America and a great three." The gallery roared after he confidently sank a yard-long putt for a par 4 on the 18th, giving him a final round of 79 and tying him with the British stars. Vardon, Ray, and everyone else congratulated Ouimet on his heroic finish and looked forward to Saturday's three-way playoff.[5]

Hagen did not stay in Boston for the tournament's conclusion, but instead caught a train for Rochester, arriving that night. Before leaving, he spoke with golf journalist H.B. Martin. Hagen hid his feelings, concluding, "I was just a little too green, I guess, but I will win this thing next year for sure. There is plenty of time ahead, and with another year's experience I'll show 'em all how to play this game." By the next day, he seemed to have regained a more honest perspective when he "stood bashfully in the caddie house of the Country Club of Rochester . . . and meekly received the congratulations of the club members." During an interview for the local papers, Hagen admitted that he had "played a pretty good game" at Brookline and said that he planned to enter next year's open if it was held within "reasonable distance" from Rochester. Reporters learned that several club members had already volunteered to underwrite his trip to the 1914 event. If Hagen disappointed himself at Brookline, it seemed he had exceeded the expectations of Rochesterians, who were noticeably proud of their golf professional.[6]

The attention made Hagen feel better, and he may have even wondered why he left Brookline so quickly, especially after news of the playoff arrived. For on September 20, Francis Ouimet fired what golf historian Herbert Warren Wind has appropriately called "the shots heard round the world." A gallery of near 8,000 (British correspondents had it as large as 20,000; in any case, it was record-size for the U.S Open) gathered in a heavy, cool mist to watch Ouimet and Eddie Lowrey, his little ten-year-old caddie, duel Harry

Vardon and Big Ted Ray through the eighteen-hole tiebreaker. They all shot 38s on the front nine, but Ouimet shocked everyone for the second straight day when he fired a 34 on the back nine to finish at 72. Neither Vardon nor Ray could keep up with him. Ultimately, the anticipation, excitement, and pressure surrounding the playoff unnerved the seasoned British professionals more than the young American amateur. Ray faltered on the 15th and finished with a 78, while Vardon lost two stokes each on the 17th and 18th to finish with 77. The *New York Times* correspondent described the scene following the final putt: "Thousands of dripping, rubber-coated spectators massed about Ouimet, who was hoisted to the shoulders of those nearest to him, while cheer after cheer rang out in his honor. Excited women tore bunches of flowers from their bodices and hurled them at the youthful winner; hundreds of men strove to reach him in order to pat him on the back or shake his hand."

John Reid Jr., Secretary of the USGA, presided over the closing ceremony. After receiving the trophy, Ouimet said, "I am as much surprised and as pleased as anyone here. Naturally it was always my hope to win out. I simply tried my best to keep this cup from going to our friends across the water. I am very glad to have been the agency for keeping the cup in America." Listening to this acceptance speech, one Brookline resident commented, "Francis is a good boy; his life is clean." If all of the reports are to be accepted, even Ouimet's mother was in the gallery and called out his name, to which he responded, "Thank you mother; I'll be home soon." Fresh-faced, modest, *and* an amateur, Francis Ouimet became an instant American sports legend. The fact that he was from a modest background, unlike most amateur golfers, further enhanced his popularity. As Vardon and Ray praised their conqueror, members of the gallery, in one last bit of drama, took up a collection of more than $100 for Eddie Lowrey. The gutsy little kid had stirred every one's patriotism by wearing a red, white, and blue ribbon throughout the playoff.[7]

With or without the melodrama, the 1913 U.S. Open was a landmark event for American golf. Ouimet's victory over two of Britain's most feared, veteran professionals was simply astounding. Its historical significance was not lost on contemporary writers, who spoke of a new "era" in American golf. Although some British writers believed Ouimet's familiarity with the course explained the outcome, most just accepted it as a natural result of the sport's growth in the U.S. Henry Leach, an Englishman, summed up the consensus on both sides of the Atlantic: "Big history was made at Brookline in the third week of September. . . . America has indeed graduated now as a first-class golfing power. . . . Britain has been complacent and America has been—if I dare say it—a little timid. There will be no more of this sort of thing." Wind's Revolutionary War metaphor is especially illustrative because Ouimet's victory was a kind of declaration of independence, announcing the rise of American golf.[8]

While contemporary golf enthusiasts appreciated the event, its immediate effect on the broader sports public is more dubious. As golf writer Charles Price and Grantland Rice biographer Charles Fountain have correctly noted, Ouimet's victory made the front page in Boston, but elsewhere it received varying amounts of coverage in the sports pages. Still, when H.B. Martin wrote that Ouimet's victory "became front page news and it created an interest in the royal game in this country that it had never known before," he was only, at most, half wrong. Even if it did not make more than one city's front pages, the 1913 U.S. Open was the biggest step yet in golf's journey from the private club to the American public.[9]

The Country Club of Rochester needed Hagen for a month or so after he returned from Brookline, so he winterized the course and pro shop and waited for the falling leaves to turn to snow. When that happened, Hagen was relieved from his duties at the club. He packed his things and decided to take his first golf tour of Florida. Because of his strong finish at Brookline, Hagen now had a reputation that could make a southern tour profitable, or at least viable. As there was little else for a northern golf professional to do, most of them either idled away their time or secured other employment for the winter. Some of the most fortunate took temporary jobs at clubs in the south, but those with a reputation could also arrange four-ball exhibitions or enter one of a handful of tournaments, such as the North and South Open.

It would be another ten years or so before the southeast could boast of a winter golf circuit, but the sport had made significant inroads there by 1913. Massive, pretentious resort hotels such as those in St. Augustine and Bellair, Florida, were constructed in the late nineteenth century before the arrival of golf. In time, the region, the sport, and the hotels developed a symbiotic relationship, combining to create a posh seasonal playground for the nation's elite, just the sort of place Hagen found attractive. On this trip, Hagen stayed in Tarpon Springs, Florida, in the house of George Clemson, a businessman and member of the Country Club of Rochester. For exhibitions, he teamed with Tommy Kerrigan, professional at the Dedham club near Boston. He did not win any tournaments, and, aside from his alleged tryout with baseball's Phillies, the only memorable thing about his 1913–1914 southern tour was that it was his first.[10]

In July he again made plans to enter the U.S. Open, scheduled for Chicago's Midlothian Country Club the following month. Ernest Willard, club member and owner of the *Democrat and Chronicle*, approached Hagen, offering to underwrite his trip to Chicago. So that he would not have to travel alone, Willard also agreed to pay the way for one of Hagen's friends, Dutch Leonard. Hagen accepted Willard's generous offer and began to practice seriously for the tournament.

He packed his best golf outfit, essentially unchanged since Brookline, and with Leonard took a train to Chicago, arriving in time for the qualifying rounds on Tuesday, August 18. Hagen remembered that he and his friend stayed in the Great Northern Hotel and that the trip was "quite an adventure" inasmuch as he had "never been out of the east before." When he arrived at the club, he found his fellow professionals grumbling about their accommodations. Midlothian's clubhouse was one of many in the world that opened its doors to amateurs, but not professionals, who were generally perceived as crude, unsophisticated, and subservient. In this case, though, the USGA itself, as reported by Wednesday's *Chicago Daily Tribune*, made the rule segregating amateurs and professionals. The *American Golfer* recorded that professionals "were not allowed to dress in the clubhouse, and the house in which they were located had only a few lockers, while lavatory conditions were poor." "Instead of lockers," most professionals "just had pegs to hang their clothes on," noted *Golfers Magazine*. Hagen and his peers were used to comfortable, if still second-class, treatment at their home clubs. Unkempt restrooms and pegs on the wall seemed degrading.[11]

Lean, strong, and twenty-one years old, Walter Hagen entered his second
U.S. Open in 1914. Courtesy: Albert R. Stone Negative Collection,
Rochester Museum and Science Center, Rochester, New York

Whatever Hagen thought or said of these provisions in 1914,
and it probably was not much, he did not make any reference to
them in his autobiography. He did recall in 1951, however, that he
"had no trouble at all getting a locker at Midlothian," because he
simply entered the locker room, ignorant of any restrictions, while
no one at the club put up any resistance. Chick Evans also claimed
that Hagen and a few of the older professionals used the club's
locker room, along with the club members and amateurs. If that
happened, it violated the USGA's ruling and was not the experience of most professionals at Chicago. In later years, the whole
episode—the treatment of the professionals, Hagen's entry into
the locker room, and the debate that followed—became known as
the "Midlothian Incident." No one will ever know exactly what
was said and done at Midlothian or the precise location Hagen
changed clothes and, admittedly, it is not that important. What is
important, though, is the legend that Hagen led a rebellion of sorts
at Midlothian that resulted in the equal accommodations for pro-

fessionals and amateurs in the U.S. There is, as Herbert Graffis has explained, no evidence to support such a claim, and, in fairness to Hagen, he never gave the story any credence. The legend probably grew because the conditions for professionals at Midlothian were unusually poor, Hagen was the star of the event, and in later years he did work to break down social barriers to professional golfers.[12]

Despite the unequal facilities, there were over 125 entries, so the USGA used the same qualifying format in 1914 that had been used at Brookline. This time Hagen played his preliminary rounds on the first day. The weather was typically hot that week, and it had not rained for some time; therefore, the course was hard and "fast." In the days before sophisticated sprinkling systems, it meant, according to conventional wisdom, that the course would generally play easier, even if putting might be more difficult. Over the cement-like fairways, players could drive the ball much farther, reaching more par 5s in two or having shorter approach shots to the green. Hagen took advantage of the dry conditions on Tuesday and easily qualified at 75–77–152, while "Long Jim" Barnes (so nicknamed because he was a lanky 6' 4" and drove the ball a long way) led on the first day with a 146.[13]

The tournament proper began on Thursday morning. Hagen, who had for the first time eaten lobster and oysters the previous evening, played the opening round on little sleep and with a severely upset stomach. He suffered through the discomfort, however, and stole the morning's headlines by breaking the course record. Hagen holed putts of forty, thirty, and twenty feet, and his 68 was five shots under par. Others posted low scores that morning too, including defending champion Francis Ouimet, who came in at 69. Charles "Chick" Evans, a local favorite competing in his first U.S. Open, finished the morning round eight shots behind. Hagen cooled off a bit in the afternoon but still maintained first place by one stroke over Boston's Tom McNamara.

Although thunderstorms strong enough to knock out the suburb's electric power flared up on Thursday night, conditions essentially remained the same for the last day. Hagen played steady golf in the third round. He teed off near the end of the field and, despite the pressure of being in the lead, held his game together for a 75. The heat took its toll on everyone; no one broke 70, and Hagen was still the leader through three rounds. The finest performance of the morning was turned in by Chick Evans, who climbed into contention with a 71 and trailed by only four strokes.

Hagen's first concern as he began his final eighteen holes was not Evans but McNamara, who was only two strokes behind. Hagen started a bit shaky and could do no better than a 38 at the turn. By that point, the tournament had tightened further; McNamara collapsed, but Evans came on strong, closing to within one stroke of Hagen. It must have seemed to Hagen, who had led all of the way, as though he was destined to lose again. It definitely seemed that way to the gallery, which swarmed around Evans, urging the local hero to pull off a tremendous come-from-behind victory. Having a "small, undemonstrative" gallery helped the still mostly inexperienced Hagen, whereas the cheering 1,000-person gallery following Evans was a distraction. Hagen could thank Mother Nature for his small gallery because at about noon, despite the outcry of the club, the Chicago Public Service Company shut off its power to fix the damage wrought by the previous evening's storm and, in the process, "marooned" some 3,000 spectators waiting to take the club's electric trolley to the course.

Whatever the gallery's influence, Hagen settled himself and came in with a 73. The highlight of his last nine holes came on the 18th, a short 277-yard par 4. After pulling his drive into the long rough about fifty yards short of the green, Hagen made a "wonderful" pitch to within eight feet of the hole. He then "walked over, got the line in one glance, and sent it down." It was a fitting conclusion for Hagen, who had relied heavily on his short game all week.

Evans, meanwhile, was doing his best to catch Hagen but came to the 18th hole requiring an improbable eagle two to force a playoff. He made things interesting after he crushed his tee shot, driving to the fringe of the green about forty-five feet from the hole. The crowd cheered Evans's drive, but he understood the difficult situation still facing him, commenting "It looks a long way off." Hagen stood at the 18th green and watched as Evans selected an iron and chipped his ball; the distance was perfect, but his ball stopped eight inches to the left of the hole. It was over. Evans and Ouimet congratulated the new champion, who had won his first U.S. Open by a single shot. Moreover, his four round total of 290 equaled the all-time low score for a U.S. Open set by George Sargent in 1909. Evans remembered that Hagen was gracious in victory: "Later, in the locker room, Walter came up and said, 'You know, I was telling everyone when I came in today that I was out last night with the boys and girls. But . . . no one was in bed any earlier than I was last night—or up any earlier today.'"

Because of the outbreak of the Great War and the lack of British entries, Hagen's achievement received slim coverage across the Atlantic. Said Britain's *Golf Illustrated*, "The British Press are too much concerned with our own trials and troubles to pay much attention to golfing events in another hemisphere, and, moreover, the American Open Championship is an event which does not particularly appeal to the golfing public on this side unless we are represented therein, as we were last year at Brookline." But if the event did not carry the prestige or the publicity in 1914 that it had carried in 1913, Hagen's low scoring, Evans's comeback performance, and the clash between amateurs and professionals made the Midlothian tournament exciting and distinctive.[14]

Although many competitors left Chicago for Minneapolis and the Western Open, Hagen and Leonard boarded a train for home. Meanwhile, across the country sports pages printed headlines like those of the *New York Herald*, "W.C. Hagen Flashes Brilliantly as New Star in Golfing World." In 1913 Hagen's rise at the Country Club of Rochester was chronicled only in the local papers; now his story was discussed throughout the nation. Still, Rochester displayed hardly a shadow of the celebrations that would accompany such an athletic accomplishment ten years later. Local newsman Henry Clune reminisced, "There was no dancing in the streets and streamers were not festooned between the lampposts with huge stenciled letters 'Welcome Home, Champ.'" A few reporters greeted Hagen at the train station in Rochester when he arrived on Monday. One asked him about his plans for the future, and Hagen only replied that they were of an "indefinite character." On Wednesday night the club organized a dinner in Hagen's honor and presented him with a gold watch to commemorate his victory. But if Clune remembered Hagen's homecoming as not being much, the *Democrat and Chronicle* characterized the dinner as "substantial" and told readers that their local golf professional was no longer referred to by members as "boy," but was now called "Mr. Hagen."[15]

In time Hagen's plans became more certain. He realized two important things about his victory at Midlothian: first, he had about a year to capitalize on it by signing endorsements and playing exhibitions; second, the accomplishment would carry him only so far, and if he wanted to stay near the top, he would need to follow it with others. Hagen's job at the Rochester club provided a steady

The 1914 U.S. Open champion. Courtesy: Albert R. Stone Negative Collection, Rochester Museum and Science Center, Rochester, New York

After winning the 1914 U.S. Open, Hagen received a hero's welcome at the Country Club of Rochester, complete with stars, stripes, and a host of admiring caddies. Courtesy: Albert R. Stone Negative Collection, Rochester Museum and Science Center, Rochester, New York

income and some local prestige, but he now had the opportunity to gain a much larger income and wider fame, and he intended to do just that. When his club closed for the winter of 1914–1915, Hagen accepted an invitation to do a tour of the west with Long Jim Barnes, the new Western Open champion. After playing in as many exhibitions in the northwest as the winter weather allowed, they traveled south to San Francisco in April and entered the Panama-Pacific Exposition Open. First prize for the tournament was a whopping $1,000. The figure was an all-time high; Hagen had received only $300 of a $900 total purse for his U.S. Open victory. That, together with the excitement and publicity surrounding the exposition, made for an attractive event.

Hagen, Barnes, and Chick Evans joined a regional cast to create a strong field. Hagen played splendidly, winning with a 286 and surpassing all sorts of marks: His second round 66 included a 30 on the front nine, both records, as was his first day's two-round total of 140. Herbert Reed, covering the event for *Harper's Weekly*, commented that Hagen had not only shot "perfect golf," but had done so displaying an "illuminating smile" and the type of "class" found in "the aristocracy of golf." Reed recognized some of the qualities that would eventually make "Sir Walter"; that is, confidence, insouciance, and charisma. The victory established Hagen as one of the nation's leading "money players" and proved that his Midlothian performance was no accident.[16]

Hagen's play in tournaments and exhibitions increased considerably in 1915. Following a second-place finish in eastern Pennsylvania's Shawnee Open, he traveled in mid-June to the Baltusrol Golf Club in New Jersey to play his third U.S. Open. He was supposed to have defended his title against another British invasion comprised of Vardon, Ray, and George Duncan, but those three, slated to travel across the Atlantic aboard the *Lusitania* on May 15, decided to postpone their trip after that ill-fated luxury liner was sunk by a German U-Boat on May 7. It was just as well for Hagen that the British stars did not show up, because he finished in an eight-way tie for tenth place, while receiving only $6.25 for his troubles. The story of the week was four-time U.S. Amateur champion Jerry Travers, who won his first U.S. Open. But if Hagen pocketed only $6.25, Travers collected no cash whatsoever; the USGA ruled that amateur champions could be given only a championship trophy plate for their accomplishment. The $300 first place prize went to second place finisher and professional Tom McNamara. Travers's victory was also significant because it made five Opens in a row won by "homebred" players.[17]

In early July Hagen rebounded from his disappointing U.S. Open performance by winning the Massachusetts Open, five strokes ahead of runner-up Mike Brady. The tournament was played at Brookline and, just as in the U.S. Open two years earlier, it rained on the last day of the event. Hagen accepted the $150 first prize and the next week headed to Long Island for the prestigious Metropolitan Open, which, aside from the U.S. and Western Opens, annually attracted the strongest players in the country. Hagen could not capture consecutive crowns, but he played well in New York's event, finishing alone in third place.[18]

Hagen took the next month off; then in mid-August he entrained back to Chicago for the Western Open. Tom McNamara led the tournament from start to finish, while Hagen finished in a tie for fourth place, five shots behind. Still, it was a solid showing in his first Western. By the fall of 1915, Hagen had won three tournaments, had competed in numerous exhibitions with such players as Jim Barnes, Tom McNamara, and Chick Evans, and had even secured his first golf equipment endorsement, signing an agreement with A.G. Spalding & Brothers to play their "Red Honor" golf ball. In short, Hagen had performed well, and it was beginning to pay off.[19]

For the first time in three years, Hagen spent the winter in Rochester. He probably needed to catch up on things at the club; certainly, over the previous season he had learned of the challenges facing a club professional who desired national competition. Although Hagen remembered getting "a kick out of all the traveling" that he did in 1915, the time away made managing the club more difficult. Actually, Hagen was beginning the transformation from a locally recognized professional who spent his time at the club selling equipment and giving lessons, to a nationally famous professional who traveled, competed for prize money and endorsements, and spent less time doing the traditional duties around the club.

A handful of other professionals shared Hagen's experience and frustrations. As the position evolved and the number of club professionals grew, the leaders of the sport recognized the usefulness of a national organization for golf club professionals. The idea had been discussed as early as 1897, and several regional organizations, such as the Eastern Professional Golfers' Association, had already formed. Then on January 17, 1916, the country's top professionals gathered at New York City to establish the Professional Golfers Association of America (PGA). Hagen was one of thirty-five charter members dedicated to organizing his profession and to promoting the sport by staging an annual match-play tournament for professionals only. It was the first significant step toward the legitimization of professional golf in the U.S. and, in time, became the foundation for a national golf tour.[20]

Despite passing on a winter swing, Hagen maintained a busy competitive schedule in 1916, entering all of the big tournaments and adding to his already enviable record. He began the season in late June, though, with a disappointing seventh-place finish in the U.S. Open, held at the Minikahda Country Club in Minneapolis. The performance was especially frustrating for Hagen, who was touted as a favorite. Yet another homebred won, as Chick Evans broke through for his first (and only) U.S. Open. As if rubbing it in on Hagen and his fellow professionals, the *New York Times* commented smugly that Evans was an idol for thousands "who love the game for what there is in it, not for what they can get out of it." Hagen took out of it $60 in prize money and headed back east.[21]

Two weeks later he won an exciting three-way play-off to capture his first Metropolitan Open. The tournament, staged again on Long Island, was deadlocked on Friday after seventy-two holes with Hagen, Barnes, and Charles Hoffner in the lead. The next day, July 15, the three played an additional eighteen holes before a gallery that included Yale football legend Walter Camp and former New York Giants' baseball player John Montgomery Ward. Hagen, who trailed Barnes by two shots at the turn, won the "memorable struggle" with a 74, one stroke ahead of Barnes and three better than Hoffner. His 35 on the back nine made the difference and represented superb come-from-behind play. Observed the *Rochester Democrat and Chronicle*, "another star [has been] fitted into Hagen's crown."[22]

He added two more stars in August when he won the Shawnee Open and the Western Open. If not as prestigious as the Metropolitan Open, the Shawnee event still attracted a strong field, because professionals from the northeast used it that year to fine-tune their games in preparation for the Western. Hagen's 298 bested the scores of Jim Barnes and Gil Nichols, among many others. The following week, on August 17–18 at the Blue Mound Country Club in Milwaukee, Hagen totaled a 286 to win his first Western Open title. What did the new champion think about his accomplishment? "In coming ahead of such men as Barnes, Hutchison, [George] Sargent, and [George] Simpson, I feel that I have won one of the greatest victories of my life. They played great golf but I was fortunate in that the shots I tried to make came off successfully." Despite his modesty, the Rochester professional had landed one of the biggest prizes of the entire season. A.G. Spalding & Brothers was thrilled and immediately paid for a half-page spread in *Golfers Magazine*, advertising that Walter Hagen, "A Great Golfer," and Bullet Honor, "Golf Ball Extraordinary," had teamed up to win the Western Open. The lesson? Amateurs needed to "Play an Honor and Excel."[23]

Hagen and his "Bullet Honors" could not sustain their success for the last major event of the year, the inaugural PGA Championship, held at the Siwanoy Country Club in Mount Vernon, New

York. Long Jim Barnes made history on October 14 when he became the first man to have his name engraved on the Rodman Wanamaker Trophy. Hagen performed well, lasting into the semifinals before Jock Hutchison beat him 2 up. The PGA offered a generous $5,000 purse, of which Barnes collected $500, plus a diamond-studded medal. (By comparison, in 1916 the USGA increased the Open purse to a total of $1,200.) Overall, the event was successful in attracting the nation's leading professionals and in generating excitement by allowing golf fans an opportunity to watch professionals compete in the match-play format. Following the Great War, it became a fixture that marked the conclusion of the professional season.

By the end of October, Hagen was back in Rochester to stay, at least for the winter. A couple of weeks before, the club's board had voted to renew his contract, and in late September it had given him $100 "toward defraying his expenses at the Open Championship Tournament." If he was gone more often than most professionals, in exchange Hagen brought the club publicity. That was a trade the club's board members were willing to make with their increasingly famous professional, for they understood that if they were not willing, Hagen was now in a position to find another club that was.[24]

It had been more than two years since his U.S. Open victory, and Hagen had successfully capitalized on that win with numerous exhibitions and a major endorsement contract. Moreover, he had solidified his competitive reputation with tournament wins in the Panama-Pacific, Massachusetts, Shawnee, Metropolitan, and Western Opens. In September 1916, J.G. Davis of the *American Golfer* ranked Hagen "the leading professional of the year." The next month, Herbert Reed, writing in this instance for *Country Life*, carefully analyzed Hagen's "fine, free swing" and putting style, concluding that he was "among the best and most daring putters in the game." He also noted Hagen's ability to scramble out of trouble, observing that for Hagen, "nothing seems to be unplayable." Beyond technique, Reed was impressed by Hagen's confidence and "true sportsmanship."[25]

The year had also ushered in some important events in Hagen's personal life. In the fall he started spending time with an attractive young woman named Margaret Beatrice Johnson. She was nineteen, blonde-haired, and the daughter of George W. Johnson, owner of Rochester's Clinton Hotel. Gene Sarazen recalled that the two met when Hagen noticed Margaret Johnson walking a "handsome" hunting dog. Hagen admired both of them and, under the guise of inquiring about the dog, introduced himself to her. After offering to buy the dog, he asked her to dinner. She said yes and even sold him the animal, which apparently became the basis for their romance. However their paths first crossed, they fell in love, and the twenty-three-year-old Hagen now had more on his mind than golf. But if the sport did enter their dinner conversations, it is likely that they discussed the exciting, history-making U.S. Amateur Championship played that September; after all, the rest of the golf world was still talking about it.[26]

At least three significant things happened at the 1916 U.S. Amateur Championship, held at the Merion Cricket Club in Philadelphia. First, Chick Evans won, becoming the first man to win both USGA titles in a single season. "The Double," as it soon became called, was the most remarkable American golfing achievement up to that time, save Ouimet's victory over Vardon and Ray. Second, more people probably read about and attended the tournament than any other amateur event up to that point in America's short golfing history. And third, the country was introduced to a young golfing phenom from Atlanta, Little Bob Jones.

Over the previous three years, Jones had gained remarkable physical strength and golf savvy. Like the rest of the golfing public, he had been energized by the events of the 1913 U.S. Open. As he later reflected, "That is the first golf I remember reading about in the papers, and I began to feel that this was a real game." In October, the Vardon-Ray tour stopped at East Lake. The eleven-year-old Little Bob was in the gallery and witnessed Ray hit what Jones would later refer to as the greatest shot he had ever seen. It was a memorable day, despite the fact that the British professionals defeated Stewart Maiden and Druid Hills professional Willie Mann by a score of 1 up. Although he did not enter any significant, organized events that year, Jones played informally and by the end of the summer could shoot 80 against East Lake's difficult par 73.[27]

Firing an 80 was a big step for Little Bob. Playing with his usual partner, Perry Adair, he completed the round at East Lake by holing a four-foot putt, quickly had his friend sign the scorecard, and headed across the course to find his father, who was putting out on the 14th green. "I had sense enough to wait until he was through putting," wrote Jones. "Then I walked up to him and held out the card. . . . Dad took it and looked at it and then looked at me. I don't remember what he said. But suddenly he put his arms around me and hugged me—hard." The episode reveals that Bobby Jones had parents who were not only caring and affectionate, but also quite supportive of his athletic endeavors. Big Bob had decided that he was going to allow his son the opportunity of an athletic career denied him by R.T. "Rob was our only child. He was a good son—no man ever had a better," Big Bob told O.B. Keeler. "Golf was the game he loved, and it became the ambition of his mother and myself to see him progress in it and to help him all we could."[28]

Yet there is no evidence that Big Bob Jones was the stereotypical controlling or domineering father of a child prodigy, the type that manipulates his dependent, vicariously pushing him to athletic greatness. Big Bob was no Papa Lenglen (the father and coach of French tennis star Suzanne Lenglen), and seemingly offered his son a healthy balance of encouragement and support, just the thing that had been absent in Walter Hagen's golf life.

Jones continued to develop his game through 1914, playing in small, local events, and the following year his parents permitted him to start serious competition. By then his temper had grown in proportion to his skill. Early in 1915 at East Lake, Grantland Rice, Jim Barnes, and Alex Smith happened to observe Jones lose control of himself. In that instance, Jones stopped his mashie (five-iron) approach shot about thirty feet from the hole and, disgusted that it was not closer, threw his club. Smith commented, "It's a shame, but he'll never make a good golfer." Barnes disagreed, convinced that "this kid will be one of the world's greats in a few more years." Rice tended to side with Barnes: "He isn't satisfied with just a good shot. He wants it to be perfect—stone dead. He has a great ambition to play every shot in the bag. But you're right about that temper, Alex. He's a fighting cock, a hothead. That one fault could prove to be his greatest hazard."[29]

Jones began the 1915 season with a dismal showing at Montgomery, Alabama, in that city's annual invitational event. Despite his poor start, Big Bob agreed to let his son enter his first regional event, the Southern Amateur Championship, mostly because the tournament was to be played at East Lake. Big Bob entered as well. The Atlanta Athletic Club (AAC) selected the younger Jones to represent it in the team qualifying competition, along with Perry Adair, his father, George Adair, and Will Rowan. The selection was an honor that proved Little Bob was considered superior in skill to the rest of the club's members, most of whom were much older.

The preliminary rounds for the Southern Golf Association's fourteenth annual championship began on Tuesday morning, June 15. Jones qualified with an 83, just one stroke higher than the leaders, Charles Dexter of Dallas and Nelson Whitney of New Orleans, the defending champion. Moreover, Jones led the AAC to the first-place trophy in the team competition. A record 215 golfers entered, but only the top sixty-four survived to play the next day in the eighteen-hole matches.

A fierce thunderstorm struck early Wednesday, leaving the course littered with hailstones, but the match play began on schedule. Jones met E.V. Patterson of Charlotte, North Carolina, in the first round and beat him 2 and 1. In the afternoon he faced "Commodore" Bryan Heard of Houston, whom he later described as a "short, stocky man with iron-gray hair [who] wore a sun-helmet." Also a seasoned veteran, Heard defeated Little Bob 2 and 1 in a match that the *American Golfer* characterized as "brilliant." The defeat dropped Jones into the second flight, where he advanced to the thirty-six-hole final round. Jones lost, however, again by a score of 2 and 1. (Big Bob barely qualified with a 94 and then, like his son, was eliminated in the second round.) Although he did not win the title and only advanced to the second round of the top flight, the Jones family took pride in Little Bob's performance. He had, after all, qualified third in a field of more than 200 of the south's best. *Golfers Magazine* thought that Jones was "the sensation of the tournament." Still, Jones remembered that his thirteen-year-old self expected more, and that being knocked out on the first day and on his home course was disappointing.[30]

He felt better after he won the Birmingham Invitational and the club championship of Druid Hills later that summer. He followed those victories with another on September 20 in the AAC's tournament at East Lake. Little Bob led the qualifiers with an 82; Big Bob also entered and qualified with an 89. As it turned out, the most exciting feature of the tournament was the Jones family final, with father and son playing against each other in the last round. Little Bob won, 4 and 3. He finished the season two weeks later in the City Championship. Jones advanced to the semifinals, where he was knocked out by George Adair. Thus, by the close of 1915 Jones had made a splash at his first regional championship and had won three local club events. The fact that one of those had come against family did not bother the *American Golfer,* which predicted, "in the course of a few years in which [Jones] can gain the necessary experience . . . he will develop into one of the very best golfers in the country."[31]

In the summer of 1916 Jones, despite an affliction of lumbago, affirmed the *American Golfer's* analysis by winning three more club championships and the Georgia state title. He began by successfully defending his Birmingham and AAC titles. Then in late July, his father let him go with the Adairs to Knoxville, Tennessee, to play in the Cherokee Country Club's tournament. The galleries were sizable, the weather was excellent, and Jones marched through the field, defeating Simpson Dean of Rome, Georgia, 6 and 5 in the final.[32]

In the midst of winning those three club invitationals, Jones made some national news early in July when he shot 68 and tied East Lake's course record, set by Stewart Maiden. The performance was noted in the *New York Times* under the headline: "Georgia Has Golf Marvel." During the first week of August, he completed his year's regional competition by winning the inaugural championship of the Georgia State Golf Association. Still being referred to in the local press as "Little Bob," he captured the qualifying trophy and then battled through the field to meet Perry Adair in the final. Both started shakily, but Jones calmed down to shoot a course-record 70 in the afternoon and defeat Adair 2 up. Jones remembered it as "the hardest match of the many Perry and I played." The victory was his fourth of the season and seventh in the last two years. In sum, Little Bob had all but mastered the southern competition.[33]

Although he was only fourteen, Little Bob was ready to test his skills on the national level. So when George Adair asked Big Bob to let his son accompany him and Perry to Philadelphia for the U.S. Amateur, he said yes. George Adair "was responsible for my first appearance in a national championship" and "did more than anyone, other than my father, to encourage my activity in competitive golf," Jones recalled.[34]

The Merion Cricket Club had previously hosted national women's events, but it held its first national men's tournament on September 4–9, 1916. The club had two courses and decided to accommodate the 157 entries by using both, requiring each competitor to play eighteen holes on each course, thereby conducting the qualifying rounds in one day. George Adair knew that Merion's fast bentgrass greens, typical of northern courses, would be nothing like the slower, heavier Bermuda greens of southern layouts on which his son and Little Bob were used to playing; so he saw to it that the Atlanta party arrived at Merion by Thursday, August 30, to give the youngsters a chance to play a practice round or two. They stayed at the Bellevue-Stratford hotel in Philadelphia and took the train each day to the club.

It was Jones's first trip to the north, and he was "simply pop-eyed with excitement and interest." Feeling proud that he was wearing his first pair of long pants (rather than knickers, the common attire for boys in that period) and confident from his recent victories, Jones "hadn't sense or experience enough to be afraid" in his first national competition. He was young but thickset for his age at 5' 4" and 165 pounds, and he was certain that he could play with anyone.[35]

When he arrived at the course on Monday morning to warm up for his qualifying rounds, the conditions were perfect; the air was so clear that throughout the afternoon the moon could be seen against a cloudless blue background. Buoyed by the weather and wearing a cap to keep the sun out of his eyes, Jones affirmed his self-confidence, firing a record 74 over the "new" course in the morning to lead his half of the field. It must have seemed to him like just another club tournament. The new course was shorter and easier than the "old" course, though. Moreover, with his morning's round came the largest gallery of the afternoon. All of that amounted to an 89, which was good enough to qualify him for the thirty-six-hole match play rounds but also a sobering finish. As the *New York Times* correspondent put it, Jones "blew up [and] the detonation was audible all over the course."

Still, the 5,000-strong gallery was energized by his play and "roared" at the end of the day when his name was posted on the scoreboard among the thirty-two qualifiers. He also impressed P.C. Pulver of *Golfers Magazine*, who wrote, "It required only a glance at Jones for one to be speedily convinced that the boy from Atlanta was a golfer from top to bottom. There were times when

"Georgia's Golf Marvel." At fourteen, Jones took his first national
competition by storm. Expressing supreme confidence,
he poses here for photographers at Merion in 1916.
Courtesy: Sidney L. Matthew Collection

with [an] easy and almost perfectly timed stroke he would get as much distance from the tee as the big chaps who had been playing the game longer and had twice his strength. Everything he did was brought off without fuss or frills of any kind." His 163 put him in a tie for 18th place along with the oldest player in the tournament, fifty-six-year-old "Monty" Ward, the one-time Giants baseball standout. Ward astonishingly shot the lowest round of the day on the old course, a 76. Jones's and Ward's low rounds, extremities in age, and identical qualifying totals made for a trio of notable coincidences.

The draw for Tuesday's first round pitted Jones against Eben Byers of Allegheny, Pennsylvania. Byers was an experienced golfer who had been national champion in 1906 and runner-up in 1902 and 1903. Although past his prime, he seemed on his game for this tournament, qualifying alone in third place. It was a difficult lot for Jones. Grantland Rice of the *New York Tribune,* a friend of Big Bob Jones, had breakfast with Little Bob on Tuesday morning before his match with Byers. Rice remembered that Jones ate little and "was restless and nervous and anxious to get out early to the battlefield."

Jones and Byers were scheduled to tee off at 9:10, only the third group of the day, but Byers, possibly employing a bit of games-manship, kept the punctual Jones waiting for half an hour. Fifteen years later O.B. Keeler would capture the humorous, surreal feeling about the match between the fourteen-year-old "boy wonder" and the crusty veteran: "As Mr. Byers and Bobby walked off the [first] tee after their drives, Bobby, in the same spirit as he would have done it in a casual match at home, offered the former champion a piece of chewing gum. Mr. Byers declined—without thanks. And Bobby, whose motive was entirely hospitable, felt somewhat abashed. He also wondered why Mr. Byers did not chew gum."

It was awkward for both of them, but more so for Byers, who was not used to playing a young adolescent, much less one who was so highly skilled and who had the enthusiastic support of the gallery. Jones, on the other hand, had for the past two years competed against opponents much older, bigger, and more experienced than he. Like nearly all of his other matches, this was one that illustrated the infancy of the sport, as the second-generation youngster competed against a man who had learned the game in adulthood.

To make things even more interesting, both Jones and Byers had short tempers. Jones later reflected, "I think the main reason

I beat him was because he ran out of clubs first. At the 12th hole Mr. Byers threw an iron out-of-bounds and wouldn't let his caddy go after it." If Jones remembered losing his temper in the Byers match, it seems that few commentators noticed it. Pulver was the only one of the major golf journal writers to mention Jones's emotions. "When he got into trouble, there were slight indications of temper; but after all, that's a good fault, for one cannot get far in this game unless he takes the thing seriously enough to occasionally get roused at his own lapses." But Pulver added, "At no time in the match did the lad from Atlanta appear rattled, though like an unbroken colt he seemed to find difficulty in restraining himself from doing things with undue haste." Pulver's latter comment was more typical of the coverage, which tended to focus on Jones's surprising confidence. The *Philadelphia Inquirer* did not note either man's temper in its brief coverage of the match, only commenting that Jones played "with all the confidence in the world."[36]

Fortunately for Jones, Byers allowed him to get a comfortable lead following the lunch break, 5 up with 14 to play. By the last turn (28th hole), Byers had cut the margin to three. The crowd, expecting Little Bob to crumble at some point, thought the momentum had finally moved in Byers's favor. But as *Golf Illustrated*'s John Anderson noticed, "Master Jones pulled his cap down a little lower over his forehead, chewed gum and looked as complacent and undisturbed as if the last of his worries was the outcome of the match." In fact, "the inward strain was telling more upon the veteran than upon the rising star of golf," and Jones closed out the match on the 17th (35th), at which point "he was regarded almost like a hero." The next morning the *New York Times*'s sports page headline read "Boy of Fourteen Beats Ex-Champ." The Byers upset was Little Bob's introduction to the nation's golfing public, and an exciting introduction it was.

So Jones survived into the field of sixteen. His opponent on Wednesday was the Pennsylvania state champion, Frank Dyer. Dyer had qualified at 161, two shots better than Jones, and had easily defeated his first-round opponent. For some, Dyer had been a tournament favorite; most thought he would at least defeat Jones. It certainly looked that way when Jones started the match by losing five of six holes. John Anderson believed that "if there had been a train leaving for Atlanta at that moment, [Jones] would have taken it at once. He smote the air with his clubs and raged internally." Fortunately for Jones and everyone else, George Adair was following the match. Sensing that his young charge was about to explode, Adair took him aside and, according to Anderson, said, "Bob, you are playing bad golf because you are not in the right mood. Now you just get your mind on the game and play for all you are worth or I'll send you right back home."

Whatever his exact words, Adair's counsel settled Jones. He rallied to square the match at the 16th and take the lead at the 17th. Then a small controversy occurred at the 18th after Jones and Dyer pulled their tee shots into the rough; their balls had stopped in the same vicinity, and they could not agree on whose ball was whose, each claiming that the ball with the better lie was theirs. Identification was especially difficult because both had taken Walter Hagen's advice and were playing identical Spalding "Red Honor" balls. After some brief argument, Jones agreed to play the ball with the inferior lie (which he forever maintained was not really his), and it cost him the hole, because Dyer squared the match. Before he began the afternoon round, a sassy Jones told Anderson, "I've put J's all over this ball so he can't help seeing them." He won the first (19th) hole and never looked back, maintaining a slim lead and finishing Dyer off, 4 and 2.

The victory set up a third round match that would be his toughest yet; he would face the defending champion, Robert Gardner. A former track and field star at Yale University, Gardner was an excellent athlete in the prime of his golfing career. Jones recalled that when he and Dyer had completed their match and were walking back to the clubhouse, they noticed off in the distance the Gardner-Max Marston match, still in progress and attended by a huge gallery. Dyer told Jones that he had just earned the right to play the winner of that match and asked him if he knew how they stood. Jones said that he did not know, but that he "supposed the result would make very little difference so far as [he] was concerned." Confident, even cocky, and probably a bit overwhelmed, Jones had become the star of the tournament.

On Wednesday evening golf dopesters wondered if the "boy" could maintain his success, while oddsmakers considered Gardner a 5 to 4 favorite. The field had been narrowed to eight, and with three more victories, the fourteen-year-old would become the U.S. Amateur champion. The next morning the "largest gallery [that] ever followed a golf tournament in [the] section" showed up to witness the "struggle" between the "boy and man." Jones, wearing a white shirt and gray trousers, "appeared almost like a midget alongside the tall and slender Gardner." To add some melodrama, Gardner's fiancee was in the gallery. Having her there may have made him nervous; on the first hole Gardner topped his tee shot, put his second shot out of bounds, hit a tree with his third shot, and in the process lost the hole to Jones. Jones also won the second, but then Gardner steadied himself, so that by the lunch break the Atlantan was nursing a 1 up lead.

They continued to play close through the front nine in the afternoon. Heavily perspiring in the afternoon heat, Jones became disheartened when, with the match all-square, he squandered excellent opportunities at the sixth, seventh, and eighth holes. The experienced Gardner quickly capitalized, winning three out of the next four holes and eventually taking the match 4 and 3 to end Jones's unprecedented run at Merion. The youthful Atlantan had never collapsed, though, and played Gardner tough to the very last stroke. "Not even Bob Gardner, who is the last word in courage, could outgame the little fellow," concluded the *New York Times.*

The *Philadelphia Inquirer* described the scene after Gardner dropped the last putt: "His little opponent tossed aside his stick and hurried to the victor's side. He extended his right hand and the pair shook heartily. To do so, it was necessary for Gardner to stoop slightly on account of the great difference in height." The defending champion complimented Jones in his post-round interviews: "He put up a better game than I had expected. He's a real one, that is sure." As for Jones, he spoke "modestly": "Yes, I am very much disappointed. I was not sure that I could beat Mr. Gardner, but I did expect to make a better showing against him. He beat me in the sixth, seventh, and eighth holes this afternoon through the wonderful manner in which he recovered. I am going to Pine Valley [Golf Club] tomorrow, and after that match I am going right home. School starts next week, you know." Besides modesty, his comments displayed an intense competitive spirit and a perfectionism. Jones may have wanted more, but golf fans were generally impressed; the "chunky, rosy-cheeked, blonde little Southerner" had taken the measure of the country's best amateurs and played well above their expectations.[37]

While Jones and the Adairs headed back to Atlanta (Perry Adair had qualified, but was eliminated in the second round of the tournament), Gardner went on to face Chick Evans in the final, which Evans won 4 and 3. Aside from Evans's completion of "The Double," the big story of the championship day was the size and enthusiasm of the gallery. Officials counted nearly 2,000 automobiles near the grounds and estimated that the gallery numbered over 5,000. It was "the largest crowd of spectators that ever witnessed a golf event in this country," according to the *Philadelphia Inquirer* and the *New York Times*. Moreover, although groundsmen used rope in an effort to control the movement of the spectators, "shrieking feminine enthusiasm" and the "golf-mad crowd" made the ropes "useless." The 1916 event had been the most exciting and closely followed U.S. Amateur in history. It was an appropriate way to cap the period 1913–1916, during which the sport of golf and its two most promising stars, Walter Hagen and Bobby Jones, had gone public.

Chapter 3
War, Metamorphosis, and Megaphones: 1917–1919

While golf, Hagen, and Jones went public in the U.S., the sport was "almost dead" in Great Britain as that country entered its third year of war against Germany and the other Central Powers. In October of 1916, *Golfers Magazine* informed American enthusiasts that their European counterparts had taken "up the gun and the sword for the brassie and the cleek," and that clubhouses were "being turned into hospitals and the fine courses into play grounds where the convalescent soldiers may regain their strength." Indeed, for the British, the Great War had precluded everything, even golf; for Americans, however, the conflict was still mostly foreign.[1]

Since the Great War's outbreak in August of 1914, President Woodrow Wilson and Congress had kept the U.S. neutral and had encouraged Americans to do the same in their hearts and minds. But neutrality, collectively and individually, became much more difficult after 128 Americans went down with the *Lusitania* in May of 1915. Still, many Americans did not want to get involved militarily. And after Germany agreed to stop its unrestricted U-boat warfare (meaning they would target only naval and not civilian vessels), the U.S. officially remained neutral, while increasing its emotional and economic support for Britain and France. In the fall of 1916, as Walter Hagen called on Margaret Johnson and Bobby Jones played in his first U.S. Amateur, President Wilson campaigned for reelection, largely on the neutrality issue. Having won a second term in November with the slogan "He Kept Us Out Of War!", President Wilson reluctantly moved the country toward the conflict in the winter of 1917 when Germany recommenced unrestricted use of its U-boat fleet. Finally, on April 6 the U.S. officially joined the British and French in the Great War to defeat "barbaric" Germany and, declared President Wilson, to make the world "safe for democracy."

During World War I, Americans generally expected everyone to do their part and did not tolerate "slackers," regardless of their motivation. Some prominent golfers, such as Francis Ouimet, whose amateur status had recently been nullified by the USGA because of his investment in a sporting goods store, eventually entered the armed forces. For most golfers, though, "doing their part" consisted of exhibiting their talents to raise charity dollars for Red Cross relief efforts. Most of the significant golf championships were canceled for the 1917 and 1918 seasons. At fifteen, Jones was too young to consider entering military service. Hagen, on the other hand, was twenty-four and ripe for the draft.

Hagen later wrote that in the spring of 1918 he tried to join the U.S. Air Service but was turned down for some reason that he did not detail. Like so many other German-Americans in 1916, Hagen may have been ambivalent about the war. He was not especially politically minded and, after all, his mother had been born in Germany. It is possible that, to some degree, all of that influenced his decision to marry Margaret Johnson and start a family of his own.

They had enjoyed a brief courtship, and by Christmas of 1916 Walter proposed and Margaret accepted marriage. The prenuptial events consisted of two luncheons, two card parties, and a tea for the bride, while her brother George Johnson served as Hagen's best man, organizing a stag "theater party" for the groom and his friends. The *Democrat and Chronicle* reported that the couple acquired their marriage license the same day of the wedding. If so, Hagen was up early, because at 9:00 in the morning of Monday, January 29, 1917, Walter and Margaret were married in the rectory of St. Mary's Catholic Church in Rochester. The fact that they were married by a priest in the rectory suggests that the Presbyterian-reared Hagen may have converted to Catholicism, or more likely, agreed to let their children be raised Catholic. The brief newspaper account did not describe Hagen's appearance but said that his bride wore a "traveling suit of blue and a Georgette picture hat, and carried a bouquet of orchids and lilies of the valley." It was a modest ceremony and only the immediate families were present. That afternoon the couple left for New York City to honeymoon and from there to the south for "an extensive trip."[2]

When they returned from Florida, where Hagen had a temporary position at the Palma Ceia Golf Club in Tampa, the couple moved into a small cottage on the club's grounds. It may have been the first time that Hagen had lived outside of Corbett's Glen and was even more likely Margaret's first move from her parents. Their little home was "usually filled with guests, particularly over the week ends." Hagen remembered, "I was very serious about golf and my wife was strictly social. She liked parties and people. None of this interested me too much, but it bothered me not at all."[3]

They had been married nearly a year when on January 11, 1918, at the Hahnemann Hospital in Rochester, Margaret gave birth to a boy, whom they named Walter C. Jr. With an attractive young wife and a first-born son, Hagen's personal life had caught up with his professional life and, seemingly, all was in order.[4]

Although the war nearly killed golf in Great Britain, it provided a great boost to the sport over here. In time, popular war-relief exhibitions would bring much publicity to Hagen, Jones, and their sport. For a while, though, things moved along as usual. In March of 1917, Margaret watched her husband place second in Florida's West Coast Open. A few weeks later, during their trip back to Rochester after their honeymoon, Hagen entered the North and South Open at Pinehurst, finishing in eleventh place. Soon after they moved into their cottage, the U.S. declared war on Germany, and news arrived that the USGA had canceled the U.S. Open and that the Metropolitan Golf Association (MGA) had followed suit by lifting its championships as well.

In lieu of its regular open, the USGA scheduled the Patriotic Tournament for June 20–23 at Philadelphia's Whitemarsh Valley golf course. All of the proceeds, about $5,000, including money that had been earmarked for prizes, entry fees, and admission receipts, would go to the Red Cross to fund field hospitals. The event was special because it was the first in which the USGA charged an admission. Hagen made plans to enter but arrived late, after the first day's round. Jock Hutchison won the tournament; Hagen spent

While serving as the club pro in Rochester, Hagen became
accustomed to playing golf in all sorts of inclement weather.
This blustery day required an overcoat and gloves.
Courtesy: Country Club of Rochester

the next month with him and Long Jim Barnes playing in Red
Cross exhibitions in the Midwest.[5]

In late July the PGA sponsored the biggest charity matches of
the year. The unique event featured four-way team play between
the nation's leading "Homebred" professionals, Scottish professionals, English professionals, and amateurs. Twelve of the leading players in each category made up the teams; Hagen played for
the Homebreds, and Jones was invited to join the amateurs. The
War Relief International Matches would last for five days, July 23–
27, and be held over four courses—Englewood, Baltusrol, Siwanoy,
and Garden City—all within a short distance of New York City.

Jones received an invitation to the matches because of the lasting impression he had made at Merion. In early June of 1917 he
strengthened his reputation as the country's best young amateur
when, in his second attempt, he won the Southern Championship
at the Roebuck Springs course in Birmingham. Jones had come a
long way since the previous summer and was considered the fa-

vorite heading into the tournament. He qualified easily and then advanced through the field. In the rain-soaked final, he faced New Orleanian Louis Jacoby and defeated him 6 and 4. Little Bob, as the *Atlanta Constitution* still referred to him, became the "hero of everyone in Birmingham, the youngest champion that has ever graced the records of southern golfdom."[6]

After his victory, Jones traveled north with the Adairs to Chicago for a few Red Cross exhibitions and his first Western Amateur Championship. The Western Golf Association (WGA) was one of the few organizations to proceed with its events in 1917. The tournament began on July 9 over the Midlothian course, which had been toughened a bit since Hagen won his U.S. Open there nearly three years earlier. Wearing pin-striped trousers, a checked bow tie, and a cap, Jones qualified with an 80–83–163; Donald Edwards of Midlothian led the field with a 150. Obviously, Jones was not playing well, despite his natty attire. In the first round of match play the next day, former champion Ned Sawyer knocked him out 3 and 1 over eighteen holes. Still, the Jones-Sawyer match was the "main attraction," according to the *Chicago Tribune*. A few days later Francis Ouimet won the tournament.[7]

Ouimet's victory further fueled the controversy that surrounded Jones's first Western. The championship had become a point of contention for two reasons: first, the WGA disagreed with the USGA's decision to revoke Ouimet's amateur status and had allowed him to enter its championship in good standing; second, the WGA received significant criticism for holding a tournament at all, given the international situation. Although most American golfers probably sided with the WGA on the Ouimet issue, viewing the USGA's amateur ruling as unfair and legalistic, they bolted from the organization in its decision to hold annual tournaments. Charles Thompson, writing for *Golfers Magazine*, felt it necessary to defend the WGA against charges of "disloyalty and sedition" by arguing that the organization was only trying to do "its bit" in keeping with President Wilson's desires for the continuation of athletic events during the war. Thompson also reminded critics that the WGA donated to the Red Cross all of the entry fees and the money set aside for trophies, and spent its surplus purchasing Liberty Bonds. "Have other associations that criticized the Western Golf Association done as much? It [the WGA] has tried by all means within its power to show its loyalty and patriotism to the country, and it challenges any statement to the contrary," he concluded.

The brouhaha illustrated the long-held independent spirit of the
WGA in relation to the USGA, as well as intensifying patriotic
pressures of the Great War.[8]

While golf writers argued over the actions of the WGA, Jones
and Adair traveled to New York to join Walter Hagen in the PGA's
War Relief International Matches. During their stay, Jones and
Adair lived at the Riverside Drive apartment of sportswriter
Grantland Rice. Rice was an avid golfer himself and had also been
invited to play on the amateur team with Jones and Adair; it was,
after all, a PGA-sponsored event, and the amateurs were
underrepresented because Ouimet, Evans, and Jess Guilford all
took a pass to do other things. As a result, Rice got an opportunity
to play. He had befriended Big Bob Jones years before while starting his newspaper career for the *Atlanta Journal* and was a willing
chaperone for Little Bob that week. Jones remembered "romping"
around the apartment, creating all sorts of "commotion and noise,"
while Rice "knocked out long poems for his column as if he were
off in some quiet and remote place." The Rices took the teenagers
to see the sights of New York, including Coney Island. "Jones was
fifteen. Rice was thirty-six. The relationship began as the naturally
awkward child-guardian mix of deference and paternalism, but
within fifteen years it would be a very deep and rich friendship,
and Rice credited its genesis to that 1917 visit to New York,"
Charles Fountain has concluded. The visit was one episode in a
summer during which Little Bob and Perry Adair "had the time of
[their] young lives."[9]

During the last week of July, they all played a lot of golf. The
PGA created a full schedule consisting of a variety of events. It
started at the Englewood course with some entertaining mixed
foursome play. Hagen was not among them, but most of the professionals (amateurs were excluded) teamed up with some of the
area's female golfers. A small gallery paid to see the competition,
which was conducted in two-ball foursomes; in other words, each
team played one ball, alternating shots. *Golf Illustrated* observed
that the experience was "an entirely different proposition" for the
professionals, who were "treated to more practice in the rough
than they usually get in a month." "Many of them were surprisingly nervous," the account continued, "and the habit of teaching
proved too strong for many of them, with the result that their
partners, themselves very nervous, became confused and suffered
rather than profited from the advice given."

Tuesday "ushered in the more serious business" of the week and the first full day of play between the men. They began with thirty-six holes of medal play at Englewood. It was purely individual competition that day, serving as a sort of warm-up, and team scores were not calculated. Scottish professional Willie MacFarlane led with a pair of 73s. Hagen ended in a tie for ninth place with two 75s, while Jones finished with an 80–78 in the bottom half of the field. Rice, meanwhile, trailed in forty-fifth place with an 83–86.

Over the next three days, at a different course each day, the men played thirty-six holes that were comprised of round-robin foursomes in the morning and singles matches in the afternoon. One unique component of the event was that the PGA decided to keep score by holes, so that if a match was won by a count of 5 up, the team received 5 points rather than 1 for the victory. Moreover, every match went the full eighteen holes, giving the loser a chance to cut into the deficit or the winner an opportunity to expand it. Inasmuch as the scoring system placed a premium on winning by wide margins, it was rarely ever used. Another problem with the format was that a team could play generally well but fall far behind on account of poor play in one match. A single player, such as Grantland Rice, could be a serious liability if he was defeated repeatedly by lopsided scores.

On Wednesday morning at Baltusrol, the Homebreds jumped out to a big lead in the morning, collecting 26 points to 15 for the English professionals, 2 for the Scots, and 1 for the Amateurs. Jones and Norman Maxwell paired to win the point, defeating an English team that included George Sargent. The first morning in some ways exemplified the whole event, at least for Jones, who also won his singles match with Cyril Walker that afternoon. Hagen won his foursome match, but was defeated by Scottish professional Jock Hutchison in the singles. Poor Rice, who must have felt as though he was constantly battling the Four Horsemen of Golf, gave up 9 points to the English professionals in his two matches. By the end of the day, the English had the lead with 44 points to 39 for the Homebreds, 14 for the Scots, and 13 for the Amateurs.

On Thursday the scene shifted to Siwanoy, where the touted match between Jock Hutchison and Jerry Travers overshadowed another impressive Jones victory, as he downed Scottish professional Freddie McLeod 2 up. Jones and Adair had also teamed up that morning to win another point. Hagen held his own, losing his foursome match but winning in the singles. The day belonged to the Homebreds; they took 50 points from their English counterparts, who ended with just 15. Going into the final day the Homebreds had a comfortable lead of 89 points to 59 for the English, 55 for the Scots, and 24 for the Amateurs.

The Homebreds, having crushed the English and Scottish professionals, turned their attention to the Amateurs on Friday at Long Island's Garden City course. In the morning team play, the professionals maintained their supremacy, sweeping their opponents, 25 points to none. Hagen and Mike Brady defeated a strong team, Travers and Kirkby, 2 up, while Jones-Adair suffered their worst defeat, 7 down, at the hands of Jack Dowling and Emmett French. The highlight of the afternoon was the singles match between Hagen and Travers. The duel brought out "the biggest crowd of the week," about 2,000, according to the *New York Times*. Both men were characteristically wild from the tee for most of the afternoon. Travers eventually got control, though, winning four of the last six holes to trim Hagen, 3 up. As for Jones, he bounced back in his singles match, edging Emmett French 1 up. The Travers and Jones victories were the only ones that afternoon for the Amateur side; the rest of the Homebred team beat the Amateurs by wide margins, totaling 38 points to 4 in the singles. The day put an exclamation point to what had been a week dominated by the Homebreds. Final scores were Homebreds, 152; Scots, 87; English, 72; and Amateurs, 28.

The Homebred professional-amateur duel provided an exciting finish to a generally successful week. It was also the first time Hagen and Jones had laid eyes on one another. Aside from their sport, they had practically nothing in common; for starters, they were separated by almost ten years in age. The impressions they made on each other that week must not have been too deep, because neither put them in writing.

Jones, who had played extremely well, probably made the bigger impression on Hagen, who had a solid but not outstanding week. Following his good medal round, Hagen compiled a 3–3 match-play record, but was just 1–2 in singles play. Jones, on the other hand, ironically followed his rather poor medal rounds on Tuesday with a match-play record of 5–1 (3–0 in singles). His performance was truly memorable; he sent some of the nation's finest professionals to defeat. Travers, by contrast, was 2–1 in singles play and Adair 1–2. "Young Bobby Jones came out with flying colors, clearly establishing the reputation which he earned last year at Merion," concluded the *American Golfer.*

The week also provided an excellent example of how the sport promoted itself during the war. In exchange for some charity, golf remained on the sports pages and cloaked itself in patriotism, while providing its players an opportunity for competition. The *New York Times* called the PGA Relief Matches "one of the most successful and interesting golf exhibitions ever" and reported that the event had raised more than $4,000 for war relief. Some thought it should become an annual event in the golf season. *Golf Illustrated* heralded it as a "week of triumphs." The *American Golfer* praised all "the players who so unselfishly gave their services, amateurs and professionals alike, inspired wholly by patriotic motives." The sport, the PGA, the Homebreds, the Red Cross, and Little Bob Jones, all gained publicity and emerged as an odd combination of winners.[10]

Since the U.S. Amateur was canceled that fall, there was no further significant competitive outlet for Jones in 1917. Besides, his fun-filled summer was nearly over, and he would soon be back in Atlanta to begin his final year at Tech High School. Unlike Hagen, it seems Jones enjoyed formal education, at least to the degree that is possible for any youth. If temperamental, a bit overconfident, and even spoiled as an only child usually is, Jones was also highly motivated, hard working, and intellectually curious. At Tech High, he compiled such an "exceptional" record that he was often exempted from taking final exams, according to the educational custom of the day. Unlike Hagen, he did not "jump out the school-house window," but stayed in the classroom, performing nearly as well there as on the golf course.[11]

Hagen and his fellow professionals could look forward to the open of the renegade WGA. The event was held in the second week of September at the Westmoreland Country Club, situated northwest of Chicago. As the defending champion, Hagen played well, posting a third-round 69. Unfortunately for him, Long Jim Barnes played a bit better to win his second Western with a record-setting 283. Hagen pocketed the $200 second-place prize and traveled back to Rochester, where he finally spent some time at the cottage, probably encouraging his wife as she moved into the last months of her pregnancy.[12]

Despite the birth of his son, Hagen traveled south in the winter of 1918. He arrived late but in time to enter a couple of events in Jacksonville and St. Augustine, Florida, before turning back to Pinehurst, North Carolina, for the North and South Open in March. The tournament attracted its typically strong field. Hagen played consistently and captured his first North and South crown. It was a timely victory because there would not be another event that year. The WGA had announced in January that it would finally follow the example of the USGA and MGA and cancel its events for the summer.[13]

Although Hagen played a number of exhibitions in 1918, from St. Paul, Minnesota, to Washington, DC, he gave his energy less to competition and more to the major changes occurring in his personal life. Hagen had been married for more than a year and now had a son, yet he had been away from home much of the time. Margaret Hagen was increasingly unhappy with her situation and undoubtedly tried to restrict his travel. Moreover, in the spring the Hagens made a fateful decision—to move away from Rochester. While at Pinehurst, Hagen was approached by Al Wallace, a charter member of the recently formed Oakland Hills Country Club, located northwest of Detroit, Michigan. Wallace asked Hagen if he would be interested in becoming the club's first professional. The course had not yet opened, but the club was anxious to land a renowned professional who could bring instant publicity.

When he returned to Rochester, Hagen shared the offer with his wife, who was, according to Rochester newspaperman Henry Clune, very excited about it. Intelligent, urbane, and socially ambitious, Margaret Hagen had grown weary of the second-class treatment she felt they still received from the members of the local club. She expected that at Oakland Hills she would be treated "just like a member." Margaret Hagen also considered her husband a bit too provincial, even homely, and the new rich set of Detroit might be just what he needed, or so she thought. Walter, Clune remembered, was not so enthusiastic and even a bit reluctant, unwilling to leave the familiar surroundings of Rochester. After some thought and pressure from Margaret, though, Hagen finally relented.[14]

It is likely that Hagen's situation at the Country Club of Rochester also entered into his considerations. The club's board minutes include several interesting references to Hagen. For example, in the summer of 1917 the caddies' payroll was stolen or lost while in Hagen's possession. Although the board "refunded" the money to Hagen, there were many unanswered questions concerning its

Margaret Johnson Hagen and Walter Hagen, Jr., early in 1919,
just after the family moved to Detroit.
Courtesy: Detroit News Archives

disappearance. Then in October, Hagen asked for permission to do some work for a neighboring club, possibly the new Irondequoit Country Club. His employers said no. Finally, in August 1918, after he had left for Detroit, Hagen requested $150 in back pay and was again turned down. Maybe the board was simply tired of his extended absences, but whatever the reason, it seems that by the spring of 1918 Hagen's relationship with the club had deteriorated. So he reluctantly traveled to Detroit and negotiated a contract that would bring the Hagens to Michigan.[15]

On May 26 the *Detroit Free Press* announced the signing of Hagen, "one of the headiest players to ever wield a golf stick." The news came as a surprise to golfdom, which apparently did not know of the negotiations between Hagen and Joe Mack, the club's president. The Country Club of Rochester, once again, was uncooperative, insisting initially that Hagen finish the season with them. On July 1, though, Rochester canceled Hagen's agreement, and as of that day he became "attached" to Oakland Hills. The contract paid him $100 per month for the remainder of the 1918 season and $300 per month for 1919. He would also receive all profits from the sale of equipment and supplies from the pro shop. In exchange, the club expected Hagen to stock equipment, be a "competent instructor," and generally "give the club his entire time and personal services." The *Free Press* did not disclose the details of his contract, financial or otherwise. Hagen implied in his autobiography that he was offered a lot more than $3,600 per year, but that is the figure listed in the Oakland Hills board minutes. It was still a much bigger salary than he had earned in Rochester.[16]

By the end of the summer the Hagen family had moved to Detroit, a city teeming with economic activity and on the verge of a boom in its automotive industry. Oakland Hills had a beautiful course that was recently laid out by Donald Ross, one of the nation's premier golf architects and the designer of Toledo's Inverness, Columbus' Scioto, Minneapolis' Interlachen, and the famous No. 2 course at Pinehurst. Because of the war, the club's board delayed the completion of the clubhouse, and when Hagen showed up there was no pro shop. During his stay at the club, he operated his business out of a "chicken coop" near a large old barn along the left side of the first fairway. Minus the clubhouse, Oakland Hills opened the summer that Hagen arrived and would soon be regarded as one of the country's best championship venues.[17]

In all, it was an excellent career move for Hagen, who was still "very homesick for Rochester . . . [and] the huge trees and the meadows and the little brook that ran through Corbett's Glen." "Detroit was a long jump for me," wrote Hagen, "and it took me a while to get over that homesick feeling. But when I did get over it, life in my new home city hit me big!" Coincidentally, Henry Clune moved to Detroit about the same time as the Hagens, leaving the *Rochester Democrat and Chronicle* and taking a position with the *Free Press.* He remembered that Hagen experienced a "metamorphosis" after he acclimated to Detroit. "Any hay that had been in his hair in Rochester was brushed away; any aspect of the yokel that may have been in evidence disappeared. Almost at once he was invested in an aura of glamour [and] unshatterable aplomb on and off the golf course." Hagen was popular at Oakland Hills, and he enjoyed the attention.[18]

Years later Hagen claimed on at least two different occasions that he neither drank nor smoked until he was twenty-six and had left Rochester. H.B. Martin confirmed that claim, which tends to support Margaret Hagen's view that her husband was a bit too old-fashioned; it also fits nicely with all of Clune's observations. Hagen turned twenty-six in December of 1918, months after arriving in Detroit. It is possible that he relied on alcohol, cigarettes, and parties to gain acceptance in his new hometown or to rid himself of homesickness. On the other hand, it may not have been anything so calculated; maybe he just discovered the night life by accident. Whatever else happened to him as a result of the move, his marriage quickly came under siege. All of this suggests that after he settled into Detroit, Walter C. Hagen of Brighton began, for better or worse, to blossom into the suave, hedonistic Sir Walter Hagen, man of the world.[19]

The year also brought some personal changes, though not as dramatic, for Bob Jones Jr. In the spring of 1918, he graduated from high school and made plans to enter the Georgia School of Technology. During the summer, he traveled all over the eastern U.S., starring in war relief exhibition matches. In June he, Perry Adair, and Alexa Stirling took a train to Chicago and joined Elaine Rosenthal for a mixed foursome match. Stirling had won the first of three consecutive U.S. Women's Championships in 1916, and Elaine Rosenthal was a former Western Women's Champion. Stirling-Adair narrowly defeated Jones-Rosenthal in an exciting match that raised more than $2,000 for the Red Cross. Following a Kansas City exhibition that raised another $2,000 for the American Fund for the French Wounded, the mixed quartet sojourned to the east.

On July 28 at Boston's Brae Burn Country Club, Rosenthal-Adair beat Jones-Stirling 5 and 3, as Jones shot an abysmal 87. Stirling remembered what happened that day when Jones missed an easy shot on the eighth hole. She "saw the blood climb his neck and flood his face. Then he picked up his ball, took a full pitcher's windup and threw the ball into the woods. A gasp of surprise and shock went through the large crowd watching us. I wished only that the ground beneath me would open and let me sink from sight." When she chastised him afterward for his outburst, he responded, "I don't give a damn what anybody thinks of me. I only get mad at myself." Jones later admitted making "a complete fool" of himself. (In another exhibition match with Jerry Travers the previous year, Jones had hurled his putter over the heads of the gallery and into the woods when he missed a short putt.) On August 2, however, Jones set a new course record at the Ekwanok Golf Club in Manchester, Vermont. For Jones, then, the war relief matches became a personal showcase of sensational golf and volatile temper tantrums. In all, the four youths played more than a half-dozen matches for the Red Cross and concluded their whirlwind tour in the middle of August.[20]

Jones had been back in Atlanta for less than a month when Chick Evans sent him a request for his help in another series of relief exhibitions. His first term in college was about to commence, but Jones decided to take a couple of weeks to answer duty's call, travel the countryside and, this time, play with the nation's top amateur. Jones met Evans at Baltusrol for a match on September 14. Throughout the next week they played their way to New Britain, Connecticut, raising thousands of dollars for the war effort. From New Britain, it was on to Boston for a return to Brae Burn, then to Philadelphia by September 22 for a match pitting Evans-Jones against the formidable Jerry Travers and Max Marston. Evans-Jones won, 2 up, in a highly competitive exhibition. Jones's minitour with Evans concluded at Philadelphia, leaving Jones only days to get back to Atlanta for the start of classes at Georgia Tech.[21]

In some ways, Jones's decision to attend Georgia Tech seemed uncharacteristic. His family had not produced any scientists or engineers. Granddad R.T. had attended business school, and Big Bob Jones had graduated from the University of Georgia and

Mercer University before admission to the Georgia bar. Little Bob would end up as a lawyer himself, so mechanical engineering had been neither his family's experience, nor did it seem suited to his own intellectual tendencies. Yet Jones had an interest in engineering and welcomed the challenge posed by the rigorous academic program at Georgia Tech. Besides, Perry Adair attended Tech, and the factor of where your friends go has always been pivotal for young people when they choose a college. So on September 24 Jones registered for his first classes.

The major Jones declared, mechanical engineering, allowed for no electives and was packed with courses in math, chemistry, physics, geology, and drawing, besides engineering. Like nearly everyone else, he struggled through Professor Lowndes's freshman drawing class. But he survived, fit in well with his classmates, and began a generally successful and enjoyable four years of undergraduate work.[22]

Jones took a break from his studies on October 10 and played in one of his last war-relief exhibitions. For this match he and Alexa Stirling traveled to Columbus, Ohio, to compete in a mixed foursome with Evans and Elaine Rosenthal at the Scioto Country Club. Evans-Rosenthal beat Jones-Stirling handily, while the match netted $8,000 for the Red Cross. Much of the profit came from an auction for the privilege of caddying for the players. Jones drew the largest amount; one buckeye paid $1,575 for the right to carry his clubs. The other three players each drew about $750. Such auctions for caddie rights, balls, or clubs had always been a common feature of charity exhibitions. The total raised at Columbus, however, was extraordinarily high and reaffirmed the drawing power of Jones.[23]

As the end of the year drew nearer, it appeared that the war would drag on for some time. In October, the National Fuel Administration issued an order "restraining golf and country clubs from using coal between December 1 and April 1 of the next year." Wood or peat could be used for heating purposes. But as the nation's socioeconomic elite scrambled for alternative fuel, American troops "over there" began their greatest engagement of the war, as more than a million men pushed the German defensive line back into the Argonne Forest and to the French-German border. The horrific, bloody campaign lasted a little more than a month and cost the U.S. some 120,000 casualties. On November 1, the German lines finally snapped, and on November 11, 1918, the newly formed German republic signed the armistice that ended the military component of the Great War.[24]

For the next several months, golf analysts wrote about their sport's contribution to the war effort as well as the effect of the war on the sport. Everyone agreed that golf had "done its bit" by lifting championships and conducting thousands of charity exhibitions. Beyond the kind of matches in which Jones, Hagen, and other famous players competed, the USGA organized hundreds of little-publicized local drives and events across the country. In a single day in 1917, the USGA collected $100,000 for the Red Cross. Chick Evans later boasted that under the auspices of the Western Golf Association, he had played in forty-one different cities, traveled about 26,000 miles, and raised $300,000. In one day the Metropolitan Golf Association raised $75,000 for the purchase of fifty ambulances. There is no way to calculate the exact total that golf raised for the war, but the amount was in the millions. Golf had been good for the domestic war effort; the reverse was also true.[25]

Although *Golf Illustrated*'s R.E. Howard concluded that one negative effect of the war on golf was to slow down play (because the military services had taken most of the young men and left the slower, elderly players to dominate the courses), most writers believed that the war had benefited the sport. Another commentator in *Golf Illustrated* discussed the value of exhibitions and argued that through the clever use of various rivalries, amateur-professional or geographic, exhibitions had enhanced the popularity of golf. Moreover, exhibitions provided necessary competition and practice for the leading players. Most astutely, the piece prophesied, "The public, first [motivated by] patriotic reasons, have 'now got the habit' and will not easily give up the pleasure of watching their favorites in action. When the war is over, will they forget this pleasure and profit, and remember only the call upon their patriotism? Will they let the professional return to his humdrum existence of teaching and club-making? Not if they are golfers."[26]

For the first time, during the war, the USGA and PGA consistently charged admissions to their events. The leaders of these organizations learned that golf could profit mightily from gate receipts. The lesson was not lost on individual golfers, either; Walter Hagen immediately recognized the financial opportunities available in peacetime exhibition tours. Hagen remembered that in 1914, after he won the U.S. Open, he received $75 for an exhibition. Just four years later, he raised his standard fee to $300. And the publicity had helped both professionals and amateurs. In sum, if at first an inconvenience, in the end the Great War had been very good to golf.[27]

Hagen began 1919 with his annual trip to Florida. The Palma Ceia Club in Tampa again provided him seasonal employment. For competition, he mostly played in four-ball exhibitions, although he did enter and win the National Mid-Winter Open on his home course.[28]

It had been nearly three years since any national tournaments were conducted. So the USGA created a stir when it announced that the U.S. Open would be held June 9–11 at the Brae Burn Country Club outside Boston. Hagen, who remembered feeling in top "shape physically and mentally," immediately made plans to attend, returning to Detroit in the spring and mailing his entry to the USGA.

The USGA also announced a new format for its open that year. Aside from the fact that it would be the first time the tournament was played over a Monday, Tuesday, and Wednesday, the players would also, for the first time, play eighteen holes on each of the first two days, and the top sixty-four would go on to play thirty-six holes the last day. (Heretofore, half of the field had played thirty-six holes each of the first two days, while the top thirty-two from each day then advanced for the final two rounds on the third day.) Under the new system, each player would have to walk only one round the first two days, while each day's gallery would have the opportunity to see the entire field, making the event more spectator friendly.

Hagen arrived in Boston the week before the tournament but did not "get much practice on the Brae Burn course [because he] preferred to be keen, fresh, and eager when play actually started." Hagen was a favorite to win, along with Evans, Barnes, Hutchison, and Louis Tellier, Brae Burn's professional. Mike Brady, professional at the Oakley club (also in Boston) was another local pick that attracted attention.

Play began on Monday morning amid gray, drizzly conditions. The course was soggy, so players got little roll on their drives. Hagen battled the weather and finished with a 78, good enough to put him in a tie for eleventh place, six shots behind the leader, Charlie Hoffner. D.J. McGuinnes of the *Boston Globe* concluded on Monday evening that, given the weather, the scores were pretty good, and "the result of the first day's play does not appear to have anybody in the favorite for the title." Conditions improved on Tuesday; the sky was blue and bright. Hagen took advantage and shot 73, missing the course record by a stroke and landing in a tie for third place. While Hoffner faded, Brady jumped into first place, three shots ahead of Hagen, who was now in serious contention for the title.[29]

Wednesday's weather proved even nicer than Tuesday's. There was sunshine and, more importantly, no wind. It looked at first as if Brady, who began early, would run away from the field. He started hot in his third round, nearly holing his tee shot on the 203-yard eighth but settling for a three-inch putt and a birdie. Brady faltered a bit on the back side, though, and ended the morning with a 73. Hagen, meanwhile, could not match Brady's start or finish and ended his morning round at 75, alone in second place and now five strokes behind Brady, who seemed poised to win his first U.S. Open.

"King" Brady, as his fellow professionals dubbed him, started his final round before a gallery that had swelled to a reported 10,000. Not all of them were watching Brady, of course, but his following was the biggest, and by the turn the pressure began to take its toll. He shot 39 on the front, five more than he had taken in the morning, and with Hagen a couple of hours behind, Brady realized that he could lose. It proved almost too much for him; he began the final side with a seven and struggled to a 41. The 80 opened the door for his pursuers. Possibly Brady's mind returned to 1915, when Hagen had overcome him to win the Massachusetts Open at Brookline. A. Linde Fowler of the *American Golfer* noticed that, during his round, Brady worried about his position and asked members of the gallery about Hagen and the rest of the field. The King had a reputation for allowing one bad round or a couple of bad holes to ruin tournaments.[30]

Hagen was well aware of Brady's collapse, but his day had its own ups and downs. He began steadily enough, before proceeding to bogey five and six. "That," as Fowler observed, "would have meant surrender for almost any man except Hagen. But he is of the bulldog mold and he simply took a fresh grip and started afresh after his rival." Indeed, Hagen got back a stroke with a birdie at the eighth and finished the front side with a 38.

Yet he had gained only one shot through nine holes and stood on the tenth tee still four behind Brady, who by then was finished and waiting anxiously in the clubhouse. As Hagen came down the stretch in the early evening, the gallery, most of which was now following him, increased to an estimated 15,000. Unflappable, he bested Brady's marks on the 10th, 13th, 15th, and 16th to pull into a tie for the lead. He had to cover the last two holes, which were long and difficult, in at least par figures. Hagen "almost swung himself off his feet," driving to the green of the long 17th; two putts followed for a par.

On the home hole, Hagen, "master of his nerve forces," drove his ball 250 yards down the center of the fairway, which was outlined on both sides by rows and rows of spectators. He then stopped his mid-iron approach within eight feet of the hole, leaving himself a shortish putt for the victory. At that point, Hagen pulled his first—and one of his most memorable—gestures of gamesmanship by asking officials to retrieve the beleaguered Brady from the clubhouse. Young Fred Corcoran, who later would become the PGA's tournament director, was working the scoreboard and witnessed the incident. "Impeccable as always in his traditional white silk shirt and silk tie, Hagen lazily drew his putter and surveyed the putt," recalled Corcoran, "then he looked up with a smile and called, 'Where's Mike?'" Hagen wanted the King to watch him hole his birdie putt. If he missed, he would at least impress Brady with his confidence and potentially gain a psychological advantage for the next day's play-off. Hagen had been deadly accurate with his putter, though, and undoubtedly thought he would make it. He stroked the ball on line but hit it a bit too firmly, bouncing it off the rim of the cup. Still, Hagen shot 37 on the back for a final round 75, tying Brady at 301. So far it had been a "great tournament," and officials hoped to see 20,000 for Thursday's play-off.[31]

Hagen later claimed that he spent most of Wednesday night and Thursday morning at a farewell party for the singer Al Jolson, who had been in Boston for a run of the musical review *Sinbad*. Brady recalled it a bit differently: "Hagen went to the theatre to see Frank Craven in his new play. Then, after the show, he and a friend picked up a couple of showgirls and off they went to a road-house about two o'clock in the morning." When reminded of the playoff, according to Brady, "Hagen just laughed and replied 'Oh when I get to sleep I'll catch up with him.'"[32]

The perfect weather held for the playoff, which Fowler later characterized as "a match of thrills second to none in the history of the USGA open championships." Hagen, clad in knickers and a bow tie, arrived at Brae Burn to find Brady on the practice tee. Because of his reputation for folding, Brady was not the odds-on favorite. Kerr Petrie of the *New York Herald* described him as "palpably nervous" on the front nine. On the second tee, Hagen remembered sidling up to Brady and advising him to roll down his shirtsleeves before the gallery detected that the muscles in his arms were quivering. Hagen's antics may have bothered Brady, who fell three shots behind by the turn. After Hagen picked up another stroke on the tenth, it seemed that Brady would implode.[33]

Brady was aided, however, by a rules controversy that developed during the 10th hole, where observers noticed Hagen picking up a cigarette wrapper in the vicinity of his ball. Gallery members informed Brady, who then lodged a protest with officials. For a time it looked as though Hagen would suffer a two-stroke penalty for violating a loose impediment rule. Hagen, unsettled, lost two strokes on the next two holes; the King had cut his lead in half. The *New York Times* reported that on the 12th hole, "a fan of Hagen's" told the ailing front-runner that Brady had violated the same rule on the ninth. When questioned, Brady admitted discarding a stone, but he was not sure of the distances and whether or not it was a violation. After both players made pars on the 13th, they and the officials went back to the ninth to take measurements and to determine if Brady had committed any infraction. Everyone agreed that Brady had indeed violated the same rule as Hagen, and that neither man should be penalized. Although the damage to Hagen's momentum was done, he clung tenaciously to his two-shot advantage going to the long, par-3 17th. "Ninety-nine golfers in a hundred would have done their driving, approaching, and putting in the clouds for the next hour, but Hagen is not built that way," concluded Petrie.[34]

Still another rules controversy developed at the 17th hole. In this case, the problem was ball identification. A gust of wind made the tee shots difficult, and neither player hit a good one. Brady pulled his shot into a difficult lie on the left, while Hagen sliced his into the edge of the woods. Initially, neither Hagen nor his caddie, Leggy Ahearn, could find his ball. The rules stated that Hagen had five minutes to locate it before being assessed a penalty. Hagen remembered that an official, made especially rules-conscious by earlier events, stood by and timed the search. Exhibiting genuine sportsmanship, Brady helped Hagen look for the lost ball and found it buried in some soft dirt. Hagen cleverly demanded and exercised the right to identify his ball, which required moving it from its resting place and loosening the dirt around it. Having made a positive identification, Hagen took his niblick (nine-iron) and hacked the ball from the dirt into a greenside bunker. He still finished with a double-bogey, losing a stroke to Brady, who salvaged a four. Hagen led by one stroke with one hole to play.[35]

It now looked as if Hagen might collapse, and especially so after he "half-topped" his tee shot, while Brady cracked a perfect drive to the home hole. But after both men left their approaches on the fringe of the green, Hagen chipped first and put his ball within three feet of the hole. Brady knew that Hagen would likely make the three-footer and that he needed to hole his chip for a three to force another tie; he made a good effort but left his ball nine inches from the cup. Hagen then coolly dropped his putt, and the tournament was finally over. Scores for the extra round were 77 for Hagen and 78 for Brady. As for the rules controversies, Hagen told reporters that he "discounted" them entirely, figuring he could still "lick" Brady, penalties and all. "Yes, Brady is the finest fellow in the world and I think so, but I certainly did want to beat him today," he added.[36]

The 1919 U.S. Open victory was significant and illustrative. For Hagen, it affirmed his 1914 triumph; indeed, he was the only professional to win the event between 1913 and 1919, so he could now claim supremacy among his peers. It was also the stage upon which "Sir Walter" introduced himself to the golfing public (although it would be several years before he would be referred to as such in the press), displaying all of his legendary trademarks. He had come from behind to win in a playoff, scrambled to make up for poor driving, made a grand gesture on the seventy-second hole, supposedly spent Wednesday night partying either with a show-business personality or a showgirl, utilized gamesmanship, exploited the rules to the greatest possible advantage, and, in the words of Herbert Reed, "proved the proverb 'God hates a coward on the putting green.'" In sum, he had won with cheerfulness, nonchalance, confidence, resourcefulness, grit, and nerves seemingly made of steel; in time the performance would become vintage Hagen.[37]

But despite the sensational victory, all was not in order with Hagen. He accepted his $500 first place prize and then surprised everyone by announcing that he had resigned from Oakland Hills to join Al Wallace's investment business. In fact, Hagen's commitment to Oakland Hills had never been deep; the club had given him a lot of freedom to travel for competition. One writer noted in 1919 that he "was practically a free lance this year." Hagen claimed that there was no problem between himself and Oakland Hills; he could simply make more money working for Wallace. He recommended that Oakland Hills hire Mike Brady, who had actually been the top candidate for the job back in 1918. The club took his advice and also made Hagen an honorary lifetime member in 1921, suggesting that he did indeed leave on good terms.[38]

When queried about his future, Hagen only said that his plans concerning competitive golf were uncertain, and that he was considering making a trip abroad the following year to play in the British Open. At the same time, rumors of his retirement began to surface. Hagen later wrote that he even considered an offer to tour the vaudeville circuit that fall, a common off-season activity for famous sports figures in that period, but then turned it down, deciding that in spite of his good looks and golf swing, he did not have much of a stage act.

Hagen was at a crossroads in 1919. Apparently motivated by a need or desire for more income, he concluded that the professional's job at Oakland Hills did not pay enough. Most certainly, he had learned from war-relief activities and was already contemplating a career in full-time professional exhibition and tournament golf. Yet such a change would be problematical, because Hagen had a wife and child to look after, a responsibility that did not fit neatly with year-round travel.

At any rate, Oakland Hills was the last club to which Hagen was "attached." Instead, he would be listed in newspaper tournament summaries as "W.C. Hagen, unattached." Hagen was the first big-name professional to hold that distinction, which clearly declared his economic independence. For years, nearly every other competitor was listed by name and club. By 1919, though, Hagen was no longer satisfied to exhibit his talents part-time, while serving the needs of wealthy club members. He determined that if he was going to play competitive golf at all, it would be as a full-time touring professional.

In the midst of retirement stories, Hagen entered and won his second Metropolitan Open in July. After mediocre play early, Hagen told reporters that he now preferred to come from behind on the last day, and he proved it by shooting final rounds of 71 and 72 to overtake the field and win the $250 first place prize. The *American Golfer*'s correspondent concluded that Hagen "played like a Vardon at his best. Never have I seen a bolder putter nor one more successful."[39]

With two of the season's big three opens to his name, Hagen entered the Western late in July. Those who hoped for a Hagen sweep were disappointed when he finished in a tie for seventh place, nine shots behind Long Jim Barnes, who took his third Western title. Hagen collected $35 and headed to Pittsburgh for the U.S. Amateur; he had recently signed to do a series of syndicated articles covering that event. Late in September he finished fourth in the Ohio Open. That ended his tournament schedule, because he did not bother to travel to Long Island for the PGA Championship in September.

He did, however, meet King Brady in a thirty-six-hole exhibition the week before the PGA. Hagen won, 8 and 7, and pocketed a $500 purse. His decision to skip the PGA, especially in light of the Brady exhibition, drew confusion and some criticism from those who believed that the U.S. Open champion's absence would "rob" the young tournament of much "luster." If he could play in a $500 exhibition, skeptics wondered, why could he not do his fellow professionals a favor and enter the PGA? Barnes eventually captured the event for the second straight time, adding to his Western and Southern Open crowns.

Having compiled a career tournament record that included two U.S. Opens, a Western Open, two Metropolitan Opens, the Panama-Pacific Open, a Massachusetts Open, a Shawnee Invitational, a North and South Open, and a National Mid-Winter Open, Hagen finished the year working for Al Wallace as a securities broker. In its November issue, the *American Golfer* reported, "Hagen intends to confine his activities mostly to the brokerage business, although it seemed settled that he will invade England next summer and try for the British Open championship." Actually, few things were "settled" for Hagen when he celebrated his twenty-seventh birthday in December 1919.

Life in 1919 was not so complicated for Bob Jones Jr. That is not to diminish the pressures of Professor Lowndes's engineering drawing class, but as a single, handsome college freshman, Jones entered the year in an enviable situation. Not old enough to have a family of his own to care for, he could still rely heavily on the resources and secure environment created by his parents. Moreover, as long as it did not interfere too much with his considerable academic responsibilities, Jones could travel and play competitive golf. Essentially an introspective, private young man, he found the increasing fame and attention bothersome at times; nevertheless, he also discovered his niche at Georgia Tech, being elected to the Bull Dog and Koseme honor societies and joining the Pan-Hellenic Council. A former classmate remembered Jones as "a fine, clean, friendly, healthy, fun-loving, smart, modest, and hard-working man on campus." His school was not especially known for its golf tradition, but what with the enrollment of Jones and Perry Adair, the athletic director wisely organized a golf team.[40]

Jones got his competitive experience in the spring by playing on Tech's "informal" varsity golf squad. In early May the Golden Golf Tornado, as the team was nicknamed, traveled to New England for a series of matches with some Ivy League schools. On the 5th, Georgia Tech narrowly defeated Columbia University. Then two days later, led by "Captain Bobby" Jones, the Golden Tornado crushed Harvard's linksmen over the Brae Burn golf course, soon to be the site of Hagen's memorable win. The team suffered its only setback of the tour on the 8th, struggling to a tie with Yale. Jones was the standout of the competition, hitting his drives much farther than anyone else and posting the lowest score of the day, a 71. "There are only a few who appear to have anything on [Jones] in these parts," concluded the *Atlanta Constitution*. Unfortunately, a match could not be arranged with Princeton, widely recognized as the powerhouse of collegiate golf. Although Tech had Adair and Jones, it was difficult to argue Princeton's supremacy after it demolished Yale and went on to win the championship of the Intercollegiate Golf Association, which Georgia Tech did not enter. In any case, Jones's presence made the Golden Tornado especially fearsome and destructive.[41]

His freshman year behind him, Jones entered several important golf events in the summer of 1919. In the last week of June, he traveled with his parents to New Orleans for the Southern Amateur. Jones, the defending champion, missed winning the qualifying medal by one stroke. He made news the next day when his tee shot from the first hole bounced into a wheelbarrow and rolled into an old shoe. George Turpee, who refereed the event, looked at the lie and decided that under the existing rules, Jones was not entitled to relief. Jones hacked the shoe and ball out of the wheelbarrow, both landed on the green, and the ball rolled free. He ended up halving the hole in four. "The [shoe] shot was all anyone talked about," remembered Turpee.[42]

With his parents proudly looking on, Jones advanced to the semifinal round, where he was knocked out, 7 and 6, by Nelson Whitney, the eventual champion. Jones was above making excuses, but his supporters were not, and they were crushed by his defeat. "Alibis" were "in vogue among the Atlanta delegation." Jones's friends and family pointed out that his hands were blistered so badly he had three fingers taped and experienced pain on every shot. Turpee confirmed this, recalling that "when a callus came off his left hand in the first round, his mother wanted him to withdraw . . . but Bobby refused." The *New Orleans Times-Picayne* described the "Atlanta delegation" as being "mighty close to tears and might have overflowed if the end had not been apparent early in the second eighteen." O.B. Keeler remembered that Jones's loss induced "utter dishevelment" among his followers. As if offering consolation, the local paper assured Jones supporters that "Walter Hagen couldn't have beaten Whitney" that day.[43]

In late July, Jones traveled to Hamilton, Ontario, to play in the Canadian Open, as well as the International Match, an amateur team competition between the U.S. and Canada. Jones was sharp in the team competition, winning his singles and doubles matches, and the strong U.S. side, which in addition to Jones included Evans, Ouimet, Travers, and Gardner, easily defeated the Canadian squad, 12 to 3. Jones did not fare as well in the open event, however. Although he finished in a tie for second place, he was still sixteen strokes behind another Atlanta representative, J. Douglas Edgar. After giving a "capital little speech" at the closing ceremonies, Jones took the silver platter (valued at $100) offered to him instead of cash and headed back south to join his father and Stewart Maiden at the U.S. Amateur.[44]

Scheduled for the Oakmont Country Club outside Pittsburgh, the U.S. Amateur Championship was the most anticipated event of the golf season. The public had grown fond of watching professionals in medal competition, but the amateur match-play event was still the crown jewel of the sport. After all, except for Hagen, the amateurs had recently dominated the U.S. Open and seemed to be the better players. Moreover, Oakmont, built in 1903, provided a most challenging venue; it was one of the best representatives of the "penal-style" golf course that became popular in America after World War I. Henry C. Fownes created the course to punish errant shots, leaving little opportunity for "scrambling." As Fownes put it, "A poorly played shot should result in a shot irrevocably lost." At 6,707 yards and a par 73, the course was long, and its fairways were narrow, bordered by very thick rough and originally some 350 bunkers (nearly twenty per hole), in which the heavy sand was raked to create deep ruts or furrows for collecting balls. Bad enough from tee to green, Oakmont had glassy putting surfaces that were regarded among the most difficult in the world. Not long before his death, Jones reflected upon the course and wrote, "Without a doubt, the fastest greens I ever putted were those at Oakmont." In sum, it presented a terrifying obstacle to any golfer, and fans were anxious to see how the nation's top players would survive.[45]

Three years had passed since Jones had gone public at Merion. At seventeen, he had dropped about ten pounds, weighing around 155, and had grown to 5' 8"; he now looked more like a stocky young man than a stumpy kid. But although he had matured physically, it would be just his second national competition, and the layout could not have been more difficult. The USGA again decided to hold qualifying over two days. On Saturday, August 16, the entire field would play eighteen holes and be trimmed to sixty-four. On Monday, August 18, a second qualifying round would cut the remaining field in half for match play.

The weather for the qualifying rounds was awful. On Saturday the players and gallery suffered through a twenty-minute hailstorm. Jones survived with an 81, but the difficulty of the course, coupled with the weather, proved too much for Perry Adair. Considered by some to be a favorite after he shot the lowest practice round of the week, Adair cracked on Saturday, taking a 50 on the front nine. Having failed to improve his score on the back side, he picked up his ball on the 16th hole, withdrew from the tournament, and literally cried his way to the clubhouse. It was a rough day for everyone; an 89 made the cut.

There was no hail on Monday, but the sky remained dark and gloomy as the players, "fortified with cotton gloves, extra towels, resin, talcum powder, and a dozen other useless articles," again struggled through the wind and rain. Jones improved on his first day's round, taking a 78 to finish just one stroke behind the qualifying leaders, including the Pittsburgh area's own S. Davidson Herron.

The big stories of Tuesday were the beautiful weather and Jerry Travers's early exit at the hands of C.G. Waldo of Detroit. As for Jones, he advanced by eliminating J.S. Manion of St. Louis, 3 and 2, after "a few bits of advice" from Stewart Maiden. Wednesday's draw pitted two stars, Chick Evans and Francis Ouimet, in the second round's most exciting match. (Under intense criticism, the USGA reinstated Ouimet's amateur standing after he joined the armed services in 1918.) To add drama, Ouimet was stricken by flu symptoms all week. Yet he played through his ailments to beat Evans 1 up and become the favorite of the championship. Jones got some revenge that day for his defeat at Merion when he "soundly trounced" Robert Gardner, 5 and 4. The Atlantan was ahead at noon, just as he had been three years earlier, and some expected Gardner to launch another come-from-behind victory. But Jones was more experienced by 1919, and he held his lead.

So once again Jones made it into the third round of the U.S. Amateur. This time his opponent was Rudolph Knepper of Sioux City, Iowa. Knepper would become one of the West's finest, but in 1919 he was less experienced than even Jones, who knocked him out 3 and 2. Ouimet, meanwhile, was upset by J. Wood Platt in a match that went extra holes. For the first time since 1911, then, the U.S. Amateur champion would not be Ouimet, Evans, Gardner, or Travers.

Jones proved the next day, however, that his appeal was no less significant; a surprisingly large gallery showed up to watch the semifinals. Beautiful weather also mitigated the effects of the former champions' eliminations. Jones faced W.C. Fownes Jr., the son of Oakmont's designer and the "last of the old timers." Despite losing his temper, manifesting what one sportswriter called "smouldering wrath" and "supreme disgust," Jones defeated the former champion 5 and 3. The next day he would battle local favorite S. Davidson "Davie" Herron, who crushed Platt 7 and 6 in the other semifinal match.

On Friday evening dopesters focused on whether or not Herron's momentum and course knowledge could overcome Jones's obviously superior form. Herron would be a tough opponent; big and strong, weighing just over 200 pounds, the twenty-two-year-old spent his summers working in a steel foundry, according to local sources. His qualifying rounds showed that he was familiar with the course—in fact, a member of Oakmont. Further, he could expect the support of the gallery. But although he had played for Princeton, Herron had also failed to qualify at Merion, and most observers believed Jones to be the better, more experienced golfer, even if he was the youngest finalist ever. In all, Saturday's match promised to be interesting. The inside "dope" was that Jones would lose his temper and the match if Herron got out to an early lead.

On Saturday, August 23, a "generally unlearned" gallery of about 6,000 turned out to cheer their local boy; Jones had only the encouragement of "his father, his faithful follower, Stewart Maiden, and a corporal's guard." Still, he began well enough and eventually battled Herron to a tie by the lunch break. Big Bob Jones watched nervously as the match remained deadlocked through the first three holes of the afternoon. Herron captured the lead at the fourth and by the final turn was 2 up. To his credit, Jones refused to crack, trying to regain the lost holes despite the partisan crowd, which even cheered at one point after he left a shot in a sand hazard. But he could only halve the 10th, before losing the 11th, 12th, and 13th to fall 5 down. Herron finished him off, 5 and 4, with a halve on the 14th amid tumultuous cheers.[46]

It is unlikely that Jones could have pulled it off, but any chance for a comeback was destroyed by an unfortunate episode at the 601-yard 12th hole. Herron was 3 up; both youths hit solid drives, but Jones's was longer. Herron put his next shot into a trap, slightly opening the door for Jones, who desperately needed to win the hole. Jones set up over his ball and began his brassie (two-wood) shot. According to the *New York Times*, as Jones reached the top of his backswing, a "horn-rimmed bespectacled official" saw a boy "400 yards away move 2 inches" and yelled "Fore!" into his megaphone. (Megaphones were a preferred tool of tournament officials in this period to direct and control galleries. Officials, for example, used a megaphone to explain the rules controversies to the crowd in the Hagen-Brady playoff.) His concentration shattered, Jones barely made contact and dribbled his ball into a nearby fairway bunker. After two failed attempts to get it out, Jones angrily picked

up his ball and conceded the hole. Thus, instead of cutting the
deficit to 2 holes, he fell down by 4. "Jones was palpably disturbed
by a deputy calling out to the crowd to hush when all near him
were mentally observing that he was the one who should do the
hushing," wrote John Anderson. "Excited" by the episode, Jones
lost the next hole as well. Jones later acknowledged that it probably did not determine the final outcome; Herron had outplayed
him most of the afternoon. But, given Jones's temperament, it is
also true that the megaphone mishap extinguished any remaining
hopes.

Among other things, the 1919 U.S. Amateur suggested that
megaphones and golf tournaments did not mix. Analysts focused
on the official's blunder, as well as on the rancorous gallery, decry-
ing the "pop-bottle partisanship" of the Oakmont crowd. The *Cherokee Advance* of Canton, Georgia, reported that Big Bob Jones was
"bitter" about the megaphone gaffe, and the paper concluded, "It
was a mighty poorly-handled affair all the way round and too much
criticism cannot be heaped upon those responsible." Sadly for
Herron, who was in no way responsible, his victory was tarnished,
particularly among those who from the outset considered Jones
the better golfer. In truth, most probably doubted that Herron
could have beaten Jones without the home-course advantage. So
the lasting story of the event was not the course or the weather,
and the tournament that began in a storm of hail ended under a
cloud of controversy.[47]

Under the circumstances, both players comported themselves
with remarkable decorum. Herron was reserved in victory, offering only the obvious, "I tried hard to win." The combustible Jones
gracefully accepted defeat. The *American Golfer* noted that the reports of Jones's "temper displays and the number of clubs he broke
in the course of a round" were "grossly exaggerated, with the exception of one brassie . . . ." The *Pittsburgh Press* observed that the
"Golden Tornado" took the loss to heart and was "crest-fallen"
after the match. (Apparently, for western Pennsylvanians, Jones
was the Georgia Tech golf team.) Moreover, the *Press* found in
Jones "a good sport [and] a worthy foeman." Experiencing what
was surely a disappointment, Jones nonetheless had advanced to
the finals of the U.S. Amateur in only his second try, and that was
no small accomplishment. Besides, he had one more tournament
that year, the Southern Open, to be played two weeks later on his
home course, East Lake.

Jones probably considered the Southern as a last opportunity to end his year on a high note. That was not to be, though; Long Jim Barnes trimmed Jones by a single stroke. Homer George of the *Atlanta Constitution* remained blindly loyal to Jones, commenting, "I go on record as saying absolutely that Bobby Jones should have been returned winner, but for breaks in at least ten shots during the tournament." It did seem that luck was against Jones and with Barnes in the third round, especially after Long Jim holed a 175-yard mashie (five-iron) shot for an eagle on the fifth. But what really hurt Jones at East Lake was what had hurt him in the final at Oakmont; that is, he missed too many short putts, any one of which would have tied Barnes.[48]

Jones proved what he was capable of doing at East Lake a week later when he equaled his own course record, shooting a 33–35–68. Willie Ogg, the club's professional, played the round with Jones and declared it "the most phenomenal" golf he had ever seen. (Stewart Maiden had resigned as East Lake's professional earlier in the year.)

Yet Jones had hoped for more in 1919 than to equal his own noncompetitive record at East Lake. It seemed a disappointing season. He had entered three important events—the Canadian and Southern Opens, and the National Amateur—and finished second in all of them. He had also failed to defend his Southern Amateur title, being eliminated in the semifinals. Jones always called it his "runner-up year." It was also true, however, that Jones had gained invaluable experience, particularly in the U.S. Amateur. To some, Herron may not have deserved the national crown that year, but in reality Jones's supporters could not make a much better case for him. He was only seventeen, and it was just his second national event.

Jones was in the midst of what his friend and biographer O.B. Keeler later referred to as the "seven lean years," 1916–1922. Keeler's neat division of Jones's career was based on the Biblical account of Joseph, who prophesied to the Pharaoh that Egypt would experience seven fat years of plenty followed by seven lean years. As Keeler's description of Jones's career goes, the first seven years were marked by disappointments, one after the other, before Jones finally broke through in 1923 to win his first major event, opening the floodgates for the seven fattest years, 1923–1930, ever experienced by any competitive golfer.[49]

The use of Biblical allusion was common in the sportswriting of Keeler's day, but his often cited metaphor is misleading. Aside from reversing the Genesis story in which the fat years precede the lean years and suggesting that Jones had seven fat years, instead of the eight he enjoyed, Keeler's summary of Jones's career breaks down on a more substantive level. There simply was not much lean in Jones's career from 1916 to 1920. Actually, he had compiled an impressive record. He had done better in national competition than anyone else ever of his age, and had won numerous state and regional tournaments. What Jones naturally lacked was physical and—especially—psychological maturity. Any frustration felt by Jones and his fans stemmed from essentially unrealistic expectations. Golf insiders understood this, and the *New York Times,* in its unofficial year-end amateur rankings, placed Herron and Jones at numbers one and two, respectively, just ahead of Ouimet, Evans, and Fownes. It was an appropriate way for Jones to finish 1919; he really was close to being the best amateur in the country. Moreover, golf and all sports were about to enter a Golden Age that would be partially defined by the outstanding achievements of Bob Jones Jr.[50]

Chapter 4

Big Debuts,
Bigger Disappointments:
1920–1921

The Golden Age of Sports was just one facet of a growing consumer culture, which, in turn, was only one product of an emerging "modern temper" in American society. Sandwiched between the deadly serious Great War and Great Depression, for years the 1920s were considered little more than "Roaring," frivolous, materialistic, hedonistic, and, generally, unimportant. Although it still breathes strong in the popular understanding of history, this stereotype is mostly inaccurate; the period is arguably more fun to study from hindsight than it was to experience firsthand. The effects of urbanization, industrialization, social pluralism, and mass consumerism were widespread by the 1920s, creating a palpable sense of uncertainty about the future. Everyone, in some fashion, was forced to reconcile to the "tyranny of change," and people moved into modern America with varying degrees of comfort. R.T. Jones, who turned seventy-one in 1920, was undoubtedly disturbed by much of what was happening, particularly the rising challenge of science to Biblical authority. Little Bob was much less bothered than his namesake, but R.T.'s morality kept him from indulging in certain aspects of the modern culture and provided a foundation upon which to deal with change. As for Walter Hagen, he did not ponder, much less dwell, on the implications of modernity; he simply decided to take advantage of its opportunities and handle the consequences as best he could.[1]

So in the winter of 1920, as Jones began the second semester of his sophomore year at Georgia Tech, Hagen once again traveled south for the region's golf events. Aside from the usual expanding schedule, he would compete in a special match with Jim Barnes that would supposedly determine the unofficial champion of the world. Barnes had captured the Western Open, Southern Open, and PGA Championship, and Hagen had won the U.S. and Metropolitan Opens—together they had dominated the professional ranks in 1919. They played against each other in only five events that year. Each had won two of them, and in the fifth, the Ohio Open, Barnes finished third and Hagen fourth. In fact, the same year-end rankings that had Jones number two among amateurs had Hagen and Barnes listed as one and two among the professionals. The thirty-six-hole exhibition was scheduled for Sunday, March 7, at the New Orleans Country Club.[2]

Barnes had continued to shine that winter and had practiced over the New Orleans layout many more times than Hagen, who went around it only once before March 7. All of that made Hagen's victory more impressive. It was hardly easy, though. Barnes led, by as much as 4 up, most of the afternoon, until Hagen fought back to take the imaginary world's championship in extra holes. Nearly 1,500 turned out, despite the chilly weather. Hagen said that the match meant as much to him as the U.S. Open. That might have been an overstatement, but it did bring a load of prestige and a $1,000 winner's check.[3]

By the end of the next week, Hagen and Barnes had returned to Bellair Heights for the second significant event of the winter, the West Coast Open. Hagen won the tournament for the first time in fine fashion, finishing twelve strokes ahead of a strong field. He spent the rest of the month playing exhibitions, making plans for his upcoming trip abroad, and just relaxing. One of his favorite morning pastimes was trapshooting. Hagen had always enjoyed hunting and had become an excellent marksman. One day he reportedly hit twenty-two of twenty-five clay pigeons at the Bellair Country Club and then predicted that the sport would experience a boom in popularity.[4]

In the last week of March, Hagen and his fellow professionals began their trip north, stopping at Pinehurst for the finale of the winter season, the North and South Open. Hagen played well again, at least up to the last hole, where he uncharacteristically three-putted from fifteen feet. The mistake cost him the tournament, because Fred McLeod totaled one shot better. Aside from Hagen's near sweep of the winter events, the big story from Pinehurst was the amount of gambling that surrounded the event in the form of pool-selling, bookmaking, and individual wagering. According to rumors, McLeod cleared $4,000, winning a hefty "pool" in addition to his $300 purse. It all alarmed the USGA, which for the first time, early in May, officially recognized the "heavy gambling" and encouraged clubs to stamp it out themselves.[5]

By mid-April Hagen was back north, although he was now "headquartered" in New York City, not Detroit. If, as Gene Sarazen recalled, Walter Hagen's and Margaret Johnson's romance occurred in 1917 because of a dog, then by the spring of 1920 their relationship had gone completely "to the dogs." While still legally joined, they had separated; in time, the divorce would become final. Hagen's travel had taken the greatest toll on the marriage. In his own words, "the kind of life I lived as a pro golfer—playing exhibitions, entering the various scheduled PGA and USGA Championships, following the winter circuit, going any place and every place where the sun was shining and the fairways green—was not conducive to a satisfactory family life." Henry Clune offered a more general explanation, suggesting that "marriage was definitely not [Hagen's] forte; he was as ill-suited for the restraints and ordinances of the conjugal state as a pirate."[6]

Indeed, more than Hagen's absence hurt the marriage. The Detroit "metamorphosis" seems to have played a role as well. There is some evidence that their marriage had never been strong, even when they lived in Rochester, but it just crumbled after they moved to Michigan. Clune remembered being invited to the Hagen home for dinner one day in the summer of 1919. He showed up on time but Hagen was late, much to his wife's chagrin. When Hagen finally arrived, he looked at the meal she had prepared and "querulously remarked, 'We got that old hacked ham again?'" "Shut up," she snapped, "I can remember [when] you had ham on the table, you thought it was your birthday."[7]

If Hagen did begin drinking and frequenting parties for the first time in 1918–1919, then it is likely more than a coincidence that his family soon fell apart. Joseph Peck was a good friend of Hagen's in the last dozen years of his life. Peck recalled that Hagen was a mean drunk, and while he never witnessed Hagen become physically violent, he did remember that when intoxicated Hagen was verbally abusive and generally intolerable. Margaret Johnson, who according to Clune also drank, later accused her husband of violent and threatening behavior. That is not to say that Hagen became an alcoholic in 1919. The evidence suggests that he drank moderately during his competitive years, but when he did indulge, he probably became unpleasant. Moreover, where there is little evidence of Hagen's womanizing prior to 1919, there is more afterward, albeit anecdotal, beginning with the "showgirl" incident at Brae Burn's U.S. Open. So while they may never have had a strong relationship, and Hagen was away much of the time, it is also true that he simply changed his personal conduct after he left Rochester. At any rate, in essentially abandoning his family, Hagen, like a small but increasing number of other Americans in the '20s, eschewed the foundation for nineteenth century Victorian society, opting instead for a different, more modern lifestyle. One of the many side effects of his decision was that Walter Jr., just turned two years, would grow up hearing much and seeing little of his father.[8]

So it was to New York that Hagen went in April of 1920. Theoretically he worked for Al Wallace, but he actually spent most of his time practicing for his first try at the British Open. H.B. Martin had covered the previous winter's events for the *New York Globe*, and, while in Florida, Hagen convinced "Dickie" (as Martin was nicknamed) to travel abroad with him and cover the American invasion. Hagen also suggested that Martin might become his full-time manager; Martin wanted to see how the European trip went before making any long-term commitments.

The British Open was scheduled for late June, after the British Amateur. Hagen wanted to arrive in plenty of time to practice and play in exhibitions because he had heard about the difficult, windy, seaside conditions at the Royal Cinque Ports Club in Deal, England. On May 23 Hagen and Martin boarded the *Mauritania* for England, where he would join Jim Barnes, who had left the previous week.

As they crossed the Atlantic, golf writers on both sides discussed the Americans' prospects. Except for Frenchman Arnaud Massey in 1907, no foreigner had ever won the British Open. American commentators agreed that Hagen had a strong chance to win, especially given his recent play, but their optimism was mitigated somewhat by the reality that Hagen had never competed in British conditions. Grantland Rice's opinion was representative; he noted Hagen's strengths, including his currently accurate driving, extraordinary iron-play, putting, and steady temperament, but he also pointed out that Hagen "is a great believer in the high pitch to the green. On this account he has paid little attention to the low shot." Nonetheless, one British observer thought that "the month of June will be fraught with great anxiety for the British nation," because "*Dame Fortune* points to Walter Hagen" as a likely champion. For their defense, the British looked to such rising stars as Abe Mitchell and George Duncan, beside the older heroes, J.H. Taylor and Harry Vardon, who together with James Braid had won sixteen British Open titles. Hagen, meanwhile, enjoyed the luxury of the spacious *Mauritania*. The most memorable aspect of his trip was that the "lovely Constance Talmadge of the famous movie Talmadge sisters was also a passenger."[9]

Upon arriving, Hagen had his first experience with the British press. Bob Howard of the *Daily Mail* met him at the train station in London and requested an interview. Hagen agreed to talk to Howard that evening over dinner. The Americans then checked into the Carlton Hotel and hired an Austin-Daimler limousine for their stay.

Whatever Hagen told Howard that evening, the next morning's *Daily Mail*, under the headline "Cocky Doodle Doo!" carried an article declaring, "Walter Hagen, boastful American champion, is boyishly confident of winning the British Cup which only once in its history has ever left British shores. Hagen says that no golfer should be over 72 around Deal," and that "he intends to show us how to play the game." Hagen claimed that he said nothing of the sort and recalled being first "hurt" and then "boiling mad." Martin later confirmed Hagen's innocence. Hagen and Howard eventually cleared up the misunderstanding, and the paper retracted the piece the next day. Still, it was a poor first impression for Hagen to make on the British golf public, much of which concluded that he was arrogant and disrespectful.[10]

Things did not get any better when he drove out to the Deal clubhouse. Professionals received even less respect and social privilege in Britain than in the U.S. The British PGA, formed in 1901, had had little success in raising the status of professionals, whom club members considered common. According to British golf historian Geoffrey Cousins, professionals were expressly forbidden from using the clubhouse with the amateurs and were relegated to "uncomfortable changing-quarters and feeding facilities which depended on the capacity of a local caterer setting up shop in a tent." When Hagen showed up, the club secretary directed him to the "few nails allotted" to professionals in the pro shop. Sir Walter, "wearing a Saville Row polo coat, with trimmings to match," said no thanks. Instead, each day he parked his limousine in front of the clubhouse against the wishes of officials and changed his shoes there. So Hagen was arrogant and disrespectful after all, at least regarding certain British golf customs. The other professionals simply accepted their place and used the overcrowded pro shop. In the end Hagen's protest of social distinctions had "no visible effect" on the immediate positions of British professionals, wrote Cousins. Still, despite the fact that everyone else did it and that the Deal authorities condescended to him, Hagen would not play the role of an inferior.[11]

Moreover, Hagen's golf stroke did not impress the British. Martin overheard Vardon and Braid critique the American invader. "Decidedly unorthodox," Vardon commented, but he added, "I am going to reserve my decision on this chap until I have seen more of his game." After the tournament Vardon rendered his judgement: Hagen's was "not a true swing, therefore it is not a good one." On June 10 Hagen and Barnes defeated Abe Mitchell and George Duncan in an exhibition, and observers decided that Barnes was "the better golfer of the two" Americans. Ironically, the British were especially disappointed with Hagen's putting. The *London Chronicle* remarked, "Both Hagen and Barnes played strong and stable golf, but there was no evidence of that genius which British champions have shown." It was a rough beginning to his first European tour, and it would get rougher.[12]

In between practice rounds and exhibitions, Hagen relaxed for a few days in Scotland, where he and Barnes took in the final of the British Amateur at Muirfield. They watched Cyril Tolley barely defeat America's Robert Gardner in thirty-seven holes. Following that exciting and inspirational match, Hagen got his first glimpse of the Old Course at St. Andrews. He played well there in foursome exhibitions with Barnes and some local talent. Then the Americans caught a train back south to Deal for the qualifying rounds of the open event. Whatever the British thought of his form, Hagen had scored well enough in his practice rounds and looked forward to serious competition.

The qualifying rounds of the 1920 British Open were held on Wednesday and Thursday, June 23–24, over the St. George's Hill and Burhill courses. Hagen qualified on Wednesday at the St.

George's Club. He shot 76, eight more than the leader of the field, Abe Mitchell. There were only seven men ahead of him, but as the *London Times* noted, "for a good score to be done at St. George's Hill, it is essential that the drives be hit straight, and Hagen's lurching swing is not the kind which will guarantee a straight drive."

Hagen finally made a favorable impression at Burhill on Thursday. He went around in 71, tying Mitchell for the lowest round of the field and putting him in fourth-place behind Mitchell, Duncan, and Ray. The *London Times* found Hagen's shots "accurate, high, [and] forceful" and his putting "bold and confident." The *New York Times* declared that Hagen's performance proved his game was not exclusive to American courses, as the British had suggested. The locals subtly observed, though, that there was no wind on Thursday, and that the Burhill layout was open and forgiving of errant drives. Aside from his score, the British noticed Hagen's "fascinatingly esoteric" attire. According to the *Times*, "His was a scheme, or maybe it should be called a creation, in black and white, with his black sleeveless jersey, white shirt, white knickerbockers, and black and white shoes." Hagen had come a long way since his Brookline outfit, and by 1920 there was nothing second-class about his wardrobe. The *London Observer* reported that Hagen's travel closet included a dozen golf suits, nine pairs of shoes, ten sleeveless jerseys of different colors, forty different pairs of hose, and a "host of other things."

The top seventy-two plus ties advanced into the championship proper, which was not scheduled to begin until the following Wednesday, June 30. So Hagen and Barnes, who survived with a 155, had a week to think and practice. On Sunday the Americans played an exhibition at the Walmer and Kingsdown course before an "enthusiastic crowd." London reports said that neither was in "particularly brilliant form," but the *New York Times* correspondent thought both Americans had played well, especially given the strong wind. Hagen did not practice on Monday, but on Tuesday he joined Barnes at Deal for a match-play event against Vardon and Tom Williamson. The British prevailed, 3 and 1, despite Hagen's hitting long drives with the power of "a horse kicking."

At 6,650 yards, the Deal layout was tough under any conditions but especially so when the wind blew. From indoors the weather on Wednesday morning appeared beautiful, even benign. The sun was shining, and small, fluffy white clouds dotted a clear, blue sky. Yet a careful look revealed that those clouds were moving

Hagen setting up for a tee shot. He became famous for hitting
powerful, if sometimes unpredictable, drives. Notice the
wide stance and strong right-hand grip.
Courtesy: USGA

along, signaling the presence of a strong wind. That was not good for Hagen's high shots, and he played poorly on the first day of his first British Open. "Extremely crooked" off the tee, he finally limped into a tie for forty-fifth place with an 82–84, nineteen strokes behind the leader, Abe Mitchell, who had been fortunate enough to begin his round early in the day when there was more of a breeze than a wind. Hagen's draw produced a later, windier start, but the conditions were not his only problem. He seemed unusually nervous. On the first hole he missed a one-foot putt and never quite recovered. The next day he totaled 78–85–329, dropping into fifty-second place, twenty-six shots behind champion George Duncan.[13]

Barnes salvaged some respect for the U.S. by finishing alone in sixth place. Barnes was Cornish, though, and had learned his game in Britain, so however much Americans had adopted him, both sides considered Hagen the truest representative of American golf. That was a lot of pressure, even for Hagen. The distractions of the press and the club (which, of course, Hagen helped create), the weather, and his inexperience resulted in an embarrassing debut. Still, in at least one respect, Thursday, July 1, 1920, was one of the finest days in Hagen's career, because he refused to "pick up" and fought hard to the bitter end, all the while knowing that he had fulfilled the expectations of his worst critics and let down his country. And Hagen refused to make excuses. When it was over, he told reporters, "I couldn't get going. I didn't have the touch. I am discouraged now, but I am coming back to England. I hope some day to play well over here."[14]

Everyone on both sides had anticipated more from him. The *New York Times* confessed that Hagen had "not borne out his high promise." Americans, wrote one Britisher, are in "dismay" over Hagen's "ignominious" finish. Some British golf writers chose to say nothing, rather than offer the obvious commentary. Others, such as the *London Observer*, were merciless: "Hagen, the American champion, was a complete failure. His long game in the wind was the feeblest thing imaginable; in his first round he was only on the course three times from the tee." Britain's *Golf Illustrated* simply concluded, "[Hagen's] form at Deal was too bad to be true." On the other hand, the British admired Barnes's "quiet, unassuming, and strictly professional style." Further, they claimed that professional golf on their side of the ocean had "not yet reached the stage where its exponents drive to the courses in motor cars accompanied by a retinue of male and female admirers and backers arrayed in highly talkative arraignment." Most in Britain probably thought the flamboyant, disrespectful Hagen got about what he deserved. Hagen recalled the last exchange he had with Deal's club secretary, who had been annoyed by his limousine antics. "I'm sorry you didn't do better, 'Eye-gen,'" the official gloated, "but golf over here is very difficult. I do hope you'll come back some future year and try again!" "Don't worry about me," Hagen replied, "you'll see my name on that cup."[15]

Thoroughly disappointed, Hagen decided to enter the French Open at the La Boulie links in Versailles. The weekend after the British Open, he crossed the English Channel for Paris. George Duncan and Abe Mitchell, two new friends, crossed with him. The course was beautiful, the weather awful, and the accommodations for the professionals even worse. According to Hagen, the professionals were supposed to use a stable that had "a vile odor and hundreds of flies swarming about." He instantly determined that was no place for his expensive New York wardrobe and somehow convinced Duncan and Mitchell to take a stand. The disgruntled trio demanded better treatment and threatened to withdraw from the event. Because each player was important to the success of the tournament, La Boulie officials reluctantly agreed to let them use the clubhouse. The other professionals stayed in the stable, though; it was a minor, self-serving victory over tradition.

The field at La Boulie was small, but strong. Aside from Hagen, Duncan, and Mitchell, it included Frenchmen Arnaud Massey and Eugene Lafitte, as well as the Scottish amateur Tommy Armour. Hagen battled the rain and finished in a tie for first place with Lafitte. On Wednesday, July 7, the day Hagen was supposed to sail for home, he and Lafitte played a thirty-six-hole playoff. Hagen posted a 75–74, good enough to win his first and only French Open; Lafitte shot 76–78. Yet the French Open was hardly the British Open. Even the *American Golfer* commented, "Doubtless Walter Hagen feels pretty much like a man who goes gunning for bear and bags nothing more than a rabbit, or mayhap a skunk."[16]

Immediately following his victory, Hagen and Martin climbed aboard the *Aquitania*. On July 18 they arrived in New York, where Hagen told the few reporters who greeted him that he was happy with his French Open victory and looked forward to defending his Metropolitan title later in the month. By the standards of future years, it was not much of a homecoming. But then, it had not been much of a trip, either.

A week after his return, Hagen teamed with Barnes against Vardon and Ray in an exhibition match at the Shennecossett Links in New London, Connecticut. The aging British stars made their final trip to America to play in some exhibitions before entering the U.S. Open in mid-August. The British won the match on the last hole when Vardon made a twenty-five-foot putt, and Hagen missed one of five feet for the halve. Nearly 3,000 turned out to witness what the *New York Times* called "possibly the greatest four-ball match ever played in this country."[17]

But American fans forgot Hagen's missed putt a few days later when he captured his third consecutive Metropolitan Open, winning once again by coming from behind to take an exciting playoff. He fired a one-under-par 69 in the third round to catch Barnes and played even with him the rest of the way. Hagen, possessing a perfect record in playoff rounds, was very confident and easily defeated Barnes in the next day's eighteen-hole tiebreaker. Ray McCarthy of the *New York Tribune* concluded that Hagen must have had the "Indian sign" or some other jinx on Barnes.[18]

The next day he and Barnes "trounced" Vardon and Ray, 4 and 2, before 5,000 spectators in an international exhibition rematch. Hagen outplayed everyone, collecting a special $100 prize for breaking the course record with a 70. On August 1, the *New York Times* declared that Hagen had completely redeemed himself and suggested that maybe the French Open was an important event after all. Hagen had indeed rebounded remarkably well from his British Open debacle. If he successfully defended his U.S. Open crown, he could wipe away any trace of his performance abroad and maintain undisputed supremacy among America's professionals. So he set his sights on the Inverness Country Club in Toledo, Ohio, host to the 1920 U.S. Open.[19]

While Hagen traveled abroad, Bob Jones spent a relatively quiet spring in Atlanta. Late in April he squelched rumors that he would leave school early to cross the Atlantic for the British Amateur. His parents, Jones told reporters, had insisted that he finish the semester at Tech. Once again, textbooks trumped golf clubs.

When not attending classes or studying, Jones "called" on Mary Rice Malone, whom he had met one day on a trolley car. Mary was just four months younger than Bob and the sister of Mat and John Malone, two of his college chums. By early 1920, though, Jones was visiting the Malone home in affluent Druid Hills less for Mat and John and more for Mary Malone. Somewhat shy, Jones had never been a "ladies' man." In high school, he had developed only one superficial, short-lived romance. As for Mary Malone, she possessed a slender but shapely figure, dark hair and eyes, a soft, pleasant smile, and was, by all accounts, simply beautiful. She loved to dance, but only in the formal style of the previous century and did not welcome the expressive, sensual moves that would come to symbolize the roaring side of the '20s. In the words of syndicated columnist Cornell Strassburg, Mary Malone "didn't go in for wild parties. She did like to dance to no end. Then again, she wasn't a 'horsey'—or athletic—girl in any sense of the word. Tennis and things, yes. But she didn't go in for them strenuously." Her family was Irish-Catholic, but that bothered neither Jones nor his parents, and whatever R.T. Jones thought of her religion, he kept it to himself. By the summer they were in love. So in the spring of 1920, it was mostly school and Mary for Bob Jones Jr. [20]

Of course he practiced regularly at East Lake, and on May 6, Inverness club officials announced that "the phenomenal golfing youngster" had entered the U.S. Open. Jones did not compete in any significant golf events until early July, when he entered the Southern Amateur in Chattanooga and his first Western Amateur at Memphis. The field for the Southern Amateur was not too deep, and Jones, hungry for competition, experienced "easy sailing" en route to winning his second Southern Championship. [21]

The Western Amateur, as usual, attracted a healthy field, including Chick Evans. Jones and Evans had never met in formal match-play competition. Memphis golf fans hoped that they would that week, and to the crowd's delight, both of them cruised into the semifinal round. What was described as the largest gallery in the state's history turned out to watch the battle, and it was a good one; Jones once called it the most thrilling match of his career. At no point in the thirty-six-hole contest was either player up by more than one hole, and they came to the thirty-fifth all square. There Evans made a twelve-foot putt, while Jones missed a four-footer to lose the hole. They halved the thirty-sixth, so Evans won the emotionally draining match and the opportunity to play in

Saturday's final. The Chicagoan had an easier time the next afternoon and collected his fifth Western Amateur Championship. Reflecting on the match a few days later, Big Bob Jones said, "Chick
will never beat [my son] again." He was right.[22]

The Southern and Western were tune-ups for Toledo. Inverness
had never hosted a major event. The 1919 Ohio Open had been
held there, but that was all. It was the most anticipated U.S. Open
since 1913; Hagen was the defending champion, Jones would be
entered for the first time, Vardon and Ray presented a serious international threat—in sum, the tournament ballyhooed itself. Grantland
Rice's "Big Four" favorites were Hagen, Barnes, Vardon, and Ray.
The 286-man field was record-size, and the only notable not entered was Francis Ouimet, the one player Vardon and Ray supposedly wanted to meet—again. Apparently, Ouimet had an offer to
cover the tournament as a newspaper analyst and would definitely
not compete. His decision raised criticism. One "prominent golfer"
was quoted in the *Toledo Blade* as saying, "we are disappointed. It
does not reflect much credit on our sportsmanship, to say the least."
Everyone else was there, though. Many of the professionals arrived
in Toledo within days of the event, having just left Chicago after the
Western Open. Hagen had been in Chicago but did not compete in
the Western. He surfaced in Toledo on Monday, August 9, one day
before the qualifying rounds began.[23]

The USGA had announced the qualifying round pairings a week
earlier. The biggest news was that Jones would play his preliminary rounds with Harry Vardon. Although it was not really a
"match," everyone was interested to see how Jones would measure
up next to Vardon. The Atlantan did not disappoint his fans, playing "whirlwind golf" on Tuesday that was "good in all departments."
He shot his first nine holes in 34 (–2), while Vardon struggled to a
41. They reversed their forms on the back nine, each finishing
with a 75. Despite his slip, Jones played well enough to please
Vardon, who had gotten his first look at the promising American
amateur. Afterward Vardon commented, "The youngster is a fine
golfer." A reporter prodded him further: "Better than Evans or
Ouimet?" "I said he's a fine golfer, isn't that enough?" snapped
Vardon. He refused to draw comparisons but admired Jones's
"sound style" and later confessed, "the possibilities of his golf impressed me enormously."[24]

On Wednesday the huge field was trimmed to a more manage-
able sixty-four, plus ties. Jock Hutchison grabbed the spotlight

that day, shooting a course-record 69 to lead the field. Hagen, meanwhile, barely survived the cut, adding a 77 to his Tuesday's 78. Jones, still paired with Vardon, had another steady performance, shooting 76. He later recalled an amusing exchange between Vardon and himself on the eighth tee. Jones had just completely misplayed his pitch to the seventh green, taking a bogey. Embarrassed, he asked, "Mr. Vardon, did you ever see a worse shot than that?" "No," answered the seasoned veteran without expression.[25]

Heavy dew greeted the players on Thursday morning for the tournament proper. The sun soon burned the greens dry, though, and by evening Hutchison was still the front-runner. With a 78–74, Jones finished in a tie for eleventh place, while Hagen improved to a 74–73, landing in fourth with Vardon and Ray. Hagen was in excellent position to win his third U.S. Open; after all, he had been telling everyone that he played best when coming from behind. Jones also remained in contention. In fact, anyone between Jones and Hutchison had a chance. "Picking the winner at this time is too much like searching for a needle in a haystack," wrote George Pulford of the *Toledo Blade*.

In the end, the 1920 Open provided what the 1913 Open had not: a British champion. The weather on Friday morning was perfect, and some 10,000 turned out to watch the final rounds. Harry Vardon shot 71 in the morning to pull into the lead, one ahead of Hutchison and two in front of Ray. The fifty-year-old Britisher stood up well over the front nine of his last round but collapsed on his final nine, taking a 42 after conditions turned windy and rainy late in the day. Still, Vardon finished just one stroke behind his compatriot, Ted Ray. As for Hagen, it became obvious early that he would be "dethroned." He posted a pair of 77s and finished alone in eleventh place. Jones began the day hot, going around in 70 to pull within four. As it turned out, a 73 would have caught Ray, but the pressure eventually got to the amateur. Following lunch, customarily topped with pie and ice cream, Jones stumbled to a 77 and finished in a tie for eighth place.

Jock Hutchison came to the last two holes needing a par and a birdie to catch Ray and keep the title "over here." Paired with Hagen, "Jock-o-the-Hutch" parred 17 and was faced with a twenty-foot putt on 18 for the tie. Hagen was also on the final green in two, and his ball was away, or outside of Hutchison's. According to Rice, Hagen holed his thirty-foot putt for a birdie and then turned to his partner, "Now go to it, Jock. You see how easy it is."

Hutchison made a good effort but narrowly missed, and the British collected yet another national title in 1920.[26]

Though a foreigner, Big Ted Ray was nonetheless a popular champion. "If the title had to go to Great Britain, it couldn't have gone to a more picturesque character or to a more likeable sportsman," declared the *New York Times*. Ray's home club, Oxhey, in Hertfordshire, England, commemorated his victory by making him an honorary member. That was "an unprecedented event in British golf which raised more than a few eyebrows in many quarters," wrote Geoffrey Cousins. "This break with tradition opened the gates," Cousins noted; Taylor, Vardon, and Braid also soon were awarded honorary memberships. If not as dramatic, Ray's honorary membership was probably a bigger step toward the "emancipation" of British golf professionals than Hagen's limousine-as-locker-room routine.[27]

For Hagen, Inverness had been another disappointment; he had given up his crown too easily. He spent the rest of 1920 playing mostly in exhibitions, some of which involved Vardon and Ray. On September 22, he captured the Bellevue Country Club's Invitational. He did not compete in the PGA Championship that fall, however, because according to the *Toledo Blade*, he had forfeited his membership, and PGA members had "decided that he was not entitled to enter" on account of his winning the 1919 U.S. Open. Hagen said nothing about it in his autobiography, but he probably had dropped his membership when he resigned from Oakland Hills to become "unattached." It is also possible that the PGA's action was a response to Hagen's ignoring the event the previous year. In any case, Hagen discovered that free agency had a price.

By the middle of October he was back at his old stamping ground for an exhibition with Barnes, Vardon, and Ray at the Country Club of Rochester. The Americans were victorious, and Hagen received a loud ovation from the enthusiastic gallery. In December, he traveled to Florida for the winter season. He had won the World's Championship match from Barnes, the West Coast, French, Metropolitan, and Bellevue events, but had played poorly in the two national opens. As one of America's top professional golfers, the expectations for him were as high as ever. So despite his victories, Hagen wrote, "nineteen-twenty was one of my lean years."[28]

Inverness had not really been "lean" for Jones. The eighth-place finish was very good for his first U.S. Open, and his 70 in the third round was outstanding. Hagen's lowest round had been 73. As Jones admitted later, he was simply "full of pie and ice-cream and inexperience." One benefit of Inverness was that Jones met Luke Ross, who would caddie for him in the U.S. Open and Amateur until the USGA banned the use of regular caddies in their events in 1926. Ross had worked for Leo Diegel at the Detroit Country Club, and it was Diegel who arranged for them to meet. The two got along immediately, and Ross, with O.B. Keeler, became a constant in the Jones camp for the next six years.[29]

The next month Jones suffered what may accurately be described as his first serious competitive disappointment in the so-called "lean years." It came in the U.S. Amateur, held at the Engineers' Country Club on Long Island. He had made it to the third round at Merion in 1916, then to the final round at Oakmont in 1919; many analysts assumed that Jones would go all the way in the 1920 Amateur. It looked promising at first, after he tied Fred Wright of Massachusetts for the qualifying medal and then breezed into the semifinals, where he faced Francis Ouimet. Jones had never played Ouimet in formal competition but was nonetheless confident from his sharp play in the early rounds. The only potential problem for Jones was his inconsistent temperament. William McNutt wrote in the *Atlanta Constitution* that although Jones was a "veritable icebox" in his first round match, by the third match his "fundamental golfing fault showed up. When his drives began swerving and his irons temporarily refused to rescue him, his face became flushed with anger, [but] when he got away a screaming drive on the long 12th that traveled a good 320 yards and came to rest in the mathematical center of the fairway, his good spirits returned to him."

About 7,000 curious fans turned out to see if Jones would assume the character of an icebox or a volcano in his first confrontation with the hero of Brookline. Ouimet jumped out to an early lead, winning the first two holes, and maintained it late into the morning when Jones's temper spilled over. At the 17th he mishit a sand shot and "socked his club back into his bag with a vicious movement." After missing a "teeny little putkkpoo" on the 18th to fall 3 down, he picked up his ball and drop-kicked it into the rough.

Jones temporarily settled himself and early in the afternoon regained one of the holes. Then a strange incident occurred at the 25th green. As Jones set up for his first putt, a yellow jacket began buzzing around his ball. He stepped back more than once and tried to shoo away the insect. At one point an official even helped Jones by trapping the wasp in his megaphone, but that did little good because the yellow jacket made its way out of the mouthpiece and once more honed in on Jones's ball. After swinging his putter and generally carrying on for the gallery, which was by now having a good laugh, Jones three-putted to lose the hole. He lost the next two as well.

The 25th hole underscored Ouimet's analysis of the outcome, which emphasized Jones's poor putting skills. In his autobiography Ouimet reminisced, "I must say he was not even a fair putter [in 1920.]" For the *Constitution*, however, the yellow jacket hole was simply another example of Jones's inability to control himself on the course. Charles Blair Macdonald also witnessed the episode. After Jones holed out, Macdonald told his friend, "Mark my words, he will not win. He lacks concentration." Jones recalled that his father, who had made the trip to Long Island, was "pretty well broken up over my defeat." The next day Chick Evans continued his superiority in the American amateur ranks, crushing Ouimet 7 and 6 in the final before an estimated 13,000.[30]

Later that fall Jones once again entered the Southern Open, conveniently held at East Lake. The tournament drew an unusually strong field of professionals after it substantially increased its prize money. The winner's check was for $1,000. It was the sort of event that Hagen liked to win, but he entered and then dropped out just before the start. His withdrawal could have been on account of the unseasonably cold, windy weather; a number of others dropped out for that reason. Jones braved the conditions and played well enough to end alone in second place, two strokes behind fellow Atlantan, J. Douglas Edgar. It was a frustrating finish for Jones because after three rounds "Little Bob" and "Long Jim" Barnes had held a two-stroke lead over the field. So 1920 ended in a valley, at least competitively, for both Jones and Hagen. Any disappointment Jones felt in the fall of 1920, however, would soon be dwarfed by what he felt in the spring of 1921.[31]

In January of 1921, golf fans were especially excited about the upcoming season, and the biggest reason was the planned American invasion of Britain. The best Americans, including Jones and Hagen, were set to cross the Atlantic in hopes of regaining some of the prestige lost the previous year. And besides the traditional events, an "informal" amateur team competition would be played just prior to the British Amateur at Hoylake in northern England. On January 8 the *New York Times* announced that George Herbert Walker had donated the "Walker Cup" as a trophy for the international event. Some even suggested that the new competition might justify the USGA's underwriting the amateurs' trip, but the governing body did not pay the team's expenses. The eight-man squad consisted of Captain William Fownes, Bob Jones, Chick Evans, Francis Ouimet, Fred Wright, Jesse Guilford, Paul Hunter, and J. Wood Platt. Late in April the *London Times* warned its nation's players to train systematically and feared an all-American final in the British Amateur. Bob Gardner, after all, had nearly won the tournament the previous year.[32]

Having made arrangements to finish his junior year at Georgia Tech early, Jones traveled from Atlanta to New York the last week of April. On the 30th he, along with the Fownes and Ouimet families, boarded the *Caronia* and set out for his British debut. Luxury steamliners could cross the Atlantic in about ten days, so on May 9, at Liverpool, Jones and the British got their first look at each other. The Americans were met by reporters from numerous London papers. After declaring the voyage "uneventful," Ouimet introduced Jones as "our baby." Jones stood before the reporters smiling and smoking a big cigar. Vardon had been singing Jones's praises since their qualification pairing at Inverness, making the Atlantan a powerful magnet for the press. Unlike Hagen, Jones made a good first impression on the British. His welcoming committee agreed that he possessed "the most lovable manner and engaging smile."[33]

The British Amateur did not begin until May 23, so the Americans had nearly two weeks to practice. They played their first round at Hoylake on the 10th and organized numerous foursome exhibitions in the days after. The British fans enjoyed Jones's accurate driving and smooth, orthodox swing. Together with Evans and Ouimet, he was regarded as the most serious American threat to win the championship. The potential for an American victory seemed substantial on May 21, when the U.S. crushed the British in the international team competition, 9 to 3. Only Evans, Platt, and Hunter lost their singles matches, and the Americans swept the foursomes.

Displaying a "steadiness which excited admiration," Jones won his singles and foursome, paired with Evans. The margin of the U.S. victory was "shocking" and "surprising" to the *New York Times*, which covered the event on the front page of its Sunday edition.

Two days later the Amateur got underway. The British format was different because there were no qualifying rounds to pare down the field, and only the final match was thirty-six holes. The eighteen-hole competitions provided enough time for all of the entries to start immediately in match play. Although they began well, the Americans generally did not like the eighteen-hole duels. The problem, as they saw it, was that favorites could be easily upset if their opponents got hot, even if only for a short time. Still, Jones won his opening match, and in fact, all eight Americans advanced into the second round. Oddsmakers had Jones a 5 to 1 favorite, Ouimet at 6 to 1, and Evans at 7 to 1.

But the U.S. invaders struggled the next day, despite warm, windless conditions. Grantland Rice called it "one of the black days in the history of American golf." Ouimet, Evans, and Guilford were defeated, and Jones barely survived, defeating E.A. Hamlet, 1 up. Hamlet was a florist by trade and an obscure amateur who possessed "a ridiculous style," according to *Golf Illustrated*'s George Greenwood. He shot a medal score of 87 against Jones, who did little better at 85. And, once again, Jones's temper flared. On the fifth hole he "kicked" a bush after mishitting a fairway iron shot, and he "dashed his putter into the ground" after missing a putt on another hole. Jones was 2 down at the 15th, looking to be eliminated, but Hamlet crumbled beneath the pressure, allowing Jones to regain his composure, win the last three holes, and close out the match. Though still not playing well, Jones won his third match. That evening the *London Times* concluded that Jones was no longer a favorite. "Jones made an amazing display of bad golf" in the Hamlet match, the paper remarked, and "it was entirely the ludicrous display of Jones that made any match of it. It was really dreadful: The crowd did not know whether to laugh or cry."

Jones joined his famous countrymen in the gallery after the fourth round. Allan Graham thrashed him 6 and 5. The Atlantan continued his poor play from the previous day; nonetheless, he showed no signs of ill temper and heartily congratulated Graham on the 13th green. Three other Americans lost in the fourth round, leaving only Fred Wright, who fell in extra holes the next day to the renowned British golf historian Bernard Darwin.

At a loss to explain their stinging defeat, the American players resorted to criticizing the course and the format. Ouimet suggested that Hoylake was "not a good test of golf" because it was too hard and fast. "Some of the finer points of the game," he argued, "such as pitching right up to the pin and stopping dead, have no place here." He further believed that eighteen-hole matches were unfair. Jones agreed, declaring, "I'll come back over again, when they play thirty-six holes." Even Captain Fownes chimed in, blaming the course for the defeat of "a great team—on paper—the greatest team ever." Fownes also thought that if the tourney had been held the previous week, "we would have won." Oswald Kirkby was the only American who refrained from displacing responsibility, remarking, "Our boys simply had a bad reversal of form, that's all." Some American writers chastised Jones, Ouimet, and the other Americans for making "alibis."

While the Americans dressed their wounds, Willie Hunter went on to win the all-British final. By the closing ceremonies the American squad had recuperated enough to display some class. Jones, Ouimet, and Fownes were on hand to watch Hunter accept his trophy. Jones told the crowd of several thousand that the American team "had a great time. I don't think we have enjoyed anything more than this competition." The master of ceremonies replied, "There is something more than golf in a match drawing together these two great countries. The true hope of the world lies in the great friendship of America and Great Britain." With those platitudes, the 1921 British Amateur came to an end.[34]

Jones and Evans, after being eliminated from the Amateur, reportedly threatened to pull out of the Open and go home early, but Fownes talked them into staying. When it was over, Jones probably wished he had followed through on his threat. Scotland's St. Andrews was the venue of the 1921 British Open, scheduled to begin on June 20. Fourteen American professionals, including Hagen, joined five American amateurs on the entry list.

While Jones suffered through the Amateur, Hagen had crossed the Atlantic on the *Aquitania*. His winter in Florida had been lackluster. He did not win any tournaments, and the most notable thing about the season was that H.B. Martin decided not to become his full-time manager. Maybe Martin thought Hagen's proposition too great a financial risk. Or he may have left Hagen because "Walter really did most of the managing, and most of the advising, too." In Martin's place, Hagen acquired Robert Harlow.[35]

Harlow was the son of a Presbyterian minister and a graduate of the University of Pennsylvania. Early in 1921, he resigned from the Associated Press in New York to become Hagen's full-time business agent. He traveled with Hagen, booked Hagen's exhibitions, and contracted endorsements for Hagen. A savvy sports promoter, Harlow would help create and then sell "Sir Walter." In April, Grantland Rice had commented that it was possible for leading professional golfers to earn from $20,000 to $25,000 per year. Actually, Hagen never made less than $45,000 a year and some years made as much as $75,000. They quickly "hit it off" and became good friends as well as business partners. "[Harlow] knew his business and he grew to know me—my good points and my shortcomings," Hagen reminisced. The two trusted each other so much that they would never require "a written contract of any sort."[36]

Hagen needed a friend on the eve of his departure to Britain. For as he traveled to New York on May 18, Margaret Johnson-Hagen stood before Judge Fred Lamb's court in Detroit and pleaded for a divorce. With her mother at her side, she told the judge that her husband had displayed a violent temper, frequently making threats of bodily harm, although he had never actually hit her. Beyond that, she claimed that Hagen had abandoned her. Her mother corroborated the charge of abandonment, saying that her daughter had lived with her throughout most of the marriage. Hagen had been in Detroit the day before his wife appeared in court, possibly to try to talk her out of the divorce, or maybe just to say goodbye; in any case, he did not stay around to contest her charges. That seemed all too much in character, and convinced the judge of the veracity of Margaret Johnson's claims. It took only five minutes to grant the divorce. Judge Lamb gave legal custody of Walter Jr. to his mother until he was fourteen years old and allowed his father only visitation privileges. He further ordered Hagen to pay his ex-wife $10,000, plus an additional $50 per month for child support. Soon after, Margaret Johnson and her son moved back to Rochester.[37]

Among other things, their divorce proved that Walter and Margaret's religious faith was not a strong influence in their lives. Divorce was especially rare among Catholics in that period. A large majority of couples who could not get along, even those of limited piety, simply separated, refusing to actually dissolve their marriage out of respect for church teaching. In fact, aside from his infant baptism, there is no evidence to suggest that the Hagen family had ever taken religion too seriously. Be that as it may, Hagen must have been sad and relieved, as he sailed to Great Britain in the spring of 1921.

Hagen and Harlow were accompanied on the *Aquitania* by the strongest American professional contingent ever to challenge for the British Open. Jim Barnes, Jock Hutchison, Fred McLeod, Tommy Kerrigan, Charles Hoffner, and William "Wild Bill" Mehlhorn were all aboard. The *New York Times* observed that their departure was "business-like," and that they did not receive the celebratory send-off that had been given to the amateurs the previous month. The professionals landed in Scotland about a week after the Amateur Championship and immediately began practicing and playing exhibitions. Like their amateur counterparts, they played their first international team competition on June 6 at the Gleneagles Golf Club—an event that would evolve into the Ryder Cup matches. Unlike their amateur counterparts, the American professionals were defeated handily, 9 to 3. Hagen halved his singles and foursome matches.[38]

Two weeks later, Hagen and Jones qualified for the British Open amid difficult, windy conditions. Jock Hutchison led all qualifiers and remained in the lead after the first day of the tournament proper. By then, Jones was five strokes behind and Hagen six. Hutchison's performance, which included a hole-in-one, was popular because he had been born in Scotland. If he kept up his form and won, both sides would be able to claim success. That is exactly what happened, but it was not an easy victory. Through four rounds he was tied with British amateur Roger Wethered. As for Hagen, he had a much better outing than the previous year at Deal. There he had finished in fifty-second place; at St. Andrews he improved his score by twenty-seven strokes, taking a 302 to come in sixth place.

Jones, on the other hand, endured his worst moment in competitive golf. He had taken a 78 and 74 on the first day, but he began the third round poorly, topping his first tee shot, taking fives and sixes on the first five holes, and finishing the front nine with a 46. Jones had played himself out of the tournament, and he knew it. Worse yet, he was looking at a debut in the British Open that would rank with Hagen's. The Atlantan hated that prospect and his imperfect play even more. He took a six at the 10th. Seething with frustration and anger, Jones simply lost control of himself at the 11th after he hit his tee shot into Hill Bunker, which guards the green. Following three or four attempts to get the ball out of the trap, Jones "tore up his card and expressed a preference for cricket," as the *London Times* diplomatically put it. In other words, he quit.[39]

According to Sidney L. Matthew, a Jones biographer who has done careful research on the affair, "reports of what transpired next are inconsistent." Some say that Jones picked up his ball in the bunker; others recall that he finally blasted his ball onto the green and then picked it up. At least one witness remembered that Jones quite literally tore up his scorecard while walking down the 12th fairway. Jones later maintained that he did not really tear up his card; he just did so only figuratively, by picking up his ball and withdrawing from the tournament. Nonetheless, he called it his "one last superbly childish gesture" and the "most inglorious failure" of his career.[40]

It is certain that Jones played out the rest of the round and the fourth as well. He took a fine—but meaningless—72 in the final round. It was an embarrassing display for anyone, but especially so for a leading amateur. The game, his temper, and the circumstances of the moment had gotten the best of him. On other occasions, Jones had cursed loudly, broken and thrown clubs, kicked and thrown balls, and gouged his putter into the turf. But in simply quitting, he displayed the supreme act of unsportsmanlike behavior.

The next day Hutchison became the first American professional to win the British Open, soundly defeating Wethered in the thirty-six-hole playoff. So for Americans generally and Hagen particularly, the 1921 British Open was a positive experience. For Bob Jones Jr., though, it climaxed a terribly disappointing British debut.[41]

On July 11, a relatively small party greeted Jock Hutchison in New York on his triumphant return from Great Britain. The celebration was not larger primarily because Hutchison was not a homebred. The U.S. had adopted him, as it had Barnes, but he also had learned his game abroad and was not a true product of the American game. Neither Jones nor Hagen traveled home with Hutchison; they had both arrived a week or so earlier to prepare for the U.S. Open, which was to be held at the Columbia Country Club outside Washington, DC. Following that event, they would face each other again in the Western Open.

The USGA decided to give the 274-man field only one qualifying round at Columbia. That was an especially controversial decision for amateurs, who had just decried the evils of the eighteen-hole matches in the British Amateur. Professionals did not like it much, either. But Columbia had only one course, and, in the interest of time, half the field qualified on Tuesday and the other half on Wednesday. (It was the only year that qualifying for the U.S. Open was conducted over just eighteen holes.) Hagen passed by comfortably on Tuesday, July 19, with a 74. Jones, on the other hand, barely survived on Wednesday with a 77; he had but one stroke to spare. Jim Barnes led everyone with a 69.

Those trends continued through the tournament proper. Barnes stayed hot, and on Thursday he came in five strokes better than Jones and eight ahead of Hagen. Still, "the temperamental Atlanta youngster" was the low-scoring amateur after the first day. Then for a brief moment on Friday, Hagen garnered attention with "one of his brilliant streaks," scorching a 34 in his first nine. That helped him finish the event in a tie for runner-up, while Jones came in fifth place. Barnes, meanwhile, simply crushed the field, winning by nine strokes, the largest margin ever to that time. After years of trying, the tall Cornishman had finally captured a national open.

Both President Warren G. Harding and Vice President Calvin Coolidge were on hand at the presentation ceremony. President Harding was an enthusiastic golf fan, and Hagen later claimed to have been "many times a guest at the White House" during his administration. Dapper as usual, Harding wore a "light summer suit and broad-brimmed panama hat" for the occasion. Cameras flashed and the Marine Band blared, as Barnes modestly accepted the trophy from the President, who declared, "If I had my wish I would want a republic where everybody could play [golf.]" "If we only apply that poise and confidence [of Barnes] to other things in life," he continued, "we will achieve even more than we have." Harding's statements brought an appropriately patriotic flavor to Barnes's triumph; the U.S. Open crown had been brought back home. On the ride to their hotel that evening, Hagen mentioned to Keeler that he thought Jones was close to winning a major event, and he further prophesied that it would be the U.S. Open, rather than the Amateur.[42]

In the last week of July, Hagen failed to extend his winning streak to four in the Metropolitan Open, finishing in seventh place. That performance came in the wake of rumors that he was again considering retirement. Nonetheless, a month later he joined Barnes and Jones in Cleveland for the Western Open.

After the first two days at Cleveland it appeared that Jones would indeed finally break through. He led the field with a 69–70. Hagen played well, too, finishing four strokes behind with a 71–72. But the weather changed, and on the last day the wind rushed across Lake Erie. Jones did not accommodate the conditions and "blew up." Hagen continued his steady play, and where Jones had taken an 83, he shot 73. He added a 71 in his fourth round, so although he did not break 70, Hagen was consistent in capturing his second Western Open. He finished five strokes ahead of Hutchison and eight in front of Jones.[43]

Throughout, Hagen displayed the temperament that Jones lacked. During an interview with Grantland Rice between the U.S. and Western Opens, Hagen discussed his steady mental approach to the game: "If I hook or slice to the rough, I always try to kid myself that I will have a good lie and will be able to get the ball out. In any event I always say to myself, 'Well, no matter where my tee shot goes, my business is to keep on scoring and at least do the best I can.' I always figure that I am going to miss a few shots in the course of a round, and so when I hook one or slice one or top one I am set for it. I just check it off and say that's one of the bunch I was due to miss." For Hagen, it was part experience and maturity, but it was also a matter of personality. Though highly competitive, Hagen did not manifest the golf perfectionism of Jones, or most players, for that matter. The Western concluded a string of medal events, the longest one yet, in which Hagen and Jones both participated. In each one Hagen finished ahead of the Atlantan. He was arguably the best golfer in the U.S., professional or amateur, and over the next two months he intended to prove it.[44]

Hagen left Cleveland and traveled north for the Michigan Open in the second week of September. The tournament provided a nice warm-up for the PGA Championship, and Hagen claimed his second consecutive title, this time edging Mike Brady. Hagen, "the man minus nerves," took a 69 in the final round. By the end of the month he was back east at the Inwood Country Club on Long Island for the PGA Championship. Hagen was still "unattached," but it did not matter that year because the PGA qualified its field by selecting the top thirty-one finishers in the U.S. Open, plus the defending champion. Having failed to win either of the national opens, Hagen welcomed the chance to play in the professionals' event, and the PGA, moreover, wanted his magnetic personality in its tournament. So the rift between Hagen and the PGA, whatever it had actually been, was bridged by the new qualification standards, and he entered the event for the second time.[45]

Hagen took advantage, sailing through his first three rounds by wide margins. He then defeated Cyril Walker 5 and 4 in a rain-soaked semifinal. Those triumphs earned him a trip to the final to face Jim Barnes. The defending champion, Jock Hutchison, had been knocked out by Gene Sarazen, a nineteen-year-old from Titusville, Pennsylvania. The victory was Sarazen's way of "going public"; he soon enjoyed a meteoric rise in golf comparable to that of Hagen. Although he lost to Walker in the third round, Sarazen's 8 and 6 win over "Jock-o-the-Hutch" was the most sensational of the week.

But the tournament came down to a battle between familiar favorites, "Dashing Walter" and "Long Jim." Both began the final in good form, and Hagen was only 1 up at lunch. With his "Indian sign" still holding sway, he extended his lead to four holes after firing a 33 on the front nine in the afternoon. Barnes must have felt hexed when he missed a one-footer on 16, giving Hagen his first PGA Championship, 3 and 2.[46]

Since the latest retirement rumors, Hagen had won three tournaments, two of them major events. If the stories had any validity, he certainly was not playing like a man about to put his clubs away for good. Given that Hagen had once again defeated Barnes and that early in September Barnes had defeated Hutchison in the "unofficial world's championship," one could surmise that Hagen was the world's best. The *New York Times* suggested as much.[47]

In late October he played a few exhibitions with Barnes, George Duncan, and Abe Mitchell, including one in New York that helped inaugurate the lavishly landscaped Westchester-Biltmore Country Club. Then he and Harlow made plans to return to Florida for the winter. Their business partnership was already evolving into a lasting friendship. Moreover, with his late season heroics, Hagen had salvaged what easily could have been a poor competitive year. For Hagen, 1921, which began on a personally sour note with his divorce, concluded on a professionally sweet one.

By 1921 the image of Sir Walter was in full bloom. Nattily attired,
Hagen lounges confidently before his gallery.
Courtesy: PGA

The year did not end so well for Bobby Jones. After his loss to
Hagen in the Western Open, Jones had gone on to the U.S. Amateur in St. Louis for his last event of the year. It was his fourth try
at the national title, and commentators expected him to win. "I am
certain that the man of the future is Bobby Jones of Atlanta. Never
has a young golfer impressed me so deeply as Jones," Vardon declared that fall. He added that Jones possessed an "inborn gift" for
the game and a swing that was "easy and graceful." Indeed, Jones
was widely regarded as the most talented golfer in the world. Still,
he had not won a significant tournament. He and nearly everyone
else associated with the game was confused about that; confusion
turned into frustration as time went by and the pressure to win
increased. Jones was now in the throes of his truly "lean years,"
1920–1922.[48]

He received no relief at St. Louis late in September, and the
event proved more exacerbating than anything else. Heading into
the tournament, Grantland Rice picked Evans, Ouimet, Gardner,
and Jones as his favorites, but only Gardner advanced to the final
round. Jones crushed a local favorite in the first round and easily
won again in the second round. He was in good form, despite suffering an accidental burn to his left hand a few weeks earlier. (On
September 7, he reportedly had shot a 42 at East Lake using only

his right hand.) By the time he arrived at the St. Louis Country Club, his hand was healed, at least enough to compete.[49]

In the third round, though, he faced a much tougher opponent in British star Willie Hunter. Hunter was the reigning British champion and hoped to capture the amateur "double" almost as much as Jones hoped to win his first national title. Clad in a white shirt, tie, and white knickers, Jones began strong. By lunch he was clinging to a two-hole lead, which could easily have been more. Yet Hunter refused to quit that afternoon and pulled ahead for the first time at the 15th green (33rd hole), where Jones missed a two-foot putt. Jones could not regain the lost ground, and the Britisher went on to win the exciting match 2 and 1. Hunter remembered that Big Bob Jones was the first to congratulate him.[50]

But Hunter did not recall an incident that occurred at the last hole of the match. That was when Jones, after misplaying his second shot to the green, lost his temper. He carelessly tossed his club toward his bag, which was on the ground not far from the gallery. Unfortunately, the club did not stop at his bag but bounced over it and struck a lady in the leg. Although the injury, if any, was slight, Jones naturally felt terrible. Few seemed to have noticed it. The *St. Louis Post-Dispatch* made no mention of it and in fact reported that "those who hoped to see Jones go into a temperamental tailspin were disappointed." Yet Jones and a few others knew what had happened, and it was a disappointing way for him to end the season. Since his "childish gesture" at St. Andrews, Jones had worked hard to improve his on-course demeanor; golf writers made no mention of any outbursts at the U.S. or Western Opens. Gene Sarazen, who played with Jones at Columbia, remembered that "we didn't let our tempers get the best of us, and returned to the locker room with the same number of clubs we had started out with." The *New York Times* reported a couple of minor flares in practice rounds at St. Louis, but on the whole, Jones had been making a redoubled effort to control his temper. Nonetheless, it got the best of him one more time.[51]

Hunter went down to defeat at the hands of Gardner in the semifinal the next day. Gardner, in turn, collapsed in the final to Jesse "Siege Gun" Guilford. The 6-foot, 200-pound "Siege Gun" used his length from the tees to destroy the two-time champion, 7 and 6. Jones watched the final and then literally limped back to Atlanta. On top of the embarrassing defeat, he was suffering from a painful case of varicose (or swollen) veins in his left leg.

As the Atlanta air turned cold, there was not much for Jones to smile about, at least concerning competitive golf. He agreed with Kerr Petrie's year-end analysis in the *Southern Golfer:* "It cannot be said that fresh honors have been heaped upon the young head of Bobby Jones. A lad of promise is Bobby, but, then, every one knows what they say about promises." To make matters worse, Jones received a letter from George Walker, president of the USGA, a few weeks after the Amateur. Walker warned, "You will never play in a USGA event again unless you can learn to control your temper." The USGA was tired of Jones's tantrums; the fact that he was apologetic mattered little to golf's ruling amateur authority. Jones's fiery determination to win, even at the price of inconsiderate behavior, had been tolerable—even admirable and endearing—to some people when he was a fourteen-year-old looking to conquer the world. Such behavior had simply become unacceptable now that he was a man, however young. It had to stop. Everyone, including Jones, understood that. Given what the Atlantan would eventually do for the organization and its game, it is deeply ironic that in 1921 Walker felt the need to chastise him for endangering the sport's image.[52]

So by late 1921, the explosive Little Bob earnestly pursued his transformation to the controlled, orderly "Mr. Jones." Grantland Rice, among others, believed that the "clincher" came at St. Andrews, and that by the Columbia tournament Jones had control of himself. That is a neat interpretation, but it ignores the incident at St. Louis. It is fair to say that the St. Andrews episode was the low point for Jones. In his last autobiographical work, *Golf Is My Game,* Jones wrote that the turning point came much earlier, after his outburst in the Red Cross match with Alexa Stirling in 1918. "I resolved then that this thing had to stop. It didn't overnight, but I managed it in the end, at least in tournaments." He added, though, that, "to the finish of my golfing days I encountered golfing emotions which could not be endured with the club still in my hands."[53]

Whatever the significance of St. Andrews, the Walker letter must have served as a cold reminder; the winter of 1921–1922 was a difficult period of maturation for Jones. Like Hagen, he experienced a type of metamorphosis. When it was over he emerged as "Mr. Jones," arguably the most admired model of sportsmanship ever.

Chapter 5

"Sweet Revenge" and Calamity Jane: 1922–1923

While Bob Jones Jr. reflected on his temper and entered his last semester at Georgia Tech, Walter Hagen spent another winter in Florida. Jones did not plan to make a trip abroad in 1922, but Hagen did, and the winter season was especially important to him as a time to prepare for another British Open. Although he finished down the list in the Florida and North and South Opens, Hagen did well in other events. Late in March he captured his second West Coast Open, as well as the Deland Open. Then in early April, Hagen won the second annual White Sulphur Springs Open in West Virginia. In fact, he collected more titles that winter than anyone else.

By the first of May, Hagen was back in New York. There he announced plans for a most ambitious golf exhibition tour. Hagen told reporters that he would team with "Australian trickshot artist" Joe Kirkwood after the British Open and that their tour might last up to twelve months. It was to begin in the United States, where they would play in the major tournaments; at the close of the season, they would set off for Hawaii, Japan, the Philippines, South Africa, France, and end up in Great Britain by the spring of 1923. The tour made sense, at least according to the annual golf schedule. The problem was that no one had ever tried anything like it.

As for his partner, Hagen had met Joe Kirkwood the previous spring at the North and South Open. Five years younger than Hagen, Kirkwood was the most promising golfer out of Australia. Before coming to the United States, he won the Australian and

New Zealand Opens. But his reputation as a "trick-shot artist" soon overwhelmed his competitive accomplishments. Kirkwood discovered his talent for trick-shot exhibitionism in Australia during the Great War, when he performed for Allied wounded soldiers. He developed a routine that included such antics as severely hooking and slicing the ball, striking two balls with two clubs at once, and hitting balls teed up on a spectator's toe. He had grossly oversized clubs for some of his shots and, generally, played to the crowd. In sum, he was something of a golf clown, as well as a skillful and entertaining showman. Hagen and Bob Harlow instantly recognized the opportunity. Inasmuch as Kirkwood was a very good golfer, he and Hagen could play an exhibition against a team of local professionals or amateurs, and then Kirkwood could conclude the day with his trick-shot wizardry, drawing thousands of spectators and their dollars.[1]

Hagen made another business decision that spring. After the North and South, he had a conference with the golf executives of A.G. Spalding & Brothers. Since 1915 he had been their man, playing their balls and equipment, and each year they had been matching his purse winnings. That provided Hagen with a nice supplemental income. By 1922, however, Hagen wanted more guaranteed money. He asked for a flat $20,000 per year for serving as Spalding's representative and "officiating" the equipment production in Spalding's Chicopee, Massachusetts, factory. Spalding declined but tried to persuade its star to stay. Hagen, though, convinced that he might make a bigger profit by starting his own equipment manufacturing business, went into partnership with former baseball players John Ganzel and Joe Tinker of Orlando, Florida. Together they formed the Walter Hagen Golf Products Corporation and located their fledgling enterprise in Longwood, Florida. The only thing that the company had going for it was Hagen's name. Given the trio's lack of capital and business experience, the venture was risky. Moreover, Hagen also signed with the Thomas E. Wilson Company to endorse its "Correct Golf Grips."[2]

So Hagen laid great plans for his golf future early in 1922. To a large degree, the success of those plans was contingent upon his competitive performance. He had shown well in the winter's events, but the real tests were the national opens. In April, the *New York Times* declared Hagen "easily the ranking home-bred pro" and "one of the greatest golfers in the world." For more reasons than ever, he needed to go to Great Britain and prove it.[3]

The American invasion was much lighter in 1922 than it had been the previous year. Only three professionals made the trip: Hagen, Barnes, and Hutchison. Hagen, Harlow, and Barnes made the journey together, leaving New York Harbor on May 29 aboard the *Berengaria*. The tournament was to be played at the Royal St. George's Golf Club in Sandwich on June 19–23. That left little time for practice and less time for exhibitions because the U.S. Open was scheduled for mid-July.

While the *Berengaria* steamed across the Atlantic, Hagen and Barnes probably spent some of their time discussing a controversial decision made two months earlier by the Royal and Ancient authorities. That body outlawed the use of "ribbed" or corrugated clubs in its championships. Hutchison, among others, had used that type of club in 1921, but the British golf authorities ruled it illegal because it allowed a player to put too much backspin on his approach shots. "Ribbed" clubs were usually the middle to short irons, and "ribs" were parallel ridges that stretched from heel to toe, protruding from the face of the iron. The "R & A" had considered outlawing the club for some time, but Americans thought the British unsportsmanlike for making the announcement on the eve of the American invasion and so close to Hutchison's win. It all brought back memories of Walter Travis's 1904 amateur win, also at Sandwich, after which the British outlawed the Schenectady putter. Hutchison said that he, like Jones and Ouimet, could pitch dead to the pin with a smooth-faced iron just as easily and that he would not miss the club. The international rivalry, which needed little stoking, received some anyway.[4]

With or without the "ribbed" club, the key to winning a British Open was the ability to hit low shots, which would fly farther into the wind and more accurately through it. Since his disaster at Deal two years earlier, Hagen had worked successfully on keeping his shots low. In fact, in April the *Southern Golfer* declared, "Hagen has a new shot that is going to work wonders for him." It already had worked wonders, improving Hagen to a sixth place finish the previous year. He had displayed it to perfection in his recent winter victories. And, just before sailing, Hagen obtained two straight-faced drivers. The clubs had no loft and were designed to keep the ball extra low into the wind off the tee; in all, it was a most confident and experienced Hagen who sought the British Open in 1922. The *London Observer* agreed, noting that Hagen was "a far different golfer from what he was a year ago," particularly because of his longer, more accurate drives.[5]

The party arrived and checked into the Ramsgate Hotel about a week before the preliminary rounds. The qualifying would be held over the Royal St. George's and Prince's layouts. After the competitors played one round on each course, the 225-man field would be trimmed to seventy-two for the four championship rounds. Hagen shot 75–72, good enough to put him in a first-place tie with Kirkwood. Writing for the *London Times,* Bernard Darwin observed that Hagen had "shortened his swing" and could now hit more compact, lower shots into the wind. "As a patriotic Briton I do not at all like the look of him," Darwin concluded.

Conditions were deceptive for the tournament proper. The players were greeted by "a blue sky, sunshine, and a light wind that looked like getting up later," according to Darwin. Hagen continued his excellent play. He stayed below everyone else, posting scores of 76–73, although British stars George Duncan and old J.H. Taylor, along with Barnes, were just two strokes behind. At home, the *New York Times* reported that Hagen appeared strong and was "not likely to fall to pieces tomorrow." The same report said that Hagen behaved modestly but was still a "delight" to behold in his black and white shoes, gray knickers, light brown jersey, and black belt.

On the final day, Hagen lost his lead for the first time when the air chilled with "blustery wind and squalls of rain." The weather made the lengthy 6,850-yard course play even longer. Hagen began the third round well enough, but then faltered on the inward nine to take a 79. That dropped him into second place, two behind the surging Hutchison. For a few hours it looked as though "Jock-o-the-Hutch" would repeat as champion, and Hagen would have to settle for coming just a bit closer. But the players reversed their positions in the final round amid a heavy downpour. Hutchison struggled to a 76, while Hagen, who had been receiving regular reports on Hutchison's score from a few holes ahead, finished with a 72. Hagen totaled 300, two shots better than Hutchison.

Hagen had gone out early, so Barnes, Taylor, and Duncan all had a chance to catch him. He sat down near the 18th green and anxiously watched his competitors complete their rounds. Barnes concluded first, missing a thirty-five-foot putt for a tie. Taylor blew up on the 17th and landed four strokes behind. Then came Duncan. Following a birdie at the 13th hole, he mounted a frightening charge. He strode to the home green needing only a fifteen-foot putt to tie Hagen and finish with a final round of 68! The patriotic, partisan gallery gasped when Duncan barely missed. Hagen recalled feeling "too weak and too shaky to move," as he became the first American-born golfer to win the British Open.[6]

The event was monumental for Hagen and American golf. "Hagen's victory at Sandwich was fine vindication of his failure at Deal," Robert Harlow wrote. Indeed, the fact that Hagen had not picked up in the face of humiliating defeat two years earlier now added luster to his crown. Darwin called Hagen a "great golfer and a great fighter," adding that his "last round was a wonderful effort of skill, concentration, and courage." At the trophy presentation ceremony, Hagen made a short, humble speech. He told the crowd that he would bring the cup back next year, and he hoped to defend his title. J.H. Taylor characterized the speech as the most "modest" he had ever heard and called it "a tribute to British sportsmanship." After his remarks, however, Hagen stunned the British by giving his winner's check (about $375) to his caddie. The action offended some people, but Hagen could not resist the temptation to display his sense of egalitarian generosity, while also suggesting that the prize was a paltry sum to an accomplished touring professional.[7]

Within twenty-four hours, he, Harlow, Barnes, Hutchison, and Kirkwood boarded the *Aquitania* and sailed for home. Just before embarking, Hagen once again thanked the British press for their reception, complimented Duncan's efforts, and said little of his own. His modesty notwithstanding, the victory elevated Hagen's status as an international sports hero and secured his place in golf history. Grantland Rice concluded, "Hagen is better known today outside the United States than Babe Ruth, and only a Dempsey covers a greater range."[8]

Jock Hutchison, on the eve of his departure to Britain, had written that the United States was the "greatest golfing nation and will continue to hold [its] place at the top for all time." Taylor agreed, saying, "Golf has taken a great hold [in America]. I can hardly believe that this is the same country which we visited twenty years ago. Hagen's victory provided the proof. Moreover, the three American challengers finished first, second, and fourth overall. The *New York Times* devoted a column on its front page to the story. The report declared Hagen "indisputably the finest overseas player who ever contested for the British Open championship" and said

the accomplishment was "an American victory outright." That was
a slap at critics who for the past year had been making an issue of
Hutchison's Scottish heritage. Finally, if American golf fans thought
the victory "sweet revenge" for Ted Ray's collection of the U.S.
Open at Toledo two years earlier, Hagen must have considered it
his own sweet revenge for all the criticism he had endured in 1920.[9]

New Yorkers prepared to meet their conquering hero.
Grantland Rice was the chairman of the reception committee. He
planned a welcome-home banquet for the Americans at the new
Westchester-Biltmore Country Club, which had already made
Hagen an honorary member. Located between Harrison and Rye,
New York, the Westchester-Biltmore possessed a $6,000,000 rec-
reation/reception center in addition to its magnificent hotel and
"sports house" or members' locker room. The Italianate structure
was set on 650 acres, containing two golf courses (laid out by Walter
Travis), a polo field, tennis courts, a lake, and "a bridle path for
the lovers of the horse." The recently opened facility would come
to symbolize golf's contribution to what economist Thorstein
Veblen called "conspicuous consumption." It was a perfect place
for Sir Walter to hold honorary membership and to be "headquartered" while in New York.

As usual with such gala events, things did not go as planned.
The four-stacked luxury liner took only six days to cross the sea,
arriving on schedule in New York Harbor on Friday, June 30, but
because of heavy fog, it could not dock until noon the next day.
Beyond that delay, the weather did not improve for the celebration; the fog gave way to a summer rain on Saturday afternoon.
Still, the Seventh Regiment Military Band was on hand to blare a
"martial tune" and a crowd of patriotic golf fans cheered "Yea
Walter" and "Hail, the Conquering Hero." Band members carried
American flags alongside a banner that read "Welcome Home,
Walter Hagen, Westchester-Biltmore Country Club." Once disembarked, Hagen and the other golfers were ushered downtown
to City Hall, where Grover C. Whalen, commissioner of the Department of Plant and Structures, gave Hagen's party an official
welcome. Acting in the absence of Mayor John Hylan, the commissioner called Hagen "an American of Americans, a golfer of
golfers, a champion of champions, the champion golf player of the
world." That about covered it, so Hagen just gave a brief speech
thanking the British for their hospitality and his fellow golfers for
their inspiration. Although similar festivities for heroes of various

kinds would be repeated almost annually during the next ten years, Hagen was one of the first to be so welcomed in New York City.

The Westchester-Biltmore banquet was held later that evening. At its climax, club officials presented Hagen with the keys to a new luxury automobile. That was a long way from the gold watch he had been given by the Country Club of Rochester following his 1914 U.S. Open victory, but Hagen, golf, and American society had changed a lot since then. Rice even invited President Warren G. Harding to the festivities; the President did not make an appearance, but he sent a letter offering "felicitations and congratulations to the American golfers."[10]

Armed with the world's most prestigious title, Hagen and Kirkwood immediately kicked off their ambitious world exhibition tour, narrowly losing the next day to Tommy Armour and the Westchester-Biltmore professional, 2 and 1. More than 1,000 turned out to watch the fourball match. Thus Hagen began the most competitively and financially successful period of his career. The twenty-nine-year-old had now won every tournament of significance in the world and was considered the best golfer on the planet. Sir Walter would remain alone at the top for another three years; then he would be joined by Mr. Jones.[11]

As Walter Hagen took the final difficult step to the pinnacle of golf, Bob Jones Jr., completed his career at Georgia Tech. On June 12, the school awarded him a bachelor of science in mechanical engineering. His academic transcript at Tech was impressive, and he graduated in the top third of his class. Jones scored 90s in math, geology, and English; he made 80s in the sciences of chemistry, physics, and electrical engineering. In his major, mechanical engineering, Jones scored consistently in the high 70s. He enjoyed his years at Georgia Tech and always maintained a strong, active loyalty to his alma mater. In 1967, Jones wrote, "I have no hesitancy whatever in saying that the years I spent at Georgia Tech were the most useful by far in my undergraduate experience." With one degree to his name, Jones decided to complement it with a second one in the humanities. He made plans to enter Harvard the following September to pursue a bachelor degree in English Literature.

He also continued to court the beautiful Mary Malone. At twenty years of age, Jones had everything a man in his position could desire except a major accomplishment in golf, the realm in which he was really making a name for himself.[12]

Jones's golf was limited in the spring of 1922 to a few exhibitions and practice rounds. In March, he teamed with Perry Adair against the touring professionals Barnes and Hutchison in an exhibition at East Lake. Some 2,000 watched Jones almost single-handedly beat the pros, 3 and 1. A short time later he underwent a series of operations to cure the swollen veins in his leg; the procedures required a two-week hospital stay.[13]

In late June, just after he graduated from Tech, Jones entered the Southern Amateur, also played at East Lake. The regional championship provided Jones a convenient warm-up for the summer's major events. He cruised through his first four rounds despite the bandages still on his left leg. On June 24, one day after Hagen won the British Open, Jones captured the event for the third time. He especially wanted to win in 1922 so that his name would be the first inscribed on the George Adair memorial trophy. The elder Adair, who had done so much to help Jones get his start in national golf, had recently passed away. The Southern Golf Association honored his contributions by establishing the championship trophy in his name. Jones, showing an early sense of timing for retirement, decided that would be his last Southern Amateur.[14]

The next week Jones and O.B. Keeler took a train to Chicago, site of the 1922 U.S. Open. Jones had sent a message to George Walker a few months earlier. In it he acknowledged the USGA's position, promising to control his temper. And O.B. Keeler would help him. Over the past two years, Oscar Bane Keeler had become almost a second father to Jones, especially since Big Bob Jones curtailed the number of tournaments he attended. The senior Jones had apparently concluded by 1922 that his presence was jinxing his son. Keeler was twenty years older than Little Bob; they became acquainted in 1916 at the Georgia State Championship, and Keeler followed Jones on some of his war relief exhibition matches. Formerly of the *Kansas City Star* and *Atlanta Georgian,* Keeler increasingly covered Jones after the war and in 1920 joined the *Atlanta Journal,* where his primary job was to write about Jones. He had accompanied Jones to Toledo in 1920 and St. Louis in 1921. In time he would watch Jones win all of his major championships and claim to have traveled 120,000 miles with him. As Jones later put it, "Keeler and I became inseparable."

The Keeler relationship was vital to Jones's competitive success. On the one hand, Keeler was the clearinghouse for Jones information and thus a type of publicity agent. Ralph Trost, writer for the *Brooklyn Eagle*, thought that "Keeler made Jones. He WAS Jones. He told us what Jones said, what he hoped, his aims." Richard Miller has written that Keeler "knew more about Jones than anyone else, including his family." Keeler always got the "scoop" first, enabling him to act as a filter for the Jones image. With the exception of family friend Grantland Rice, journalists had to go through Keeler to reach Jones. So Jones had one less thing with which to concern himself as he rose to superstar status.

Beyond his role as amanuensis and agent, however, Keeler became a trusted confidant and encourager. Jones described him as "my dearest friend," adding, at "tournaments we lived together in the same room most of the time, except when either or both of us had his wife along." In truth, Keeler was something other than just a surrogate father or chaperone. He might better be characterized as an older brother or a youngish uncle. Although his formal education had not gone past high school, Keeler was a self-made, widely read, skillful writer with a sharp wit and a dry sense of humor. In other words, he could more than hold his own intellectually with Jones. He was also completely loyal to Jones, who reciprocated with deep, warm respect. At the time, it must have appeared to most observers that Jones was doing a lot for Keeler, especially professionally, but as Miller has commented, in hindsight "it's hard to say who did more for whom." In at least one way, Keeler was to Jones what Harlow was to Hagen: "the ideal companion."[15]

So Jones arrived in Chicago with a renewed commitment to manage his temper and with Keeler at his side. Thus far, he had done well in the U.S. Open, landing in eighth place in 1920 and fifth place in 1921. The venue for the championship was the Skokie Country Club in the suburb of Glencoe. The Skokie event contained several interesting "firsts." For example, the USGA decided to charge a daily admission of $1.10 in an effort not only to make a profit but also restrict the crowd to the most dedicated, educated fans. Also, for the first time, the number of entries climbed over 300, and qualifying had to be done over three days. Finally, the third qualifying day of the tournament was rained out, so that the final championship rounds had to be played on Saturday. James D. Standish Jr., vice-president of the USGA, assured everyone, however, that if a tie occurred the playoff would not be staged on the Sabbath. "It is contrary to the traditions of the USGA to play tournament golf on Sunday," he declared.[16]

Hagen, who took a break from his busy Kirkwood tour, and Hutchison were the favorites to win. Hagen did lead his qualifying field, which included Jones and Gene Sarazen. Then Hagen and Jones were paired together on the first day of the tournament proper. Hagen opened with a blistering 68 to take a commanding lead through the first round, although he faded to a 77 in the afternoon and ended in a tie for third place with Sarazen. Jones played well too, taking a 74–72 and finishing one stroke behind Hagen and Sarazen and four behind the leader, the little-known, fifty-one-year-old John Black. The *Chicago Tribune* estimated the Hagen-Jones gallery to be 3,000 and the total crowd to be 10,000, including "graybeards, 10-year-old boys, flappers, ministers of the gospel, and army and navy officers."

Sarazen began the second day slowly, but in the final round he matched Hagen's 68 and finished with the lead. Hagen, meanwhile, posted consistent rounds of 74 and 72 to come within just four strokes of capturing both national opens. As for Jones, he played better than Sarazen in the third round and took a 70. He started later than Sarazen that afternoon and knew exactly what was required in the final holes to catch him. By the 17th hole, Jones needed a par and a birdie to tie for the lead. The 18th was a rather short par 5, so it seemed that he had a good chance—at least until he pulled his drive into the woods at the 17th and took a bogey five. He made his birdie on the last hole, finishing one stroke behind, in second-place with John Black.

Joe Davis of the *Tribune* called Jones's golf "immaculate" and made no reference to any temper problems, even after his inaccurate drive on the 71st hole. Grantland Rice described Jones's performance as "the greatest display of his brilliant career." He was the low amateur, had finished ahead of the favorites, and had come within one shot of winning; not since 1919 had he been so close to capturing a national event. More importantly, Jones controlled his emotions in the midst of a loss. So although he failed to win, the Skokie open was a significant step forward for Jones. It was a big success for the USGA as well, which gathered more than $15,000 in gate receipts.[17]

A month later Jones and Keeler journeyed to the northeast for the first official Walker Cup matches and the U.S. Amateur. The Walker Cup was contested in the last week of August over the beautiful, challenging National Golf Links of America on Long Island. The strong American squad included Jones, Chick Evans, Francis Ouimet, Jesse Guilford, Jess Sweetser, and Bob Gardner. On the first day, the U.S. won three of four Scottish foursomes. Jones and Sweetser took their match 3 and 2. The Americans continued their dominance in the singles the next day, capturing five of eight matches and winning the cup 8 to 4. Jones won a tight match against Roger Wethered, 3 and 2. To be sure, the British team was not nearly as strong as it might have been; Willie Hunter did not compete, while Captain Robert Harris contracted tonsillitis and was replaced by Bernard Darwin at the last moment. Nevertheless, for the second straight year, the American amateurs soundly defeated their British counterparts. As he had done after Hagen's British Open triumph, Darwin harped on the superior putting skills of America's golfers, believing that to be the reason for the growing disparity between the two nations.[18]

On the second evening, a banquet was held for both teams. The next morning the entire group boarded a yacht for New London; there they caught a train for Boston, site of the U.S. Amateur. Like at Oakmont in 1919, the qualifying at historic Brookline was held over two rounds on Saturday and Monday, September 2 and 4. Jones carded a 73 on Saturday, two strokes more than the leader, Bob Gardner. Then he and everyone else took the next day off. Massachusetts still had Sabbath laws prohibiting golf, but Jones would not have practiced anyway. He had come to the conclusion that one of his problems in big events was that "he overgolfed himself before the tournament started." On Monday he added a 72 to finish one stroke behind the qualifying medalist, Jesse "Siege Gun" Guilford.

Jones then gingerly made his way through the field in the early match-play rounds, where he again triumphed over Gardner. The victories set up a semifinal match with Jess Sweetser of New York. A senior at Yale, Sweetser held the Metropolitan Amateur Championship and would be a tough opponent. In fact, the New Yorker shot a 69 in the morning round and took a 5 up lead on the Atlantan. All the momentum was with Sweetser. Although Jones played him tighter in the afternoon, Sweetser won by the lopsided score of 8 and 7. The next day Sweetser defeated Evans and won his only U.S. Amateur title.

Big Bob Jones had reluctantly made the trip to Brookline and so came away completely convinced that he was bad luck for his son. It must have seemed that way to the family, too. Several little-known golfers had played Jones extraordinarily tough, and then he suffered one of his worst match-play defeats ever. Yet as D.J. McGuiness of the *Boston Globe* observed, "Jones couldn't win, but he wasn't disgraced." For certain, through another frustrating event, Jones held himself together and graciously accepted the loss. Whatever the particular psychological gymnastics involved, Jones had finally learned to curb his fiery, perfectionist temperament.[19]

Jones journeyed to Atlanta for a few days before the start of another academic year. On Saturday, September 16, he obliterated his old record for East Lake, negotiating the 6,700-yard layout in 31–32–63. It was a phenomenal score, even if it was made in a meaningless practice round. By the 25th he was back north in Cambridge, Massachusetts, and enrolled at Harvard.

A few weeks later Jones made his golfing debut as a Harvard student by setting a new record at the Charles River Country Club. He also played in practice rounds and in an exhibition to help raise money for the Harvard Golf Association's new $150,000 layout. Jones did not compete on the Harvard golf team, however, because he had exhausted his college golf eligibility while at Tech. The Crimson could have used him; on one occasion he took on the entire six-man team and won. Instead, Jones volunteered to serve as the manager-coach of the squad. He traveled with the team, occasionally offering instruction, and the position kept him close to the sport he loved.

In the spring of 1923, Jones reportedly petitioned the dean's office for permission to go abroad for the British Amateur, but Harvard authorities turned him down inasmuch as the trip conflicted with his final exam schedule. It was not until the summer of 1923 that Jones played in any formal competition. Still, his time at Harvard had been beneficial to his game because he spent hours putting on the region's bentgrass greens; when Jones emerged from Cambridge in the spring, he was more familiar than ever with the slick greens of northern layouts.

Jones did not join Harvard's chapter of the Sigma Alpha Epsilon and, in fact, spent less time than usual socializing. As he later put it, "I came to Harvard in something of a hurry to complete the requirements for a degree in English Literature in the least time possible, and so did not expect to have much time for outside activities." Jones did not write about why he was in a hurry, but it may have been because he wanted to get back to Atlanta to wed Mary Malone. Their courtship was going on four years, after all, and he had already experienced "fraternity life" at Tech. He recalled spending "all my surplus allowance" in the bookstores "around Scolley Square or, when I was a little better heeled, in Lauriat's basement." In short, Jones's time at Harvard was consumed by academics and golf.[20]

Sir Walter had never been bothered by college term papers, reading assignments, or essay exams, and he certainly did not have to worry about maintaining his game; the most ambitious golf exhibition tour the country had ever seen would soon provide him with more than enough practice. Following Skokie, he and Kirkwood traveled throughout the northeast, playing exhibitions in such places as Springfield, Massachusetts, and Syracuse, New York. They won eleven consecutive matches in the Chesapeake Bay area during the last two weeks of July, but that streak came to an end on Sunday, August 6, when they were defeated by Sarazen and Armour at the Westchester-Biltmore. Hagen and Kirkwood usually played a foursome match against either well-known competitors or obscure local talent. Their opponents might be fellow professionals, amateurs, British, or women; Harlow exploited whatever rivalry was available. Newspaper accounts usually estimated the crowds between 500 and 3,000.[21]

Besides Kirkwood's trick shots, another gimmick the team used to draw spectators was the "Reddy Tee." The little peg soon became a staple on the links, but up to that time, most golfers had relied on caddies to create a tee from a box of dirt and a pail of water available at each "tee box" or tee area. Caddies sculpted a small mound from the moistened dirt that served as a tee for drives. By 1915 golfers had experimented with various rubber and wooden tees. Then in 1920 William Lowell, a dentist, developed a standard wooden peg with a concave platform that provided players an instantly ready, red tee. His product hit the market in May of 1922, and a package of eighteen sold for twenty-five cents.

Like nearly every other golf innovation, the Reddy Tee initially met with ridicule, especially from purists. But the pegs soon caught on after Lowell paid Harlow $1,500 to make them a part of the Hagen-Kirkwood tour. Of course, the Reddy Tee would have been successful even without Hagen's help, but he was one of the first well-known professionals to use it. He and Kirkwood would typically leave them on the ground, so that the spectators (*usually* young boys) could scramble for the souvenirs. It was another little way of creating excitement and anticipation for the exhibitions.[22]

Hagen and Kirkwood were making too much money to stop and play in formal tournaments, where they might or might not collect a paycheck. The only tournament in 1922 that Hagen and Kirkwood entered after the U.S. Open was the Southern Open, and Hagen's refusal to defend his PGA or Western crowns brought him more criticism. Officials at Oakland Hills, site of the Western, were especially disappointed. A club spokesman said that Hagen "owed" it to the club and his Detroit fans to do the "ethical" thing and play in the Western. Harlow retorted that he had tried to schedule exhibitions for Hagen and Kirkwood in the Detroit area so that they could enter the event without losing stride in their exhibition tour. Local club owners, though, believed that Detroiters would see enough of Hagen when he defended his title; apparently, they did not think a Hagen exhibition so close to the Western a profitable venture. Some suggested simply paying Hagen the money he would lose in exhibition receipts. Yet that would have amounted to little more than an "appearance fee," which was determined unfair to the other professionals and, frankly, too commercial for most golf organizers.

"There is a harmful tendency attaching itself to the game," one unidentified player warned. "Golf is essentially an amateur game. Even its professional side is based on the rules of amateurism— love of the sport for the sport itself and fair play. Love of the sport would make it appear almost an obligation for the title holders to defend their titles." However noble, that view was anachronistic and basically out of touch with reality, especially where Hagen was concerned. From his vantage, the only entities that stood to lose money would be the Western Golf Association and Oakland Hills, and Hagen supposed they could absorb the loss much easier than he. As for the fans, they could blame their local clubs for not scheduling exhibitions; besides, he would be back in the area at some other time.[23]

Although most of his fellow professionals easily forgave him for skipping the Western, they were still upset by his decision to pass up the PGA. Sarazen won the event at Oakmont, but the defending champion's presence is particularly critical in a match-play event, and, without Hagen, Sarazen's victory was tainted. Sarazen raised some eyebrows himself when, after winning the PGA, he announced that he was too tired to enter the Western or defend his Southern Open title and would instead exploit his two major championships in exhibitions. He soon joined Hagen in deflecting charges of commercializing the game.

Amid all of this, between the PGA and the Western, Hagen and Sarazen signed to play for the "unofficial world's championship" in early October. The seventy-two-hole battle would carry a purse of $3,000, the biggest ever for such a match; it was almost too much for the sport's purists to handle. Nonetheless, exhibition golf had arrived, and the sport's brightest stars could afford to snub the ruling bodies and clubs that sponsored the events. All of this put pressure on event sponsors to increase prize money, a trend that alarmed the USGA. "If [golf] is allowed to be commercialized by the professionals, the phenomenal interest now taken by the ordinary golfer in the game will be nullified to a great extent," cautioned the organization. Seemingly unaffected, Hagen went his own way in late 1922, making a big profit while embracing what one critic called "creeping commercialism."[24]

The Sarazen match was scheduled for October 6–7, and the first thirty-six holes were played at Oakmont. From there the men took a train to New York, where the next day they played the final two rounds at the Westchester-Biltmore. They were the world's best; Hagen was the first American homebred to win the British Open, while Sarazen had the U.S. Open and PGA Championships behind his name.

The match lived up to its billing. After the first day, Hagen led by two holes. Then, during the train ride to New York, he pulled one of his most legendary acts of gamesmanship. According to Sarazen, Hagen told him, "Kid, I can beat you at anything." He next sent Sarazen a loud necktie with a note, supposedly written by a secret admirer, asking that Sarazen win with the tie. Sarazen naively showed up the next morning wearing the bright tie and, as Hagen recalled, "grinning from ear to ear." Yet if Sarazen spent some of his free moments trying to find his secret admirer in the gallery, it did not affect his game, because he fought back, eventually winning 3 and 2. Moreover, Sarazen did it all while experiencing some severe stomach pain. A few observers noticed that he was in discomfort; indeed, early the next morning he went to the hospital for an emergency appendectomy. The surgery concluded one of the most famous events in either man's career.[25]

Even in the loss, Hagen collected forty-five percent of the $3,000 purse, or $1,350. But if the contract was designed so that both men were guaranteed a lot of money, the match still carried significant prestige and there was plenty of incentive to win; now Sarazen could claim to be the world's best golfer. Hagen had been favored, but Sarazen was not intimidated and did what Barnes, among many others, never seemed quite able to do—overcome the infamous Hagen magic and beat him at match play. For Hagen, it was a disappointing, even humiliating, defeat. After all, his opponent had won while on the verge of an appendicitis attack. The *New York Times* remarked that Hagen seemed "overgolfed" and lacked his characteristic "fire and dash" in the Sarazen duel. In truth, Hagen was exhausted. His golf odyssey with Kirkwood had maintained a grueling pace, yet it was not half finished.

Two weeks later, on October 24, Hagen and Kirkwood played their last match of the year in the East, and the next day the Harlow troop boarded a train for Kansas City, where they would enter several matches before heading out to northern California. From there they would make their way to southern California, then to Texas, and finally into Florida. Upon leaving New York, the duo confessed that they would not make it around the world on this tour but were planning to do so the next season. They probably changed their minds because of fatigue and having made enough profits in the States. Moreover, the South tempted professional golfers with several new juicy plumbs that winter, not the least of which was San Antonio's $6,000 Texas Open.[26]

As Hagen played his way west, the *New York Times* published its year-end analysis of the golf season, concluding that the two biggest stories were Hagen's victory abroad and the rise of Sarazen. There was no mention of Bobby Jones. Golf analyst William Hicks still rated Hagen above Sarazen—a conclusion based on Hagen's low medal scoring. As he calculated it, Hagen compiled a 71.75 in some 200 rounds, broke 70 thirty-five times, won three opens, and finished runner-up in three others. *Golf Illustrated*, however, declared Sarazen "the supreme golfer of the year." Hagen would soon confirm Hicks's vote of confidence.[27]

By the first week of 1923, Hagen, "feeling fit and well," was in Sacramento for several exhibitions and the California Open. On January 4 he and Kirkwood trounced Hutchison and Sarazen 8 and 7. Hay Chapman of the *San Francisco Chronicle* noticed that Sarazen, who had recovered remarkably from his surgery, was wearing the necktie that Hagen had given him during their world's championship contest. "But," as Chapman concluded, "the spell didn't work"; Hagen shot a medal score of 139 and was the star of the event. Kirkwood went on five days later to win the California Open, defeating MacDonald Smith in a playoff. After finishing in a tie for third, Hagen relaxed on the day of the playoff by duck shooting at the Wild Goose Club. John W. Hession, a champion rifleman, observed that Hagen was "a hunter of no mean ability." The next day Hagen and Kirkwood played a benefit match at the Mare Island Country Club for the U.S. Navy. It was a good beginning to the western swing, and apparently, Hagen had once again found his game.[28]

The team made its way south to Los Angeles for more exhibitions and then started back east late in January. By the end of the month they were in San Antonio for the second annual Texas Open. Hagen played well throughout the tournament, despite having never practiced on the Brackenridge Park layout. He shot 65 in the third round and won the event in vintage Sir Walter style, coming from six shots behind after two rounds to defeat William "Wild Bill" Mehlhorn in an exciting playoff. The *San Antonio Express* reported that Hagen sat on the apron of the 18th green "in one of his most elaborate sportcoats, and with the same old smile," and watched Mehlhorn miss a three-foot putt for a victory on the final hole of regulation play. After he won the playoff, Hagen autographed his ball for the *Express*'s Bruce Layer as a memento of the event, pocketed the world's record $1,500 prize, and generally enhanced his reputation as the toughest money player around.

Yet Hagen's win at San Antonio was important for another reason. The Texas Open has been widely regarded as the birthplace of modern tour golf. The event was the first permanent "big money" tournament and became the anchor for a winter circuit that followed the same path Hagen and Kirkwood traveled in 1922–1923. The "southern swing" eventually was strengthened by the addition of the Los Angeles Open in 1926, which took its cues from the San Antonio event. If Hagen was the "Johnny Appleseed" of professional tour golf, then his victory at the Texas Open in 1923 was most appropriate.[29]

Over the next month Hagen and Kirkwood journeyed from southern Texas to Florida, playing exhibitions in such places as New Orleans and Mobile, Alabama. The *New Orleans Times-Picayne*'s Gordon Hebert included a full summary of Kirkwood's trick-shot display in his coverage of a March 3 exhibition. According to Hebert, Kirkwood drove the ball standing on either foot, successfully negotiated stymies "from all distances" (and both left- and right-handed), stacked balls three high and then struck the middle one without much disturbing the other two, drove a ball teed up on a watch's crystal, and, finally, launched a ball from beneath a spectator's foot. The show, which lasted for about an hour, included many other shots and was, Hebert declared, a "wonder."[30]

Hagen and Kirkwood eventually arrived safely in the St. Petersburg area and promptly entered the West Coast Open. Hagen won the event on March 17 in sensational fashion and for the second straight year. His red-hot 276 was ten shots better than any other score in the field and only two strokes more than the unofficial, but widely regarded, all-time open tournament record. Most stunning was his third-round 62, which was a world's record for a single round in an open. To be sure, Bellair Heights' No. 2 layout was no Oakmont; par for the shortish course was only 69. The course was narrow, however, so Hagen's 33–29 was still impressive.[31]

In the next two weeks, Hagen won the Asheville-Biltmore Open in Asheville, North Carolina (another recent addition to the winter circuit), and the North and South Open at Pinehurst. In the North and South, he broke the world's record for two consecutive rounds in an open when he fired 70–68; then he set the tournament record with a 289 total. In between those victories, he finished second in the St. Augustine Open.[32]

The North and South capped Hagen's most successful winter ever. It also put an exclamation mark on the Hagen-Kirkwood barnstorming venture. The pair had to cancel their last few matches after Kirkwood sprained his shoulder while trying to land a four-foot kingfish in the Gulf of Mexico late in March. Nonetheless, their whirlwind tour had been the most extensive and profitable in the history of golf. On the one hand, they did well competitively. The *New York Times* figured that the pair played in 120 matches and lost only 16. In the West they were 50–4–2. A Harlow-designed advertisement for their fall 1923 tour appeared in the *American Golfer*, proclaiming that between July 1, 1922, and April 10,

1923, Hagen and Kirkwood played 115 exhibitions and compiled a record of 97–14–4. The ad noted that Hagen had won four opens and Kirkwood three, and it highlighted Hagen's 62.

No financial records were published, but in mid-March the *Southern Golfer* simply reported that the troop was "highly satisfied from a money standpoint." In his autobiography, Hagen recalled that their base appearance fee during the tour was $500, although sometimes they received an additional cut from the gate receipts. If Hagen's memory is correct (and the figure does seem in line with contemporary rates), then the group easily cleared $50,000. It is a fair estimate that, after expenses, Hagen collected in the vicinity of $15,000, plus a few thousand dollars more in open-purse winnings. Moreover, it seems everyone got along as they traveled thousands of miles on trains, automobiles, and occasionally airplanes. Kirkwood, who had only lived in America for two years, could claim to have set foot in every state of the union by the spring of 1923. The tour had been a lot of hard work, but it must have seemed worth it because Hagen and Harlow immediately scheduled another for the fall.[33]

So with a grand tour and four winter victories to his name, Hagen arrived in New York on April 12. That city's *Times* declared Hagen "right now in his greatest golfing form" and the southern season a success, since it now could boast of having a legitimate circuit. Innis Brown, writing for the *American Golfer*, amplified that observation: "Time was when it was customary to speak of the *golfing season*, referring primarily to that period from spring to autumn during which competitive golf raged through the land. But nowadays the golfing season's pretty much always here." In New York, Hagen completed his plans to travel abroad in defense of his British Open crown, and, shortly after he arrived, the Westchester-Biltmore finally presented him with his new Cadillac sports model (the keys for which he had received the previous summer). He promptly drove it north to Rochester.[34]

Hagen went to Rochester for several reasons. Among them was to spend some time with his son, who had turned five years while Hagen was in California. During the stay, Albert Stone of the *Rochester Herald* snapped pictures of Hagen and his new Cadillac, and he also took some photographs of Hagen and his son at the Country Club. The photos show Junior, wearing a nifty little golf outfit of shorts and an overcoat, receiving instructions on the golf grip and stance from his world-famous father. Although it was rarely publicized, Hagen probably passed through Rochester whenever possible to see Junior during his childhood years. There is no way of knowing how often Hagen did this. It is certain, though, that he sometimes would go months, such as during the Kirkwood tour of 1922–1923, without seeing his boy. The *New York World* reported that Hagen also went to Rochester to visit his mother. He probably used the occasion to inform his family that he had decided to marry again.

The second Mrs. Hagen would be Edna Crosby Straus, a Jewish widow of a leather manufacturer from Newark, New Jersey. She was slender, with dark hair and eyes. Her husband, I.T. Straus, had died in 1919. A year later, after becoming acquainted in Canada through mutual friends (possibly the Wallaces of Detroit), and after his separation from Margaret Johnson, Hagen and Edna Crosby began their romance. According to the New York newspapers, they spent a lot of time together in Florida during their two-year courtship. She had been born in Philadelphia and was thirty-two years old. Hagen was thirty, despite the figure of twenty-nine he listed on their marriage license.

They announced their engagement on a Friday, a few days after Hagen returned from Rochester, and were married the following Monday morning, April 30, 1923. The brief ceremony was performed at the Westchester-Biltmore at 10:00 and was followed by a "wedding breakfast." Al Wallace and his wife served as the best man and matron of honor. Joe Kirkwood and his wife and H.B. Martin were among the small number of witnesses. The couple drank from the British Open cup, and Hagen presented his bride with a diamond pendant bracelet during the celebration that afternoon. Although they probably left early, the Hagens were guests of honor at the farewell dinner given for the golfers. After the meal, a letter from President Harding wishing Hagen, Sarazen, and the other American professionals the best of luck was read aloud to the crowd. The next day the newlyweds boarded the *Aquitania* for Scotland. Edna Hagen must not have minded too much organizing her honeymoon around the British Open; at any rate, unlike Hagen's first marriage, this one would produce no children, and, for a while at least, his wife would travel with him.[35]

Just before climbing onto the *Aquitania*, Hagen told New York reporters that he was playing "good enough golf to win the [British] event" and that he "was certainly playing better than [he] was a year ago." But he added, "Unless I happen to get a break now

During his visit to Rochester in April 1923, Hagen showed off his new Cadillac and shared some time with his son at the Country Club. Courtesy: Albert R. Stone Negative Collection, Rochester Museum and Science Center, Rochester, New York.

and then and unless my putts are dropping I can't win." Hagen's forecast proved accurate. After narrowly qualifying, he played well at Troon in the second week of June. In fact, Hagen missed repeating as champion of the British Open by only one stroke. Arthur Gladstone Havers, a young English professional, thrilled the 10,000-person gallery by bringing the Claret Jug back to the Isles for one last time in the '20s. Havers finished early, and Hagen came to the last hole needing a birdie three to force a tie. But he hit his approach shot into a bunker (at which point a few British fans cheered) and could only salvage a par 4. Regarding his bunker shot, the ever-confident Hagen later told *Golf Illustrated*'s Patterson McNutt, "I had a mental picture of my chip dropping into the hole. I could see that ball going in. I was really surprised when it didn't go in." "It wasn't my year," he philosophized, "I was just beginning to play real golf when the tournament ended."

It was still a gallant title-defense, and the failure did nothing to tarnish his reputation. Conditions had been characteristically rough for the event. As Bernard Darwin recorded them one day, "The sea was lead coloured; so was the sky. The rain swept across the course, as if it never would stop, and it was very cold." Although the weather improved by the end of the competition, the gallery, which had been especially raucous that week, did not. For example, after Hagen took a double-bogey on the short eighth, the "Postage Stamp" hole, and then missed a very short putt on the ninth green, a woman in the gallery laughed loudly at him. Hagen "calmly strolled across the green and quietly admonished her with the remark 'I don't think that was a sporting thing to do.'" At least that was the way George Greenwood recorded the exchange in *Golf Illustrated*.[36]

Moreover, the international rivalry had once again been fueled by controversy. Just before the tournament began, the Royal & Ancient golf authorities handed down another poorly timed equipment ruling when it outlawed punched irons (which had small, round cavities indented on the face) as it had the corrugated or ribbed clubs in 1922. Although Harlow later denied its accuracy, a story appeared in the *London Daily Mail* just before the tournament under the headline "Hagen Flays British Club Ban: Sees Hostility To U.S. Golfers." In the story, Sir Walter criticized not so much the ruling as its timing and the inconsiderate attitude shown by the R & A toward the Americans, who, reportedly, spent the night before the event filing the faces of their irons smooth.

Walter Hagen and Edna Crosby on their wedding day, April 30, 1923.
Courtesy: Sydney L. Matthew Collection

The whole experience upset Edna Hagen. Upon her departure
to the United States, she told reporters that, while enjoying much
of her stay, she was "not impressed with Scottish sportsmanship.
When the British golf champion arrived there was not a soul to
meet him and take him to the clubhouse, or show any interest in
his comfort." Then she concluded, "If Scottish golfers visit America
I hope they will be received very differently." Harlow later confirmed much of this, recalling, "Not one of the [American profes-
sionals] was ever invited into the clubhouse." For that reason,
Hagen did not join Havers or tournament officials in the clubhouse for the trophy presentation and concluding ceremonies. He
figured that if he was not good enough to enter during the week,
he was not good enough to enter at all, even if the defending champion and runner-up was expected to attend. Instead, Hagen walked
to the entrance of the clubhouse, where he turned abruptly and
announced that he was going to a nearby pub. Before leaving he

told the crowd: "If the committee likes, they can present the trophy to the new champion over there."

When the party returned to New York a week later, Hagen simply said, "I am sorry to say that I did not receive the treatment which would make me anxious to return. Whenever I missed a shot, the gallery applauded and some of them cheered, which in my opinion was very unsportsmanlike." Sarazen had a different opinion, though, and said that the gallery had treated him "splendidly." But then Sarazen had posted an 85, failing even to qualify for his first British Open. Hagen added that the trip was so expensive he might only make it biennially in the future. It was not like Sir Walter to gripe or offer alibis, and, according to H.B. Martin, that made Hagen's complaints all the more credible. Thus ended Hagen's first effort to defend his British Open crown. Once again the tournament provided an exciting finish and an assortment of brouhahas, in all of which Hagen took center stage. At least for a while, it seemed the British had stemmed the rising tide of American golf.[37]

After returning to the States, Hagen played three weeks of exhibitions. Then in mid-July it was on to Long Island for the U.S. Open. Despite his failure to retain the British Open, Hagen was still considered "the greatest competitive golfer in this country today, if not in the world," and was a favorite at the Inwood Country Club. Other professional challengers were Barnes, Kirkwood, Hutchison, and Sarazen. The finest amateurs, including Ouimet, Evans, and Jones, would be there too. It was the first competition of the season for Jones, who had recently finished his first year at Harvard.

On Monday, July 9, qualifying for the Open got underway. Sectional qualifying had still not arrived, so the huge 360-man field had to be qualified on site that week. Ninety men would play two rounds each on either Monday, Tuesday, Wednesday or Thursday, with the lowest eighteen, plus ties, each day advancing to Friday and Saturday's rounds. Hagen qualified on Wednesday with a 156, six strokes behind leader MacDonald Smith. Hagen was not at his best, at least in his scoring. He still entertained the crowd, though, donning a "sun-helmet" in the morning round because, he said, he was spending so much time in the rough. William Richardson of the *New York Times* thought that the only thing missing from Hagen's African safari was an elephant and a carbine. Jones played his preliminary rounds the next day and, like Hagen, shot a 77 and 79 to finish six behind the leaders. Richardson noted that Jones had neither chased insects nor torn up his card in a rage; rather, the young Georgian had become "gentle and docile on the links." That was good, he concluded, but not nearly as entertaining as "Dr. Livingston's African exploration," his name for Hagen's "screamingly funny comedy."

H.B. Martin made an interesting, if informal, survey of the seventy-seven men who qualified. He found that only twenty were Scottish or English. Twenty-one of the contenders were "homebreds," while the other thirty-five were Italian, Spanish, Irish, or German. Gone were the days when golf events in America were dominated by the British.

Hagen and Jones were paired together for the first rounds on Friday morning, and the professional had still not recovered his edge. He shot 77–75 and did not putt well, missing a two-footer at the eighth in the afternoon and taking three putts from twelve feet on the ninth green. Then Hagen uncharacteristically lost control of himself, picking his ball out of the hole and throwing it out-of-bounds. He did improve his position by the end of the day, however, moving from twentieth place at the break to ninth by the evening. Jones, meanwhile, played much better, carding 71–73 and finishing in second place, two strokes behind Jock Hutchison. That day it was Jones who chipped and putted with deft control and deadly accuracy, so the pairing produced more than one ironic moment.[38]

One reason for Jones's improved short game was his new putter. A few days before the event, Jones had complained about his putting woes to Jimmy Maiden, Stewart Maiden's brother and the professional of the neighboring Nassau Country Club. Maiden produced a Condie-branded putter with a "semi-goose neck" and a blade "that had a little more loft than most putters of the day." The blade was nicked-up and a bit rusted, and the shaft contained a hairline crack; obviously, the putter was not new. By the time Jones touched it, the soon-to-be-famous tool had already been dubbed "Calamity Jane." It was common for golfers in that era to name each of their clubs; after all, they were not yet manufactured

At age twenty-one, Jones had suffered several years of frustration and disappointment. By the summer of 1923, he was eager to break through for his first national championship.
Courtesy: Emory University

in uniform sets. The finest clubs were still hickory-shafted and individually handcrafted. In fact, each club in a player's bag looked, felt, and was even weighted differently from all of the others. Jones immediately liked the feel of the putter. He took it to the practice green, where he supposedly sank twenty-four of his first twenty-five putts. The discovery proved monumental for Jones who, when he won his thirteenth major championship in 1930, was still using a Calamity Jane putter. By then he would also have acquired his fabled driver, "Jeanie Deans"; the pair of clubs would eventually become the most famous in the history of golf.[39]

So far the putter had done the job for Jones, and the magic continued the next day. He added a pair of 76s, good enough to put him in the lead with only a few golfers left on the course. One of those yet to come in was Hagen. He started very hot, but although he had made up a lot of ground, rising from ninth place to fourth, he cracked in the final round and took an abominable 86. He finished in a tie for eighteenth.

As for Jones, he may have had the lead in the clubhouse, but he was not happy with his position. Going into the last three holes of the tournament, he needed all fours to complete a round of 72. Such a mark would have put him safely out of the reach of anyone left on the course, but instead of fours, the Atlantan went 5–5–6. Rice described Jones coming into the clubhouse as having "deep circles under his eyes, a weary sag to his body, and the look of one who had been mortally hurt." When O.B. Keeler met his young companion at the door and tried to console him, Jones snapped, "I didn't finish like a champion. I finished like a yellow dog. I don't deserve to win." The weak finish left the door open for little Bobby Cruickshank. At 5' 5" and 125 pounds, Cruickshank was not a formidable-looking Scotsman. He also had troubles on the final nine holes, but he pulled himself together and caught Jones with a six-foot birdie putt on the 18th to force a play-off.[40]

Francis Ouimet roomed with Jones that week. He remembered that on Saturday evening, Jones read a few chapters of a book and then "turned in for a fine night's rest." With the USGA having overcome its qualms about Sunday golf, the play-off was decided the next day, July 15, at 2:00. Keeler remembered that the sky was overcast, occasionally flashing with lightning, while the air was hot and sultry. Despite the ominous weather, nearly 10,000 people turned out to see if Jones would finally break through for his first major victory. The match was one of the most exciting tiebreakers in U.S. Open history. Jones and Cruickshank each fired 37s on the front nine in what Rice called a "ding-dong, nip-and-tuck battle." They were still deadlocked heading to the 18th.

The immense pressure finally took its toll on the "wee Scot." Luke Ross, Jones's caddie, remembered that Cruickshank rubbed dirt into his palms before hitting his last tee shot, which he topped and pulled only 150 yards. Jones then pushed his drive into the spectators who lined the right side of the fairway. Cruickshank had little choice but to lay up short of the creek crossing the fairway just in front of the green, and he did that nicely. Jones, though, had a tough decision. Or so it seemed. He was about 190 yards from the green. If he gambled and left his shot short, it could be wet, and, despite Cruickshank's troubles, he might still lose. On the other hand, if he could clear the water and put his ball on or near the putting surface, he would instantly grab the advantage. Richardson reported that Jones's ball was "perched" up with a decent lie. Ross later recalled that Jones was intensely focused and did not think long about the decision before asking him for the driving iron (one-iron). Ouimet, standing nearby, "shuddered" at the thought of using the "hardest club in the bag" to play such a pressure-ridden stroke. In his characteristically quick fashion, Jones set up over his ball, went through his routine, and then fired possibly the most important shot of his career. It came off perfectly. The ball stopped only six feet from the hole. The beleaguered Cruickshank pulled his pitch into a bunker and ended with a six for a 78. Jones easily two-putted for a four, a round of 76, and his first U.S. Open.[41]

When queried later about what he thought just before hitting his epic shot, Jones replied: "I don't remember what I thought. I suppose I ought to say that I made up my mind heroically to win or lose with one shot—that magnificent gamble stuff. But I can't say that and be honest. I did think of playing safe . . . . But it seems I didn't do it. I guess I just banged away at it." Jones did say that he had set out to play Inwood, not Cruickshank. In other words, he made his enemy Old Man Par. It was a strategy that would work for him again and again. Years later Jones wrote that his first conscious thought after the play-off was "I don't care what happens now." He had finally won a national championship, and in most dramatic style.[42]

The trophy presentation immediately followed the play-off. Cruickshank graciously praised Jones: "My what a golfer that boy is. He's the greatest champion of them all. To be defeated by him is glory enough." Jones was too choked up to say much of anything. Moments earlier, the gallery had swarmed on the 18th green and carried him off on its shoulders, while a "kiltie" played the bagpipes somewhere on the grounds.

The next day, accolades began pouring down on Jones from around the world. A *New York Times* editorial declared Jones "the shining stylist of golf. His form is so excellent and correct that it stands by him in stead when fate frowns upon him, or when for any reason his nervous coordination is not perfect." Moreover, Jones had acquired the proper temperament "*tranquilus saevis in undis*," translated as "calm even in cruel bunkers." The victory also aroused the British. "Nothing but delight was expressed everywhere when the cables flashed the news that Bobby Jones had won the United States Open Championship," George Greenwood relayed. The reason was twofold. "Jones is admired not merely because he is a great and wonderful golfer, but because of his attractive personality. An Englishman loves a man who is frank, boyish, and unspoiled, and Jones is all of these." Britishers also liked Jones's swing, which was "Vardonesque" in its "purity." And Hagen, in one of the articles that was now regularly appearing under his name in the *Metropolitan Golfer*, wrote that Jones had "accomplished as a man what he failed to do as a boy," and was "entitled to all the credit that goes with winning the blue ribbon of golfdom."[43]

Of course Atlantans agreed; when Jones's train pulled into the Brookwood Station on July 17, he was greeted by hundreds of fans and paraded home with a brass band. Moreover, the lower house of the state legislature adopted a resolution congratulating him, and Governor Clifford Walker announced "Georgia is proud of [Bobby Jones]." A week later nearly 500 of the city's elite gathered at East Lake Country Club to honor their hero. The *Atlanta Constitution* observed that the dinner was an "elaborate affair" and that "nothing was spared." Aside from the dinner, a number of people, including Mayor Walter A. Sims and Big Bob Jones, gave speeches lauding Jones's "sterling qualities," "golfing prowess," and the "manly traits he [has] displayed for years whether in victory or defeat." It seems that where Jones was concerned, everyone's memory, especially in Atlanta, was short or at least selective. A telegram from Charles Blair Macdonald stated that a "cleaner, finer" sportsman did not exist. A congratulatory letter from Governor Walker was read aloud, and then O.B. Keeler received a gold watch for his role in the victory. Jones, who never enjoyed speaking on such occasions, stammered through a few modest words of thanks and received a silver service to commemorate his triumph. The *Constitution* concluded that Bobby Jones is "nothing less than an idol to the people of the city, the state, and the south." His four lean years had come to an end; Jones had finally broken through. The only remaining uncertainty was the level of greatness to which he would rise.[44]

Jones skipped the Western Amateur that summer so that he could recover from the "mental and physical ordeal" of Inwood. Instead, he played several exhibitions with Perry Adair in Atlanta and Memphis. In September he traveled to Chicago's Flossmore Country Club for the U.S. Amateur, where, after tying Chick Evans for the qualifying medal, he was stunned in the second round by Max Marston, Pennsylvania's state champion. Jones had never been eliminated so early in a national amateur. Hugh Fullerton of the *Chicago Tribune* placed part of the blame on the legions of mosquitoes which plagued everyone in the second round. The bugs were so bad that "Siege Gun" Guilford wore a leather jacket and gloves for his match. As usual, Jones offered no alibis. He was still riding high from Inwood and, in fact, had not yet rebounded emotionally. Moreover, Marston was simply a tough opponent. After eliminating Jones, Marston went all the way to the final, where he took the measure of defending champion Jess Sweetser in thirty-eight holes.[45]

By the end of the month, Jones was back in Cambridge, feverishly working to finish his degree in English Literature. On the academic fast-track and striving for graduation after the fall term, he desperately missed his family and wanted to get back to Atlanta for good. Still, he had time that autumn to enter a few golf exhibitions, which were to benefit charity and to maintain his game. On October 11, for example, he and Marston teamed up to defeat Ouimet and Guilford in a match for the State's Caddie Welfare Fund.

Nearly two weeks later, on October 29, Jones-Sweetser defeated the formidable pair of Hagen-Sarazen 1 up in an exciting thirty-six-hole four-ball match at the Winged Foot Country Club in Mamaroneck, New York. The Rotary Club organized the exhibition and designated the proceeds for the city's "crippled children's fund." Approximately 3,000 spectators watched the professionals take a five-hole lead in the morning. The amateurs fought back in the afternoon, mostly because of Jones's play. Hagen, who had shined in the morning, looked dull and tired late in the day as his own score ballooned to an 81. The *New York Times* noted that Hagen was "forced to play second fiddle to Jones," who shot 73 in the afternoon, five strokes better than either his partner or Sarazen. Following the match, the organizers awarded Jones and Sweetser wristwatches. For them, the event was a complete success, raising nearly $7,000 for charity; for Hagen, though, the Winged Foot exhibition was a disappointing conclusion to his competitive year.[46]

After his embarrassing finish at Inwood, Hagen struggled late in July to sixth-place in the Metropolitan Open. Two months later, at the end of September, he lost to Sarazen in the final round of the PGA Championship at the Pelham Country Club in New York. Hagen had cruised through his early matches; he certainly did not hand the final to Sarazen, who had to defend his title on the second hole of a sudden-death playoff. For one of the few times in his career, Hagen displayed his nerves on the final hole when he failed to clear a bunker with a short greenside pitch. And throughout the match, Hagen was not his typical, nonchalant self; at one point he got into a sharp exchange with Sarazen over the rules. It was especially frustrating for Hagen to lose another big man-to-man competition with Sarazen, who now seemed able to beat Hagen almost at will. Writing for *Golf Illustrated,* Richardson concluded that Sarazen was now "Hagen's master at match-play."[47]

About two weeks before his exhibition with Jones at Winged Foot, Hagen again finished runner-up in an important event, the Western Open. He could take pride in his final-round 67, but it was not good enough to overcome his third-round 78. The 78 happened because Hagen took an abysmal 44 on the back side, including an eight on the 13th hole. One reporter noticed that, after carding his eight, Hagen's "interest seemed to be far away from the game" as he three-putted the 14th, 15th, 17th, and 18th greens. The final-round 67 was a testimony of his competitive fire and determination to win just one major event in 1923.[48]

He failed to do that, though. Since his white-hot winter performance, Hagen could only talk of second-place finishes. To be

Jones and Hagen competed in a number of amateur-professional charity
matches in the 1920s. In late 1923, Jones teamed with Jess Sweetser,
while Hagen joined Gene Sarazen for an exhibition at the
Winged Foot Country Club.
Courtesy: Sidney L. Matthew Collection

sure, two of them came in the British Open and the PGA, but runner-ups carried little prestige and brought few spectators to exhibitions. Moreover, his U.S. Open showing was particularly weak. There can be little doubt that he was, indeed, "overgolfed." Harlow had organized a series of exhibitions for Hagen and Kirkwood that fall, so he had been playing or traveling to play almost every day since the summer of 1922. It could not have come as a surprise when Hagen slipped behind Sarazen in the year-end rankings for professionals, at least as William White of *Golfers Magazine* ordered them. The same rankings put Jones number one among the amateurs, slightly ahead of Marston. The *New York Times* and *Metropolitan Golfer* offered season-concluding analysis that echoed White's but stopped short of specific numerical rankings.[49]

In a short time, however, such analyses would mean nothing, because neither Sarazen nor anyone else would be able to keep up with Hagen in 1924. In fact, Sarazen would soon struggle with the "flash in the pan" label, while Hagen would shake off the mediocrity of 1923 and recapture the glory of 1922. If Hagen had slipped, he was about to go right back to the top and, once again, amaze the world of golf.

Chapter 6

"The Greatest Ever" and a

Return to Merion:

1924–1925

With his own runner-up year behind him, Walter Hagen headed for his winter base along the west coast of Florida. Accompanying him early in December 1923 were his wife and a chauffeur, who drove their Cadillac southward from Philadelphia to St. Petersburg. It was Hagen's first automobile trip along the Atlantic coast, and he immensely enjoyed the scenery, especially in the Carolinas. He had traveled the same path many times by railroad but found that it "did not compare in any way, shape or form with the motor car" as a means of transportation.

After he arrived in St. Petersburg, Hagen struck one of the most fortuitous and lucrative financial arrangements of his life. Jack Taylor, a gulf coast real estate developer, approached Hagen with the idea of constructing another country club in the St. Petersburg-Tampa Bay area. Taylor owned some 350 acres surrounding Bear Creek and bordering the town of Pasadena. He planned to put a course on the land and sell small plots for homes to create a "splendid, aristocratic resort community." Taylor asked Hagen to help design the course, serve as the club's first president, and represent it in tournaments throughout the regular season. For his name and trouble, Hagen would receive $30,000 annually. Hagen did not think long before accepting the offer and spent much of the winter of 1924 organizing the

Bear Creek Golf and Country Club, later renamed Pasadena-on-the-Gulf. The plans called for thirty-six holes to be ready by the spring of 1925.

According to an advertisement in the *Southern Golfer*, Hagen sent personal invitations to "a selected list of golfers whose reputations make them highly desirable [and who] will add great prestige to the club and will attract other members of equal standing socially and financially." The club was to be "exclusive," not "semi-public." That winter Hagen characterized the project as the "dream of my life." "This being the first time that I have had a finger in the pie," he went on, "I hope to make the most of it." Pasadena-on-the-Gulf and the Spanish villa-style home that the Hagens occupied were certainly a long way from the old homestead in Corbett's Glen.[1]

The Bear Creek land deal came at a good time for Hagen. Although he had poured thousands of dollars into his golf equipment company in Longwood, it had struggled. At one point in the company's short life, his sister, Freda Hagen, even came to Longwood to help manage the business. But neither her efforts nor anyone else's could make the venture successful. Hagen later wrote that the company failed because of Florida's humid climate, which caused the clubs' hickory shafts to swell. When the products were shipped north, the shafts contracted, permitting the iron heads to slip free. That may have been a problem, but it is more likely that the enterprise simply suffered from poor organization and inexperienced leadership. Hagen had started the factory after leaving A.G. Spalding & Brothers, but by the spring of 1923 he had returned, endorsing the "Spalding 50" ball. And in the spring of 1924 Hagen again dabbled in the brokerage business. All of that suggests that Hagen's business discipline was not necessarily on par with his golf skills, so the $30,000 salary was a welcomed, steady income.

Not surprisingly, Hagen had a relatively light competitive winter season. He did play in a handful of four-ball exhibitions. In tournament play he finished fourth in the St. Petersburg Open and second in the West Coast Open, which he had won the previous two years. Hagen got back into the winner's circle at the last event of the season, the North and South Open. He did it in impressive style, shooting a pair of 68s the first day. He collected the paltry first-place prize of $300 and then motored back to New York City for the country's first National Golf Show.[2]

Bob Harlow, along with several wealthy golf boosters, organized the exposition, which was held May 5–7 at the Seventy-First Regiment's armory building. The show's objectives were to create greater interest in the sport and give some sixty equipment and clothing manufacturers an opportunity to exhibit their latest lines. Models strutted the most recent styles of golf-wear twice a day; trophies for the PGA, U.S. Open, U.S. Amateur, U.S. Women's Championship, and the Walker Cup were showcased. Beyond that, visitors were awed by the 240-foot miniature golf course, complete with bunkers, rough, and water hazards. Most of the holes, which ranged from thirty to forty-five feet, required only putts, but a few called for pitches. Some of the stars, Hagen among them, played matches over the little course to the delight of the galleries. Approximately 8,000 golf enthusiasts paid for tickets to the show, prompting the *Southern Golfer* to declare golf "the greatest American sport, a sport which in the last few years has surpassed interest in even automobiles, baseball, and football, while tennis has been left even farther behind."[3]

It had taken a while, but golf finally had risen to new heights as a participatory and spectator sport. R. Hay Chapman, writing for *Southern Golfer*, highlighted the sport's "miraculous growth" in California, where he claimed that there were over 25,000 club members, 5,000 municipal golfers, and another 10,000 visiting golfers annually. *Outlook* carried an article by golf editor J. Lewis Brown that counted nearly 2,500 golf clubs and 1,500,000 golfers in the United States. New York City alone possessed 250 courses; Chicago, 105. Brown believed that the "demand is greater than the supply" because "the baseball and football fan of today is the golfer of tomorrow." "Baseball and tennis have long scoffed at the Royal and Ancient game," Brown concluded, but golf "is rapidly overhauling them [and] is destined to become the center of the limelight of popularity as America's National pastime and one in which Uncle Sam's players will reign supreme the world over." Sol Metzger picked up on Brown's conclusion when he wrote in *Country Life* about the "Rapid Rise of American Golf" vis à vis the British game; to be sure, American golfers had gained significant respect abroad.[4]

The USGA's decision to hold its open early in June was another sign of American golf's strength. Until 1924 the USGA organized its events around what was considered the global championship, the British Open. Traditionally, the Royal and Ancient authorities staged their event in May or June, leaving July–September, the hottest, driest months, for the U.S. Open. In what amounted to yet another declaration of independence, the USGA decided to hold its 1924 Open early in June, forcing the British to move theirs. Of course, the R & A could have left its Open in early June as well, but that would have cost it the entry of American players, who by then would choose to play in the U.S. Open. The R & A did not like the schedule change, but in the end there was really nothing that it could do.

That year qualifying for the U.S. Open was finally done regionally. So the 287-man field was divided into an eastern and western section, with the top forty-two from each area advancing to the tournament proper. Hagen, who badly wanted to win his third title, qualified in the east region at the Worcester Country Club on May 28 with a mediocre 76–78. The USGA announced that Jones automatically qualified as the reigning champion.

While Hagen signed on with Pasadena-on-the-Gulf and entertained New Yorkers at the first National Golf Show, Jones put the finishing touches on his second academic degree and eagerly awaited his marriage to Mary Malone. He began 1924 at the Hotel Astor in New York as the guest of honor for the USGA's annual organization dinner. A few weeks later he completed Harvard's requirements for a B.A. in English Literature. His course work had included French, German, and English history, as well as Roman history and Continental Europe, 1817–1871. Jones also took classes in Comparative Literature, Composition, Dryden, Swift, and Shakespeare. That emphasis in the humanities nicely complemented his engineering degree from Georgia Tech and made him one of the most intellectually well-rounded athletes ever. A short time later, the Harvard Athletic Committee awarded Jones a crimson "H" for winning the U.S. Open as a student at the institution.

On February 8, during his trip back to Atlanta, Jones visited with reporters in New York. He told them that he had given little attention to golf over the last two months and that he did not plan to play in Europe that year. "Naturally," he said, "I'd like to go abroad, but since I am just starting out in business, I want to devote myself to that and to get launched on my career as soon as possible." The career that Jones referred to was real estate. When he returned to Atlanta that spring, Jones took a position in the

Adair Realty and Trust Company. George Adair had started the profitable business; Perry Adair had worked in it for several years. Now Jones would join his friend and, reportedly, begin his career at the "bottom" like everyone else, taking "his place in the renting department."[5]

Jones kept his word and did not go abroad that spring, but he did play in several exhibitions and a regional open tournament. His well-publicized exhibition matches occurred in March and April. On Saturday, April 5, in what some called a world's championship match, British Open titleholder Arthur Havers beat Jones 2 and 1 in thirty-six holes at East Lake. In late April Jones played another exhibition to benefit the American Fund for the 1924 Olympics. Then on May 21 he won the Alabama-Georgia Open, played at Druid Hills in Atlanta. Kenneth Sapp of the *Atlanta Constitution* wrote that Jones performed "like a machine" and was "easily the big attraction of the tournament," finishing fourteen strokes lower than the runner-up, David Spittall. A few days later he arrived in Detroit and took a room at the Oakland Hills Country Club, site of the U.S. Open.[6]

Jones and Hagen got about a week's worth of practice at Detroit, and both were considered heavy favorites by golf dopesters. After taking a 74 in his first practice round, Jones told Buda Baker of the *Detroit News* that the layout was "tough," especially because of its "unusually" large and undulating greens. Jones played six practice rounds, scoring between 73 and 77. The *Atlanta Constitution* noticed that during an informal four-ball competition on Monday, "Jones and Hagen indulged in a slugging match from the tees, taking turns leading the way." Another observer recorded that Hagen was using "wooden pegs" instead of sand for his tees and that he still left them in the ground for souvenirs.

Jones maintained his consistent form on June 5 when the event got underway. After the first two rounds, he and "Wild Bill" Mehlhorn were tied for the lead; Jones carded a 74–73. The gallery following him was large and cumbersome, and the *Atlanta Constitution* reported that Jones lost his patience while waiting for the crowd to be cleared from the 10th fairway. "Oh well, I'm going to drive anyway," he declared, hitting his ball and then adding, "that ought to nail one of them." It may have, because he hooked it into the rough and suffered a double-bogey. For the most part, though, Jones played with "new poise" and a "calm" demeanor. Hagen scored well that day too, posting a pair of 75s and landing in fourth place. Cyril Walker, a professional from Englewood, New Jersey, was between Hagen and Jones at 148.

Similar to Bobby Cruickshank, Walker was slight in build, standing 5' 6" and weighing 120 pounds. But he possessed "wrists of steel," and could hit the ball a long way. On the final day, he played better than anyone else and captured the title. His 297 was three shots lower than Jones, who finished alone in second place. Jones praised Walker, declaring, "this guy is good. He can shoot a game of golf and won by shooting a damnsite better than anyone else in the show. Naturally I am disappointed at not retaining my title, but I have no excuse to offer and no complaints to make." One writer thought that Jones's comment in defeat "epitomizes the American ideal of sportsmanship." Kenneth Laub of the *Detroit News* dissected Jones's play and concluded that the large, difficult greens had caused his defeat; Jones had missed a half-dozen putts of less than ten feet, and on the fourth hole he three-putted from fifteen feet. As for Hagen, he "broke" in the final round after putting his ball in the water and taking a double-bogey on the infamous 16th. He finished where he had started, in fourth place at 303.

Post-tournament analysis focused on Walker's courageous, upset victory and the solid performance of Jones. Previously, Walker's best tournament finish had been runner-up to Hagen in the North and South Open. Although Jones had won the U.S. Open only once, the *New York Times* pointed out that in his five attempts he was seventeen shots lower than his nearest rival, Hagen. Jones was already building a record in the U.S. Open that suggested he was the country's finest medal player. The event was also a success for the USGA, which claimed that 10,000 had turned out for the final day, and that it had collected $20,000 in gate receipts throughout the week. Jones may not have accepted the second-place prize check, but others certainly made a nice profit from his appearance.[7]

Given what was on their minds, Hagen and Jones both performed well at Oakland Hills. Neither remained long in Detroit: Hagen rushed to New York to catch a ship bound for England, where he would make another run at the British Open; Jones had to hurry back to Atlanta, where he would finally marry after a five-year courtship.

At 8:30 on Tuesday evening, June 17, Bob Jones and Mary Malone were wed in what the *Atlanta Constitution* described as "a social event of rare beauty." The ceremony was held on the lawn behind the spacious Malone home because Jones would not convert to Catholicism. Father James Horton of the Sacred Heart Church performed the ceremony, though, suggesting that, like Hagen, Jones had at least agreed to allow his children to be reared Catholic. The event illustrated the tension and compromise inherent in their Protestant-Catholic union. It also proved that however traditional, intolerant, or inflexible R.T.'s religious outlook may have been, his grandson, like an increasing number in his generation, was more ambivalent about his own religious convictions.

The Malone house was decorated with palms, baskets of summer flowers, Madonna lilies, and an altar of lilies and tiny electric lights shaped into a four-leaf clover. The grounds were lined with pink flowers and illuminated by strings of lights. A "brilliant reception" followed, and guests ate pieces of a three-tiered cake. The *Constitution* carefully traced the couple's "prominent" family backgrounds, noting the Confederate officers in Mary's family tree and R.T. in Bob's. In sum, the evening was an attraction on Atlanta's high society calendar. The newlyweds left the reception early and traveled to Asheville, North Carolina, for their honeymoon. After that, they returned to live with Big Bob and Clara Jones, until Bob Jr. could establish himself in the real estate business.[8]

As Jones honeymooned in North Carolina, "Sir Walter" looked to make more history abroad. (By the spring of 1924 sportswriters occasionally called Hagen by that nickname, although his other one, "The Haig," had been used regularly for several years as well.) On June 10, just three days after the U.S. Open concluded, he and his wife sailed for England. They had hurried to New York City via Rochester, where on Sunday Hagen may have spent a few hours with his son. The Hagens were accompanied on the *Mauretania* by the Sarazens (who had been married the previous day) and professionals Johnny Farrell and Al Espinosa. They would all join Jim Barnes, who was already in England.

By the 21st the party was settled in Liverpool, and Hagen had shot 68 in a rain-soaked practice round at Hoylake. That score was quite impressive; his 83 in the first qualifying round two days later was not. Still, observed the *New York Times*, Hagen "walked away with his wife, seemingly not bothered and with an air of confidence that everything would turn out all right tomorrow." Hagen did respond in characteristically cool fashion the next day, showing up late for his tee time and then posting a 73 to make it into the tournament proper. The shot of the day was his sinking of a fifty-yard pitch for eagle on the seventh hole. Sarazen, who had failed to qualify the previous year, led the field.

Hagen teed off at 10:00 the next morning in his first rounds. He "cut a picturesque figure in lavender 'plus-fours' [knickers] and sweater and black and white shoes." Edna Hagen's appearance neatly complemented her husband's; she even wore heeled shoes with black and white wing tips, matching those of Sir Walter. His game was not quite as consistent as his wardrobe, though, and one reporter described Hagen's play as "brilliantly erratic." With rounds of 77–73, Hagen finished the day three strokes behind the leader, British professional E.R. Whitcombe.

A strong breeze kicked up the next day, June 27. When it was over, that afternoon would stand out as one of the greatest in Hagen's career. Nattily attired in gray and white, he started hot, taking a 74 in the third round and catching Whitcombe in the lead. Both men then finished the tournament strong. Whitcombe came in first with a 78, so Hagen, who had a 41 on the front nine, knew that he needed a 36 to win.

He hit a solid drive to the 10th, a lengthy dogleg with an elevated green. The wind gusted as he took his mashie-iron (four-iron) and set up over his approach shot. Hagen rifled his ball through the breeze and onto the green, but it just trickled off the slick surface and down a steep slope into the rough. When asked later if that break "jolted" him, Hagen replied: "No, it didn't. And for two reasons: in the first place, I knew in advance that the green was treacherous under the conditions and that even a good shot might not stay on. I had underwritten that possibility. And in the second place, that was no spot for me to fret over any bad break. I needed all the concentration I had to get my next shot close and drop my putt for a par 4." Hagen's chip left his ball eight feet from the cup. He focused on the line and then confidently dropped the putt for his par.

Despite his tee shot at the 10th, Hagen was not driving accurately, but he continued to scramble his way to the 18th hole, where a par 4 would give him the tournament. He finally split the fairway with his tee shot, but his approach was too long and over the green. His chip was a little short, leaving his ball six feet from the hole. Again, Hagen needed a tough putt; the intensity of the moment was severe. He calmly surveyed the green and then hit the ball squarely into the back of the hole. The crowd roared; Hagen waved his putter in the air. Edna Hagen, heeled shoes and all, ran out on the 18th green and kissed the champion. Moments later, during the trophy presentation, Hagen received a deafening ovation; the crowd even sang "For He's a Jolly Good Fellow" to cornet music. George Greenwood wrote that, "no more dramatic and no more thrilling finish to a championship has ever been witnessed on any links. The most thrilling scene ever depicted in the 'movies' pales into insignificance before it."[9]

The victory brought, among other things, more legitimacy to his runner-up finish the previous year; Hagen had now won two of the past three British Opens and had come within one shot of winning all three. The man the British crowd carried on its shoulders from the green that day had wiped away any lingering doubts about his being the world's greatest competitive golfer. In the following two weeks, Hagen affirmed his status by winning the Belgian Open and finishing third in the French Open.

By July 21, the day that the Hagens returned to the United States aboard the *Leviathan*, Sir Walter had been trumpeted from both sides of the Atlantic. London's *Daily Express* declared Hagen's victory "marvelous," adding that "golf in Great Britain is much overshadowed." Bernard Darwin wrote in the *Times* that, "other people may play more blameless and accurate golf and make fewer bad shots, but in pure fighting ability Hagen has no equal. We can only salute the conqueror as our unquestioned superior." The *Daily Mail* and *Sporting Life* simply concluded that Hagen "has become the world's best golfer."[10]

The U.S. analysis was much the same. The *New York Times* lauded Hagen, already "the greatest competitive golfer of the present age," as "the greatest competitive golfer that ever lived—bar none." John G. Anderson thought that "America's foremost golfer has no counterpart in golf history for determination, resourcefulness, courage and golfing brains." Hagen's finish was "the most superb and stout-hearted golf which it has been my lot to witness in twenty-eight years." The victory, remarked Innis Brown of the *American Golfer*, entitled Hagen "to rank with the greatest that the game has ever produced here or elsewhere." Brown also pointed out that Hagen was the first man ever to repeat victories in both national opens. Finally, Hagen's hometown paper, the *Rochester Times-Union*, labeled him "the greatest competitive golfer of his time." What did Hagen think of his accomplishment? "I just had a great big piece of luck. I had the breaks when I needed them most." Putting his previous year's experience behind him, he added that the gallery's demonstration on the final hole proved "that the British are as fine sportsmen as can be found in the entire world. It almost made me ashamed of what I had done."[11]

Following a victory banquet at the Westchester-Biltmore and a few days of relaxation, Hagen set out to capitalize on his refurbished reputation. He made money that summer by endorsing such items as a five-album golf instructional series entitled "Golf Secrets by Walter Hagen." For $10, a golfer who wanted to break 100 could purchase the long-playing records, supposedly containing ten years of Hagen's experience and $10,000 worth of lessons. Winning golf was not "magic," according to Hagen, but the ability to "separate good practical golf from intricate and sometimes harmful theory." Hagen also put his signature to a solid sterling-silver putter, "an exact replica" of the club "which won four open championships here and abroad." Lambert Brothers Jewelers of New York crafted and sold the putter for $35. But Hagen mostly profited by playing exhibitions with Kirkwood in Canada and the United States. To accommodate his schedule, Hagen withdrew from the Canadian Open and skipped the Western Open. The only significant tournament he entered in the second half of 1924 was the PGA Championship.[12]

The PGA followed the USGA's lead and held regional qualifying events for its tournament. Late in August, Hagen played his preliminary rounds in the New York district, posting a 70–78 and surviving by only one stroke. A few weeks later, he traveled to French Lick, Indiana, for the tournament proper. Two additional qualifying rounds were played on site to slice the field in half for match play, and on September 15 Hagen shot 70–71, just one more than leader Johnny Farrell. When the match play started, Hagen cut his way through Tom Harman, Al Watrous, Johnny Farrell, and Ray Derr. In an astounding upset, defending champion Sarazen was eliminated in the second round by a youngster named Larry Nabholtz.

So the anticipated rematch between Hagen and Sarazen did not materialize; rather, on September 20 Hagen faced his old rival

In the summer of 1924, the *New York Times* declared Hagen
the "greatest golfer that ever lived—bar none."
Courtesy: Country Club of Rochester

Jim Barnes in the final. Hagen still had Barnes's number and beat
the lanky Cornishman 2 up en route to his second PGA crown. As
William Richardson described it, "Barnes failed in crises; Hagen
generally rose to the occasion." Besides outplaying Barnes that
day, Hagen also outdressed him. W. Blaine Patton of the *Indianapolis Star* noted that Barnes's long, loose-fitting pants provided
a "strange contrast to the immaculate Hagen," who wore his usual
knickers and bow tie. The triumph underscored Hagen as the
"outstanding golfer of the year."[13]

Following exhibitions in Indianapolis, Muncie, Richmond, and Terre Haute, Hagen played his way back to the northeast. Late in October he teamed with Sarazen to defeat Ouimet and Sweetser 1 up in an exciting thirty-six-hole struggle at the St. Albans Golf Club on Long Island. The event was a rematch of the professional-amateur duel in which Ouimet-Jones had defeated Hagen-Sarazen. Staged again for the "benefit of the crippled children" of New York, the match raised nearly $4,000. Sarazen carried the professionals to victory, while the *Metropolitan Golfer* thought that Hagen appeared a "trifle stale." That should have surprised no one, because it had been a busy period for Hagen since returning from Europe. He and Kirkwood had played many exhibitions that fall, and Hagen later estimated that they had played 220 matches since teaming up in 1922.[14]

Yet exhibitions provided guaranteed money, so a few days after the professional-amateur charity match, Hagen and Harlow announced the formation of the Professional Golfers League of Florida. Harlow said that the league would "afford the professionals the best opportunity for competition as well as a means of making money." He also promised that the matches would not conflict with the Texas Open and other southern big-money events. Teams representing some of the most prestigious clubs, including Hagen and Kirkwood from Pasadena-on-the-Gulf, would compete against each other in four-ball exhibitions. The league format was experimental; nothing like it had ever been tried in golf. If successful, it would allow top players to essentially bypass the tournaments and make a more reliable income from exhibitions. Moreover, it represented an attempt to bring a coherent schedule to the winter's competition, which until then had been managed haphazardly by various tournament organizers.

The league, plus Hagen's barnstorming, once again raised criticism among traditionalists. British star veteran J.H. Taylor sounded the old alarms concerning the commercialization of the game. Taylor admitted that Hagen's barnstorming exhibitionism probably aided him in tournament play, inasmuch as it allowed constant, competitive practice. But Taylor also believed that "it is only by [club duties] that [the professional] justifies his existence and renders himself worthy of being an essential part of the game." As for Hagen, he cared little to nothing about Taylor's opinions. In late November he started south, stopping at Norfolk, Virginia, where he captured the Princess Anne Country Club's Open. From there it was on to Bear Creek and the Professional Golfers League.[15]

With a beautiful new wife, Bob Jones Jr. had been distracted from golf in the summer of 1924. Following his honeymoon, Jones refocused and began preparing for the Walker Cup and U.S. Amateur, which was returning to the Merion Cricket Club, site of his first national event back in 1916. He passed up an invitation to the Western Amateur, so his preparation came in the form of casual practice rounds and charity exhibitions. On July 17 he played a thirty-six-hole four-ball match at Druid Hills for the benefit of the "Women's Club building fund." The following week he traveled to Savannah with Perry Adair; there they defeated some local professional talent 1 up in eighteen holes. In another four-ball contest on August 8, Jones smashed the course record at the Newman Country Club. Three days later his 67 set another record, this time at the Ansley Park layout. Finally, on the 28th, Jones played in an exhibition for the Educational Society in Albany, Georgia. In sum, if Jones "launched" his career in real estate, he also spent much of the summer of 1924 launching golf balls and practicing for the fall's events.[16]

On September 12–13 the Walker Cup matches were played at the National Golf Links of America on Long Island. Bob Gardner captained a U.S. team that included Jones, Evans, Ouimet, Guilford, Marston, and Sweetser. The American side once again defeated their British counterparts, this time taking three of four Scottish foursomes and six of eight singles matches to retain the cup, 9–3. As usual, the home side was stronger because of the convenience of playing in the event, while the visitors were not as well represented. Most notably absent were Roger Wethered and E.W. Holderness. Still, the British team put up a gallant struggle, and most of the individual matches were in doubt until the final holes.[17]

By the following week, Jones, Keeler, and Luke Ross were in Philadelphia, gearing up for the Amateur, with Jones and Keeler sharing a room in the Greenhill Farms Hotel. The USGA scheduled the qualifying rounds at Merion for Saturday and Monday, September 20 and 22. Every player would play one round each day, and the top thirty-two would advance to Tuesday's match play. Jones shot 72 on Saturday and on Monday to qualify easily.

Although not the medalist, the Atlantan was in excellent form for match play, and on Tuesday he ripped through his first opponent, Canadian Amateur Champion W.J. Thompson. That set up a second-round match against the red-hot D. Clarke "Ducky" Corkran, who had edged Jones for the qualifying medal. After a slow start, Jones clipped Ducky, 3 and 2. In the third round he beat Rudy Knepper to advance into the semifinals.

There he met his friend and American golf hero, Francis Ouimet. The last time Jones had played Ouimet in the Amateur was in 1920, when, following the yellow jacket incident, he lost 6 and 5. Jones had overcome a lot since then, and his affection for Ouimet did not protect the living legend from an 11 and 10 thrashing. As William Richardson summed it up, "Brilliant Bobby" simply "humiliated" Ouimet. When it was over, the loser was characteristically courteous: "There's no disgrace in going down before such a golfer as Jones was today." George Von Elm of southern California beat defending champion Max Marston in the other semifinal, earning the opportunity to play Jones in the championship round.

By now nearly every golf writer had made numerous allusions to 1916 and Jones's first visit to Merion. Sports editors around the country juxtaposed photographs from 1916 of the capped, gum-chewing, world-beating, sassy, hot-headed, husky fourteen-year-old Little Bob with recent pictures of the suited, modest, controlled, matured, educated, lean twenty-two-year-old Mr. Jones. It was easy to see that the all-American boy had grown admirably into a young gentleman. Von Elm, on the other hand, was the first golfer from west of the Mississippi to make it to the final of the U.S. Amateur, and Jones's experience made him the solid favorite. Actually, both men were playing well.

Philadelphia's weather had been beautiful all week, and it stayed that way for championship Saturday, September 27. Jones ate a light breakfast that morning, consisting of only fruit and cereal. There was a feeling of destiny in the air when the USGA's official starter introduced Jones and Von Elm to the anxious gallery of 10,000. Ross even carried two clubs—an old mid-iron (two-iron) and a mashie-iron (four-iron)—that Jones had used in 1916. Probably a bit nervous when the match began, Jones lost the first hole. He soon settled down, though, and went 4 up by the break. Then Jones came out sizzling in the afternoon, winning five and losing none of the first nine holes, extending his lead to 9 up. They halved the tenth, where Jones won the match 9 and 8 and his first U.S. Amateur crown. It was also the first time that the U.S. Amateur trophy had journeyed below the Mason-Dixon line, so two regional "firsts" were recorded.

The end had been almost uninteresting. Nevertheless, it was an appropriate finish to a week in which Jones simply destroyed the competition. His aggregate score versus his opponents was 35 up, for an average of 7 up. The difference that week was threefold. First, Jones was putting exceptionally well with Calamity Jane. Second, he utilized the strategy for which he would become famous; that is, Jones made Old Man Par his adversary. Third, once in the lead Jones did not back off of his opponents in the afternoon but only increased the pressure. The last two factors are illustrated in the following statistic: Jones had forty pars, eleven birdies, and ten bogeys to play his sixty-one afternoon holes in one under par.

Perry Lewis of the *Philadelphia Inquirer* observed that "Jones never let up on Von Elm. Instead, he was out there shooting par all the time, regardless of what Von Elm was doing, for he knew that as he drew close to regulation figures the certainty of his triumph was assured." William Richardson also noticed Jones's "new plan" and commented that Jones was "machine-like when it comes to playing against par." Keeler later wrote that one night, just before the light was turned out in their room, Jones commented, "I've discovered something about golf. . . . If you keep on shooting par at them, they'll crack sooner or later." Keeler also suggested that Jones's new eating habits had helped. Forsaking large breakfasts and lunches topped with *pie a la mode,* Jones ate much less during competition and saved his big meal for the dinner hour.[18]

Lewis of the *Inquirer* hit upon another theme common to the post-tournament analysis: Jones's extraordinary sportsmanship and amateurism. "It is not the golden glow of commerce coveted by the money-changers which Bobby clutches to his bosom this morning," Lewis commented. "It is gold unalloyed with selfish greed—gold of accomplishment in its virgin state—gold of an ambition realized—a long-denied honor gained at last after a series of sickening discouragements." The fact that it took eight years to win the event now played to the advantage of Jones's image. According to commentators, he had won by overcoming obstacles through discipline and hard work. The *Inquirer* included the following biographical piece in its Sunday edition:

Bobby Jones, New Golf King Is Fine Sportsman
Who Is Jones?

Bobby Jones, of Atlanta, Georgia, is a democratic champion.
Born in Atlanta, he went through the public schools of his home town.
Then he matriculated at Georgia Tech Prep, and after graduating went through Georgia Tech.
He then took a B.A. at Harvard.
Out of Harvard, he was at work two weeks later for an Atlanta concern, pressing the asphalt as he collected rents. His advancement in the business world has been remarkably rapid since he made his start from the foot of the ladder.
Jones was a splendid student, he is a progressive young American business man. He is destined to be one of the most popular champions America ever had, for he is the finest type of sportsman.

Golf fans were left to themselves to reconcile Jones's "democratic" nature with his Georgia Tech degree in engineering and Harvard degree in Dryden, Swift, and Shakespeare. In truth, if Jones "made his start from the foot of the ladder," then his was a ladder that most Americans never even touched.

As for the new champion, he remembered thinking during the trophy presentation: "Now I've won the blamed thing. And I didn't do anything, either." Jones believed that he had played no better than in earlier events; the difference in 1924, he maintained, was simply that no one got hot or "went crazy" against him with an especially low round. To be fair, Jones was the one who had played extremely hot golf that week. Additionally, he was a more emotionally disciplined, consistent competitor than in any previous match-play event. Not surprisingly, the victory at Merion reinforced in Jones a growing faith in fate or destiny; his career was assuming a neat, circular, even storybook quality.[19]

Although it was raining when Jones and Keeler returned to Atlanta, they were greeted by nearly 4,000 admirers at the Brookwood Station. The fans, including the Georgia Tech football team, surrounded Jones's wife and parents, and an estimated one thousand automobiles lined both sides of Peachtree Street. Once the star emerged from the train, cameras began flashing and the crowd cheered. According to the *Atlanta Georgian*, it was a larger reception than the one given in 1923, after Jones had won the U.S. Open. When it was finished, Jones quickly retired to his parents' house for some rest, while Atlantans spent a "half-hour trying to get out of the worst traffic jam in the annals of our narrow streets."[20]

Early in November, Jones again set aside his responsibilities at Adair Realty to play in the annual foursome match for the benefit of the "crippled children's fund." A month later he and Ouimet lost to the British professionals Abe Mitchell and George Duncan in an exhibition at Asheville, North Carolina. That ended a busy and productive golf season for Jones. He had not entered many tournaments in 1924 but had played in numerous exhibitions and, for the second straight year, had won a national title. H.B. Martin of the *Southern Golfer* ranked him number one among amateurs, adding, "There is no question as to his supremacy."[21]

Joe Horgan, writing for the same publication, put Walter Hagen first among the professionals, as "everyone would agree who was not deaf and blind." *Golf Illustrated*'s James Harnett concurred, adding that Hagen was not only the best among the professionals but the "golfer of the year." Sarazen had been little more than a "flash in the pan," according to Harnett, while Hagen's performances in the last three British Opens had made the "world his [golfing] kingdom." At thirty-one years of age, Hagen had won no less than twenty-five tournaments, including two British Opens, two U.S. Opens, two Western Opens, three Metropolitan Opens, and two PGA Championships.[22]

At twenty-two, Jones had a U.S. Open and U.S. Amateur, along with a number of regional titles; he had also compiled an astonishing scoring average in the U.S. Open and had just discovered how to win major tournaments. At the close of 1924, Sir Walter was the emperor of golf. Mr. Jones, though, was about to challenge him for that crown. Moreover, that struggle fueled another major change: the U.S.'s consolidation of its golfing superiority over the British.

It would take another two years, however, for those changes to become apparent. There were actually few competitive surprises in the 1925 season, probably the least eventful of those between 1919 and 1930.

For the first time, Jones began the year with some Florida golf. The Florida real estate boom was at its zenith, and the state could now boast of 120 golf courses. Adair Realty and Trust was actively involved in the market. So Jones spent much of February and March ostensibly promoting his company's sizable land holdings; along the way, he kept his game in shape. Jones and Perry Adair made their headquarters in Sarasota, where early in February they played several well-attended exhibitions.

A couple of months later, Grantland Rice, writing for *Collier's* magazine, perpetuated an increasingly popular perception that, since entering the real estate business, Jones was "playing less golf than he had ever played before." Fans were told that with "little practice" Jones "tore through the field" at Merion. Rice's article ironically appeared in April of 1925, just after Jones finished his first Florida swing, hardly a sign of decreasing play. Jones may have been playing less golf than during his college days; he was certainly not playing as often as Hagen and other professionals. Nevertheless, Jones was playing plenty, much more than admirers who were determined to highlight his amateurism wanted to admit.[23]

On February 27 Jones entered his first West Coast Open, joining the professionals, including Hagen, at Pasadena. The event, which had been moved from Bellair that year, was played at Hagen's course for the first time. Jones, displaying "ragged golf," neither started nor finished well. Hagen was not in top form either, and when the tournament concluded on March 2, he was in seventh place and Jones in fifteenth. Soon after, Jones returned to Atlanta, where he continued in real estate and prepared for the U.S. Open, which was scheduled for late May.[24]

Hagen's poor finish in the West Coast Open punctuated an especially hectic season. On January 10, he had joined Kirkwood to play in a match that officially opened the Pasadena-on-the-Gulf Golf and Country Club. The occasion brought out Pasadena's and St. Petersburg's mayors, as well as the Pasadena band. The home team lost 1 up to Cyril Walker and Jim Barnes in eighteen holes. Still, Hagen shot the lowest round of the day, and aside from the loss, the match provided a successful start for the club.[25]

A week later Hagen and thirteen other leading professionals began competition in the Florida Winter Golf League. By then the league consisted of seven teams that were located in Tampa,

Miami, and Orlando: Hagen-Kirkwood, Barnes-McLeod, Sarazen-Diegel, Farrell-Cruickshank, Walker-Eddie Loos, Mehlhorn-Armour, and Kerrigan-Dow L. George. The inaugural match was played between Hagen-Kirkwood and Sarazen-Diegel at Pasadena, with the home team losing 5 and 4. Over the next month and between open tournaments, the teams competed in home-and-home, round-robin competition. The winners took sixty percent of the gate, the losers forty percent, and tickets to each match sold for $2. Hagen-Kirkwood began slowly and finished in the middle of the standings, while Sarazen-Diegel went on to win the league championship. Yet despite the significant promotional efforts of Harlow, Hagen, and H.B. Martin, the new league did not draw satisfactorily. One problem was the sheer number of matches—seventy-two in all. Harlow still declared the project a success, adding that he was "certain that there would be a league next year worked out along different lines."[26]

When not competing in league matches, Hagen entered several open events. He failed to win any and his best finish was runner-up in the North and South. Part of the explanation for his inconsistency may have been that Hagen had lost his mashie-iron (four-iron) the previous December. It was a club that Hagen relied on both for chipping around the greens and for approaches of about 190 yards; he had used it to win all four of his national opens. The *Southern Golfer* announced the loss, stating that, "Walter is willing to pay a liberal reward for its return."[27]

With or without his mashie-iron, Hagen had to face Cyril Walker early in February for the so-called World's Championship. Had it not been for that event, the 1925 winter season would have been dismal for Hagen. But on Sunday, February 1, and Wednesday, February 4, the reigning British Open and U.S. Open champions clashed for the world's title; Hagen demolished Walker 17 and 15. One commentator described it as "an exhibition of class against mediocrity." The match was not official, yet golf writers agreed that Hagen's margin of victory had to represent some sort of record. The triumph answered all questions concerning Hagen and his recent lackluster performances and made the winter competitively successful for him.

Hagen's time off the course was spent in his Pasadena office, where he filled the role of club president. He remembered that the suite came complete with a "beautiful blonde secretary," who sat on her desk, playing the ukulele and always leaving the visitors smiling. Hagen also recalled being there infrequently, and that his duties "consisted chiefly of lining up the afternoon golf and perhaps a few telephone calls to plan some doings for the evening." In late April the *New York Times* reported that Hagen had signed a two-year contract extension with Pasadena to serve as its club president and representative through 1925 and 1926. The terms paid him another $30,000 each year.[28]

That news coincided with Hagen's sale of his struggling equipment manufacturing company. He claimed to have lost $100,000; in any case, he was glad to be out from under it. Al Wallace had connected Hagen with L.A. Young, a businessman in Detroit, who owned a steel and wire company that produced automobile parts. Young agreed to purchase the golf manufactory and paid Hagen $75,000 for his name and equipment line. It "was just like the bonus paid [to] outstanding young baseball players," Hagen wrote. The Young agreement also guaranteed Hagen royalties on the sale of any equipment carrying his name. Moreover, Hagen was made a "director of engineering" and was to be involved in club design. His greatest value, however, was as a winning golfer. Young soon moved the company to Detroit, emphasizing the fact that the purchase was one of a name and not so much a business. Given the Pasadena club presidency, the increasing number of syndicated articles appearing beneath his name, and his endorsement of everything from equipment to long-playing records to sweaters and socks for knickers, the stories that Hagen made as much as $75,000 per year in the 1920s seem credible.[29]

By April, Hagen was fielding inquiries every day about plans to defend his British Open title. Throughout the winter he had hinted that he would go to Scotland, and then he said that he would make up his mind after the U.S. Open. Finally, on May 15 he announced that he would not travel abroad in 1925 but promised that he would go in 1926. Jim Barnes, who had also made the trip every year since 1920, was the only notable American, besides Macdonald Smith, who went abroad late in June. "Long Jim" was finally rewarded, capturing his first and only British Open.

For Hagen, Jones, and most leading American golfers, the U.S. Open was the national medal event of the year. The 1925 tournament was staged early in June at Boston's Worcester Country Club. The USGA had almost 450 entries, by far the largest number ever, and qualifying was again done regionally. Recognizing another new financial opportunity, the USGA charged $1.10 per ticket for the preliminary competition. That was not the only development of the 1925 Open; *Golf Illustrated* reported some interesting equipment trends as well. First, nearly all of the players had adopted wooden tees. Second, and more significant, approximately twenty percent of the players had steel, instead of hickory, shafts on their clubs.[30]

Although the midwestern and southern region qualified at the Onwentsia Golf Club in Lake Forest, Illinois, Jones played his preliminary rounds in the east region at The Lido Golf Club in Lido Beach, New York, possibly so that he could combine a business trip with golf. If Jones had wanted to take the easiest path to Worcester, he would have traveled to Illinois; his presence at The Lido made a strong field, including Hagen, even stronger. In a downpour on May 29, the "distinguished Atlanta realtor" and "sometime golfer" qualified with a 72. That, added to his 71 from the day before, put Jones in second place, a stroke behind Mac Smith. Hagen's 75–72 was plenty good enough to qualify, if not as sensational as Jones's score. Both men were considered favorites to win the tournament proper, but Jones's habit of scoring low in the event made him the heavier pick. At any rate, the gallery would be treated to a Hagen-Jones pairing for Wednesday, June 3, the first day of the Worcester competition.

The players got in practice rounds over the Worcester layout on Monday. At dusk, it did not look good for the professionals; Jones shot a 66, tying the course-record. Playing with Jones and carding a 72, Hagen made news that day as well when he scored his first career hole-in-one at the 180-yard sixth hole, using a driving-iron (one-iron). In an informal poll conducted at Worcester, Hagen was also voted the best-dressed player. Hagen's achievements notwithstanding, dopesters were even more convinced that the horde of "money-changing" professionals could not defeat the Atlanta amateur. William Richardson of the *New York Times* wrote that the professionals were counting on Hagen and Smith to "deliver them from the Joneses. In this commercial day and age, possession of the open championship is a business. To Jones it means nothing but a bit more honor to his already princely fortune; to professionals the title means not only fame but money—lots of it." The conventional wisdom by 1925 was that a professional wearing a U.S. Open crown could make at least $25,000 on exhibitions.

Hagen shot a 68 in Tuesday's practice, while Jones took the day off. On Wednesday they shook hands at the tee box of the first hole and together began the 1925 U.S. Open. After exchanging pleasantries, they probably commented on the sultry conditions. The weather was a factor that week; the eastern U.S. was in the midst of a heat wave that would be blamed for the deaths of 225 people. The temperature on Wednesday reached ninety-four degrees, and the sun was scorching hot.

Hagen outplayed Jones in the morning, but in the afternoon it was the other way around. Actually, neither man performed very well. Hagen sweated his way into twelfth place with 72–76; Jones labored in the morning to a 77, but followed it up with a 70 to end in a tie for tenth. Despite their performances, the pair attracted most of the 5,000-person gallery that day. Commentators agreed that if anyone could come back from a poor start, Hagen or Jones could.

Both men tried on Thursday, but only Jones succeeded. In fact, it was more a matter of the leaders slipping than anything else. First-day leader Willie MacFarlane shot a final round 78 to finish at 291. Hagen posted consistent rounds of 71–74, tying him with Sarazen for fifth place, only two shots behind the leaders. Jones began the day with another 70 but ended with a 74. His final nine holes were riddled with errors, including missed short putts on the 11th and 14th holes. After the mistake on the 14th, Jones manifested some of the old fire when he "indicated his disgust by flinging his putter down on the green." Nonetheless, in spite of the mistakes, his 74 was still good enough to put him in a tie with the ailing MacFarlane.

MacFarlane was like so many other American professionals in that period: he had been born in Scotland and had learned his game there. He was also what later would be termed a "journeyman." That is, the thirty-six-year-old MacFarlane did not have an especially impressive style or tournament record, but he played consistently enough to compete with his more talented colleagues. He did not enter as many events as the leading professionals and essentially fulfilled the traditional role of golf professional at his club, Oak Ridge in Tuckahoe, New York. Grantland Rice reported that MacFarlane had played only about ten rounds since the previous October. His last U.S. Open had been at Toledo in 1920, when he came in eighth place behind "Big Ted" Ray and, coincidentally, in a tie with Jones; since then he had only finished runner-up in the Shawnee and Metropolitan Opens. The near-wins established MacFarlane as a weak finisher who never quite completed an event. He was tall but thin and wore glasses, adding to his benign persona. Sportswriters were fond of referring to him as the "bespectacled Scot" or the "pedagogical-looking Scotsman." The consensus was that he looked more like a schoolmaster than a professional golfer, and that Friday's eighteen-hole playoff against Jones would be the biggest moment of his career.

With his wife and ten-year-old daughter looking on, MacFarlane took a few deep breaths and then rose to the occasion. At 11:00 he met Jones and some 5,000 spectators on the first tee to begin the deciding round. The sun was hotter than in previous days; the mercury climbed to ninety-five in the shade. Both men played well, and MacFarlane's 37 on the first nine was one stroke lower than Jones's mark. The battle shifted to and fro throughout the back nine. When that side was finished, the competitors had simply reversed their front nine scores, so that after eighteen extra holes, they were still tied with 75s. Surprised USGA officials declared that another eighteen holes would have to be played following a break. The playoff, which was the first of thirty-six holes in either the U.S. or British Open, had now assumed epic proportions.

Playing like a "perfect machine," Jones jumped out to a four-stroke lead by the turn of the afternoon round. Both men were exhausted, and it seemed that MacFarlane had finally succumbed to Jones's superiority. Yet the "studious-looking" Scot dug a bit deeper. He birdied the 10th and the 13th holes to pick up three shots on Jones. After Jones gave up another stroke on the 15th, they remained tied until the 18th hole, where MacFarlane made another par for a final round of 72. Jones missed a ten-footer for his par and had to settle for a 73. It was finally over. The scores through 108 holes: MacFarlane, 438; Jones, 439. Apparently, MacFarlane's reputation as a weak finisher had been greatly exaggerated.

For days, commentators discussed the courage of both players, but the most common topic was MacFarlane's so-called overachievement. For that he garnered respect, even if many felt he did not exactly deserve the title. MacFarlane also received substantial praise for what he said after the play-off: He had been "lucky" to win, and "defeating Bobby Jones is a greater honor than winning two or three open championships." When a reporter asked MacFarlane if he planned to "make a tour [and] give the almighty dollar a chase," MacFarlane responded, "I don't know what I am going to do. This much I do know, however. I am scheduled to do some teaching at the club tomorrow and I've got to get back to Tuckahoe!" "Imagine" that, exclaimed Richardson of the *Times*, adding that MacFarlane's "strong feeling of devotion to duty" would make him a beloved champion. As for Jones, the loss did nothing to hurt his standing. In fact, Richardson declared Jones "the greatest golfer that ever appeared in the United States. The professional who beats him one year is far down the list the next, but Jones is always either first or second." Therefore, "popular opinion will award the greater glory to Jones."

Although his amateur image needed no boosting, it got some anyway at Worcester when Jones called a penalty stroke on himself in the first round of the tournament. The episode occurred at the 11th, a par 3. Jones put his tee shot in the rough to the left of the green. While addressing the ball for his chip shot, it moved, or so Jones said. No one else, certainly not his partner Hagen, witnessed any infraction. Jones, however, insisted that his ball had moved and that he deserved the one-stroke penalty provided for in the rules. The officials reluctantly assessed the stroke. The episode made the tie with MacFarlane all the more interesting. Keeler wrote that when observers lauded Jones for his integrity, the Atlantan replied, "You'd as well praise me for not breaking into banks. There is only one way to play this game." To Jones, it seemed honesty and sportsmanship mattered more than money or glory. Six hours after the conclusion of the MacFarlane play-off, Jones and Keeler boarded a Pullman sleeper car and headed back for Atlanta. If exhausted and disappointed, Jones was a loser in only the strictest definition of the word.[31]

A few months later, early in September, Jones solidified his challenge to Hagen as the country's number-one golfer by winning his second consecutive U.S. Amateur. Mighty Oakmont, where in 1919 Jones had battled chubby Davie Herron and a megaphone, was the venue for the 1925 event. The USGA experimented with a new format that year; the number of qualifiers for match play was reduced from thirty-two to sixteen, and all of the matches would go thirty-six holes. Jones thought the new plan a good idea inasmuch as "no unheralded 'dark horses' may in one inspired burst eliminate the best men in the field." The top players still disliked eighteen-hole matches and believed them to be poor tests of golf. The problem with the new format, though, was that it made it more likely that a top player would not even survive into match play; 128 men would compete for only sixteen slots.

Although he was the defending champion, Jones had to qualify like everyone else. He did that on the first two days of September, finishing in a tie for second place with Jesse Guilford and again displaying his top form. The previous Saturday, his practice round 67 had tied the course record. On Sunday he had attended church before spending "the rest of the day reading and lounging." While that routine paid off for him, other notables suffered. Five former champions—Ouimet, Evans, Herron, Marston, and Gardner— failed to make it into match play. As Richardson's hyperbole put it, "The wreck of Hesperus, the fall of Troy, and the burning of Rome were mere trifles compared to what happened at Oakmont today." Whatever Jones or anyone else thought of the new format before the tournament started, everyone now agreed that it was not such a good idea after all.

On Wednesday Jones started his march through the field, easily eliminating William Reekie, Clarence Wolff, and, for the second straight year, George Von Elm. It had been an easy road for Jones, probably his easiest ever. But he was not the only star that week; the other was his young friend and fellow Atlantan, Watts Gunn.

Gunn was yet another golf prodigy to come out of East Lake and one of the South's finest young players. A few weeks before the trip to Pittsburgh, Jones had intervened between Gunn and his father, a Macon judge, convincing Judge Gunn to permit his son to enter his first U.S. Amateur. Watts Gunn had performed much better at Oakmont than anyone had anticipated; in fact, the final that year became an all-Atlanta one when he played his way into the championship match. Stories of how Gunn came to Oakmont and his relationship to Jones were printed over and over in sports pages around the country and brought some interest to an otherwise predictable event. Southerners, Atlantans specifically, were nearly beside themselves with excitement on championship Saturday.

Gunn had sustained an extraordinarily high level of play in getting to Jones, who was fond of Gunn and like everyone else was impressed by his grit. Nevertheless, as Westbrook Pegler reported in the *Atlanta Constitution*, Jones planned to go after his friend aggressively the next day. "Yes, I'm going to bear down on him in tomorrow's match, I'd be a fool if I didn't," Jones said. "I am more proud of Watts and what he has done than I ever was of anything I did, but I'll beat him if I can." As he had done with Ouimet the previous year, Jones showed no mercy. Before teeing off, Gunn asked Jones if he was to receive the usual two strokes, as when they competed in friendly practice rounds at East Lake. Jones good-naturedly but seriously replied, "I'm going to lick you today." And he did. Gunn fought hard but fell 4 down by the lunch break. When play resumed, Gunn's timing appeared off, and the pressure began to tell. Jones closed the match 8 and 7. He immediately shook Gunn's hand and put his arm around him, then the pair walked back to the clubhouse.[32]

On the following Monday, a band played "Dixie" when the train carrying Jones, Keeler, and Gunn arrived in Atlanta. Several thousand greeted the party at about 4:00 that afternoon. The *Constitution* thought that it was the largest such gathering yet, and the players were paraded down Mitchell, Whitehall, Peachtree, and Ivy Streets before escaping to their homes. Jones was particularly glad that day to get back to his family because it now included his first child. Mary had given birth the previous April 18 to a daughter named Clara Malone, who, like her namesakes, had dark hair and eyes.

Jones was not in Atlanta long, however, before he announced that he would again spend the winter season playing golf and promoting real estate in Florida. He and Mary were already in Sarasota by late November, when the clubhouse at East Lake was destroyed by fire. It was the second time in eleven years that the clubhouse had burned to the ground, but on this occasion the USGA's Havemeyer Trophy went with it. If disturbed by the disaster, Jones tried to put it out of his mind; he was entering his busiest winter ever, the one that would include his Battle of the Century with Walter Hagen.[33]

Following the U.S. Open, Hagen and Harlow had launched a six-week exhibition tour that took them from Boston northwest through Canada and into Minnesota, where, at Pequot's Breezy Point Lodge, Hagen competed in a unique event. The exhibition combined golf and trapshooting. His team won the golf match but, despite Hagen's hitting eighteen of twenty-five targets, lost the shooting portion of the competition. From Minnesota, Hagen and Harlow journeyed into western Canada, playing exhibitions in Winnepeg, Regina, Saskatoon, Calgary, and Edmonton. In late July they surfaced in Toronto for the Canadian Open, where Hagen finished in third place.[34]

By the end of the summer, Hagen's golf standing had slipped. He had not won an event all year, except for his pummeling of Cyril

Walker in the Unofficial World's Championship. It was easy for golf writers to begin referring to Jones as the "golfer of the year" and the "greatest golfer in the land." Hagen had just one more chance to prove that he still belonged on top: he could equal Jones's match-play performance by retaining his PGA crown. Such an accomplishment, coupled with the fact that he finished only two strokes behind Jones in the U.S. Open, would provide his supporters an argument that he still deserved the number one ranking.

As the defending champion, Hagen was exempt from the regional qualifying for the PGA Championship. Yet he still had to qualify on site with sixty-three other professionals at Chicago's Olympia Fields. On September 21, Hagen shot an unimpressive 75–76 to finish eleven strokes behind the leader, Al Watrous. Though not scoring so well, Hagen was confident at Olympia Fields. It was at the start of that event when Sir Walter supposedly strode into the locker room and asked Watrous and Leo Diegel which of them planned to finish second.

On Tuesday Watrous did; Hagen beat him 1 up on the 39th green. Watrous had held a slim lead for most of the match, but Hagen eventually squared things at the 32nd hole and took a temporary lead at the 34th, only to lose it again at the home hole and force a sudden-death play-off. Nonetheless, Hagen's win at the 34th became legendary: he purposefully hit an easy mashie (five-iron) to the hole in an effort to confuse Watrous, who had been carefully observing Hagen's club selection. Watrous then followed with a full mashie of his own and put his ball behind the green. The come-from-behind performance was the story of the day. "Hagen was the Hagen of old," proclaimed one report.

The next day, Hagen eliminated Mike Brady. That victory led to a third-round clash with Diegel. Nearly 3,000 turned out to watch the match, which proved to be the most exciting in the event's short history. Hagen again started slowly, falling to 5 down at the break. But when they reached the 33rd tee, Hagen had closed the deficit to three. He continued to claw his way back into the match, courageously winning three of the last four holes and squaring the match with a long putt on the 36th. By then, Diegel was on the verge of imploding. Somehow, they halved three more holes. Finally, on the 40th green, Diegel missed a ten-foot putt that would have extended the duel. Hagen had pulled off one of his finest victories in a match that, at lunchtime, was shaping up to be one of his worst defeats.[35]

Everything following the Diegel slugfest was anticlimactic. In the semifinal round Hagen defeated young "Lighthorse" Harry Cooper, and in the final he easily knocked out "Wild Bill" Mehlhorn. Hagen's defense of his PGA title was stunning. Commentators revived the old Hagen themes. Richardson of the *New York Times* declared that the victory would "outlive everything else" that Hagen had done. "For all things that combine to make a really great golfer—skill, power, endurance, nerve, will-to-win, sportsmanship in defeat or victory—the golf world has never produced a man like Walter Hagen. He is in a class by himself—Hagen, Coeur de Lion." The *American Golfer's* Innis Brown believed that Hagen, "however the debate may range along other lines of supremacy in golf, is the world's champion over-time golfer." And A.T. Packard, writing for *Golfers Magazine*, decided that, "there is no place to put Walter Hagen except at the top of the professionals." But, Packard added, "No man can say that he is better than Bobby Jones. His scores indicate that he is as good, but Hagen never makes a really impressive showing unless he must. With Bobby, the impression grows while watching his play, that no man in the world can beat him. He wins impressively. As between Bobby and Walter, it would take an extended series of matches to pick the superior player." As if in reply, the 1926 season provided just such a series. It started with the Battle of the Century.

Chapter 7

Passing the Crowns:

1926–1927

Two things would become clear by the end of the 1926 season: first, the best golfer in the United States was Bobby Jones; second, the greatest golfing nation in the world was the United States. For several years, those two matters had consumed golf analysts around the globe, but there would be little room for debate by December of 1926.

A year earlier, however, there was plenty of argument, especially on the first issue. Hagen had won two British Opens and finished runner-up in three attempts; he also had won the match-play championship for his class the previous two years. Jones had won a U.S. Open and finished runner-up three times in his last four attempts; he, too, had won the match-play championship for his class in 1924 and 1925. Their accomplishments since 1922 were remarkably comparable. Hagen's pounding of Jones on March 7, 1926, in the Battle of the Century only added fuel to the fire, because many commentators had considered Jones the better player.

Both stars competed in a number of four-ball exhibitions along the Gulf Coast in the winter of 1925–1926. Jones played many of his with professional Tommy Armour. The *Professional Golfer* had even reported late in December that Jones-Armour would represent Whitfield Estates in the second edition of the Florida Winter Golf League. Owned by Adair Realty, Whitfield Estates was situated near Sarasota and had just opened for business that season. Early in January, though, the *Southern Golfer* informed fans that there would be no Florida League after all because of a lack of interest.

One can only speculate as to how Jones's presence in the league would have affected, or jeopardized, his amateur standing; the issue was not raised in the press. Possibly in response to the *Professional Golfer*'s report, however, rumors circulated in December that Jones might become a professional. He quickly put those stories to rest with a letter to *Golfers Magazine* that stated: "I never have considered nor ever expect to consider turning professional." Nonetheless, Jones did play with Tommy Armour and Watts Gunn in about a dozen exhibitions scattered around the Battle of the Century, mostly to promote Whitfield Estates. He also finished third in the Miami Open, an event that Hagen did not enter.[1]

On February 21, Jones-Armour defeated Hagen and Gil Nichols in an eighteen-hole four-ball affair at Pasadena. The event was characterized as a "curtain-raiser," designed to create interest in the Battle of the Century. Planned as thirty-six holes, it was reduced to eighteen because of Hagen's ill health. He was suffering from flu symptoms and was reportedly under doctor's orders to remain in bed for a few days after the match.[2]

Despite the four-ball loss, it seemed that by early April Hagen had put down Jones's claim to the throne—and not just because of his convincing 12 and 11 victory in the Battle of the Century. Two weeks after that epic dual, in mid-March, Hagen and Jones met again in the Florida West Coast Open, played over Hagen's Pasadena layout. Hagen won, while Jones finished a close second. The narrow victory notwithstanding, the *American Golfer* concluded, "Jones has crumpled before the wizardry of Walter's game."

By then, both Hagen and Jones had announced that they would travel abroad for the British events. Beyond the National Amateur and Open, Jones would join a team of American amateurs to play for the Walker Cup, and Hagen was to select and captain a squad for international professional matches. In other words, it would be a full-scale amateur-professional invasion, such as was launched in 1921. Aside from those international rivalries, golf fans would be treated to an individual subplot, a sustained competition between Hagen and Jones. Having apparently settled the question of match-play superiority in the Battle of the Century, they agreed to engage in a medal contest. The two stars made a good-natured bet on the 252 holes in the Florida West Coast, British, and U.S. opens (seventy-two holes in each tournament proper, plus thirty-six holes in qualifying rounds for the British Open). The loser was to buy a "fine hat" for the victor; "the joke," the *Metropolitan Golfer*

Golf's brightest stars in the Golden Age of Sports. Bobby Jones and
Walter Hagen meet in Florida during the winter of 1926.
Courtesy: Jones Family Collection.

chuckled, was that "Walter never wears a hat—he goes bareheaded practically all the time."

The point, though, was that the real prize was the crown worn by the world's best golfer. Hagen's two-stroke margin in the West Coast Open prompted H.B. Martin to suggest that Jones's medal prowess had been exaggerated. In an article entitled "Golf Records Make Interesting Comparison," Martin examined their records in the ten medal events in which they had both competed. He found that Hagen actually led Jones 2,863 strokes to 2,868. Martin also reported that Hagen had captured twenty-three of sixty opens during his career and had won two U.S. Opens in eleven starts, compared to Jones's one victory in six attempts. All of that had been mostly overlooked; still, Jones's scoring in the U.S. Open suggested that he would eventually finish on top.[3]

In April Jones returned to Atlanta, where he continued working for Adair Realty and Trust and made preparations for his European excursion. Jones booked passage on the *Aquitania* for May 5. Meanwhile, Hagen sharpened his game, finishing seventh in the North and South Open. Then on April 15 he released the invitations to his international challenge team, requesting Mac Smith, Al Watrous, Gene Sarazen, Leo Diegel, "Wild Bill" Mehlhorn, Tommy Armour, Bobby Cruickshank, Al Espinosa, Joe Kirkwood, "Long Jim" Barnes, and Johnny Farrell. The next day the *New York Times* reported that an anonymous golf enthusiast was preparing to donate a challenge cup, similar to the Walker Cup, for the professionals. A month later the world learned that the donor's name was Samuel Ryder and that the first competition would be held June 4–5 at the Wentworth Golf Club near London. With anticipation growing, Hagen made another announcement on May 19: he had accepted a challenge from British professional Abe Mitchell to play a seventy-two-hole match for a hefty purse of 1,000 pounds sterling (about $5,000 in contemporary exchange). Mitchell, whom the British regarded as the finest match player in the world, had issued the challenge the previous January to any U.S. golfer who was man enough to accept it. Having just defeated Bobby Jones in a similar event, Hagen felt even more manly than usual.[4]

So with an increasing number of lines drawn in the sand, the Americans began their trek across the Atlantic. Most of the amateurs, including Jones, Watts Gunn, Jess Sweetser, Jesse Guilford, Roland Mackenzie, Francis Ouimet, George Von Elm, and Walker Cup Captain Bob Gardner, left on schedule aboard the *Aquitania*.

Bob Harlow was along, too; he left to help plan the professional team event. Jones-Mackenzie passed the time aboard the *Aquitania* by taking on all comers in shuffleboard. In an effort to maintain their form, team members also drove golf balls into the Atlantic. They disembarked in England on May 11 to discover that the country was still virtually paralyzed by a prolonged labor strike. For Britishers, golf was not the only matter of importance that summer. One editorial asked, "What's it all about? Is it essential to the welfare of the nation to win one of these [golf] contests? Is it to be made a business?"

A week later the American amateurs commenced competition. On May 16–17 the Walker Cup team defeated the Cambridge-Oxford Society. That, plus other performances, led Britain's *Sporting Life* to call "the American Walker Cup team the strongest combination we have ever entertained." By Friday the 21st, the Americans had arrived in Scotland and were playing practice rounds over the Muirfield layout, site of the Amateur. Jones suffered from a cold but still practiced; Von Elm and Sweetser were also bothered by similar ailments. The Atlantan shot another round on Saturday that was reportedly unimpressive. Out of respect for the Sabbath, everyone received a forced break on Sunday.

The Amateur began the next day. Chick Evans once described Muirfield as "a genuine Scottish seaside links with a sort of roughness—a wild, desolate, treeless beauty unknown to the prettified courses we know so well." Actually, Muirfield was not as unlike American layouts as many other British courses. The location was slightly inland and the breeze often light, at least relatively speaking. Still, on a dark day, when the wind bellowed from the Firth of Forth, the long layout could be frightening. The Americans, though, were determined to inspire some fear themselves, even if no Yankee had won the event since "Old Man" Travis had stunned the British in 1904. Evans, Jones, and Von Elm were heavy favorites.

Jones started well enough. After drawing a bye for the first day's play, he defeated Major C.B. Omerod 3 and 2. The narrow margin of victory proved that Jones was not in top form; one report had him "far from his best." He nonetheless won two more matches the next day, prompting the *New York Times* to declare that finally "he was the real Bobby Jones of whom Britain had heard but not seen." Yet he raised some eyebrows when, because of the heat, he discarded his sweater and played in his white dress shirt. Jones continued to improve his play on the third day, winning two more matches by even wider margins. In the afternoon, some 5,000 watched Jones put out Robert Harris, the defending champion.

Just eight golfers remained in the tournament. The only Americans still playing were Jones and Jess Sweetser, who had been too ill the previous weekend to practice. Jones's quarterfinal opponent, Andrew Jamieson, was a local player, inexperienced in major competition and clearly the underdog. But on the morning of the match Jones awoke with what he described as a "stiff neck." He later wrote that it was so painful he considered withdrawing from the match. A masseur worked on him for over an hour, and by tee time, Jones said that he felt fine. Yet something was certainly wrong; Bernard Darwin described Jones's play as "rather limp and spiritless." Jones was so off form that he did not win a single hole from Jamieson, who took the match 4 and 3.

Jess Sweetser, still ill and possibly feeling worse than Jones, somehow managed to play himself into the championship match, where he confronted Alfred Simpson. On Saturday, May 29, Sweetser made history by becoming the first American-born golfer to win the British Amateur, soundly defeating Simpson 6 and 5. The Scottish crowd responded well to Sweetser, carrying him on their shoulders for a quarter mile to the clubhouse. Sweetser modestly thanked the throng, and Britain's *Golf Monthly* replied: "The Americans have so often accepted failure with such modest grace that in their hour of victory we extend the sincerest congratulations . . . ."[6]

Five days later, on June 3, the U.S. retained the Walker Cup at St. Andrews by a score of 6.5 to 5.5. That made the U.S. 4–0 in the amateur competition (5–0 if one counted the preliminary matches of 1921). "The old gray town" closed its businesses; hotels flew the American flag; 5,000 spectators turned out daily; and although it should not have, the warm, enthusiastic welcome at St. Andrews surprised the U.S. team. Jones shined, easily winning in both the foursome and singles competition. "Mr. Jones," Darwin observed, displayed "perfectly steady and faultless golf, not without a certain deprecating air as if he felt sorry for his adversary, but, very properly, not allowing his sympathy to take any practical shape." The margin of victory was quite narrow, though, and fortunately for the U.S. side, George Von Elm halved his match, which allowed the U.S. to keep the cup. Hours later, Sweetser collapsed from illness. He immediately sailed for home, where he would be bedridden for days. Given that, his accomplishments abroad seemed nothing less than heroic.[7]

The next day, June 4, the professional team matches got underway at the Wentworth Club. So far, the amateurs had led a successful invasion, and the professionals hoped to sustain it. Some of them, including Hagen, had arrived in England just three days earlier aboard the *Aquitania*. His late arrival implied that the matches were not a top priority because Captain Hagen and the professionals traveling with him—Watrous, Armour, and Mehlhorn—were unfamiliar with the Wentworth layout and had left themselves only a few days to practice. The British team, captained by "Big Ted" Ray, intended to make the Americans pay for their negligence.

After the first day, the Americans found themselves down 5 to 0, having lost all of the two-ball foursome matches. Hagen at least looked good during his embarrassing defeat. He cut "quite a picturesque appearance in an attire of shades of white and brown" when he and Barnes were humiliated 9 and 8 by George Duncan and Abe Mitchell. Things did not improve much the next day for the U.S. in the singles competition. Mehlhorn captured the only point, while Emmett French battled to a draw in his match. As for Captain Hagen, he played "mighty poor golf" against George Duncan, suffering a stunning 6 and 5 defeat. Overall, the British thoroughly thrashed the Americans, 13.5 to 1.5 points. The lopsided defeat occurred, in part, because the U.S. team was not as strong as Hagen had planned. Darwin recognized the fact that several leading American players, such as Sarazen, Farrell, and Diegel, did not compete, but "still . . . they had a fine side, and to trounce them thus was a proud feather in the caps of the British team. It ought to do British golf all the good in the world."[8]

Actually, the professional team matches were arguably the least significant battle in that summer's international golf war. What the British really needed to soothe the sting from their loss in the amateur events was a victory in their Open, the most important tournament of the campaign. British oddsmakers had Jones a 6–1 favorite; Hagen and Barnes were quoted at 12–1. Von Elm, Watrous, and Mehlhorn, however, were given little chance at 200–1.

Qualifying for the Open began on the 16th. The tournament proper would be held at the Royal Lytham and St. Anne's Club, located north of Liverpool. For the first time, the Royal & Ancient

authorities held regional qualifying rounds. Some of the competitors, such as Hagen, qualified on site, while others, including Jones,
qualified at the Sunningdale club to the south. Hagen posted two
fine rounds of 72–71, leading the section at St. Anne's. In addition,
his "cool and imperturbable mannerism made a hit with the crowd."

But if Hagen's qualifying rounds were good, Jones's were excellent. Playing "without spot or blemish" at Sunningdale, he shot
his two lowest rounds ever in major medal competition, 66–68–
134 (–10). Years later Jones characterized the 66 as "about as
perfect a round of golf that I ever did in my life." The weather was
ideal, yet Sunningdale was long and widely-regarded as Britain's
toughest inland layout, more difficult than St. Anne's. The length
may actually have worked in Jones's favor because he preferred
long-iron shots to the greens rather than pitches. At any rate, he
smashed the course record, while also establishing new lows for a
single round and qualifying total in the British Open.

One British writer, searching for the words to describe Jones's
"almost super-human" performance, bubbled, "It's not a fact, but
it's true." Once they recovered from the shock, the British loved
it. "Mr. Jones," declared one editorial, "had become popular enough
to be placed on the Privy Council." His "steadiness" suggested a
"wonderful state of physical well-being, and of mental and moral
tranquility." Regardless of what he did in the tournament proper,
Jones had "already won for himself imperishable fame on the links
and set a record for which his rivals will be shooting hopelessly for
years to come." Moreover, Sir Walter and Mr. Jones were not the
only Americans making news; in fact, eleven others—Kirkwood,
Von Elm, Mehlhorn, Gunn, Barnes, Armour, Watrous, McLeod,
Walker, French, and Mackenzie—had also qualified, some in impressive fashion. "The primary object of the British now is not to
gain glory, but rather to avoid great disgrace," Anthony Spalding
grimly concluded.[9]

Throughout the following week, most of the competitors practiced at St. Anne's, while Hagen and Mitchell played their international grudge match at Wentworth. Despite appearing nervous,
Mitchell grabbed a 4-up lead after the first day. The final thirty-six
holes were played the next day at the St. George's Hill layout.
About 2,000 had turned out for the first rounds, but twice that
number showed on the second day to watch Hagen storm back.
He shot a medal score of 68 in the morning; by the sixth hole he
had pulled even with Mitchell, and on the 10th he took the lead

for the last time. He won the match 2 and 1, providing some vindication for the professional team's humiliation.

Unfortunately for Hagen, the biggest story of the exhibition
was not his characteristic come-from-behind victory but the gamesmanship that he allegedly employed in the process. On the second
day, Hagen appeared at the first tee twenty minutes late. He had
done the same thing a week before at the Northern Professionals
Championship. Tardiness was a problem for Hagen that summer;
he also had been late for a farewell luncheon aboard the *Aquitania*,
just before it was to set sail for Britain. In each case, Hagen offered no excuse and behaved as though he had done nothing wrong.
Missing the Cunard line's luncheon was simply embarrassing, but
showing up late for his tee time at the Northern almost disquali-
fied him. His tardiness for the Mitchell match was unacceptable
to the British, especially because he offered no explanation. Rather,
Hagen "sauntered to the first tee and chatted with friends until
the referee drew his attention to the fact that the match was in
progress." The British thought that Hagen was trying to disrupt
Mitchell's concentration. If so, it worked.[10]

Hagen was early for his tee time five days later, on Wednesday, June 23, to begin the Open. The weather was nice and warm,
with a fresh, northwesterly wind. He arrived with a "diamond and
sceptre" look of victory, and backed it up with another sizzling 68
that took the first-round lead. Jones, who seemed "a bit nervous
and unsettled at the start," finished alone in fifth place with 72.
R.A. Whitcombe turned in the best round of the natives, a sixth-
place 73. Bernard Darwin felt that on the first day the Americans
"piled on the agony and rubbed our noses in the dirt."

Darwin and the rest of the British press pinned their hopes on
a possible "counterattack" the second day, but none was forthcoming. The weather remained pleasant, except for the wind, which
was stronger and more unpredictable than on the first day. Hagen
ballooned to a 77 and Darwin concluded, "It is difficult to lay a
finger on any particular weak spot, the strokes just slipped away.
[Hagen] is incapable of a Jones-like steadiness." The Atlantan, on
the other hand, posted another 72, good enough to put him in a tie
for the lead at 144. Hagen was next at 145, then came Al Watrous
at 146. The closest Britisher, Archie Compston, was in a seventh-
place tie with two Americans. The Europeans, who by now were
conceding an American victory, began rooting for Jones because
"in spite of his greatness, his cap still fits his head."

Jones did not disappoint the next day, one that Hagen would later dub "Black Friday for the British." Shortly after 9 A.M., Jones and Watrous teed off in the third round. Hagen, who always said that he preferred finishing after the leaders so as to have a target, teed off an hour and a half later. The front-runners stood up well under the intense pressure as they dueled through the day, with Hagen lurking close behind. Watrous was in the lead by the break, two strokes ahead of Jones and four ahead of Hagen—they alone occupied the first three places.

Watrous played steadily through the 13th hole of the last round, maintaining his two-shot lead. Then he cracked and, as Darwin described it, "quite unexpectedly, began throwing away the championship," allowing Jones to draw even with him. They both parred the 16th hole. Things seemed to turn back in Watrous's favor at the 17th, another par 4, after he hit his drive down the middle, and Jones hooked his tee shot into a sand bunker. Watrous hit his approach first, a fine shot to the edge of the green. Jones paid no attention, however, focusing on his own shot, which would be from a clean lie. He stroked his ball perfectly, picking it out of the sand and landing it on the center of the green. The *Lytham St. Anne's Express* later called it the "greatest shot in golf history." It seemed to "slay poor Watrous," who responded with a three-putt that gave another shot to Jones. The Atlantan gained one more stroke at the home hole and went to the clubhouse with the lead.

Hagen, meanwhile, was still on the course with a chance to catch Jones. But despite an admirable effort in windy conditions, he came to the home hole requiring an unlikely eagle two. After hitting a nice drive, Sir Walter gave one of the finest "shows" of his career. With Jones watching from the clubhouse balcony, he paced off the yardage, leaving his caddie at the green, and returned to his bag, where he paused before selecting and reselecting his iron. After yelling to his caddie to remove the flagstick, he rifled a remarkably accurate mashie (five-iron) shot, landing his ball just inches from the cup. The ball had no backspin, though, and bounded through the green and into the rough. The crowd, which had been shamelessly cheering for Jones and wishing ill on Hagen, let out a collective sigh of relief. Hagen took a six and finished four shots behind Jones and in a third-place tie with Von Elm. It was Hagen's worst result in a British Open since 1921. Of course, if he had been concerned about that he would have played the last hole differently to be the runner-up. Abe Mitchell was the top British player, alone in fifth place.

When it was over, Hagen accepted the defeat with a smile, graciously concluding, "the best man won." For his part, the new champion admitted feeling "nervous all day and dazed when putting" and apologized if he appeared "fidgety." His pace had been dizzying. Jones's 291 tied the all-time record set by James Braid at Prestwick in 1908. Moreover, Jones was only the third amateur overall, and the first American amateur, to win the event. Americans could take additional pride in the fact that no British amateur had ever captured the U.S. Open. Back in the United States, a *New York Times* editorial crowned Jones the "Emperor" of golf and praised the other American competitors who had dominated the tournament and established U.S. supremacy in the sport. The British agreed, albeit reluctantly on the second point. They considered Jones a "genius" and "in a class by himself, judged either from a professional or amateur standpoint." J.H. Taylor simply said, "The greatest golfing prize has been won by the greatest golfer." Gordon Harkness thought that "Jones's victory, without a doubt, is a popular one with the British, much more than if one of the American professionals had won." Concerning the "American Avalanche" that swept the tournament, Britain's *Golf Monthly* declared that it "cannot be explained away by any paltering excuses. Our players are not good enough." The publication confessed that if Diegel, Farrell, Hutchison, and Cruickshank had made the trip, the result would have been even worse for Britain, concluding that "on the professional side there is not one man on the horizon to whom we can turn our faces and vision hope."[11]

Aside from the professional team competition, the invasion had been a complete success. The top four finishers in the British Open—and seven of the top eight—were Americans; an American had won the British Amateur; and the U.S. had retained the Walker Cup. Hagen had even defeated Mitchell in their grudge match. It was one of the most impressive manifestations yet of the rise of American golf. The U.S. had completely wrenched the international golfing crown away from Great Britain. Now Bobby Jones was about to go home and do the same thing on the national level.

The one consolation for the British that summer was that their events had been swept by amateurs. It was easier for them to accept Jones winning their Open than Hagen, because tradition-conscious British golf fans loved the Atlantan's "unobtrusive, unassuming, and studious" disposition. Less than forty-eight hours after the British Open concluded, Jones, Hagen, and most of the Americans boarded the *Aquitania* and headed for home. Their national open was scheduled for July 8. Just before leaving Britain, however, Jones and Hagen gave revealing press interviews that magnified their very different public images.[12]

Jones told London reporters that "life seemed rosey" and that he had not yet given "vent to [his] excitement." One writer then asked Jones if he had ever made money from the sport. Jones replied that he had not made a cent from golf and never would. He also claimed to have recently declined an opportunity to write a series of syndicated newspaper articles, as well as a business executive's position worth $40,000. (Later that year, *Golfers Magazine* reported that in 1925 Jones had turned down an offer of $12,000 to write a series of articles.) Jones surmised, "I reckon this trip will leave me $1,500 out of pocket, but it has been worthwhile. There is no monetary value, so far as I'm concerned, to winning the British Open championship, but it is an honor which an American in particular is proud to hold." Jones concluded his interview by announcing that he intended to leave the real-estate business and enter law school, because he wanted to follow in his father's professional footsteps. The *London Observer* declared Jones a "genius." The *Daily Telegraph* of London editorialized: "Mr. Jones, a quiet young man dressed in brown knickers and jersey, is a worthy champion in every respect. He is extremely modest, hates to talk about himself, and shuns the limelight as he would the plague."[13]

While Mr. Jones garnered British admiration by eschewing material gain and proposing more formal education, Sir Walter pricked the British by carelessly philosophizing on the "American Avalanche." In an interview with the *Evening Standard*, Hagen said that the British simply did not work hard enough at their sports. He went so far as to use the term "lazy." "You have to get more pep. It angers me when, after I have beaten some Englishman, someone says, 'But he is a pretty good sport.' What he ought to be is a good golfer." He added that it would be healthier for golf if the British could occasionally win their own open, suggesting that the

The British Open champion, Bobby Jones, returns home in July 1926,
flanked by Walter Hagen and Al Watrous.
Courtesy: USC Department of Special Collections

event had become an uninteresting showcase for American
strength. The *Observer* characterized Hagen's "gratuitous little lec-
ture" as "ridiculous nonsense" and "condescending frothiness."
Outlook described the comments as "braggadocio couched in the
language of the prize ring."[14]

Hagen's analysis, along with his entire behavior during the visit,
naturally angered British fans. Sir Walter had, after all, hired a
chauffeured Rolls Royce and lodged at the luxurious Savoy in London and the Majestic in St. Anne's. His American caddie had carried "an enormous bag" that was "four times larger than the average
caddie bag." And, of course, Hagen's wardrobe on and off the links
was dazzling. Some of the British public had come to tolerate Sir
Walter's flamboyance, but everyone was bothered by his tardiness
in the Mitchell match. If he had never learned his "place" as a
professional, the British thought, then at least he could display
some sense of fair play and modesty in victory. One anonymous

"British golf star" said that, "Hagen's reception stands decidedly frigid. His characteristics of largeness, newness, and expansiveness did not appeal to the blunt but very generous Northern heart."[15]

Some American commentators agreed. *Living Age* feared that "the wardrobes and manners of some of our wandering athletes might well strain the alleged friendly sporting relations between the two great English-speaking democracies." A *New York Times* editorial, entitled "To Defeat Adding Bitterness," concluded that Hagen was not only a great golfer but a "master of the gentle art of making the English thoroughly dislike him." The *Independent* stated that his "dubious sportsmanship [in the Mitchell match] may be excused on the part of a professional out to win under any circumstances or conditions. But one can hardly forgive Hagen for his stupid, arrogant, and ill-considered remarks." The *Independent* further suggested that Hagen be reprimanded by the USGA with a temporary ban from tournaments for "unsportsmanlike behavior and speech harmful to American golf." *Outlook* summarized, "Unfortunately, while Bobby Jones was earning his laurels, Walter Hagen was proving that he had well already earned his unpopularity. Hagen's conduct and language have had at least the one good effect of heightening Americans' gratification in Bobby Jones's victory." Whatever Hagen actually said in the aftermath of the British Open (quotations and reports varied), he had been roundly criticized on both sides of the Atlantic by the time the *Aquitania* entered New York Harbor.[16]

To a degree, Hagen had lost the British Open but stolen the show. On July 2, with Edna Hagen at his side, he alighted from the *Aquitania* "grinning his famous grin." He claimed to be surprised by the furor over his remarks, saying that they had been exaggerated, that he had not used the term "lazy," that he simply had been asked for a "frank" analysis of the British decline, and that he did not mean to "dig" the British for their loss. "It's all news to me. I don't know a thing about it, and I didn't make any such statement as was attributed to me." Then Hagen waffled a bit: "Even if I said anything like it, which I don't think I did, it was absolutely without intent to be critical." As for the Mitchell match, Hagen explained that he showed up ten minutes late, not twenty, because his driver had simply taken a wrong turn. "I have always liked Abe Mitchell," Hagen maintained, "and wouldn't try to make him nervous by waiting even if I thought doing so would give me an advantage."

The *New York Times* reported that "Hagen's statements were backed up by Bobby Jones, President Fownes, and Al Watrous."[17]

Two days later Hagen felt the need to make a much stronger denial. In the second statement he said that he had been tardy for the Mitchell match because of heavy traffic. He stopped short of apologizing for anything but concluded, "I like the British very much indeed. They are fine sportsmen, and American golfers always have a glorious time over there and are eager to return."[18]

While much controversy surrounded Hagen when the *Aquitania* arrived, the crowd poured out affection on Jones. More than fifty Atlantans, including Jones's grandfather, parents, and wife, made the trip to New York. Jones disembarked at about 1:00 P.M. amid scattered rebel yells and the customary "Dixie." After greeting his family, Jones was ushered down Broadway to City Hall. The reception, including a full-blown ticker-tape parade, complete with motorcycle police escort, band, and flying confetti, was given primarily in honor of Jones, although Hagen, Gunn, and Watrous followed behind him.

When the party reached City Hall, it was introduced to Mayor Jimmy Walker. The mayor told the crowd that New York was proud of Jones's accomplishment for "American sportsmanship and American sporting skill." Walker considered Jones "a splendid example to the young men of America [because he had] played the game well and cleanly until [he] reached the very top." The proceeding was broadcast live on WNYC radio. Jones, "bashful as a schoolboy and speaking in a voice which was almost inaudible," responded into the microphone: "This is the most remarkable reception I have ever experienced. I can't tell you how much I appreciate it. It isn't necessary for me to tell you how I feel about it. You can tell by just looking at me." Someone called for three cheers for Mayor Walker and three more for Atlanta. The celebration lasted until 3:00; then the Joneses retired to their suites at the Hotel Vanderbilt where a banquet and dance were given that evening in Jones's honor.

The *New York Times* described the festivities as "the greatest reception in the history of sports" and suggested that it was a testimony to the popularity of golf. Jones seemed a bit surprised and uncomfortable during the reception. That was understandable; he had never received such an outpouring of admiration outside of Atlanta and genuinely disliked being the center of attention. But his life had changed forever. In "Bobby Jones," Americans had found a new sports hero whose extraordinary popularity was based on a modest, unassuming personality, the ideals of amateurism, and unprecedented natural skills.[19]

One week later at the Scioto Country Club in Columbus, Ohio, Jones consolidated his position at the top when he became the first golfer to win both national opens in the same season. He began hot and cold, carding 70–79; the opening mark represented his lowest first round ever in a U.S. Open, and the afternoon score was his highest ever. The 79 occurred, in part, because Jones called a penalty stroke on himself after he accidentally moved his ball on the 15th green. On the final morning the weather was as ominous as Jones's "grim, taciturn, fighting" expression. Six strokes behind the leader, the Atlantan was determined to pull off a Hagen-like comeback performance. Maintaining his intensity, Jones shot 71–73 to edge Joe Turnesa by one stroke and claim the title, while Hagen finished alone in seventh place.

It was a stunning victory but also a major ordeal. Within fifteen days Jones had won the British Open, sailed home, endured a ticker-tape parade, and won the U.S. Open. He was drained emotionally. At Scioto, Grantland Rice described Jones as "nerve-racked and weary to exhaustion." During the first day of the event, a number of spectators thought Jones's face looked "drawn and tired" and that there were "deep lines around [his] eyes." On the last morning, he could not hold down his breakfast and visited a doctor before the start of the third round. After completing his final round, Jones had to wait for the rest of the field to finish. He spent the time alone in his room, where, as he later put it, I "blew up completely for the first time in my life." Jones's mother found him weeping uncontrollably and declared that that was enough tournament golf for her Little Bob. At the presentation ceremony, he accepted the trophy without comment; in fact, Jones had asked tournament officials not to call on him for a speech. Hagen, rarely at a loss for words, picked up some of the slack by congratulating the champion: "Well, you've got to hand it to Bobby. He's certainly a great golfer. The wonder is that he hasn't won all the opens of recent years."[20]

Two days later the "monarch of golfdom" arrived in Atlanta for one more crowded celebration. The usual parade, with whistles, cheers, and band, escorted Jones and Gunn in a convertible down Peachtree Street to the Atlanta Athletic Club. There Mayor Walter Sims lauded Jones, who "slouched" in a chair and "blushed." Jones smiled and waved a few times but was otherwise even less demonstrative than usual. When his turn came to speak, Jones briefly thanked the crowd and said how good it was to be back home.[21]

Following his last round at Scioto, Jones had told reporters that he was "tired of golf," and that he did not "want to see a niblick or any other club" until the U.S. Amateur in September. Aside from quiet practice rounds at East Lake, Jones played little the rest of that summer. Instead, he gave an "intimate" interview with O.B. Keeler, who later became an honorary member of the Associated Press for landing the story. Jones supposedly said that it "was the only interview he [had] ever given out or probably ever [would] give out." Keeler claimed that the story was made difficult by Jones's modesty; he just did not like talking about his own achievements. Actually, as *Golfers Magazine* noted, although the interview occupied "double-column space in, let us say, all American papers," there was "nothing at all new, radical, or greatly explanatory" in what Jones said. He spoke mostly of the difference between "golf and tournament golf," his swing, and his mental preparation for competition. The interview concluded with Keeler asking about Jones's habit of calling penalty strokes on himself, to which Jones replied: "That is absolutely nothing to talk about, and you are not to write about it." Then, repeating one of his most famous golf maxims, he added, "there is only one way to play this game."[22]

Early in August, Jones vacationed with his father and Keeler in Sarasota before making final preparations to enter law school at Emory University in Atlanta. The Sarasota trip was highlighted by some tarpon fishing and another parade in his honor. To show their appreciation in a tangible way, the citizens of Sarasota presented Jones with a beautiful Pierce-Arrow sedan. The commemoration occurred despite the fact that Jones would no longer be involved with the promotion of Florida real estate.[23]

After spending two years with Adair Realty and Trust, Jones decided that sales was not his forte. Eugene Branch, Jones's law partner, said that Jones left real estate because he did not like "puffing up" property as one would used cars. Others have suggested that whenever Jones sold a piece of land he felt as though he had sold a part of himself. In any case, it is easy to understand why he was unhappy in a business that required an aggressive, intrusive, even coercive personality; Jones was a relatively private individual, and, except for his good-looks and natural charisma, he did not manifest the character of a successful salesman.

On the other hand, he did not seem to possess the qualities of a trial lawyer. Just before beginning his classes, Jones said that he would not become a trial lawyer because he "was not the sort of fellow who can do much standing on his feet, spouting a lot of words." He added, "I don't believe that a sporting champion, as a rule, is much good at anything outside of his game—but I've got a family to support." So he set aside real estate and prepared to pick up law.[24]

Jones was scheduled to begin classes at Emory on September 28, about two weeks after the U.S. Amateur. The USGA finally had decided to follow the lead of tennis and seed its match play draw. With that in mind, the Associated Press released its ranking of the top ten American amateurs. Jones was first, followed by Sweetser, Von Elm, Ouimet, Guilford, and Evans. With Sweetser still too ill to compete, Jones was considered a heavy favorite to win his third major event of the year. He already held what sports-writers were calling golf's "Triple Crown," the two national opens, plus the 1925 U.S. Amateur, and he had an opportunity to break more new ground, because no one, not even Jerry Travers or "Old Man" Travis, had captured three consecutive U.S. Amateurs. Jones may have been tired, but there was plenty of incentive for him to win one more title.

So by the end of August, Jones was gearing up for the Amateur, which was to be played that year at the Baltusrol Country Club. In addition to practice rounds, he competed in several exhibitions, including a hospital benefit with professionals Hagen, Sarazen, and Mac Smith in Indianapolis, Indiana.

The U.S. Amateur began on September 13, and at first it appeared that Jones would indeed make more history. Performing "just like a machine," he won the qualifying medal and then advanced all the way to the championship round. Few thought that George Von Elm would be able to keep up with him in the final, but the Californian won the exciting match 2 and 1. "I was playing too good of golf to lose today," boasted the new champion. Analysts praised Von Elm for his courage but suggested that Jones was not in top form for the match; the *New York Times* commented that despite the loss, Jones was still the best. All of that must have grated on Von Elm, who was jealous of Jones's standing. Von Elm once admitted to golf writer Lester Rice that he "hated Jones's guts." For his part, Jones had "no illusions about Von Elm's real feelings." He added, "He always impressed me as having a chip on either shoulder." Nevertheless, both generously conceded putts in the final match, manifesting some sportsmanship and concealing any ill feelings.[25]

Within days Jones left New Jersey for Atlanta to begin classes at Emory. He generally avoided publicity that fall, hitting the books hard once again. On September 30, newspapers reported that he had been made an honorary member of the Royal and Ancient Club of St. Andrews because of his victory at St. Anne's. That award notwithstanding, late in October Jones announced that he would not defend his British Open title, nor would he spend a third consecutive winter in Florida. His education came first, and he would be too busy to travel either south or abroad. "The United States Open and the United States Amateur are all I can see for 1927, and [I will have] darn little chance to win them. They seem to me to be getting tougher and tougher," Jones said. With that statement, he closed what he once characterized as "the greatest year I'll ever have" and retired into academia. A month later, on November 30, Mary Jones gave birth to their second child, a boy named Robert Tyre Jones III. He was a handsome baby with a big smile, chubby cheeks, and dark features.[26]

Hagen, meanwhile, worked to recapture some of the prestige he had lost to Jones. After leaving Columbus, he won the inaugural Eastern Open with a sizzling 65–67–74–69 (–13), which just missed tying the all-time record of 274 (–10) that was set during the 1922 Ohio Open. The runner-up, Johnny Farrell, finished nine shots behind. William Richardson believed that the victory "proves [Hagen] to be alive and kicking despite his Scioto failure and the long, bleak period when Jones was taking bows that Walter is in the habit of taking. There is one thing about Hagen. He may be down, but he won't stay down. He always bobs up, and generally he bobs up with something worth while."[27]

Hagen kept bobbing up for the rest of the season. At Indianapolis he finished nine strokes ahead of Gene Sarazen to win his third Western Open. Hagen's total included middle rounds of 68–66. Jones, who was in town to play their charity exhibition the following day, said: "That's the sort of golf Hagen played last winter when he defeated me, and when he is right, he can lick anyone." Hagen shook Jones's hand and replied, "The same to you."[28]

In September Hagen entered the PGA Championship at the Salisbury Country Club in Garden City, Long Island. After taking the qualifying medal, he marched through the field to win his third straight professional match-play event. Unlike the previous two PGAs,

Walter and Edna Hagen appear happy in this photo with
Yankee pitcher Bob Shawke at the 1926 World Series.
Courtesy: Corbis-Bettman

Hagen was not pressed in any of his matches. He had now done what
no one else had—win the same major title in three consecutive years.
Hagen's accomplishment was highlighted by the fact that reigning
champions were being dethroned everywhere in the fall of 1926: Jones
had lost in his bid for a third Amateur; Jack Dempsey was outboxed
by Gene Tunney to lose the heavyweight title; Babe Ruth's powerful
New York Yankees lost the World Series to Rogers Hornsby's St.
Louis Cardinals; even "Big Bill" Tilden lost a major tennis match in
France to Rene LaCoste. Hagen had stunned even the most loqua-
cious observers. Jack Hoag of *Golfers Magazine* again anointed Hagen
the "Match-play King of the World." Richardson simply wrote, "Bobby
Jones tried it and failed; Hagen tried it and succeeded. That ought to
start and end a lot of arguments."[29]

Having done about all he could to refurbish his competitive
reputation, Hagen, like Jones, took a break from tournament play

in the fall of 1926. Not to be surpassed by Jones's Pierce-Arrow, he bought himself a new Cadillac convertible coupe. On October 9 he showed up in New York for the debut of French tennis star Suzanne Lenglen's professional U.S. tour. He also played several charity exhibitions before beginning a trip to the west coast on the 15th. For the first time since 1923, Hagen would visit southern California. In November he went west through Canada, giving exhibitions and indulging in some duck hunting on Lake Manitoba. By mid-December, Hagen was in Los Angeles for several more exhibitions; two weeks later he left for Texas and then for Florida. In a four-month whirlwind tour Hagen literally traveled around the contiguous U.S.[30]

By the time Hagen reached Texas, the country's golf dopesters had published their end-of-season analysis. The consensus was that Jones's unprecedented sweep of both national opens, together with his making the U.S. Amateur final and the British Amateur quarterfinal, eclipsed all other golf and most other sports achievements in 1926. The only golf records that came close to it were Chick Evans's victories in the U.S. Amateur and U.S. Open in 1916 and Harold Hilton's winning of the U.S. and British Amateurs in 1911; yet everyone agreed that Jones's double was the most impressive of the three. Little mention was ever made of the hat wagered between Hagen and Jones following the Battle of the Century. A few noted that after Jones finished two strokes behind Hagen in the West Coast Open, he had gone on to better Hagen's scores by nine strokes in British Open qualifying, four strokes in the British Open, and five strokes in the U.S. Open. Still, Hagen had ended the season exceptionally strong in both medal and match play events, prompting the *Southern Golfer* to remark, "Hagen dominates the professional field like Mussolini dominates Italy." Sir Walter, it seemed, could beat everyone—except Mr. Jones.[31]

So even though Hagen's late season heroics left his fans an argument, most analysts now considered Jones the best golfer in the world. Moreover, the devastating U.S. invasion of Great Britain had signaled the rise of American golf to a position of international supremacy. 1926 had been a pivotal year for golf; two crowns had been passed.

The upcoming season confirmed the 1926 transfers of power. On the international front, America continued to flex its golf muscles when the USGA once again joined the R & A in a clash over the scheduling of the national opens. The conflict began in November 1926 when the USGA announced that its 1927 open would be held during the last week of June, after the northern U.S. had warmed up and before the region's courses dried out. The R & A had already scheduled its open for the same week. Although the U.S. had unilaterally moved its open in 1924, the R & A had fought the change, religiously clinging to the traditional time slot of late June for its national open. The two ruling bodies had gone back and forth over the issue for more than two years, and by late 1926 the USGA simply decided to hold its event when it wanted.

Throughout November and December, golf writers discussed the meaning of the USGA's "defiance" of the R & A in "throwing down a glove" and forcing a "showdown" over the national open schedule. One commentator noted that the Royal & Ancient might always have an advantage in terms of tradition, but it had to accept the fact that "American golf has assumed a position of even greater importance than British golf." But Harold Hilton, now the editor of Britain's *Golf Illustrated*, thought it "unreasonable" for the USGA to ask the R & A to move its open; after all, the British Open had always been in the third week of June. The brouhaha finally cooled down in January of 1927 after "extensive cable negotiations." Both sides compromised, although the USGA clearly got the better side of it. The U.S. Open would be staged from June 14–16, and the British Open would be held the week of July 11. The arrangement reflected reality, and it was appropriate that the U.S. came closer to its original demands. Simply put, the British Open needed American stars more than the U.S. Open needed British players.[32]

While golf's governing authorities slugged it out over the national open schedule, Walter Hagen experienced some tumult of his own when his second marriage disintegrated. Edna Hagen would eventually state in divorce proceedings that she became estranged from her husband in March of 1927. Unlike Margaret Johnson, Edna Straus-Hagen never testified to experiencing any verbal abuse or cruelty. She said only that Hagen abandoned her. Henry Clune, Hagen's friend from Rochester, recalled the popular explanation for the breakup: "The story is that [the] dissolution began one night in a Florida hotel, when Walter, returning at a very unseemly hour, was discovered by Mrs. Hagen, as he hastily prepared for bed, to be without underwear." Hagen's only explanation, according to Clune, was that he had been "robbed."

From hindsight it is impossible to know precisely what caused the collapse of Hagen's last marriage. Divorce records show that *both* parties charged abandonment. Most likely, it was the same thing that destroyed Hagen's first marriage: that is, extended periods of separation and—if there was any truth to the rumors—infidelity. Reflecting on his competitive years, Hagen wrote, "Romantic affairs had a pleasant habit of developing quickly in those days and I usually managed to overcome any obstacles barring the way to my 'pursuit of happiness.'" Whatever the specifics, by April of 1927 Hagen had separated from his wife of four years. Unlike his first divorce, his second was a complicated, lengthy mess that would not be resolved until 1937.[33]

Things went a little better for Hagen in his professional life. He lost a much-publicized exhibition to "Lighthorse" Harry Cooper and finished far down the list in the Texas Open. In March, however, he finally defeated Gene Sarazen, 8 and 7, in a particularly satisfying seventy-two-hole match. He skipped the West Coast Open but entered the Southern Open, held at East Lake. Hagen and everyone else finished far behind Jones in that event. Early in April, he managed a runner-up in the North and South Open.

Besides personal problems, another explanation for Hagen's inconsistent play in the winter of 1927 was a foot ailment. After visiting an orthopedic specialist in April, Hagen was ordered to stay off his feet for several weeks. The ailment was described in the papers as a "growth on the sole of his left foot" which created significant swelling and pain. It was probably the reason that he shot an 82 and withdrew from the Metropolitan Open in May. At any rate, early 1927 had not gone well for Hagen, who was limping in more ways than one when he arrived at the Worcester Country Club in Massachusetts to captain the Ryder Cup team.[34]

The PGA organized its international team matches for the second consecutive season in order to put them in the odd-numbered years, opposite the Walker Cup. In June of 1927 they also served as a warm-up for the U.S. Open. The team competition was the only event that the Americans had failed to capture during their 1926 British invasion, and Hagen desperately wanted to make up for the embarrassing loss. In 1927, though, Hagen's team was comprised of only homebred professionals. Naturalized citizens—such as Barnes, Kirkwood, and Hutchison—were ineligible to play on what was to be as purely an American team as possible. Typically, the visiting team was much weaker than the home squad. It was especially so in the 1927 Ryder Cup matches because Abe Mitchell did not make the trip. His presence may have made no difference, however; the determined American team demolished the British 9.5 to 2.5 points. Captain Hagen won his foursome and singles matches. The performance "completely avenged" the previous year's disaster, according to P.C. Pulver of the *Professional Golfer of America*. With America's professional golf pride properly restored, Hagen traveled to Pittsburgh, where he joined Bobby Jones for the U.S. Open.[35]

Jones had played less golf than usual in the first half of 1927. O.B. Keeler wrote in the *American Golfer* that Jones played "precisely two and one-half rounds of golf between November 20 and February 20 and was going to school steadily every weekday." Still, on February 24 he made his first hole-in-one in a practice round with Stewart Maiden at East Lake. The following month he destroyed the professional field in the Southern Open, finishing eight strokes better than runner-up Johnny Farrell and eighteen ahead of Hagen. The amateur's victory was ironic because the Southern Open offered the largest purse ever, a hefty $12,000 that included a winner's check of $4,000.[36]

On March 30, news arrived in Atlanta that Jones had again been honored abroad. This time the Sunningdale club awarded him a lifetime membership. By then, sportswriters were universally referring to Jones as "Bobby." Jones never liked that nickname, telling a fellow competitor that he preferred "Bob" now that he was past his twenty-fifth birthday. Jones thought "Bobby" was "too kiddish." Nonetheless, he could not shed the label, which came to epitomize his boyish, unassuming, amateur image.

When he traveled to New York City on business in mid-April, the *Times* reported that "Bob" had left his clubs at home but brought along his law books. Jones told William Richardson that he planned to play at Oakmont and reaffirmed that he would not travel abroad in 1927. Jones refrained from making any predictions for the U.S. Open, saying only that he loved Oakmont. As though he could not help himself, Richardson was again referring to the Atlantan as "Bobby" by the end of his report.[37]

Later that month, golfdom experienced some interesting controversies concerning the boundaries of amateurism. Newspapers reported on April 21 that the USGA had declared Mary K. Browne ineligible for its events, because the California tennis and golf star had joined Suzanne Lenglen's professional tennis tour. The USGA claimed that Browne had acted in a "manner detrimental to the best interests and true spirit of the game," capitalizing on "her skill in amateur athletics." Ever the maverick, the Western Golf Association announced that it would allow Browne to play in its events. Sportswriter John Kiernan, though deferring to the USGA's right to make its own policy, believed that public opinion was not behind the ruling.

Two days after the Browne decision, the *New York Times* reported that Jones had signed a contract worth an unknown amount of money to write a series of articles for a newspaper syndicate. The USGA immediately responded that Jones's authorship did not violate its amateur rules. Nonetheless, the *Times* observed that, "news of his action was received here with surprise . . . as Jones is known to have declined many such offers to profit by his reputation." Readers were reminded that a few years earlier Jones reportedly had said, "I am not a writer, and I refuse to sell my name for $25,000. If I were not fairly well-known as a golfer, anything I might write would not be worth $10, and I do not intend to trade on my reputation, regardless of whether my standing as an amateur is affected." If Jones had ever made that statement, he had obviously altered his view. Of course, the line between amateurism and professionalism had always been blurry, and, as with every other amateur athlete of note, there had always been a certain amount of delusion in Jones's amateurism. One moment he could accept a luxurious Pierce-Arrow sedan from the citizens of Sarasota, and the next explain that he had to pick up his third academic degree because "I've got a family to support." Some surprised fans may have recalled Jones's comments to London reporters the previous summer, in which he said that he had never made a cent off the game and never would. Still, few people could bring themselves to resent Jones and his decision to write for money.

In fact, if it had been anyone other than Jones or if it had not come in the wake of the Browne affair, the decision to write the articles would not have created such a stir. Jones was only doing what others had done before him. Chick Evans and Francis Ouimet had signed similar contracts, and U.S. women's amateur tennis star Helen Wills not only wrote articles but also made a nice profit from the sale of her paintings. Wills fancied herself a serious artist, although she was an obvious novice with oil and brush; she sold her paintings for a lot more money than they ever would have brought were she not a famous amateur athlete. Yet people were sensitized by the Browne controversy, and Bobby Jones was regarded as not just another amateur athlete but the ultimate model of amateurism. In sum, if at times Jones was a bit disingenuous about his amateurism, it is also true that the public held him to a higher standard than any other amateur athlete.[38]

The U.S. Open was held just days after Americans welcomed home Charles Lindbergh, who, in his *Spirit of St. Louis*, had recently become the first aviator to fly solo across the Atlantic Ocean. Jones was wise not to have made any predictions about his play. He gave his worst performance in any national open, except for the 1921 British event from which he withdrew. Oakmont's extralong rough and 193 furrowed bunkers brought out his recent lack of competition. Jones failed to break 75 and ended in a tie for eleventh place, eight strokes behind the winner, Tommy Armour. Hagen did a little better, coming in sixth place.

The leaders' inability to break 300 proved how difficult Oakmont was that summer. In light of his scoring average in the U.S. Open, though, the expectations for Jones were extraordinarily high and the pressure on him to win was immense. William Richardson commented that Jones's failure was "one of the biggest disappointments in modern golf history." Despite that and the fact that he refused all invitations for dinner and interviews while in Pittsburgh, Jones did find time to visit a young fan named Rody Marshall, who had been paralyzed in a diving accident several years earlier. Marshall, it was reported, could not come to the course, so Jones went to him with a "word of cheer."[39]

Mostly because of his showing in the U.S. Open, Jones changed his mind about traveling abroad. On June 22 the *Atlanta Constitution* reported that he was considering going to Britain because he had lost two of his crowns and did not want to give up the third without a fight. By the 24th, Jones was in New York. The next day he climbed aboard the *Transylvania* to defend his British Open title. Big Bob Jones and Stewart Maiden accompanied him; O.B. Keeler had left a few days earlier. Before departing, the Colonel told reporters that his son had fared poorly at Oakmont because he had practiced so little, studying for law exams instead.[40]

On July 3 the party arrived in St. Andrews, Scotland, leaving Jones about a week to get his game in shape. He shot numerous practice rounds and was reported to be in "splendid form" by tournament time. Indeed he was; Jones led from start to finish and successfully defended his British Open crown. His first-round 68 tied the course record and was highlighted by putts of 90 and 150 feet. At 285 (–3), Jones also became the first man to win either national open in under-par figures. Few other Americans made the trip that year, and British professional Aubrey Boomer was runner-up. It was a convincing and popular victory for Jones, who, as one newspaper pointed out, "is known on the program as Mr. Robert T. Jones Jr., but to all, he is 'Bobby.'" When he holed out on the last green, the gallery of 12,000 swarmed around Jones and carried him on their shoulders to the clubhouse.[41]

Jones delighted the Scottish crowd at the trophy presentation when he announced that he would leave the Claret Jug in the care of St. Andrews. That, as well as his acceptance speech, brought more loud cheers from the Scots. "I have achieved the ambition of my life," Jones said. "Whatever I have done in the past, or whatever I do in the future does not matter two straws. I am happy, supremely happy, not because I am supposed to have accomplished something that has never been done before, but because I have won at a place where golf was played nearly five centuries ago. This wonderful experience will live in my memory until my dying day. If I never win anything again, I am satisfied." Britain's *Golf Illustrated* thought Jones a "better man than he is a golfer. One cannot help but love him." *Golf Monthly* added, "The character of Mr. Jones has captured the hearts of golfers of two hemispheres with his modesty and the sincerity of a nature as honest as the sunlight." For weeks after, British publications praised Jones the man.

The win, of course, was special because it occurred at St. Andrews, golf's mecca and the site of Jones's most ignominious moment in tournament competition. As sportswriters noted over and over on both sides of the Atlantic, it was a triumph for Jones over his temper as much as over the course or the field. William Richardson wrote that between Jones's two trips to St. Andrews, the Atlantan had undergone "a complete mental metamorphosis." In 1921, Richardson believed, Jones was a "fretful, impetuous youth—golf's bad boy, a lovable, forgivable, bad boy," but by 1927 he was a "man grown-up—cool, calm, calculating—the very epitome of stability."[42]

Yet all the talk about his overcoming his temper bothered Jones. Just before leaving Britain, he told reporters, "Honestly, I don't think it's fair for newspapers at home to talk about my 'uncontrollable temper.'" Jones admitted making a "fool" of himself "only twice," once in the 1921 British Open and once during a war-relief match in Boston ten years earlier. But Jones asked, "What's the sense of throwing Boston at me now? Two breaks in ten years of playing does not seem to be evidence of such 'uncontrollable temper.'" If Jones forgot his other temper tantrums, he was also a bit uncomfortable as a role model. "Of course it's nice to have people say nice things about you, but honestly, when New York papers make me out such a glowing example of moral discipline I don't know what to make of it." Then he remarked, "Golf undoubtedly is one of the best forms of moral discipline, and the more one plays it the better disciplined he becomes—or ought to become. . . . I have no recipe for discipline. . . . I only know that you can break any habit if you try hard enough, except smoking." The Colonel reminded reporters that, "life isn't all golf and [my son] will start his studies as soon as he gets back." With those parting words, on July 23 the Joneses boarded the *Acetone* to sail for home.[43]

A few weeks later—but before the start of the academic year—Jones traveled to Minnesota's Minikahda Golf Club for the U.S. Amateur. Despite his loss to Von Elm in 1926, he was the number-one seed for the match play. He validated the seeding, again winning the qualifying medal before advancing to the championship round, where he beat Chick Evans 8 and 7 to collect his third U.S. Amateur title in four years. A humorous incident occurred in the second round after Jones's first tee shot struck a spectator, Dr. D.F. Gosin. After being helped to his feet, Dr. Gosin inquired as to who had hit the shot and then said, "It's all right, as long as it was Bobby." Apparently Jones's popularity had reached such heights that he had a license to nail galleries with errant drives.[44]

The championship round, though, was marked by a tension that peaked on the last green of the tournament. Evans had just lost three holes and was about to lose the match when he and Jones came to the 11th (29th); Jones was 7 up with 8 to play. Faced with a short putt for a halve that would have made Jones dormie 7, Evans nudged his ball with his putter, lost a shot, the hole, and thus the match. Contemporary coverage described the movement of the ball as an accident.

Years later, however, Evans and Jones offered different versions. Evans said that he had put his putter down close to the ball and looked up at Jones, who was glaring at him. Evans told Jones that his ball had not moved, to which Jones supposedly responded, "It sure did." With that, Evans reached out his hand to congratulate Jones, conceding the hole and the match. Jones's recollection was that Evans nonchalantly but intentionally moved the ball with his putter and then said, "I guess it moved, didn't it?" Jones answered, "Yes, Chick, I guess it did," whereupon they shook hands. Jones never considered the incident an accident, believing instead that Evans "preferred being the apparent victim of a misfortune to playing the long twelfth hole up the hill away from the clubhouse." Jones also remembered that Evans became frustrated when Jones refused to concede a breaking three-foot putt. Evans "tipped his hat" mockingly to Jones when the Atlantan had his back turned. (In match play, of course, it is not uncommon for a player to "concede" or simply give his opponent very short putts that would be made anyway far more often than not.)

Evans's antics were so blatant, according to Jones, that the referee, William Fownes, considered talking to Evans about his behavior. The episode was the most obvious sign during their competitive days of bad feelings between Evans and Jones. Many years later, Evans would cast aspersions on Jones's amateurism. Like Von Elm, Evans resented Jones's popularity and success. Whatever was actually done or said between Jones and Evans, the Georgian impressed William Richardson with his "business-like seriousness" in competition. Richardson believed that Jones had "turned from a golfer who was both human and humane into a mechanism."[45]

By the end of August, Jones was back in Atlanta, preparing for his second year at Emory law school and commenting, "I'm going back to work now. There's a lot of law to be read, and I guess I've had my vacation." Having captured his second major championship of the season and the seventh of his career, Jones ended his competitive year. He played golf only occasionally that fall. Besides concentrating on his studies, he probably also enjoyed reading the reviews of his recently published autobiography, *Down the Fairway,* on which he collaborated with O.B. Keeler. The book covered Jones's life and career through the 1926 season, including some chapters on instruction. The *American Golfer* called it "the most enjoyable book on golf it has been our good fortune to encounter."[46]

Jones had told reporters that he planned to complete Emory's three-year law course and join his father's firm, Jones, Evins, &

Moore. The program was rigorous and ranked in prestige with Columbia, Harvard, Yale, and Michigan. Jones had performed exceptionally well his first year, finishing second in his class of twenty-five. Professor H.M. Quillian, Jones's instructor in "contracts," said that the golfer had "one of the finest legal minds of any student I've ever known." Quillian was especially high on Jones's vocabulary and writing skills. In fact, Jones's intellect impressed all of his professors.

Jones was doing so well by the end of the 1927 fall term that he decided to take the Georgia bar examination. On December 28 Jones learned that he had passed, and, although he said that he would still complete his degree at Emory, he did not return to school the following term. There was no practical need for him to finish the program because he was free to enter Jones, Evins, & Moore and to begin practicing law immediately.[47]

Late in November, members of the Atlanta Athletic Club held a banquet in Jones's honor. The event was staged so that leading citizens of the city could present Jones with the most generous expression of admiration yet given him. For being not only the greatest golfer in the world but also a fine sportsman, Atlanta's sports boosters gave Jones $50,000 for a new house. Five thousand Atlantans supposedly contributed to the fund. The plan was for Jones to pick a piece of property, where a house would be built to his specifications. It was a big gift, but then Jones had brought the city an incalculable amount of free advertising on both sides of the Atlantic. Jones gratefully accepted; after all, he, Mary, Clara, and Robert III were still living with Big Bob and Clara Jones. He must have suspected that the USGA would have something to say about the unprecedented cash award. Still, it was an appropriately happy way for Bob Jones to end 1927. He was a well-educated lawyer, the best golfer on the planet, and one of the most admired athletes in America and Europe. That year even Walter Hagen declared Jones the "greatest ever."[48]

Sir Walter had started the year quietly but would finish it with a bang, just as in 1926. For a while, though, following his disappointing finish at Oakmont, he continued to languish in mediocrity. Late in June he finished third in defending the Eastern Open, and in August he took sixth place in the Canadian Open. It seemed that he could not regain the edge in his game.

Hagen spent the end of August covering the U.S. Amateur for a newspaper syndicate. It was there that Hagen called Jones the greatest ever. Given Jones's year and Hagen's, sportswriters drew the obvious conclusions. John Kiernan commented that Jones had outdone Hagen, who "seems to have slipped." Kiernan also feared that Hagen had lost "the indomitable determination, the fighting spirit, the will to win that once marked his play."

Kiernan was essentially correct, but Hagen was still capable of brief winning binges. In September, at Chicago's Olympia Fields, he successfully defended his Western Open crown. It was his fourth victory in that major event and he did it with characteristic flair, dropping a sixty-five-foot putt for eagle on the home hole of the second round. His 281 included a 67 and 69. Later that month, Hagen entered and then withdrew from the Chicago Open. He did not have to bother with regional qualifying for the upcoming PGA Championship, which was to be held in Dallas.[49]

Hagen played less than usual in the weeks between the Western and PGA. One reason was that he had indulged in another ill-fated business venture, the purchase of the Rochester Tribe of baseball's International League. Hagen's hometown minor league club was on the verge of bankruptcy and relocation when he, Bob Harlow, and John Ganzel, a former manager of the team, offered to play the role of local heroes, purchase the franchise, and keep it in Rochester. By September 22 Hagen owned a substantial interest in the ball team, contingent upon his and Ganzel's producing the rest of the purchase price. Reports had Hagen putting up about $27,000, with the understanding that if the difference—about $40,000—could not be raised, his money would be returned. As the club's intended president, he tried hard to secure the financing for a modern ballpark and poured much energy into making the team solvent. Hagen remembered that he "was beginning to think of himself as a baseball magnate." Later in the year he attended organized baseball's winter meetings in New York City and was officially approved as the Tribe's president. Ultimately, however, neither he nor Ganzel could raise the $40,000, so, despite their efforts, the team went bankrupt (but remained in Rochester) and was eventually sold to the St. Louis Cardinals. Renamed the Red Wings, the club became an important part of Branch

Rickey's farm system. Hagen later claimed to have lost more than $37,000 on his brief investment in the Tribe.[50]

The baseball venture was not the only distraction for Hagen in the weeks before the PGA; he also spent the last week of October fishing for black bass in Michigan. Thus preoccupied, he considered not defending his PGA title. Kerr Petrie reported in *Golf Illustrated* that Hagen had not touched a golf club for ten days before the PGA. But he made an eleventh-hour decision to go to Dallas (just as Jones reportedly had done for the British Open) and showed up at the Cedar Crest Golf Club on October 30, one day before the event started. His Sunday arrival left little time for practice, but Hagen was already familiar with the layout, which had been the venue for his exhibition loss to Cooper the previous winter.

Hagen led Monday's field in the on-site qualifying. The next day he began making his way through the field, winning his first three rounds. He nearly lost on Friday in the semifinals, when Al Espinosa took him to extra holes. Hagen was particularly fortunate in that match because he was 1 down heading to the 36th hole. But Espinosa three-putted from twenty-five feet, handing the 36th to Hagen, and then missed a four-footer to lose the match at the 37th. Afterward, Hagen admitted being lucky. "But," he added, "what are you going to do about it? You give these boys a chance and they don't take it." Thus Hagen advanced to his fifth consecutive PGA final, and on Saturday, November 5, he won the tournament for the fourth straight year, defeating Joe Turnesa 1 up in another exciting, come-from-behind effort. It had been a difficult, most unlikely victory. Golf writers believed that Hagen's superior mental approach made the difference. Although his skills were not what they had once been, his "headwork" still allowed him to excel in match play.

Hagen had compiled an awesome PGA record. From 1924–1927, he had won twenty consecutive PGA match-play victories. Analysts reminded fans that if Hagen had not lost to Sarazen in the 1923 final, he would have won five crowns in a row. Overall, in seven attempts since 1916, Hagen had won the PGA five times and lost twice, once in the final and once in the semifinal round. His match-play record in the event was 32–2, and both of his losses came in extra holes. Richardson considered it the "greatest record in golf."[51]

Following the victory, as pledged, Hagen gave his "famous dun-colored sweater" to the Dallas policeman who had patrolled the club during the event. He had also promised a fourteen-year-old fan the pick of the clubs in his bag; Hagen lost his "favorite brassie." Leaving those souvenirs, he headed back to Rochester, where he would spend the winter attempting to save the Rochester Tribe.

As in 1926, Hagen put a nice shine on what might have been a dull season. The *Southern Golfer* ranked him second for the year, behind U.S. Open champion Tommy Armour. Hagen's career was becoming one marked by long periods of drought interrupted by spurts of brilliance. He was especially inconsistent in medal-play competition, and despite his determined efforts, he could not win his third U.S. Open. All of that should have surprised no one. Hagen was, after all, about to turn thirty-five. But if his career had been reduced to flashes of success, then those flashes would be some of the brightest ever.

Chapter 8

The "Atlanta Golf Machine" and the "Lion-Tamer": 1928–1929

The primary reason that Walter Hagen traveled around the United States in the winter of 1927 and to Rochester instead of Florida in the winter of 1928 was that he had lost his position, or at least his salary, at Pasadena. Hagen's lucrative arrangement with Jack Taylor became a casualty of the Florida real estate market. The market had peaked in 1925, and by the summer of 1926 it was in serious trouble. A deadly hurricane ripped through southern Florida in September of 1926, killing 400 people and finishing off much of the state's speculative enthusiasm. Hagen summarized his and many other Americans' experience: "The Florida boom paid me off well for three straight years, then the bubble burst." Actually, because Hagen had not invested in land himself, he lost only a regular income and a comfortable winter base.[1]

Hagen returned to Rochester in the winter of 1928 to prepare the Tribe baseball team for the upcoming season. It was even reported that its soon-to-be president would work out with the club in spring training. But Hagen's stint as a "baseball magnate" did not last long enough for that. On January 5 the *Rochester Times-Union* revealed that the Hagen-Ganzel offer was dead and that the St. Louis Cardinals were interested in buying the Tribe.[2]

Without the Tribe to hold his attention, Hagen fled the snow in Rochester and headed for the sunshine in southern California. For the next several years, Hollywood would be Sir Walter's win-

ter retreat. Hagen loved spending time with movie stars and pro-
ducers, being seen with them, and, occasionally, working with them.
He had already "starred" alongside Marge Beebe in a silent golfing
comedy entitled *Green Grass Widow*. The sum of Hagen's memory
about the experience was that "Marge Beebe's form was as good
on the course as off." Hagen recalled that while in Hollywood, he
leased a large house on King's Road above Sunset Boulevard. The
four-bedroom "villa" was staffed by two "Philippine houseboys"
and served Hagen's "big-scale entertaining" quite well. He also
remembered that many "film beauties," including Bette Davis, Bebe
Daniels, Norma and Constance Talmadge, and the "curvaceous
blonde" Thelma Todd, would "often drop in for tea." Hagen went
to Hollywood early in 1928 to do another picture, but although
several sequences were made, the project went overbudget and
was never completed.[3]

In mid-March he announced that he would journey abroad to
enter the British Open and to meet Archie Compston in another
international grudge match. Compston, like Abe Mitchell two years
earlier, had issued a challenge the previous November from across
the Atlantic; this one, though, was specifically for Hagen. The
"Welsh Giant" (Compston stood around 6' 5") was considered the
best match player in Great Britain. In his brief challenge, Compston
declared: "I am willing to play Hagen over seventy-two holes for
the world's championship, with a substantial side bet and a percentage of the gate receipts." Hagen hesitated but finally announced
that he would face Compston for "a stake of $2,500 a side." The
match was scheduled for April 27–28, 1928, about a week before
the British Open. Bob Jones had already said that he would not
defend his title, so the British were especially happy to have Hagen's
commitment. He was scheduled to leave for Britain on April 18
aboard the *Aquitania*.[4]

Hagen played little golf between his acceptance of the
Compston challenge and his boarding the *Aquitania*. In fact, he
had played only occasionally since winning the PGA the previous
autumn. Two days before the *Aquitania* departed, Hagen arrived
in New York. An already tight schedule became tighter when Hagen
realized en route to New York that he had left his passport in
California, so he had to spend the next two days acquiring a new
one. Before boarding, he gave an impromptu press conference and
told reporters that he would ask Compston for a postponement of
their match. Because of his filmmaking, he had been unable to

practice and would "need a little time to get back into shape." He added, "No one who is not in good shape should play Archie." Someone brought up Bobby Jones's decision not to defend his British Open crown and asked Hagen what he thought of the Atlantan's impressive play as of late. Hagen said that he was sorry Jones could not make the trip, and as for Jones's good form: "Tell me something new, that boy always plays good golf."[5]

Compston received Hagen's request with little sympathy. Having practiced for weeks, he was in top form and saw no reason to postpone the match. If the American professional had frittered away time in Hollywood, failing to prepare himself for the biggest international match of the season, then he would have to suffer the consequences. "I am as good as any golfer in the world today. And I am going to prove it," Compston declared. The competition would be held on time, two days after Hagen's arrival in London. When Hagen learned of Compston's rebuff, he simply smiled and commented: "Well, I suppose I must do my best." Hagen also admitted that he wanted "to put himself right" with the British public for his tardiness in the 1926 Mitchell match. To ensure Hagen's timely arrival at Moor Park, Harlow hired a private detective, formerly of Scotland Yard. Harlow told the British press that if Sir Walter wanted "another forty winks" in his bedroom at the Savoy, the detective was to "haul him out from under the bed-clothes." The British loved it. So, having rarely touched his clubs for a month and with bodyguard in tow, Hagen practiced for a day at Moor Park, site of the impending battle.[6]

The next morning, as Hagen remembered it, Compston's caddie appeared holding the Welsh Giant's mascot and good-luck charm, a black cat. Informed about Hagen's match-play magic, Compston was determined to cast his own spell, and it worked. He demolished Hagen; after the first day the American was 14 down. The press noted that at least Sir Walter showed up on time. He was punctual the next day, too, when Compston closed him out by the count of 18 and 17. To make matters worse, the humiliating performance was constantly before the gallery in unusual fashion; Moor Park officials had struck upon the idea of having a boy carry a scoreboard. Britain's *Golf Illustrated* later sold copies of a photograph showing a dejected Hagen being followed by the roving scoreboard, which read "Compston 16." By the second day, the gallery was giving Hagen "sympathy applause" in response to his executing the simplest of shots.[7]

Naturally, British fans reveled in Hagen's loss, probably more than in Compston's victory. British golfers were not "lazy" after all, at least not Archie Compston; on this occasion it was Hagen who had been unprepared. The American remembered some of the local headlines: "Hagen Submerged!", "American Gets His Own Medicine!", "Hagen's Ghost Is Laid," and "The Eclipse of Hagen!" British cartoonist Tommy Webster had been drawing a series for the Hagen-Compston match. His last sketch showed Hagen in bed, struggling to get past his bodyguard, with the caption: "Harlow Should Have Paid Scotland Yard to Keep Hagen in Bed . . . 18 and 17!" The *Morning Post* noted that the victory deserved "more than passing celebration to a British golfer's heart, which for a long time has been uncheered by any challenge to American ascendancy." The *London Observer* mocked the American professional, stating that he had been "badly mauled [and] ignominiously crushed" in his quest for more money and he "now knows better." The *Observer* also quoted an anonymous "compatriot" of Hagen: it was a lesson that "has been coming to [Hagen] for a long time, and one that he will never forget."

But while they savored the victory, Britishers also respected Hagen's attitude in defeat. "I got what I deserved," Sir Walter admitted. "I am supposed to have said that British professionals did not work at the game, and I have discovered one of them has been working very hard indeed, while I, who am getting on for 40, have allowed other interests to interfere with golf." Did Hagen's lack of practice explain the outcome? "[I] do not want to make any excuses, because I know that if I had played par golf I would have been down, for Archie played super golf." Hagen concluded that he was going to work hard for the British Open. Once in his limousine, however, he assured Harlow, "Archie was good, but I can beat him any time."

The hypercritical *Observer* was not much impressed by Hagen's public statements, commenting that practicing for the Open could not "wipe out this debacle." Most British analysts, though, admired Hagen's pluck and serenity. The *Times* of London noted that during the lunch break on the second day, when he was down 18 with 18 to play, Hagen courteously "signed autographs for young and old alike." That, the *Times* declared, was the mark of "a great golfer and sportsman."

Moreover, British writers acknowledged that Hagen was indeed tired from the trip and in no shape to face Compston. Generally, the lopsided margin was interpreted less as a manifestation of British superiority and more as a case of one golfer playing extremely well and another playing unusually poorly. Still, *Golf Monthly* believed that Hagen's loss "inspired hope among British golfers that in the forthcoming Open Championship, the cycle of American successes will be brought to an end." Maybe Compston could keep the Claret Jug in Britain; it certainly seemed that Hagen was no threat. The *Observer* thought it a pity that Jones had not tried for the "hat trick," adding that, given Hagen's "annihilation," an American victory was remote. Bernard Darwin of the *Times* cautioned restraint, however, suggesting that Hagen would "likely prove every whit as dangerous" in the Open, and would play as if the Compston match had never taken place. Hagen was, after all, the master psychologist of the game.[8]

Aside from Hagen, Darwin may have been the only man in Britain who gave Hagen a chance. Yet Sir Walter had two things in his favor: the tournament would be held over the Royal St. George's links at Sandwich, where he had won his first British Open in 1922; and Hagen had more than a week to practice—and practice he did. He remembered being "serious about winning the British Open. That defeat by Compston had been a terrific blow to my pride." The following week he "refused the tempting phone calls." Harlow confirmed that Hagen "became serious" after the Compston match: "He went to work. He followed a strict routine of practice, diet, and sessions with a masseur. And he even locked his address book in a valise."

On May 6, Hagen took a 73 over the par 72 layout, driving and putting accurately. He had putted dismally in the Compston match; now he seemed to have his favorite part of the game in tune. By the preliminary rounds, even Compston considered Hagen a favorite. On May 7–8, Hagen qualified with 76–77. One reporter noted that Hagen wore the same blue sweater and stockings that he had worn in the Compston match, apparently unaffected by superstition.

The tournament proper began the next day, amid a "strong and bitter northerly wind." The weather was so cold that some forecast snow for the tournament. Hagen shot 75 to end the day in fourth place. Darwin recorded that his round contained "some characteristic mistakes and characteristic recoveries." Conditions improved for the second round, and so did Hagen's play; he moved into second place after a slow start, adding a 73. That evening he nonchalantly reflected, "I played quite well. I might have done better, but then I might have done worse."

Hagen saved his best performance for the final day. He came from behind, posted a pair of 72s, and won his third British Open title. Darwin thought that the unexpected victory "showed what amazing courage, vitality, and recuperative power Hagen possesses." Any other golfer "would have been at least temporarily crushed by that fearful beating from Compston only a short while ago. To Hagen it only acted as a spur. There are other golfers as good as he is, and perhaps one better; but as a fighter he is in a little class all by himself." That probably summed up the views of most golf fans around the world. The *Daily Express* thought that, "Except for Bobby Jones, Hagen must be reckoned the world's best tournament golfer." *Sporting Life* believed that "no finer display of determination to overcome difficulties was ever witnessed," and that Hagen's performance represented "the most dramatic comeback in the history of the game."[9]

Hagen enjoyed a special treat at the closing ceremonies when he received the Claret Jug from Edward, Prince of Wales. Hagen modestly told the crowd that he had been "lucky" to win. Prince Edward had been an interested spectator all week and was seen several times chatting with Hagen and Gene Sarazen. In one episode that has become part of Sir Walter's legend, Edward invited Hagen into the clubhouse for a drink. They chatted at the grill for a while before the club's secretary politely reminded Edward that professionals were not allowed in the building. The Prince supposedly brushed off the comment, saying that he would drink with whoever he wanted, wherever he wanted. The clubhouse-storming incident became another basis for Sir Walter's reputation as golf's "Great Emancipator." For the most part, though, Hagen comported himself dutifully, and, when he left Britain for France a few days later, he had garnered new-found admiration, even affection, from the British golfing public.[10]

Before returning to the United States, Hagen and Harlow toured Continental Europe. Through the rest of May, Hagen played exhibitions in Paris, Vienna, Berlin, and Zurich. On his way back through France, he played a few rounds along the Riviera. By the end of the month, he was in the British Isles for more matches in Ireland and England. Hagen had announced that he would compete in the Irish Open, but he changed his mind at the last moment, saying that he was too tired from his Continental tour. That angered the Irish event's sponsors, particularly because it came after the pairings had been arranged. Declared Alan Kidd, secretary of the Golfing Union of Ireland: "Hagen not only has injured his name as a sportsman here but indirectly has hurt the good name of all Americans." Despite his best efforts, Hagen could not escape Europe without alienating some segment of the British populace. Nonetheless, the trip did his competitive and personal image good with most foreign fans and added to his 1928 income; Hagen-Harlow reportedly made $15,000 for their troubles.[11]

On June 8, Hagen arrived in New York Harbor to a hero's welcome. William Richardson of the *New York Times* considered it "second only to that received by Bobby Jones" two years earlier. Golf writers ludicrously had resorted to comparing every aspect of Hagen's and Jones's careers. "It lacked the scope of the Jones reception," but, Richardson reminded, "allowance must be made for the fact that Hagen's ship docked early in the morning, whereas Bobby's came up the bay in the afternoon." Although Hagen arrived at 9:00, he had to wait until 2:30 for his formal welcome at City Hall by Mayor Jimmy Walker, because according to the *Times*, "that was the only time that Mayor Walker had open on his calendar." Still, immediately after landing, Hagen was paraded up Fifth Avenue, while a band played "Yankee Doodle Dandy." When Mayor Walker finally greeted Hagen, he handed him the keys to the city.[12]

If Hagen's reception was not quite up to Jones standards, then neither was the rest of his season. The British Open proved to be its highlight. He finished a solid fourth place in the U.S. Open later that month and runner-up at the Canadian Open in July. In the fall, Leo Diegel knocked him out of the PGA in the third round by a count of 2 and 1, ending Hagen's consecutive match-play winning streak at twenty-two. (Diegel went on to win the tournament.) In between those major events, Hagen finished third in the New York Open; he skipped the Western Open, playing in fewer tournaments than he once did.[13]

Instead, Hagen capitalized on his British crown through exhibitions. In July he beat Compston 6 and 5 in a rematch of their Moor Park duel. *Canadian Golfer* reported that Hagen received $5,000 for his victory over the Welsh Giant. Hagen also defeated Johnny Farrell in the Unofficial Championship of the World; the best-of-five marathon called for 180 holes, spread out over five days and five cities. The series went the distance and brought in more than $9,000 in gate receipts, of which Hagen took the lion's share. Some skeptics suggested that Hagen had let up on Farrell in the fourth match to guarantee the additional receipts of a fifth match.[14]

Hagen amused even skeptical fans, though, late in August when he drove "300 miles out of bounds," showing up in Menominee, Michigan, for an exhibition that was to be played in Menominee, Wisconsin. Hagen could only telephone his apologies. He then covered the Walker Cup matches for *Golf Illustrated* and the U.S. Amateur for the *Boston Globe*. In Boston he was regularly besieged by autograph-hunters.[15]

By early November, Hagen was again playing his way to southern California, a region that now challenged hurricane-battered Florida as the sport's winter haven, boasting opens with lucrative purses in Long Beach, Catalina Island, and Los Angeles. He and Harlow traveled with Johnny Farrell, who had joined Hagen in exhibitions throughout the northwest. As they often did, Hagen and Harlow took a break with some duck hunting on Tulie Lake in Oregon. The deliberate Hagen, Harlow recalled, was always the first one to spot the mallards and say "Mark," but the last one to fire his shotgun. Still, he was exceptionally accurate and adept at hitting birds just as they seemed to fly out of range.[16]

From Oregon the Hagen party went south to San Francisco for another exhibition, finally arriving in the Los Angeles area early in December. On the 11th, the PGA announced that Hagen would captain the third U.S. Ryder Cup team, which meant that in 1929 he would travel abroad and defend his British title. A few days later, Hagen relaxed with some more hunting, this time shooting seven wild goats on Catalina Island. He then finished 1928 on a high note, capturing the Long Beach Open. Nonetheless, the *Metropolitan Golfer* ranked Hagen third among professionals for the season. Minus the British Open, the year would have been mediocre at best. Only that victory sustained his reputation, facilitated the Farrell matches, and generally kept Hagen near the top of his profession for another season.[17]

As the comments following the British Open illustrated, Bob Jones continued to wear the emperor's crown through 1928. He began the year by revealing that he would not finish school but rather would join his father's law practice. He took the same opportunity to inform his fans that he would not be traveling abroad that summer.[18]

On January 4 Jones was in New York City for a sportsmanship banquet at the Hotel Commodore. There he joined some of the decade's most illustrious sports figures, including Gene Tunney, Babe Ruth, Bill Tilden, and Johnny Weissmuller. Mayor Jimmy Walker emceed the "Champions' Dinner," during which Jones spoke briefly. In his characteristic style, Mayor Walker introduced Jones as the "greatest golfer ever known." The Atlantan responded with a few sentences about the "greatness" of the occasion, thanking the committee for his invitation.[19]

Three days later, Jones announced that he would return the generous $50,000 housing allowance given to him in Atlanta, because it might cast aspersions on his amateurism and sport. While most of the public thought the gift acceptable, "another still respectable part entertains some doubts." Criticism had "come to his notice, [and] to avoid any chance of misunderstanding," he "decided that the best thing to do was to return the home." Jones thanked his Atlanta friends again and reminded them that their gift was significant only because of the affection it represented. As he likely expected, the $50,000 had raised many eyebrows at the USGA. Supposedly, cheers went up at the USGA convention in the Hotel Astor when news arrived of Jones's decision. President Melvin Traylor called the choice "magnificent," because Jones was neither a rich man nor the son of a rich man. The press association in London declared that Jones's action "will be much admired in this country, where he is held in equal admiration with any of our own amateurs."

William Fownes also lauded Jones, characterizing his decision as a "voluntary act." That is not so clear. In truth, some concerns were voiced in the weeks before Jones's trip to New York. While there, he met with USGA officials, who advised him that, although there was nothing technically wrong with accepting the money, it clearly would not be in the "best interests of the game." Jones concurred, and a few weeks later he was named to several USGA advisory committees, including those on course selection and membership and reinstatement, and was made captain of the 1928 Walker Cup squad.[20]

Of course, Jones could have resisted the USGA; after all, its advice had been muddled and inconsistent. Other star athletes, particularly tennis players, had led rebellions against the constraints of amateurism. Jones might have asked, "What's the difference between a luxury sedan and a house?" The USGA might have responded, "about $45,000." Ultimately, Jones's amateur standing could have been rescinded, as had Francis Ouimet's a decade earlier.

Given Jones's status, it is interesting to contemplate what might have happened if he had challenged golf's authority. The fact that he did not, however, says a lot about him. By nature, he was a conservative person who easily deferred to the game's authority and traditions, even if it meant significant short-term economic loss. His dutiful sacrifice for the sport underscored his image as a traditional amateur. But his decision also illustrates that Jones understood the unique basis of his fame and influence: his amateur status. He wanted and needed to protect his image as a simon-pure athlete. If Jones could do that and continue to compile an unprecedented competitive record in the process, he eventually would be in a position to make far more than $50,000 from golf and still retire with stellar, impeccable standing in his sport. Jones's thinking proved wise; much more cash did come his way, and all the while he maintained the public's deep admiration and respect.

In the meantime, Jones and his family needed a house of their own. Mary Jones was especially anxious to relocate. The couple purchased a home on Northside Avenue in northeast Atlanta and moved in the spring of 1928.

Richard Miller has written that Jones borrowed approximately $50,000 from granddad R.T. to finance the house. If Jones did consider obtaining the money that way, he changed his mind. Lewis Jones Jr. of Canton, Georgia, has an interesting letter dated January 11, 1928, in which "Rob" thanked R.T. for his offer to help him buy a house. Jones also thanked R.T. for approving his "action in turning back the home" that his friends had given him. "I felt I was right," Jones wrote, "but I feel more certain of it now." As for R.T.'s offer to finance a new house, Jones was "awfully grateful" but declined, because "Mary and I should make some effort now to shoulder responsibilities . . . [and] scratch for ourselves for a while." He assured R.T., "If I need any help and feel that I am justified in asking it, I may call on you later."[21]

With a new house and his amateur status above reproach, Jones looked forward to the 1928 golf season. He skipped the Southern Open that spring because he wanted to practice a month to get himself in "tiptop shape." In March he played an exhibition at East Lake with Frank White, U.S. Treasurer. After the match Jones autographed White's scorecard and White reciprocated by signing a brand new dollar bill. Ten days later in Atlanta, Jones received a portrait of himself, done by Margaret Fitzhugh Browne. At the unveiling ceremony, Jones was credited with the "sportsmanship of medieval knighthood" because he had returned the $50,000 and played golf solely for "the love of the game." The next month he played a handful of exhibitions with Watts Gunn for the American Olympic Fund. Those exhibitions, plus a "month's hard practice" prepared Jones for the U.S. Open.[22]

The 1928 U.S. Open was held at Chicago's Olympia Fields. As usual, both Jones and Hagen were favorites. The USGA had ruled that the top thirty finishers at Oakmont were exempt from regional qualifying, so neither Hagen nor Jones dealt with that inconvenience. Hagen liked the course—he had won the PGA Championship and Western Open there—and wanted to duplicate Jones's feat of winning both national opens in the same season. But whereas Jones showed up the weekend before the event for some final practice, Hagen waited until one day before the tournament began. Still, dopesters agreed that if he could stay close to Jones and turn the medal event into a man-to-man struggle, he would gain the advantage.

Once again, Hagen's fans were disappointed. Until the 71st hole, it looked as though Roland Hancock, a young, unknown professional, would capture the event of his career. The crowds had been most enthusiastic that week, prompting William Richardson to note: "A prize ring has nothing on the modern roped green of the golf course." "One more tournament like that," wrote John Kiernan, "and the spectators will rush from the last green to the nearest insane asylum and give themselves up." Hancock was forced to wait for thirty minutes on the 17th tee, while officials cleared the fairway. With more time to think than he wanted or needed, the inexperienced Hancock double-bogeyed 17 and bogeyed 18 to fall one shot behind Jones and Johnny Farrell, who had both already finished at 294. Hagen's 296 put him in a fourth-place tie.

For the third time, Jones would be involved in a play-off for the U.S. Open championship. He and Farrell met for thirty-six holes the next day, Sunday, June 24. Most of the 8,000 spectators rooted for Jones and were frustrated when he came up short. Only one stroke separated the competitors through 108 holes; Jones bogeyed the 106th, and that proved to be the difference.[23]

Although he lost, Jones had fought hard, recovering the U.S. Open form that had eluded him at Oakmont in 1927. A *New York Times* editorial commented that Jones's designation as the world's greatest golfer was still unchallenged. Golf was a sport of "upsets and miracles," and after all, for Jones "there would have been nothing in it [a U.S. Open victory] but glory, of which he has already had enough to turn his head, if it were not so firmly set on his sturdy shoulders." Still, the editorial concluded, no one could "begrudge Farrell" the opportunity to "add greatly to his income."[24]

Throughout July, Jones practiced regularly, but he engaged in no serious competition until late August, when he returned to Chicago for the Walker Cup matches. Robert Gardner, the former captain, stepped aside, and Jones was his natural heir. The Atlantan badly wanted a victory in his first captaincy and prepared with a sense of mission. The week before coming north, Jones played six practice rounds, all between 69 and 71. In Chicago, he compiled an average of 69 for ten more preliminary rounds. Observers suggested that he resembled a "golfing automaton" or a "machine" more than a mortal man, and compared his cool determination to that of Helen Wills, the icy "Miss Poker-Face" of women's tennis.[25]

The rest of the American squad—Chick Evans, Jess Sweetser, George Von Elm, Harrison Johnston, Francis Ouimet, Watts Gunn, and Roland Mackenzie—also looked strong. By the end of the week, Jones was confident. "We ought to win, but this is golf, and you know the old saying about golf being a humbling game." As it turned out, the British were the ones humbled or, actually, "humiliated." Britain's *Golf Monthly* likened the defeat to Waterloo, concluding that its team had been "beaten, crushed, [and] annihilated." On the first day, the U.S. swept the foursomes. Evans was the only American to lose in the singles the next day, and the U.S. retained the cup, 11 points to 1. In his singles match, Jones thrashed the reigning British Amateur champion, Thomas Philip Perkins, 13 and 12.[26]

Two days later, Jones, Keeler, and nearly everyone involved in the Walker Cup competition departed from Chicago's LaSalle Street Station on the *Twentieth Century Limited* for Boston and the U.S. Amateur championship. The tournament was scheduled for the Brae Burn Golf Club, site of Hagen's 1919 U.S. Open victory.

On the way, Jones and Keeler spent some time in New York as the guests of USGA Vice President H.H. Ramsey. By September 4, Jones was practicing at Brae Burn, and it was obvious that he had not lost his Chicago form. The following day he teamed up with Farrell against Hagen and Sarazen for a thirty-six-hole exhibition to raise money for the Ryder Cup team's 1929 travel expenses. Five thousand turned out to watch Hagen-Sarazen win by the narrowest margin, 1 up. More than $10,000 was raised, and Jones shined in the loss, shooting a 67.[27]

The following week, Jones advanced through the field at Brae Burn. After finishing fifth in the qualifying rounds, he survived the first day's eighteen-hole matches, edging his afternoon opponent, Ray Gorton, 1 up. Jones breathed easier in the thirty-six-hole affairs, crushing his next two adversaries. That set up a rematch of the Walker Cup duel between Jones and Perkins. The British star again fell to Jones; the score was 10 and 9, one of the widest final round margins in U.S. Amateur history.

For Jones, it was his eighth national title, surpassing the mark of seven held by Britishers Harold Hilton and Harry Vardon. Moreover, he had collected at least one national crown in each season since 1923. It was also his fourth U.S. Amateur title in five years and the second time he had repeated as champion. Essentially, the event belonged to the "Atlanta golf machine." It seemed that the rest of the world's amateurs had succumbed to the "Jones complex." Some feared that his dominance would lead to a lack of interest in future amateur events. Grantland Rice likened Jones to a "cyclone" and proclaimed: "The amateur golf championship of the United States might as well be handed to Bobby Jones at the start of each fiscal year to save any number of people a lot of time and money and bother." Jones's victory had become so common that much of the post-tournament analysis ignored his achievement, focusing instead on the format of the event, specifically whether or not the eighteen-hole matches should be retained.[28]

By October, Jones was at home in Atlanta practicing law. He played infrequently the rest of the year, although late in November he joined Democratic politician Alfred Smith for a publicized round at East Lake. (Smith had lost lopsidedly to Republican Herbert Hoover in the presidential election a few weeks earlier.) Jones then spent the holidays in southern Florida, where, between fishing trips, he played one more charity exhibition. With that, Jones concluded another sparkling season.[29]

"The Atlanta Golf Machine." By 1928, Jones was ranked widely
as the number one golfer in the world.
Courtesy: Sidney L. Matthew Collection

Jones thoroughly enjoyed his Miami vacation. On January 6, the *Atlanta Constitution* reported that he lost four sailfish but landed a seven-foot, thirty-four-pound barracuda after an hour-long struggle. He returned to Atlanta the following week for a match involving Glenna Collett. Collett had played a number of exhibitions with Jones and Hagen, but this was her first in Atlanta. By early 1929 she had taken Alexa Stirling's place as the best female golfer in the country, winning the U.S. Women's Amateur championship in 1922, 1925, and 1928. (She would go on to make it three in a row, winning the title again in 1929 and 1930.) Golf writers would eventually refer to her as the "Bobby Jones of women's golf" because of her record and gracious manner in victory or defeat. Her fame, together with that of Alexa Stirling, Maureen Orcutt, Edith Cummings, Mary K. Browne and others, proved that the rise of American golf was not a purely male story. Collett was teamed with Chick Ridley, former Georgia state champion, against Jones and Mrs. Dalton Raymond, a former southern champion. Collett-Ridley won, with Collett firing an 80 from the men's tees.[30]

Aside from occasional exhibitions and practice rounds, Jones continued to play little golf that winter. During a business trip to New York City early in April, he reaffirmed that he would not travel abroad in 1929 but would journey to the Pacific Coast for the U.S. Amateur in the fall. On May 8 Jones was admitted to the bar of the U.S. District Court in Macon, Georgia, to try his first federal case, which he won on May 17. Jones appeared before Judge Bascom S. Deaver representing an Atlanta company to whom Herbert Pearson, a "receiver of a Macon bank," owed $4,000. Pearson claimed the right to delay payment on the loan, and Jones argued that it should be given immediate priority. In spite of his victory, the case was just the sort that counselor Jones found unpleasant.

Jones soon fulfilled his 1926 prediction and decided that trial practice was not for him. He was simply much more comfortable attacking "Old Man Par" than an old man or young woman or anyone else on the witness stand. Just as real estate necessitated intrusiveness, trial lawyering required personal confrontation and aggression. Although Jones possessed more than enough intellect for either career, neither suited his personality. Late in his life,

Jones remarked that he believed litigation to be "distasteful." By the summer of 1929, he concluded that he most enjoyed the behind-the-scenes work of giving legal advice, especially to the family businesses in Canton.[31]

So, having discovered another career path that did not agree with him, Jones resumed competitive golf. In mid-June, he received a unique offer when the Japanese Foreign Ministry invited him to play in Tokyo. The invitation declared that "all Japanese golfers are anxious to welcome [you.]" Although Jones said that he would "love to go to Japan," he did not "see at present how he could be away from the office that long." He never made the trip, and Asian golfers had to settle for Sir Walter a few years later.[32]

On June 17, three days after he courteously refused the Japanese invitation, Jones made his way north on the *Birmingham Special* to the Winged Foot Golf Club in Maramoneck, New York, site of the U.S. Open. Grantland Rice informed fans that Jones had "played only six or seven rounds between September and April"; Keeler put the number around ten but also reported that Jones had been practicing regularly throughout April, May, and early June. Nonetheless, Jones felt that his game was rusty, and so he showed up at Winged Foot about ten days before the tournament to get in some more "hard practice." On the 21st he played a round with Sarazen, Farrell, and Kirkwood. At one point, the foursome passed another that included baseball superstar Babe Ruth and Ruth's teammate Waite Hoyt. In his irreverent, brash way, Ruth shouted to Jones's group, "I'll take on the four of you!" Despite his considerable golf skill, the Babe was a bit out of his element at Winged Foot, and his challenge, according to William Richardson, was simply "ignored."

Given the way that Jones had been playing, he probably would have beaten the best ball of the entire New York Yankees team. He shot two 69s in practice. Winged Foot seemed tailor-made for Jones, requiring both extraordinary length and accuracy off the tee. The character of the "man-sized" course, plus Jones's practice scores, made the Atlantan a huge favorite, while commentators predicted that Hagen would struggle over the long, narrow, heavily bunkered layout. Jones was so satisfied with his game on Wednesday, June 26, that he passed on a final opportunity to go around the course, opting only for some time on the putting green.

The tournament began the next day in nearly perfect weather. The sun was so hot, though, that Hagen wore a Panama hat. Maybe the hat threw off his balance; at any rate, he played poorly, while Jones jumped into the lead with another 69. Al Espinosa was next, just one stroke back. A "torrential downpour" hit Winged Foot on the afternoon of the second day. Some of the players, such as Espinosa, were fortunate to finish before the storm struck. Espinosa took advantage and grabbed the lead. Jones, meanwhile, battled the waterlogged course and finished two strokes behind. The rain killed Hagen's chances; his embarrassing 81 put him fifteen shots to the rear.

Jones started fast on the final day, amassing a three-stroke lead by the lunch break. But he floundered on the last nine, and when he reached the 72nd hole, Jones was in a precarious position. He had given away four strokes to par on the previous five holes and was in danger of firing his first 80 in U.S. Open competition. The tournament came down to a slippery, downhill, breaking twelve-foot putt for a 79 to tie Espinosa. O.B. Keeler was too nervous to watch, so he turned away, listening for the crowd's response. "The breathing ceased," he recalled. "A thin click, and the beginning of a kind of sigh—the ball was on its way. The sigh grew louder . . . . it changed to a gasp. . . . Missed! No! The gasp changed to a roar." Jones had struck the ball so delicately that it rolled to the edge of the hole and seemingly suspended itself before falling in. Al Watrous later called the putt the "finest" he ever saw; Keeler thought it the "most important shot of Jones's career," because, had he missed, he might never have recovered the confidence lost on his final nine.

The putt put Jones in still another U.S. Open play-off. Coincidentally, Jones and Espinosa had tied at 294, just as Jones and Farrell had the previous year. That was where the similarities between the two opens ended, however, because the next day Jones regained his composure and beat Espinosa all over the course. At Jones's suggestion, the play-off had been postponed a couple of hours so that both competitors could accompany their wives to mass. Although he smiled at his wife moments before the play-off began, saying that he "felt fine going after Bobby Jones," Espinosa was actually an emotional wreck, and whatever prayers he uttered that morning went unanswered. En route to his ninth national crown, Jones mercilessly pummeled his professional friend, shooting 72–69 to Espinosa's 84–80. If he lost in humiliating style, Espinosa received some compensation when he collected the top prize, recently increased to $1,000 by the USGA. With tickets at

$3 and total gate receipts a reported $36,000, the organization could afford to be a bit more generous with the players.[33]

As for Jones, he traveled back home to more superlatives and accolades. At the trophy presentation, USGA President Findlay Douglas had called the Georgian "the greatest golfer that ever lived," adding that "there never was a more ideal sportsman than Mr. Jones." For a change, no band or parade awaited the Jones party at the Brookwood Station in Atlanta, possibly because the city figured that once a year was enough and he would win the Amateur in the fall when it might be cooler. The modest reception was nonetheless "magnificent in its sincerity," and plenty of friends, fans, and family, including little Clara Malone and Bobby III, showed up to greet their hero. If the city did less than usual, the Georgia House of Representatives adopted a resolution congratulating Jones. Upon arrival, he announced that "Calamity Jane Jr." would be given a rest; he planned to refocus on his law practice until the U.S. Amateur in the fall.[34]

In spite of his announcement, Jones continued to play as much as possible during the six weeks between his triumphant return from Winged Foot and his departure for Pebble Beach, site of the Amateur. Just two days after forecasting a break, Jones played in an exhibition at East Lake. He played three more exhibitions that week, and at least two more by the end of July. Early in August, he competed in another at a new course in Highland, North Carolina. Amid all of that, Grantland Rice wrote in *Collier's* that Jones entered national championships "in spite of a still greater devotion to the practice of law."[35]

On August 17 the Joneses—Big Bob, Clara, Bob Jr., and Mary— left in a "special car" from Brookwood Station for the West. California golfers eagerly awaited the Emperor's arrival but were again warned by local papers that Jones had "played little golf this year because of his growing law practice." It was the first time that the Amateur championship was played in the far west. It was also Jones's first trip to the region, so the party spent a day sightseeing at the Grand Canyon before arriving in Los Angeles. While in L.A., Jones played in a charity exhibition and was a guest at Will Rogers's ranch. His train pulled into San Francisco the morning of the 26th, and that afternoon he tied the Pebble Beach course record of 73, while praising the beautiful and challenging layout. The *San Francisco Chronicle* reported that Jones immediately won the hearts of Californians with his "slow, boyish smile and marvelous golf shots."

"Mr. Bobby Jones conquered," the *Examiner* noted, and "made a million more friends."[36]

Jones was the number-one seed for the impending event, and he had about a week to practice. As in 1926, he was in a position to set a record of winning three consecutive amateur titles. Although Hagen's string of four in the PGA took some luster away from Jones's potential achievement, most analysts then still considered three U.S. Amateurs more impressive. A year earlier, California native George Von Elm had predicted that there would be some surprises at Pebble Beach, a "real he-man's course."

Jones looked unstoppable in practice; once again it was "the field against Bobby." On Tuesday, September 3, he tied Gene Homans for the qualifying medal and then looked to his first-round match with Johnny Goodman, an unknown twenty-year-old from Omaha, Nebraska. As usual, the first two match-play rounds were at eighteen holes. In 1921, Jones had despised the eighteen-hole format used in the British Amateur. At Brae Burn in 1928, he had barely survived an eighteen-hole affair with Ray Gorton. Unfortunately for Jones and his "10,000 worshippers," who flocked to the Monterey peninsula on trains, automobiles, and yachts, Von Elm had been correct about potential surprises, and Johnny Goodman proved better than good. He stunned Jones by a count of 1 up, pulling arguably the upset of the century in U.S. Amateur match play.[37]

"If an earthquake had suddenly rocked the peninsula," wrote Alan Gould in the *San Francisco Chronicle*, "the shock could hardly have been any greater . . . ,[and] there was as much gloom around the home green at the finish as there was enthusiastic appreciation for the astonishing feat of Goodman." The defeat of Jones, remarked the *New York Times*, was "nothing short of a calamity"; O.B. Keeler recalled that the gallery appeared "heart-broken." To make matters worse for Californians, Jones was not the only big name to fall on the first day; Jess Sweetser and George Von Elm also lost. The USGA did not like Jones's early exit either. Gate receipts at Pebble Beach turned out to be lower than anticipated, and the blame was affixed to Jones's elimination. Later that week, William Richardson characterized the semifinals as "the most uninteresting that ever were played in the championship," while E.M. Adams commented in *Golfers Magazine* that "the champion's early defeat took most of the spice and enthusiasm out of the tournament." Concluded the acerbic Ring Lardner, "The ancient Scottish pastime in this age is a one-man sport, and the one man is public property, like Lindbergh, or Charlie Chaplin, or Babe Ruth. If you're giving a show, don't kill the star in the prologue." A year earlier, analysts had feared that Jones's domination would lead to apathy for the event, but in 1929 they discovered that his absence made the tournament even more boring.[38]

In one of his finest moments, Jones congratulated Goodman and told reporters: "We can't win all the time. I didn't do so well today. The clubs weren't working. We had a great match, though, and Goodman is a fine golfer and a game boy." Jones did not blame the course, the gallery, the breaks, or even the format. When queried a few days later about the eighteen-hole matches, Jones replied, "A real champion should be able to play two to seventy-two holes." The response reflected his maturation. Moreover, rather than immediately getting back on board the train for Atlanta, Jones remained at Pebble Beach to watch the rest of the tournament, even serving as a referee for one of the semifinal matches.[39]

Jones's behavior in defeat endeared him to northern Californians; in fact, the Golden Gate city decided that a first-round loss to Goodman was no reason to rob its citizens of a Bobby Jones celebration. So, less than a week after his defeat, Jones, puffing a cigar and wearing a panama hat, blue blazer, and white knickers, was received in San Francisco with a parade and motorcycle police escort. He told reporters that he was "tickled to death to be here" and that he just wanted to relish the city. One evening Jones and his wife tried to slip unnoticed into the Geary Theater to take in a "burlesque melodrama" entitled "After Dark." Although they were discovered and it created a distraction, the Joneses seemed to enjoy the show.[40]

On September 12, the Jones family began its journey back east. Because they had cut through the southwest on the way to California and wanted to see as much of the country as possible, they traveled home through the northwest. The party spent time in Wyoming and at Yellowstone National Park and in Colorado Springs before arriving in Atlanta at the end of the month.

Jones closed out the 1920s in relatively quiet fashion. In mid-November, while in New York for a meeting of the USGA executive committee, he announced that he had become part-owner of the Atlanta Crackers minor league baseball club. Baseball was still the national pastime, and Jones, like Hagen, found it a pleasant distraction from the links. Some observers speculated that

Jones was looking for a permanent diversion. Following his return from California, a few stories suggested that "Bobby Jones [is] losing interest in golf" and even contemplating retirement. Jones assured fans that he was not ready to quit, saying that he would continue to compete as long as he could "walk and earn a living as a lawyer." When someone asked how much longer Jones would play, O.B. Keeler answered: "Of course, Bobby is not going to come out and say he will continue competitive play for five or ten years. He doesn't know what may happen, but if he is chosen on the American Walker Cup team in 1930, he will go to Britain and compete not only in the international match but also in the British open and amateur."[41]

At twenty-seven, Jones was young enough to at least double his major championship crowns. Yet, despite public statements to the contrary, he was indeed tired of competitive golf. It was time-consuming as well as expensive, and he had never been happy in the limelight, which by late 1929 was brighter than ever. Mary Jones had grown weary of it, too. She was jealous of her husband's time and, like him, did not enjoy having her family on national display. Jones said that his priorities were family first, vocation second, and golf third, with the game never being a life unto itself. Like his father and grandfather, Jones absolutely believed in the Victorian ideal that men should be available for their family. The record of his life, however, suggests that he was capable of rearranging his priorities, because competitive golf had always required extended absences from home. If it continued, he would become miserable. In terms of his physical condition, he could easily compete another ten years; in about every other way he had had enough.

So if things had unfolded differently at Pebble Beach, maybe he would have seriously entertained retirement; after all, a win there would have given him three consecutive U.S. Amateur championships, a nice note on which to exit the stage. But Jones could not retire on a loss; too much of his life had been given to building the greatest amateur golf career ever. Besides, after his tremendous 1926 season, the thought of winning all four national titles had crossed his mind. Jones understood that time was running out, and that he had one last opportunity. The 1930 Walker Cup matches would be played abroad, providing him an excuse to enter all four national championships. Jones determined to win as many of them as possible and then reevaluate his future in competitive golf. It proved to be a very good plan.

While Jones reflected on his first-round loss to Goodman, the nation was coming to grips with Black Tuesday, October 29, 1929, the day the stock market crashed. As Frederick Lewis Allen put it, "an old order [gave] place to new." Historians and economists now generally agree that Black Tuesday did not cause the Great Depression, as was once so widely believed; nonetheless, it was a frightening and painful signal that the country was headed into a long period of "hard times." The survival of sports businesses in the 1930s, however, illustrates that the Depression did not hit everyone so hard; in fact, many middle-to-upper-income families, who survived the initial dislocation, actually experienced a rise in their standard of living as prices for consumer goods nosedived. There is no evidence that the Depression hurt the Joneses much. Rather, R.T.'s textile mills continued to crank out denim, much of which was simply stored and then sold at a huge profit during World War II.[42]

If the Joneses were well equipped to handle "hard times," Walter Hagen had proved that he was capable of taking the kind of financial risks that led some people to jump out of windows. Fortunately for him, golf had always been a sport sustained by rich people; Hagen could line up a string of exhibitions at posh country clubs, and the well-to-do would continue to purchase the equipment he endorsed. For those reasons, Hagen, too, came through the "hard times" with minimal discomfort.

Yet 1929 was another rocky year for Hagen. It opened with his filing for divorce from Edna Straus on January 31. Hagen, the *Los Angeles Times* commented, had once again been "stymied by matrimony." Estranged from his wife since the spring of 1927, Hagen wanted to make the separation official. In his divorce suit, Hagen charged that his wife had deserted him, despite his "indulgence, kindness, and generosity." Undoubtedly, Sir Walter was concerned about potential alimony. According to his wife, Hagen had agreed to pay her $500 per month when they had separated. If he had made such a promise, he broke it, and his suit was only the first step in a long divorce process. In September of 1929, a Los Angeles judge awarded Edna Straus $9,300, essentially the monthly allowance that Hagen had failed to pay. Hagen did not appear in court to contest the decision, but his wife soon discovered that winning a legal judgment and collecting alimony were two very different things. As far as Hagen was concerned, paying one ex-wife at a time was enough.[43]

Hagen also stepped into more professional controversy that winter. This time the issue was the composition of the Ryder Cup team. He spoke out against the requirement that members be American-born. Hagen argued that it was unfair and discriminatory to some professionals, such as Tommy Armour, Macdonald Smith, Jim Barnes, Jock Hutchison, and Joe Kirkwood, all of whom were naturalized American citizens. Although he was willing to abide by the restriction one more year in order to "demonstrate sufficiently the strength of our native-born professional golfers," he wanted foreign-born players to have an opportunity to make the 1931 team.[44]

Hagen seemed to be in the minority, though. U.S. Open champion and homebred professional Johnny Farrell, for example, thought his captain "mistaken," because the foreign-born professionals "really developed the fundamentals of their games before coming to the states." The British, who were little less than mortified by Hagen's suggestion, agreed, arguing that "financial allurements" had brought their best players to the U.S. and that if Hagen's suggestion were implemented, the U.S. would be buying the Ryder Cup. Thus, the British found another way to blame Yankee materialism for their decline in world golf competition. Still, British fans made a convincing point. Most of the players Hagen was concerned about had learned their game in Great Britain, had come to the U.S. to make money, and would otherwise have uplifted the depleted British professional ranks. On the other hand, the British argument was flawed in that several of the foreign-born professionals had been a part of the 1926 U.S. team that was humiliated abroad.[45]

The PGA decided that protecting the integrity of international match play was its supreme interest. Thus, Hagen's wishes were never realized and the Ryder Cup teams would thereafter remain exclusively homebred. The 1929 team included Captain Hagen, Leo Diegel, Ed Dudley, Al Espinosa, Johnny Farrell, Johnny Golden, Gene Sarazen, Horton Smith, Joe Turnesa, and Al Watrous. The selection process assumed another controversy when Bill Mehlhorn became angry over his being dropped from the team, despite his solid performance in recent winter tournaments.

Mehlhorn did not blame Hagen, who was "one of his best friends in the profession" but was upset with the PGA, which had made the final selections.[46]

Unfortunately, Hagen's competitive season was rough as well. In California, he finished ninth in the San Diego Open, tied for sixteenth in the Los Angeles Open, and came in eighth in the Pasadena Open. He skipped February's Texas events and by early March arrived in Florida. There Hagen finished fourteenth in both the West Coast Open and the Florida State Open, although he and Leo Diegel captured Miami's International Fourball tournament. By Hagen's standards, it was not a good winter.[47]

There was certainly no reason to expect great things from him when he took the Ryder Cup team abroad in April of 1929. The team sailed aboard the *Mauretania* on the 10th, wearing splendid navy-blue, double-breasted jackets and grey trousers (picked out by Captain Hagen) and carrying team golf bags (also Hagen's idea). The U.S. Army gave Hagen permission to put a patch consisting of the official government eagle ensign crossed with golf clubs on the breast pockets of the blazers. Just before leaving New York Harbor, Hagen told reporters, I am "confident that we will win." To stay in form, the professionals drove golf balls into canvas nets which had recently been added to the *Mauretania*'s deck. Despite the Cunard line's sophisticated practice facilities and Hagen's efforts to build team spirit, the 1929 U.S. Ryder Cup team was doomed.

The team arrived in Leeds, England, on the 16th with more than a week to practice over the Moortown course. The weather was so cold that snow fell during one of the practice rounds. Still, the Americans liked the layout and maintained their hopes for a victory. On the 25th, the day before the matches got underway, an enterprising filmmaker with a new sound camera caught rival captains Hagen and George Duncan in a casual discussion. They were reportedly "overwhelmed" by the "talkie." Hagen "stammered," commenting, "The only thing I have to say is here's to a great match." The forty-five-year-old Duncan seemed even more frightened by the newfangled machine but shook Hagen's hand and replied, "I wish you luck, Walter. May the better team win." At the end of the day, a more relaxed Hagen predicted, "I shall win. I usually do and I have a fighting team."

Two days later, the British proved Hagen wrong. The matches were the closest and most exciting in the event's short history. On the first day, the sides split the foursome competition, 2 points each. Playing with Golden, Hagen won his match. The next day, however, he was pummeled 10 and 8 in his duel with Captain Duncan. That delighted the *London Observer*, because during the match Hagen had "assumed a jaunty air and on one or two occasions laughed aloud when he failed to hole a putt." Duncan had been confident that day, too. E.M. Cockell of Britain's *Golf Illustrated* reported that before his match with Hagen, Duncan said, "This guy has never beaten me in a serious match and he never will." In all, the Americans lost five of the eight singles, and Britain reclaimed the Ryder Cup by a final count of 7 points to 5. The captain's battle proved pivotal; had Hagen won, the Americans would have tied the score.

Afterward, Hagen said that the galleries had "witnessed some of the greatest golf ever played," except for his match. "The best team won," and "it's all for the good of the game." He was not "down-hearted" and looked forward to winning the trophy back two years hence. Hagen's good sportsmanship and die-hard self-confidence concealed his deep disappointment. His caddie in Britain that year was a youngster named Ernest Hargreaves. He remembered that Hagen was "complimentary about his opponent's play and humorously deprecating about his own; but he could not disguise from himself or anyone else that he [had taken] a thrashing."

Some observers criticized Hagen's decision in not using Horton Smith in the foursomes. The twenty-one-year-old Smith was America's newest golf star and one of the three Americans to win his singles match. George Greenwood surmised in *Golf Illustrated* that Hagen had played Dudley (who teamed with Sarazen for a loss) instead of Smith on the first day, because, as Hagen put it, Dudley had made the long trip, and each team member deserved a "chance to deliver a blow for his country." Cockell concluded, "In the matter of captaincy, I think Britain was better served." Others second-guessed the PGA's decision to leave Mehlhorn off the team. To all of that, Hagen simply responded, "I think I have disposed of the men at my command to the best advantage" possible.[48]

When Bob Jones heard of the demise of the U.S. Ryder Cup team, he remarked that "probably in the long run it was a good thing [for international competition] and in the open tournament to follow, the American team will be on edge, trying hard to recoup their lost prestige." That was exactly what Hagen's men hoped to do as they set out northward for Scotland in the first week of May. The British Open was to be held at Muirfield. A few observers took note of the fact that Hagen had again suffered a humiliating match-play loss, similar to the one Compston had dealt him in 1928. They wondered if Hagen might repeat history a step further and pull an encore in the British Open. Young Hargreaves recalled that Hagen sensed destiny. Immediately following his loss to Duncan, Hagen told his sixteen-year-old caddie, "I have a feeling that I am going to be lucky at Muirfield."[49]

Hagen's team had lost in the Ryder Cup, he had been embarrassed by Duncan, and critics had surfaced on both sides of the Atlantic to question his judgment and leadership. Beyond that, Hagen probably did not like the fact that his Ryder Cup team had to qualify for the British Open, inasmuch as the USGA had exempted the British team from the preliminary rounds for the 1927 U.S. Open. The Royal and Ancient Golf Association simply could not bring itself to "shatter" tradition and exempt the Americans. So, if he smiled on the outside, Hagen's inner spirit was probably as "vile" as the weather when the Open qualifying commenced. Actually, the weather was a big story that week. As Bernard Darwin described it, "Both sea and sky were grey, and there came a melancholy booming from the foghorn on the Bass Rock [as] a cold rain was coming down quite relentlessly—nothing much more unpleasant could be imagined." Hagen quietly qualified in eighteenth spot, ten strokes behind the leader, Leo Diegel.

Sir Walter continued to pose little threat after the first round of the tournament proper, finishing six strokes off the pace. But he surprised everyone the second day when he fired a record-smashing 33–34–67 and climbed into second place, two behind Diegel. As the crowd gathered around him on the last green, Hagen coolly inquired, "What's all the fuss about? The championship has just started." Darwin noted that Hagen's round was not the usual wildness followed by amazing recoveries but rather a round of "sheer perfection. It was not Hagen golf, but Bobby Jones golf."

By that point in his career, Hagen had learned how to play in all kinds of British conditions. It had been nine years since he had "cracked wide open," finishing in fifty-second place at Deal, and during the interim he discovered how to keep the ball low into the wind, recover from trouble, and win. So, when the Firth of Forth was stirred and the wind began to blow hard, Hagen was ready as few others could be. The weather was simply morbid for the last two rounds; big blackened clouds—the kind that appear to be within arm's length—hung ominously low over the fairways. Providing a nice contrast, Sir Walter appeared at the first tee wearing a "symphony in blue and brown" that included a light brown sweater vest and bright blue shirt, with plus fours and stockings to match. Unintimidated by the forbidding conditions, Hagen asked sportswriter Al Laney: "You coming with the winner? I figure about 150 will do it today. What do you think?"

Indeed, on the final day Hagen kept his balance in a gale to shoot a pair of 75s and win his fourth British Open crown. As Jones had suspected, the Americans again took their revenge, dominating the event. Farrell was runner-up, and Diegel came in third. Abe Mitchell and Percy Alliss took fourth and fifth place, but the next five spots were filled by Americans. Moreover, eight of the top ten and eleven of the top fifteen finishers were Yankees. One Scottish professional remarked, "The Americans have licked us. Tom Morris would have wept bitterly to see this." "It was a glorious win for Americans," noted E.M. Adams in *Golfers Magazine*, "but a greater accomplishment for Hagen."[50]

Hagen could not resist the opportunity to gloat a little over his spectacular title defense. "One of the things I like to do is to disappoint people [and] make them eat their words," he admitted with a smile. "In this championship I may have disappointed some folk, but you have no idea how full of joy I am at winning after the Ryder Cup match, when people put me out of the reckoning." At the trophy ceremony, Hagen pointed out that the Americans had "brought two cups to England and lost one of them, so we've got to cling to this one." He remembered that Harry Vardon had six titles and James Braid five; thus, "I am down, and I must come back again." Then, regaining a touch of diplomacy, he told the British throng that he had been "lucky" to win and that they "had been very good to me." Recalling his numerous hubbubs in Britain, Hagen concluded, "I hope I have done nothing to offend you. If so, believe me, I never intended it." After those comments, he accepted the winner's check and promptly handed it to his young caddie.[51]

The British did not like Hagen's suggestion that he might match Vardon's or Braid's records, but golf fans everywhere again admired Sir Walter's fighting heart. They agreed with Adams, who wrote: "There isn't another golfer in the world who could have gone out in the gale that blew across Muirfield and reel off two miracle rounds of 75 each." Hagen looked "more majestic and massive than ever," observed the *London Evening News*. The *Times* of London was convinced that "no reverse, however severe, can shake [his] nerve or ruffle his equanimity." P.C. Pulver called the thirty-six-year-old Hagen "the man who never is through," while Grantland Rice simply dubbed him "the Lion Tamer." *Golf Illustrated*'s George Girard revealed that "some feel that suffering under the sting of defeat, [Hagen] becomes invincible." Britain's *Golf Illustrated* offered Hagen its "heartiest congratulations," and advised fellow countrymen: "Let us in the future lull him into a comatose state. We must see to it that Hagen plays no public matches over here previous to the Championship. Or, if he does he is allowed to win."[52]

On May 12 Hagen relaxed with a day of trout fishing on Loch Leven. Then, on the 18th, he teamed up with the Prince of Wales—who had given up hunting and polo for golf—to defeat Sir Philip Sassoon and Aubrey Boomer in a private match near Sunningdale. Hagen told reporters that "the Prince telephoned me at my hotel and it certainly was a great and pleasant surprise." Afterward, Hagen "irreverently" noted that the Prince was a quick study, who played the game with his "bean." The next day news arrived that both he and Duncan had been made honorary members of the Moortown Golf Club. Hagen expressed "deep appreciation" for the honor; as he pointed out, he belonged to five American clubs, but Moortown was his first British membership.[53]

Hagen spent the following week on the Continent, flying for exhibitions from France to Germany to Austria to Hungary to Switzerland and back to France. He enjoyed himself to the fullest, specifically recalling a "beautiful little number" in Berlin. "Since I had been a free man the past several years," he wrote, "all these extracurricular activities were legal passes."

He returned to Britain by June 1 for the first of two thirty-six-hole matches with Archie Compston. Hagen lost the first match 8 and 7 at Moor Park, where Compston had humiliated him the previous year, but won the second exhibition at the Blackwell Golf Club near Birmingham. If Hagen had had his way, he would not have faced Compston either day; he was exhausted from his Continental tour. The matches had been scheduled, however, and when Hagen publicly suggested that they might be canceled, the British press instantly reacted, reminding Hagen of his offense in snubbing the 1928 Irish Open and the "tremendous responsibilities [he] bears because of his unique position in his profession." Britain's *Golf Illustrated* called Hagen's effort to avoid the matches an "unfortunate incident" and "gross discourtesy" that "put a slight on the British golf public." Hagen eventually acquiesced, although he took his time, showing up at Moor Park twenty minutes late.[55]

On June 8, the *Leviathan* brought a tired Hagen and his Claret Jug into New York Harbor. He told reporters all about his match with the Prince of Wales and, specifically, how he had helped the Prince correct his slice. "I'll bet he is hitting a great ball by now," Hagen guessed. He also announced plans to make an exhibition tour of the Pacific rim early in 1930 that would preclude defending his British Open a third consecutive year. He finished by confessing that he was "immensely pleased" with his fourth British victory. In all, Hagen seemed poised to extend his success in American events.[56]

As in 1928, though, the British Open would be the highlight of Hagen's season. He conducted an exhibition tour through Michigan and Ohio with Horton Smith prior to the U.S. Open, in which he tied for sixteenth place. He again skipped the Metropolitan and Western Opens but finished thirteenth in the Canadian Open. Late in August Hagen captured the inaugural Great Lakes Open in Charlevoix, Michigan. That tournament came at the end of a two-week fishing trip on the Georgian Bay in Ontario. For most of the summer, Hagen spent his golf energies on an extended tour with Smith. In September the pair played their way to the west coast via Canada, Idaho, and Oregon. By October 1, Hagen-Smith had compiled a record of 45–5 in exhibition play. Hagen later recalled playing eighty-two matches and personally collecting $17,000.[57]

Their tour ended early in November, when Hagen-Smith began gearing up for the PGA Championship. The PGA had followed the USGA's lead in going to the Golden State, holding its event at the Hillcrest Country Club in Los Angeles. In between practice rounds, Hagen indulged in some acting, making several golf instructional-comedy film shorts and pocketing another $3,600. Despite the diversion, Hagen performed respectably in the PGA after barely qualifying; he advanced into the semifinals, where he was knocked out for the second straight year by defending champion Leo Diegel. The event was a hit in southern California, attended by a galaxy of movie stars and other Hollywood personalities. Actress Fay Wray was even given the task of introducing the players for the semifinals. She did well, at least until she became "tongue-tied," referring to Hagen as the reigning "British Opium champion."[58]

Following the PGA, Hagen finished twenty-second in the Catalina Open and nineteenth in the Pasadena Open. On those flat notes, he closed his golf season. Yet given his age and the year's rocky beginning, Hagen could not have been too disappointed. He had proved that he could still compete with the world's best and win major championships. The "entertainer of princes [still] has the knack of coming through when least expected" and "galleries continue to follow him," observed the *Professional Golfer of America*. "Hagen is like Ruth in that he is as interesting in defeat as in victory." Moreover, Hagen was excited about his upcoming tour to Australia, New Zealand, and Japan. As Harry Vardon had done in the U.S. almost thirty years earlier, Hagen, in the twilight of his career, planned to take the good news of golf abroad and make a tidy profit in the process.[59]

Chapter 9

"Completing the Cycle":

1930

The Hagen-Kirkwood Pacific tour was not scheduled to begin until February 1, so Hagen spent most of January working on his golf instructional-comedy short, which included Leo Diegel, as well as Mack Sennett (who also directed) and actresses Marge Beebe and Jean Fay. He and Diegel were so busy with the film's production that they both missed their tee times in the Long Beach Open. As *Golfers Magazine* put it, Hagen did not "movie" fast enough to satisfy the tournament's officials. On February 1 he and Kirkwood left San Pedro, California, bound for Honolulu, then New Zealand, Australia, the Philippines, China, and Japan. Just before embarking, Hagen told reporters that he would use the unprecedented tour to sharpen his game for the summer's major events; the team planned to be back in time for the U.S. Open. As the reigning British Open champion, Hagen also hoped to make a lot of money in the South Pacific.

Things did not go that well. On February 24, after several matches in Hawaii, Hagen-Kirkwood boarded the *Arangi* for New Zealand. En route, the ship's passengers experienced a mild outbreak of small pox, which forced a three-week quarantine and the cancellation of about half of the duo's March exhibitions. Moreover, when Hagen and Kirkwood finally reached Sydney, Australia, and began their tour in earnest, they discovered that Aussies were not much inclined to purchase tickets for mere exhibitions. That was of particular concern to Kirkwood, who reportedly had a contract with Hagen guaranteeing Sir Walter $16,000 for the tour. Near the end of the trip, however, Hagen generously "tore up" his contract with Kirkwood and agreed to split the receipts fifty-fifty, so that both men "barely made expenses."[1]

But if his first grand tour of the Pacific did not pay off as hoped, it was still an enjoyable time. On March 19 the "globe-touring" professionals won two matches in Adelaide, Australia; Hagen played well and seemed to have his game in shape. Beyond his competitive successes, he enjoyed traveling through the Fiji Islands, bartering for pearls in the Philippines, hunting kangaroo in Australia, and meeting both the Prime Minister of Australia and the Emperor of Japan. On June 8, following a three-week stay in Japan, Hagen-Kirkwood gave a private exhibition for Emperor Hirohito in Tokyo at the Shinjuku Imperial Garden links. Hagen presented the Emperor with a set of golf clubs, and the Emperor responded with an engraved gold cigarette case.

Hagen fancied himself something of a golf missionary. "Golf was in its infancy in Japan at the time of our first visit," he wrote. "Our tour undoubtedly inspired many of the young professionals and amateurs to work harder at their game." In all, Sir Walter played fifty-three matches in Australia, China, and Japan and spent fifty-eight days at sea. On June 21 he and Kirkwood returned to North America aboard the *Empress of Russia*, arriving in Victoria, British Columbia, with a "carload of Japanese kimonos and other trinkets" for their friends.[2]

Two interesting things involving Hagen had occurred while he was on tour. First, by late April Americans could "see and hear" Sir Walter in "Match Play." The "great short-feature talking comedy" was billed as a "double treat" of "good, wholesome fun [and] championship golf." Second, on May 14 Hagen's lawyers brought suit against the Rochester Red Wings baseball club. Hagen had always claimed to have lost a large sum in his attempt to purchase the team. Specifically, the suit charged that the ball club had not returned to Hagen $8,500 of his down payment. The Red Wings, led by Warren Giles (whom the St. Louis Cardinals had installed as president), fought Hagen's claim, and it would take another six years to resolve the matter.[3]

The timing of Hagen's action against the Red Wings suggests that he, like so many others, had felt the "hard times" and needed to play all of his financial and legal cards. It is impossible to know exactly what Hagen's motive was in suing the ball club. He did not mention the proceeding in his autobiography (except that he lost $37,500 in the failed arrangement) and never actively involved himself in the case, opting instead to let his Rochester lawyers take care of the matter. As for his own financial situation, it is likely that Hagen was sufficiently solvent. To be sure, his Pacific tour had been economically disappointing, and by now he had probably spent the $3,500 payment for his appearance in "Match Play." Nevertheless, for the last several years Hagen's material resources had not depended on competitive earnings or even on nongolf product endorsements, which were undoubtedly still lucrative for him, but rather on the annual subsidy he received from the L.A. Young Company's sale of Walter Hagen Ultra golf equipment.

As of 1930 the Ultra line was doing very well, endorsed and played by Horton Smith, Craig Wood, and, of course, Sir Walter himself. Like most other consumer products, golf equipment had changed significantly with the rise of mass manufacturing, and the L.A. Young Company was on the cutting edge. Most notable was the development of steel shafts, uniformly produced so that each club in a set looked and felt the same. Ultra clubs boasted "high-carbon, spring steel shafts; deep-faced, powerful heads; and scientific matching and balancing." Ultra irons had more powerful "compact blades," and the new Hagen ball ensured "longer carry and absolute accuracy." Beyond that, the Ultra line included a unique concave-faced sand wedge. Although eventually outlawed by golf's authorities because it "scooped" (or double-hit) balls out of hazards, the Hagen sand wedge was the rage for several years. The Ultra line sold thousands of sets after 1928, providing Hagen a healthy income for the rest of his life.[4]

Some traditionalists, of course, disliked the modern equipment because gone forever were the days when *each* club in a golfer's bag possessed its own shaft flexibility, weighting, balance, and look. In the place of Calamity Janes, Jeanie Deans, mashies, spoons and the like, came putters, drivers, five-irons, six-irons, seven-irons, three-woods and so on. But like the "Bounding Billy," matched sets with steel shafts made the game easier, more accessible, and thus more popular. In one sense, though, the old-timers were correct; the game had changed, and the new equipment precluded much of the creative shot-making skill that golfers had to develop in the days of individualized, idiosyncratic club-design.

At any rate, the Ultra royalties helped soothe Hagen's loss of Robert Harlow as manager. By 1930 the famous Harlow-Hagen team had formally broken up, and on May 1 Harlow became the PGA's full-time Tournament Bureau Manager. The break with

Harlow is difficult to analyze, except to say that it seems the split was mutual and involved no significant hard feelings. Certainly Hagen was looking to downscale his competitive activities; also, the PGA desperately needed a full-time event coordinator, and Harlow was a natural to fill the position. Whatever the motivations, the Hagen-Harlow separation, along with other events, signaled the devolution of Hagen's competitive career.[5]

Sir Walter's seventeenth-place finish in the U.S. Open was another sign. In fact, the 1930 season did not include any flashes of Hagen brilliance comparable to his winning the British Opens in 1928 and 1929; some suggested that he had been relegated to "has-been" status, that his vision was blurring, and that he needed glasses. Hagen called such observations "bunk."[6]

Determined to come back yet again, Hagen improved to sixth place in the Canadian Open, finished fourth in the St. Paul Open, and took another sixth place at the Western Open. He made headlines in Detroit when he fired 66–67 in rounds preliminary to the Western Open. Hagen's best finish of 1930 was runner-up in the St. Louis Open (where a young "midget golfer" from Texas listed as "Bennie" Hogan withdrew). On the final day, he showed up at the first tee twenty-five minutes late, "faultlessly clad in white plus fours and shirt, and deep blue stocking and tie, [and] with the aggravating insouciance that has broken down many opponents in other golf finals." Of course, a runner-up in the St. Louis Open hardly constituted another comeback. The most visible evidence of Hagen's competitive decay was his failure even to qualify for match-play in the PGA Championship, the event which he had once owned. Still, in November he was again named captain of the 1931 Ryder Cup team.[7]

As the *St. Louis Post-Dispatch*'s coverage illustrated, while Hagen's competitive career declined, the legend of "Sir Walter" started its rise. In February of 1930, Grantland Rice wrote an article about Hagen for *Collier's* magazine entitled "Golf's Bad Boy." Rice summarized Hagen's career from Brookline in 1913 through his most recent British Open victory, touching on such episodes as Hagen's limousine locker-room at Deal in 1920, his tardiness in 1926 for both the Cunard line's farewell luncheon and the Abe Mitchell match, his gamesmanship in PGA matches, and his supposedly showing up late one morning for a "big tournament on the west coast" wearing his "dinner clothes" from the previous evening. Hagen, the story went, played the round in his formal wear, amazing everyone by shooting a 69 and leading the field. "The Haig" had been the "stormy petrel of golf, one of the most widely praised and one of the most keenly criticized competitors in any game." To some he was "one of the greatest fellows"; to others he had been "a goat-getter and a bum." Sir Walter, Rice believed, was simultaneously an "irresponsible playboy" and a "keen competitor." That dichotomy was "the foundation of Hagen's golf greatness." And so the legend of Sir Walter began to grow.[8]

Two months after Grantland Rice stirred memories of Sir Walter, the readers of *Collier's* perused another article entitled "Not My Business," which reminded sports fans that golf was not really Bobby Jones's primary concern. The piece was written by Jones, and along with Grantland Rice's "Golf's Bad Boy," it reinforced the stark contrast between the decade's two greatest golfers.

In "Not My Business," Jones advised that the average American "should not choose his sport with the same care he would use in deciding what business or profession he will devote his life [to]"; sports "should be no more than a means of obtaining diversion, recreation, and exercise." Jones did recognize the modern realities of sports as big business, however, and did not question "the right of an individual to commercialize his proficiency in sport if his happiness and well-being [would] be promoted by so doing." "If enough people [would] pay to see Walter Hagen play golf to make it profitable for him," Jones could see no difference between that and "Caruso being paid to sing or a lawyer receiving money for drafting a contract."

He understood that some people considered him a "jackass" for "refusing to grasp the bonanza of wealth" by turning professional, while others "commended" him for "maintaining the ideals of amateur sport." As for Jones, he admitted that "there was no temptation in professionalism until I had all but completed the college education which my father had determined I should have." He decided, though, that "night after night on Pullmans, round after round of golf played before thunderous crowds, and little possibility of enjoying home" did not appeal to him. Concluding that the option of professional sports was a live, legitimate one for youths in modern America and that the decision ultimately rested with the individual, Jones "chose to follow the law, at a safe distance, rather than golf as a profession."[9]

"Not My Business" offered a fascinating look into Jones's views of professional sports, showing a thoughtful athlete whose general mind-set was rooted in tradition but shaped by modern relativism. So it is easy to see the influences that two generations—his grandfather and father—had had. Jones disliked the idea of constantly performing before large crowds and cared too much about his family to travel year-round. For him, full-time professional sports was wrong. But by 1930 he was not so pious or openly judgmental of others. Professionalization and commercialization of sports was a fact; if Walter Hagen or anybody else wanted to capitalize on golf, so be it.

Aside from writing "Not My Business," Jones also took some time to give an interview to the noted biographer William E. Woodward for the *American Magazine*. Woodward's job was to "take Bobby Jones apart and see what makes him tick." He reviewed Jones's sickly childhood and extraordinary golf career. Woodward was impressed by Jones's modesty, his "tacit lowering of his own personal value." In a fit of complete candor, Jones told Woodward: "I don't know what I would have done without golf. I owe everything to it, I suppose." The confession notwithstanding, however, a few lines later Woodward hit on the old theme that Jones "plays golf much less frequently than the average business man who has golf on the brain." He reviewed how Jones rarely practiced between November and April, which Jones affirmed. "I don't like to play in the cold, and there are cold winds here in the winter. Besides, I haven't the time. Got to take care of my law business."

February 15, 1930, must have been a mild day in Atlanta, because Jones not only played at East Lake but shot 63, tying his own record for the layout. In truth, just as "Not My Business" and the Woodward interview appeared in newsstands across the country, Jones ironically began one of his busiest golf seasons ever. As Jones later confessed, "golf was my paramount concern" in the winter of 1929–1930. He worked himself into shape during the coldest days by regularly playing a unique game called "Doug." Supposedly named after its inventor, the screen actor Douglas Fairbanks Sr., the game was described as a cross between "indoor tennis and badminton." Woodward reported that Jones had swelled to 186 pounds after the holidays, but that by March he had trimmed down to 165, mostly because of vigorous "Doug" matches.[10]

A few days after his 63 at East Lake, Jones made a "last-minute decision" to enter the Savannah Open, in which he expected to receive "a tidy licking" from the professionals who had been active all winter. Actually, Jones bested most of the professionals at the Savannah Golf Club, but Horton Smith was more consistent and one shot better than the Atlantan. In a unique gesture, tournament officials presented Jones with a twelve-gauge shotgun, passing on the customary silver plate or gold watch.[11]

The Savannah Open was Jones's first official winter event since the 1927 Southern Open, and his decision to enter it underscored the seriousness with which he was approaching the 1930 season. While in Savannah, Jones announced that he would also enter the upcoming inaugural Southeastern Open at Augusta. In between those tournaments he continued to practice. In March he played a round at East Lake with Judge Kenesaw Mountain Landis, Commissioner of Organized Baseball. Aside from golf, the pair probably discussed the Atlanta Crackers as well as Jones's new role as "executive vice-president and legal counsel" for the recently-formed Atlanta Baseball Association. Jones also took a break from the links to join the Crackers at their spring training camp downstate in Douglas, Georgia. Photographs in Atlanta's *Journal* and *Constitution* showed Jones in batting practice and behind the plate warming-up pitchers. The workout must not have been too intense; in all of the photos, Jones is wearing a business suit and tie.[12]

On March 28, Jones appeared in Augusta for the Southeastern. By tournament time he had his game in shape; he destroyed Smith and everyone else, winning the event by thirteen strokes. Bobby Cruickshank, who was also in the field, told O.B. Keeler that Jones would "go to Britain and win the amateur and the open, and then he'll come back over here and win the open and the amateur. He is playing too well to be stopped this year." Sportswriters once again spoke of Jones as a "golf machine" and looked forward to his trip abroad. Rice wrote that Jones's "game now was sounder and surer than it ever was before. He is starting better equipped in every way than he ever faced a single season before." Rice concluded that there was "at least a first class chance that this will be the best year he has ever had, and that will mean the best year any individual golfer ever had."[13]

On April 21, the Joneses were bid farewell at a banquet organized by members of East Lake and Augusta country clubs. After saying goodbye, Atlantans presented Jones with a gold chain and

four-leaf clover. The evening came to a climax when Augusta officials, improving on Savannah's shotgun, moved some palms to re-
veal an "imposing grandfather-clock," Jones's trophy for winning
their open three weeks earlier. "Blushing modestly," Jones spoke a
few words of gratitude and left three days later for New York City
with his wife and the ever-present Keeler.

Following a brief stay in Washington, DC, the Joneses arrived
in New York on April 28 to make final preparations for their journey aboard the *Mauretania*. It was Mary Jones's first trip to Europe with her husband, and the couple planned to visit the
Continent. Accompanying the golfers was Douglas Fairbanks Sr.,
who simply "had" to go and watch Jones play. A handful of well-
wishers saw the party off on the 30th; so while Walter Hagen barnstormed through the South Pacific, Bob Jones Jr., set sail for
England in quest of his first British Amateur Championship.[14]

The *Mauretania* steamed to Southhampton on May 6, and from
there the Joneses "motored" into London. The first official event
Jones faced was the Walker Cup. Besides Captain Jones, the squad
included George Von Elm, Dr. O.F. Willing, Francis Ouimet,
Harrison Johnston, and newcomers Donald Moe and George Voigt.
Jones believed that "England has got the strongest team she has
ever put out against us for the trophy." Nonetheless, the captain
had been easy on his men prior to sailing, encouraging them not to
"over-golf" themselves with too much practice. The Americans had
about ten days to prepare for the international competition, and
team members played warm-up rounds at Sunningdale and on-site
at Royal St. George's club in Sandwich.

On May 8, Jones played in a foursome at Sunningdale with the
Prince of Wales. Four days later he turned in a 75 at Sandwich and
learned that he had drawn a bye into the second round of the
British Amateur. On the 14th news arrived from home that Jones
had been elected to the board of directors of the First National
Bank of Atlanta. Now, the *New York Times* declared, it is Bobby
Jones, "lawyer-banker-golfer."[15]

By the start of the Walker Cup matches, the Americans were
in good form, and so were the conditions. "The Americans always

bring their own weather with them for this match," complained Bernard Darwin of the *London Times*. "However much we may pray, patriotically, for an icy wind, the balmiest and lightest of zephyrs arrive on the morning of the match." With the Prince of Wales looking on, the U.S. side took three of the four foursome matches. Jones-Willing easily won theirs. The Atlantan was "outdone" in only one respect, and that by the Prince, whose "plus four suit of chocolate, red, and beige checks" made Jones's "blue sweater and stockings" look "mid-Victorian."

The U.S. finished off the British the next day, winning seven of eight singles matches to retain the cup 10–2. Jones performed like a "well-oiled machine," trouncing rival captain Roger Wethered 9 and 8. Darwin summed it up best, admitting that the Americans "were just too good for us. At the end of the day there was nothing left to do but acknowledge the superiority of the victors and drink to the health of Miss Fishwick." (On the same day, Britain's Dianna Fishwick defeated Glenna Collett for the women's championship.) Yet Darwin also believed that there was "life in the old dog [Britain]," and that "it by no means follows that either our amateur or open championships will be won this summer by Americans."[16]

The British Amateur was scheduled to begin on Monday, May 26 at St. Andrews. During the intervening week, Jones won the *Golf Illustrated* Gold Vase tournament at Sunningdale and was a guest at Sir Philip Sassoon's Trent Park estate, which included a private nine-hole layout. Jones played an informal match there with Sir Philip, the Prince of Wales, and the Duke of York. On Saturday, Jones practiced at St. Andrews, but Sunday golf was still illegal in the "old gray city," so on the 25th he drove sixty miles to Gleneagles for another preliminary round.[17]

It was Jones's third attempt at the British Amateur title; in 1921 he was eliminated in the fourth round, and in 1926 he was defeated in the quarterfinals. The event was especially difficult to win because the champion had to survive nine matches, eight of them at eighteen holes. It was also the only major event that Jones had not yet won, and he was more determined than ever.

He carefully made his way through the early rounds. Following his bye in the first, he slipped past his second and third round opponents. Then Cyril Tolley, "the greatest personality in British golf," battled Jones to nineteen holes in the fourth round. "A breathless crowd of 10,000" watched Jones lay Tolley a perfect stymie to win the match. When the "epic struggle" was finished, Jones confessed,

"I have been very lucky. The breaks were mine." Indeed, Jones had been extraordinarily fortunate in his clash with Tolley. On three holes he had shot errantly and hit a spectator, keeping his ball from landing in desperate straits. It seemed as though Jones was destined to win the British Amateur. As Sir James Lieshman, a Scottish knight and golf enthusiast, put it: "The stars are with Jones in this tournament. His luck is fixed as the orbit of a planet. He cannot be beaten here."[18]

After an easy victory in the fifth round, Jones eliminated reigning U.S. Amateur Champion Harrison Johnston 1 up by sinking an eight-foot putt on the home hole. "I never felt more thankful in my life than when that putt dropped into the cup," said Jones. He had played well, but three of his five matches had taxed him emotionally. George Greenwood, who covered the Johnston match for the *Daily Telegraph*, noticed that Jones looked "shaken [and] a little gray about the cheeks as he stepped to the eighteenth tee. He wiped the corners of his mouth with his handkerchief, pulled down his cap well over his forehead—but there was no sign of nervousness in his drive."

The next day, Jones beat Englishman Eric Fiddian 4 and 3 in the seventh round and George Voigt 1 up in the semifinals. Guy Campbell thought that Fiddian was just "too overawed by the occasion to play great golf." Voigt, on the other hand, gave Jones all that he could handle. In fact, Jones was 2 down before storming back to win 14, halve 15, win 16, and halve 17 with a curling twelve-foot putt. Jones, beginning to sense his fate, believed that "the putt was going to go in no matter how I hit it." Voigt needed a six-footer on the home hole to send the match to extra holes; he missed, and Jones escaped into the thirty-six-hole championship round, where he would face British favorite Roger Wethered. Jones later wrote that he fell behind Voigt early in the match because he was a bit tipsy from the glass of sherry he had consumed during the lunch break. He had "never before touched a drop of alcohol before playing a tournament round" but thought that the "experiment might steady my nerves, quiet the butterflies, or rid me of some of that tired feeling." In the end, the sherry almost rid him of the British Amateur Championship.[19]

As a public course, St. Andrews did not charge admission to the matches that week, including the final. So an estimated 20,000 turned out to see if Jones could duplicate the feat of "Old Man" Travis and Jess Sweetser and become only the third American to win the British Amateur Championship. Conditions remained pleasant for the final day. The competitors battled to a draw over the first nine, but then Jones grabbed a 4-up lead by the lunch break. Wethered was putting poorly, and by the turn in the afternoon, the Atlantan had extended his lead to five holes. Much more relaxed in the thirty-six-hole format, Jones never let up and closed out the match 7 and 6. Six policemen ushered the champion through the mass of humanity to the clubhouse, where Mary Jones was waiting, while the brass band which had assembled at the 14th green to meet the champion was trampled and dispersed, so that not one note was played.[20]

Thus on May 31, 1930, Jones won his tenth national championship and made history; he became the only golfer ever to win all four national titles. After accepting the trophy, Jones once again said that he had been "lucky" to win. "I never have been happier to get any cup," he added, "and I never worked so hard, nor suffered so much either." Emotionally and physically exhausted, Jones later told reporters that he needed "extensive resting and sleeping" and planned to get them on the Continent with his wife. When asked about the British Open, he replied that he planned to do his best but added, "The way I feel right now, nothing else matters much."[21]

Meanwhile, Jones fans lauded their hero. Big Bob Jones, who happened to be baby-sitting little Clara Malone and Bob III in Atlanta, simply said: "I am mighty happy and mighty proud of my boy." The Georgia Bar Association immediately cabled its congratulations to Jones. Walter Hagen did the same from Tokyo, saying that he was "highly elated that Bobby finally crashed through and rounded out a collection of crowns such as no other golfer has ever acquired."[22]

Of course, admirers could not refrain from drawing comparisons between Jones's embarrassing St. Andrews debut in 1921 and his recent victory. An editorial entitled "More Than a Golfer" appeared in the New York Times. It argued that Jones, in evolving from a "petulant, irascible, passionate, explosive" youth to a "model of sportsmanship, poise, and self-control," represented a "splendid example of self-mastery." In addition, Jones had "kept his amateur status without taint or suspicion." He was "as much loved as a man as he [was] admired and wondered at as a golfer," because "whether in victory or defeat, he bears himself with smiling modesty and is regarded on every links of Great Britain not only a

competitor but a gentleman and a friend." That, the editorial concluded, explained why he had "become an international figure."[23]

The Joneses had about two weeks before the British Open commenced at Hoylake, England. The Atlantan was in an enviable position. In one respect the pressure was off; even if he failed to win
the Open, his victory in the Amateur made the trip a success. "A
big load had been lifted off my chest," Jones later wrote. So he and
Mary Jones enjoyed their stay on the Continent, mostly in Paris.
He played a few exhibitions to keep his timing sharp, but the order
of the journey really was "extensive resting and sleeping."[24]

By Wednesday, June 11, Bob and Mary Jones were at Hoylake.
It rained that morning, but Jones still practiced at the Royal
Liverpool links, located literally on the shores of the Irish Sea. He
spent about an hour the next day on the driving range, hitting
both woods and irons that had troubled him the day before. His
session was interrupted by the legendary British professional J.H.
Taylor, who "begged" a ball from Jones's supply and then asked
the Atlantan to autograph it for him. On Saturday the press announced that for the first time, O.B. Keeler would provide fifteen-
minute transatlantic radio summaries of the Open, starting at 6:45
each evening.

Qualifying began on Monday, June 16, and the *New York Times*
declared that "the tournament once more is a case of 'Bobby Jones
against the field.'" People were thus surprised when Jones qualified nine strokes behind the medalist, Archie Compston. Jones
was also caught off guard by his twentieth-place finish; he considered Tuesday's 77 to be his worst ever in Great Britain. The circumstances of the event partially explain Jones's high score. His
gallery was so large and raucous that he had to be accompanied
throughout the day by an armed policeman. To be sure, Jones's
galleries had always been among the biggest, but in the aftermath
of his Amateur victory, they were even larger and more trouble-
some. An unfortunate incident at the eighth green proved how
uncontrollable the crowd was. Just as Jones was about to putt, a
few members of the gallery trounced across the putting surface,
prompting the otherwise silent Atlantan to yell: "Please do not
walk across the green," or something to that effect. He missed the
twenty-footer and settled for a bogey. If not impressively, Jones
had nonetheless qualified, and as Bernard Darwin pointed out, his
77 "is not a fact upon which any sensible patriot would base his
hopes."

The first round of the tournament proper was played on Wednesday. It was almost like two days in one, however, because in the morning the weather remained "still, grey, and sultry, almost too still and hot for golf," then in the afternoon thunderstorms rolled in off the Irish Sea. In another stroke of luck, Jones was scheduled to play his round in the morning. Taking advantage of the conditions, he grabbed the lead with a 70. The gallery was still pesky; on several occasions Jones had to stop his take-away and calmly readdress his ball because spectators clicked their cameras during his swing.

The tee times were reversed for the second day, but that mattered little because the weather cooperated again. Still, Jones struggled to a 72. If Calamity Jane had not been on fire that day, he would have fallen behind, but he dropped some lengthy putts and maintained a one-stroke lead. "It was one of the hardest rounds I ever had to play," Jones told reporters, "and as I always have one such in a tournament, I hope it is over and done with."

So despite his lack of form and innumerable distractions, Jones was in excellent position on the final day to capture his third British Open. History was not in his favor; no one had won both British events in the same season since John Ball in 1890. Moreover, because of his erratic play of late, Jones was not confident when he teed up on Friday morning. The weather was not encouraging either; the gray sky occasionally emitted raindrops, lingering reminders of the previous night's storms. Jones carded a 74 in the morning, only good enough for second place. He found himself one shot behind Archie Compston, who, "playing like a frenzied giant," came from five shots behind, scorching Hoylake and electrifying the crowd.

In the afternoon, though, the tall Welshman shriveled. Compston followed his white-hot 68 with a chilling 82, a "pathetic come-down," wrote Darwin, "after his heroic work in the morning." Jones remained steady, posting a 75 to finish six strokes ahead of Compston. American professional Mac Smith shot 71, the lowest final round, but still finished in second place. Jones had won— or one might say Compston had lost. Either way, the Atlantan had collected both of Britain's national championships and could sail back to the U.S. in the best competitive shape of any golfer ever.[25]

Jones remained in the British Isles for another week before heading home on the 27th aboard the *Europa*. He spent the last days in England playing several charity matches and trying to recuperate from winning back-to-back titles. George Greenwood had observed that moments before accepting the trophy at Hoylake, the champion "flopped in a chair with his face as grey as stone and cheeks fallen in. I never saw a man closer to the point of collapse than was 'Bobby' Jones." Later that evening, Jones told the British press that he was so exhausted from the stress and strain that he doubted he would compete in Britain ever again.[26]

Meanwhile, the British scrambled to put Jones's feat in perspective. *Golf Monthly* decided that Jones's victory was more impressive than Ball's because in 1890 the Open was played at only thirty-six holes. "Bobby Jones," thought Bernard Darwin, "has no more records yet to conquer. He can retire with a quiet mind." An editorial in the *Times* of London declared Jones "the greatest of all living golfers," concluding "there seems to be no reason why he should not crown his career by doing in America what he has done here and thus win four of the biggest events of the game in the same season."

Back home, members of the U.S. House of Representatives listened as Georgia Congressman Robert Ramspeck proclaimed that "Bobby Jones is admired most and is loved most for his modesty and saneness and the manner in which he wears his fame." Walter Hagen, while literally stepping off the *Empress of Russia* in Victoria, British Columbia, again called Jones "the greatest golfer in the world," adding that no professional had a chance against him in a four-day medal test. When Big Bob Jones heard of his son's achievement, he said, "Of course, we are very happy and proud. But we got a bigger kick out of the amateur."[27]

As for the champion, he was so tired the day he left London that he forgot his golf clubs in his hotel room. Despite a bellboy's valiant efforts, the clubs did not catch up with Jones before the *Europa* set sail, so they were immediately placed on the *Aquitania,* which brought them to New York soon after Jones's arrival on July 2. Jones was reportedly nervous about his New York reception; it was the sort of occasion that had always made him apprehensive, particularly so in 1930 because it was to be broadcast nationally on NBC radio.

When the *Europa* finally pulled into New York Harbor, Jones, clad in a navy-blue suit and carrying a motion-picture camera, was greeted by several hundred Atlantans and thousands of New Yorkers. Among the Atlanta contingent were R.T., Big Bob, and Clara Jones. A band played "The Star-Spangled Banner," and firecrackers exploded when Jones disembarked and entered a waiting convertible. He and Mary Jones were paraded through a "ticker-tape blizzard" down Broadway to City Hall, where less than two weeks earlier Admiral Richard E. Byrd had been celebrated for "bringing two poles together." Jones was told that his achievement ranked with Byrd's; for ninety minutes Mayor Jimmy Walker cackled into an NBC radio microphone, saying things like, "Here you are, the greatest golfer in the world, being introduced by the worst one," while the crowd yelled "Attaboy Jimmy." Walker summed up the public's feeling when he said that the British titles would "never [again] be won by a finer sportsman or gentleman." Jones replied that he "had never experienced anything like this before," and after admitting that he really did not know what to say, concluded, "I have never been so impressed." That evening Jones and 400 of his admirers attended a banquet in his honor at the Hotel Vanderbilt.[28]

The New York reception may have been more difficult for Jones than either the British Amateur or Open. Nonetheless, he had little time to recover, because the next afternoon he and his parents boarded the Broadway Limited for Chicago, and then Minneapolis, Minnesota, site of the U.S. Open. A prominent Atlantan, Asa Candler of the burgeoning Coca-Cola empire, offered to fly Jones to Minneapolis, but the golfer passed, figuring that he had had enough adventure for one week. Mary Jones, on the other hand, hurried south to rescue her parents from Clara Malone and Bob III. Before Bob Jones left New York, he told reporters that despite what he had said in Britain about never returning to compete, he did not have any plans to retire from golf. When asked if he would quit after winning the summer's U.S. championships and "completing the cycle," Jones replied, "Well, I haven't won either one of them yet, nor have I given any thought to either one." Changing the subject, Jones said that he was pleased to hear that his Crackers had improved to fourth place while he was out of the country, joking that he had "cabled advice from time to time" to the club's manager. As for his golf abroad, it was "ragged," and he had been "lucky all the way through."[29]

On Saturday morning, July 5, a ragged, lucky, but somewhat rested Jones arrived in the Twin Cities. Declaring, "I'm feeling fit," he joined Walter Hagen, who had just motored in from Detroit, to play his first round at the Interlachen Golf Club. The *St. Paul Pioneer-Press* reported that when Jones entered the clubhouse, he immediately looked to secure a locker. He inquired about the matter to Interlachen's professional, Willie Kidd, who curtly responded, "What's the name, please?" The Atlantan simply answered, "The name's Jones." According to the local paper, Kidd "stammered his apologies" and assigned the world's most famous golfer a locker. But if Willie Kidd did not recognize Jones, seventeen-year-old Donovan Dale did. A few days earlier the local youth's name had been drawn from a hat, making him Jones's caddie for the U.S. Open. Apparently quite knowledgeable about his hero, Dale assured reporters after the first practice round 72 that Jones was not "even trying" because he "doesn't want to get too hot now. It's too early."

Actually, Jones appeared to be hitting his stride. On Monday he shot 70, the lowest round of the day and a new course record. Hagen, using a full set of steel-shafted clubs for the first time in his career, looked good that day too; his blistering 32 set a record for the front nine, although he followed it with 40. After his round, Jones chatted with Frank B. Kellogg, former U.S. Secretary of State. Kellogg wished Jones "all the luck in the world" for the coming championship, but when queried by reporters if he wanted Jones to win, Kellogg hesitated before responding, "Well, Jimmy Johnston [of St. Paul] is another fine boy." A few feet away, young Dale was receiving more attention than he may have bargained for. Besieged by the press, Dale said that Jones was "a swell guy" but that "he only spoke to me twice" to ask "Where's the water? What's your name?" Dale's man undoubtedly needed the water more than once that day; aside from Jones, the biggest story that week was the weather, which was typical in July for the "Land of 10,000 Lakes," hot and extremely humid.

Conditions were so intolerable on Tuesday that neither Jones nor Hagen practiced much. Both stars also limited their workouts on Wednesday when the temperature climbed over one hundred degrees; Jones played only nine holes that day, commenting, "I never felt such heat since I was born." The Atlantan, along with Johnston, spent the morning fishing on Lake Minnetonka.

The other item of note on Wednesday was Hagen's wardrobe. He appeared at the first tee wearing "white flannel trousers, black and white leather golf shoes, a black belt, a white silk shirt, and a white four-in-hand tie with small dots." For the most part, it was one of Sir Walter's favorite combinations. The primary difference, though, was his choice of "slacks" over knickers, or plus-fours, which had been the fashion since the Great War and which many golfers, including Jones, still wore. Always the trendsetter, Hagen signaled another change in the golf subculture. A few of the younger entrants were even sporting "open-necked polo shirts" with their "long breeches." As for his golf, many thought that Hagen had the best chance of anyone to stop the "Atlanta golf machine," who, dopesters agreed, would have to improve upon his Hoylake performance to win at Interlachen.

The country's ever-developing media were certainly determined to improve upon their Hoylake showing. Not only would NBC radio again carry O.B. Keeler for a fifteen-minute summary each evening, but the Columbia Broadcasting System planned to break new ground on Saturday with a live broadcast from 6 P.M. to 8 P.M. Columbia selected Ted Husing to be its roving reporter; he would cover the leaders, wearing a backpack that included "a portable thirty-pound transmitting apparatus," while his "caddie" would follow with an antenna. U.S. Open golf coverage had come a long way since Ouimet fired the "shots heard 'round the world" at Brookline in 1913.[30]

On Thursday, July 10, the tournament began. There were no surprises the first day. Mac Smith and Tommy Armour took the lead with 70s; Jones came next at 71, and Hagen was in a group at 72. Caddie Dale, who by then had contracted for an Associated Press column syndicated under his name, wrote, "We started pretty well on Thursday—I mean Bobby Jones did." Dale claimed that his man's only weakness was putting. Because of the heat, the round was an ordeal for everyone. One reporter noted that when he finished his round, Jones looked as though he "had been dipped in one of the ponds on the course." Chick Evans nearly quit because of dizziness, and a Red Cross doctor treated ten spectators for heat prostration. Hagen was so bothered by the conditions that he pledged to wear a "huge straw hat" the next day; Grantland Rice, who began referring to the tournament in his columns as "Dante's Inferno," wrote that "the gallery of 10,000 was in casual water from start to finish." Still, the fact that 10,000 turned out in such weather (a record number for the first day of a U.S. Open) was a testament to Jones's drawing power. The *St. Paul Pioneer-Press* proudly reported that cars from Montana, Nebraska, the Dakotas, Wisconsin, and Illinois, filled the club's parking lots.[31]

The mercury slipped into the low nineties on Friday, so the weather was not such an issue in the second round. Horton Smith's

70 dominated the headlines and put him in the lead, two shots ahead of Jones, who posted a 73. Hagen, meanwhile, dropped into ninth place with a 75. The most interesting thing about Jones's round and, as it turned out, the most discussed of the event, was his second shot to the par-5 ninth. The hole was reachable in two but required a competitor to hit his second shot some 200 yards over a pond. Jones hit his drive in good position and decided to go for the green. During his take-away, however, he was distracted by a little girl moving in his peripheral vision. He followed through with the stroke anyway, half-topping the ball so that it knuckled along the surface of the pond. About forty yards from land the ball skipped once and then twice along the water, deflecting up onto the fairway in front of the green. Jones chipped to the hole and dropped his putt, scoring a birdie and finishing two shots behind Smith rather than four or five.

That evening most sportswriters made some reference to the pond's lily pads. Many observers believed that the plants had kept Jones's ball from submerging. Hagen, no mean expert on such freakish strokes, told Grantland Rice: "He never topped the shot, or it would never have crossed the water. He caught it with an overspin, half smothered, and when you do that, water is the same as concrete or rubber. It wasn't as bad as the gallery thought it was. But it wasn't the type of shot that Bobby usually plays." In his column, caddie Dale said that the shot reminded him of "skipping a rock down the creek." Jones used the same metaphor in *Golf Is My Game*, describing the shot as "a considerable stroke of luck" and claiming that "no lily pad was involved." When asked about the lily pad break years later, Jones called it "poppycock," adding, "I never like to spoil a good story, but I don't remember seeing any lily pads on that pond." Nonetheless, the "Lily Pad Shot" would become possibly the most famous stroke of his season.[32]

Saturday, July 12, was another hot day. Jones's morning round matched the conditions; he blistered the layout with a 68 to grab a five-shot lead. The mark was a personal best for the event, and he did it in spite of making bogeys on the final two holes. No one could keep up with him, especially Hagen, who three-putted the ninth green from four feet while blowing up to a 76–80–303.

Jones stumbled in the final round, too, even encountering some controversy on the monstrous 262-yard par-3 17th hole. He began by badly slicing his tee shot with a crosswind, and his ball crashed into some trees to the right of the green before dropping into a marsh. Literally hundreds of spectators joined Jones in a search, but no one found the ball, which had likely been trampled under foot. USGA Secretary Prescott S. Bush was following Jones and ruled that he should take a one-stroke penalty and drop another ball in the fairway. Jones did that, took three more strokes to get down, and finished with his third double-bogey five of the afternoon.

The errors opened the door for the surging Mac Smith, and Jones knew that he needed a strong finish. He maintained his composure on the final hole, hitting the green in regulation but leaving his ball some forty feet from the cup. Jones later wrote that he was "quivering in every muscle" as he set up over his ball. Calamity Jane was steady, though; he drained his birdie putt and again extinguished Smith's hopes of a comeback. Jones's final round 75 gave him a 287 total, two shots better than Smith, sixteen better than Hagen, and only one more than Chick Evans's Open record, set at Minikhada in 1916.[33]

No one said much that evening, but later some suggested that Jones's lost ball on the 17th should have brought a two-stroke penalty and that Secretary Bush had been too easy on him. Bush had deferred to a local rule that defined the swampy marsh as "a parallel water hazard." Had Jones triple-bogeyed, the pressure on 18 would have been even greater and things might have turned out differently. On the other hand, Jones might just as easily have gotten down in two from the fairway instead of three and still taken a five. Winning by two strokes did a lot to muffle the criticism of Bush's ruling; in the end, one stroke did not seem to matter much. Still, it was the sort of incident that lent some credibility to the occasional charges that Jones was pampered, and even favored by golf's authorities.

Few in the 14,000-person gallery contemplated the difference between USGA and local rules and its potential effect on the outcome of the tournament. Some may have felt sorry for old Mac Smith, who in 1910 had lost the title in a play-off, but the moment that Calamity Jane dealt the final blow, cheers, hats, and all sorts of other things went into the air. Thousands of fans congregated near the clubhouse for the trophy presentation to hear USGA President Findlay Douglas introduce Jones as "the man who is being watched by the whole world." Jones gave one of his "characteristic" little speeches, thanking everyone and concluding, "I was just a little lucky, that's all." Donovan Dale, in his last installment for the AP, wrote, "Right now I'll predict that he wins the National Amateur this year." As usual, Grantland Rice summed it up best: "Last Stop—Merion."[34]

Within hours of accepting the trophy, Jones, his parents, and Keeler were on a train bound for Atlanta, where the temperature was 103°. Mary, Clara Malone, and Bob Jones III had listened to the radio coverage of the tournament and were anxious to greet the champion. Despite the oppressive heat, other Atlantans were determined to give their hero a proper welcome, too. Some 20,000 had turned out to see him return from his 1926 "Double"; 60,000 showed up to honor Charles Lindbergh the following year, and in 1928 the Georgia Tech football team was greeted by 75,000 screaming southerners after returning Rose Bowl champions. The *Atlanta Constitution* predicted that all of those welcomes would "pale into insignificance" next to Jones's reception on Monday morning.

Organizers decided that it was not such a good idea to have Jones enter the city as usual. Instead, he would get off his special train car near Chattahoochee, a few miles north of Atlanta, and motor to the starting point of the parade. Each step of the way Jones would be escorted by a fleet of small aircraft with pilots waving in Lindbergh style at the throngs below. The entire Jones family was to be paraded down Peachtree, Whitehall, and Mitchell Streets to City Hall. Preceding them would be no less than twenty various groups, including the 122nd Infantry, the Chamber of Commerce, a motorcycle police escort, the Georgia Tech alumni, the Woman's Club, the American Legion, the Crackers, the Boy Scouts, and caddies with signs reading "Welcome Home Mr. Bobby. You Sho' Brought Back the Bacon."[35]

Things went remarkably well, and it really was the Bobby Jones parade to end all Bobby Jones parades. Armistice Day, wrote one experienced reporter, was the only other celebration even comparable. The *Constitution* was right; an estimated 125,000 (about half of the city's population) lined the parade route, cheering their "Bobby," who sat on the rollback top of his chauffeured convertible and smiled back at them. The confetti was so thick that it appeared to be "snowing along Peachtree Street." At City Hall,

Mayor I.N. Ragsdale assured Atlantans that the welcome was "greater than [in] New York." Jones confirmed that observation, accepted a gold key to the city, and told his fellow citizens, "This is the proudest moment in my life [and] I shall never forget it." In complete honesty, Jones added: "I am always a little backward about expressing myself. If I had known of this celebration when I came back to New York, I might have cut out going to Minnesota and slipped back home unnoticed." Those who could hear him cheered all the louder, almost feeding upon his bashful modesty, and those who could not hear him mindlessly cheered along any- way. "I just want to say you don't think any more of me than I do of you," Jones concluded. Then he, Big Bob, and R.T. Jones posed for a three-generation photograph. In a kind of postlude, all of the bands on hand joined in playing the "Star-Spangled Banner" while the crowd slowly dispersed in mid-afternoon.

Jones was certainly happy to be home. He had not been in his house on Northside Drive since the last week of April, nearly three months earlier. Jones was intentionally vague about his plans for the immediate future, but it was reported that he escaped to the hills of North Carolina for a vacation with his wife and children. Jones did say that the golf clubs would be ignored for a while; nevertheless, he played his first round after the U.S. Open the following Saturday, and through the rest of July and August, Jones, along with his father and friends, played regular practice rounds at East Lake; Sapeolo Island, South Carolina; and the Highland Coun- try Club in North Carolina.

Try as he might to focus on law, his family, the First National Bank of Atlanta, or even the Crackers, Jones had a hard time find- ing a diversion from golf. Although not a particularly religious man, he often spoke of fate, purpose, and design. By then his beliefs were almost deterministic; Jones seemed to feel that it was his destiny to win at Merion in 1930, just as it had been his fate to lose there in 1916. All of that seemed to be reaffirmed in the months before Merion, when on three occasions Jones literally brushed close to death. In the fall of 1929, during a practice round at East Lake, a violent thunderstorm erupted; lightning struck the course as Jones's group scrambled to safety. A bolt hit the clubhouse chim- ney, blasting rocks over 300 yards, some of which showered down on Jones, ripping his shirt and barely missing his head. Then, dur- ing the trip between Minneapolis and Chicago following the U.S. Open, Jones's train narrowly avoided a serious accident. Finally,

With three of the season's major titles to his name, Jones poses with his
friend and ever-present companion, O.B. Keeler, in the summer of 1930.
Courtesy: Sidney L. Matthew Collection

just weeks before the U.S. Amateur, while Jones was walking in
downtown Atlanta, a car ran off the street and crashed into a building within feet of him. Not surprisingly, Jones traveled to Merion
with a purpose.[36]

Yet Jones's entire career, beyond his "near-death" experiences,
explains his sense of mission in the fall of 1930: "Going public" at
Merion in 1916, winning his first U.S. Amateur title there in 1924,
and returning to Merion with an opportunity to make history in
1930; debuting in 1921 in humiliating fashion at St. Andrews, the
sport's Mecca, before winning the British Open there in 1927,
and going on to capture his only British Amateur title there in
1930; winning no national tournaments for seven years and then
amassing twelve in eight seasons; beginning his career with the
image of a spoiled, cocky, temperamental child and ending it with
an image of a dutiful, modest, controlled gentleman. Clearly, it

would be fitting for Jones to win at Merion and "complete the cycle" in 1930. He had been completing cycles all of his golf life.

So, almost as a pilgrim, Jones left for the Merion Cricket Club on Monday, September 16, while still recovering from what doctors considered a mild attack of appendicitis the day before. Jones rested on the train as it carried him first to Washington and then to Philadelphia. He stopped long enough in the nation's capital to play a benefit match on Tuesday and to visit the White House, where he met the unfortunate President Herbert Hoover, who undoubtedly wished Jones better luck than his own.[37]

By Wednesday afternoon, Jones was at Merion. That evening all across the country sportswriters began their coverage something like this: "Fourteen years ago this month, a clear-eyed, tousle-haired school boy with a soft drawling voice that left no doubt as to what section of the country he was native, arrived in the city of Brotherly Love and boldly inquired the locality of the Merion Cricket Club. . . ." Grantland Rice entitled his article in the *American Golfer* "From Merion to Merion," recalling how he and Jones had eaten breakfast together before the famous Jones-Byers club-throwing contest.[38]

Jones was not the only one who sensed destiny in the breeze at Merion. His every stroke was analyzed that week as he made the final adjustments in his game. The headlines were generally like that on Thursday, "Jones Turns in 73," or, on Friday, "Jones Cards a 78." It was all Jones, Jones, Jones. The spotlight had never been brighter or the hopes and expectations to win higher. Maybe that was the reason Mary Jones did not accompany her husband on the final leg of his golf journey. At any rate, it was appropriate that Jones could look instead to his father, who back in 1914, on the 14th green at East Lake, had hugged his excited Little Bob when he shot his first 80. And besides his father, Jones could always turn to O.B. Keeler for encouragement and support. To get some semblance of peace, the Atlantan traveled to South Jersey on Friday for a practice round at Pine Valley (where he had given an exhibition following the 1916 Amateur) and then took in a ball game, watching the St. Louis Cardinals beat the Phillies at the Baker Bowl in Philadelphia.[39]

On Monday and Tuesday, Jones won the qualifying medal for the fifth time and impressively tied the tournament record with a 69–73. Even Mother Nature showed up beautifully, and the conditions brought out "mighty galleries." The *Philadelphia Inquirer*

put Monday's at 5,000 and Tuesday's at 10,000, where the estimates hovered until championship Saturday. Tuesday's crowd
seemed to get to Jones, who had to be escorted over the course all
week by a Marine guard. Philadelphians learned, according to Stan
Baumgartner, that "Bobby Jones is human after all! He breathes,
he smiles, he frowns, and he perspires." At one point in his round
he also "glared" toward someone in the gallery who clapped at the
wrong time. To Baumgartner and most other observers, though,
such displays were understandable.

Despite playing somewhat inconsistently on Wednesday, Jones
crushed both Ross Somerville, the reigning Canadian Amateur
champion, and Fred Hoblitzel over eighteen holes. Since his loss
to Goodman at Pebble Beach a year earlier, Jones had won nine
straight eighteen-hole matches. The next day he beat Fay Coleman
6 and 5 in his first thirty-six-hole test, and in Friday's semifinal
Jones faced his old friend and competitor Jess Sweetser. It was not
much of a match; Jones trounced him 9 and 8. Meanwhile, in the
other semifinal Gene Homans eliminated nineteen-year-old Charlie
Seaver (father of the future baseball Hall of Famer Tom Seaver).

An estimated 18,000 turned out on Saturday, September 27,
in anticipation of witnessing golf history. They were not disappointed. "There was never a time that Jones was not in command
of the situation," Perry Lewis wrote. The Atlantan won the first
hole and never trailed, going 7 up by the lunch break and eventually knocking out Homans 8 and 7. Within minutes, telegrams from
around the country began pouring in, including one from his asso-
ciates at the First National Bank and another from R.T., sending
his grandson the "entire family's sincere congratulations."

Jones had done it. He had finished what one sportswriter called
the "impregnable quadrilateral." Later, of course, the feat would
be universally known as the "Grand Slam," but few journalists actually used that term in the fall of 1930; most did not know what
to call it, and some wrote simply that Jones "completed the cycle."
Whatever it was called, Jones had become the first (and only) golfer
to win four major championships in one season. Moreover, his
total of thirteen major crowns surpassed everyone else's (unless
one counted Hagen's Western titles as "majors"). Yet, it was all
somewhat anticlimactic. The victories seemed to come easily; he
was never really pressed, the final was a blowout, and in the end
he did seem predestined to win. The *Philadelphia Inquirer* noted
that even Atlantans were "calm" about the victory and, per Jones's

request, made no special fuss when he returned home the follow-ing week.[40]

The only question left was whether Jones was destined to win more titles or to retire. While accepting the trophy, he had said that he expected to continue to play golf, although he could not predict when or where and added that he might play one more year and then quit. In the locker room minutes later, however, Jones told Jimmy Johnston that he was "through" because "the strain of golf is wrecking my health, stunting me in my business ambitions, and I am sick of it all." The reported confession to Johnston proved accurate, and it certainly did not come as a shock to Keeler. For several years Jones had intimated that deep down he wanted to retire, but the time had never been right.[41]

In the fall of 1930 it could not have been more right, so on November 17 the twenty-eight-year-old Jones officially announced that he would retire from competitive golf. "I certainly shall never become a professional golfer," he said near the end of a lengthy statement. Yet he also renounced his amateur status, reporting that he had recently signed a contract to do twelve golf film "shorts" with Warner Brothers Pictures. (A few months earlier, Jones had allowed his swing to be filmed for free in an educational project sponsored by the Professional Golfers' Association.) His deal signed on November 13 with Warner Brothers paid him a lot of money and included an option for six additional films. Exact figures were not published, but estimates ranged between $100,000 and $500,000. The *Atlanta Constitution* reported that "reliable" sources put the amount at $250,000, which may have been a bit conserva-tive because Jones received $120,000 up front, plus a percentage of the gross.[42]

Years later, Chick Evans again manifested his jealousy of Jones by charging that the Atlantan had accepted money from Warner Brothers prior to his victory at Merion. Jones, who had carefully protected his status throughout his career, vehemently denied Evans's claim. Rumors about the movie deal did circulate at Merion, and at one point Jones was even asked about the impending deal. The published story, though, was that Jones would be offered a huge contract *after* the tournament. When queried about it in Phila-delphia, Jones replied, "I haven't got the offer, but I'm not turning down $200,000 contracts if they do come along." In *Golf Is My Game,* Jones disclosed that he had been approached at Merion "about doing a series of motion pictures on golf, but I declined even to discuss the subject." Beyond that, there is no reason to believe that Jones made any agreement, much less accepted money from Warner Brothers before November 13 and thus no reason to believe Evans's allegations. In truth, Evans never produced a shred of evidence to substantiate his charge.[43]

But if that allegation was false, Evans, like George Von Elm and many others, remained frustrated over the hypocrisy that seemed to permeate Merion. Dollar signs were everywhere but accessible to only a few. Von Elm made his own announcement of turning professional immediately after the tournament (possibly in an effort to steal some of Jones's thunder), saying that it had cost him $10,000 annually to play as an amateur and have the "'Mr.' stuck before his name." He further characterized the Merion event as "show business in a big way." The USGA, Von Elm accurately pointed out, had made more than $55,000 off the gate at Merion but had paid the players nothing. Other observers were bothered by the hundreds of thousands of dollars gambled on Jones and his fellow amateurs.[44]

As for Von Elm, what Walter Hagen and others had realized long ago seemed finally to dawn upon him: amateur sports were expensive, exploitative, and completely impractical—unless your name was "Bobby Jones." For him, there was an unprecedented pot of gold at the end of the journey. Indeed, what really grated on Von Elm, Evans, and many other amateurs and professionals who were wise enough to hold their tongues, was the fact that Jones was not only a more accomplished golfer than they but also a so-called "simon-pure amateur" who had nonetheless profited along the way. The *London Observer* once noted that for years many professionals had considered Jones the "best paid professional," mostly because of the money he made from syndicated writings. By 1930 George Trevor estimated that the figure was no less than $25,000. To be sure, Jones had exercised impressive loyalty and discipline in passing on a $50,000 home, but that only turned into a quarter-million-dollar Hollywood contract. Yet, less than a week after his win at Merion, Jones told a reporter from the *Daily Princetonian* that professionalism was a healthy thing for golf, adding: "Without [it] men would not have the opportunity to make an honest living at golf, and in their stead there would be a great many 'crooks' falsely pretending to be amateurs."[45]

While some scratched their heads at that comment, few seemed to begrudge Jones's commercializing on his amateurism; to the contrary, he did it all, even the film contract, while garnering the deepest respect of the USGA and the public. To Jones's few jealous detractors, it was an extremely irritating irony. But to his more numerous admirers, it was easily reconciled and justified. Most fans agreed with *Golf Monthly* that "only a fool would have turned down such a [film] offer because of a sentimental regard for the status of amateurism."[46]

Immediately after Jones read his retirement statement, in which he frankly admitted that money had been a determining factor in his decision, the accolades poured in one last time. A *New York Times* editorial, entitled "Bobby Holes Out," noted that "there was a pretty general feeling expressed" that Jones had done the right thing. Although the *Times* doubted "whether these new pictures of him in action will add much," the paper summed up Jones's action favorably: "With dignity he quits the memorable scene upon which he nothing common did or mean." W.O. McGeehan of the *New York Herald-Tribune* called Jones the "Champion of Champions."[47]

The British went even further with their encomiums. Jones's "personal charm and modesty in triumph are assets making him an invaluable traveling advertisement of the finer and rarer qualities of the human race," concluded the *London News-Chronicle*. The *Times* of London compared Jones to none other than the father of his country. Like President George Washington, "Mr. Jones . . . having finished the work assigned to [him]" can "retire with the blessings of his fellow-citizens." "There has been no player, professional or amateur, including the illustrious Walter Hagen, who has been able to hold a candle to [Mr. Jones] in the years since the war," the *Times* declared, "[and] his decision to make a film cannot be criticized." The *London Observer* simply thought it best that Jones retire with "dignity" while at the "zenith of power."[48]

Reaction was much the same from various quarters within the sport. Former outstanding American amateur Jerry Travers called Jones's move "wise" because he had "won everything there is to win." *Golfers Magazine* credited Jones with doing "much to popularize golf" and emphasized the financial security that the film contract would at long last bring to his family. Generally, the reaction from golf was one of understanding, yet sadness at the thought of not seeing Jones compete in the open championships. The USGA, some writers pointed out, would be particularly sorry to see gate receipts fall, as everyone expected they would. Opportunistic voices from within the PGA suggested that Jones could now enter its match-play tournament and defeat the Hagens, Diegels, and Smiths, as he had the Von Elms, Sweetsers, and Ouimets.[49]

At least one observer believed that Jones would return to competitive golf. Walter Hagen told Joe Williams of the *New York Telegraph*: "Jones is fed up on the game right now, [but he] will be back. And the crowds will be bigger than ever," he added, citing the example of boxer Jim Jeffries's 1910 comeback to fight Jack Johnson. Hagen said that if he was wrong, he still considered the Atlantan "the perfect example of what a real sportsman ought to be, one of the grandest fellows any sport knew, [and] a swell fellow [as] I call him. Everybody calls him that." What did Hagen think about Jones's cashing in and signing with Warner Brothers? "What's wrong with it? Why shouldn't he market [his golf style]? Well, I think Jones is just as much an amateur, in the sense that it is ethically interpreted, as he ever was." Sir Walter believed that it would be an "outrage" for golf's authorities to "professionalize" Jones because of the instructional films. "I don't claim to be a deep thinker, a moralist, or a distinctionist," Hagen concluded, "but it seems to me that if there is to be a caste system in sports, it ought to be founded on something higher than dollars and cents. Somewhere the matter of character ought to come in for consideration."[50]

Despite Sir Walter's prophecy and rare venture into the realm of ethics, Bobby Jones did not make a comeback (except for his annual efforts in the Masters), nor did he compete again as a "simon-pure" amateur. The reign of Emperor Jones was over, and although Sir Walter did not seem ready to admit it, his time had passed too. The lives and public images of Sir Walter and Mr. Jones were to be as different in the years ahead as they had been in the Golden Twenties. The "Dixie Wonder" from East Lake would finish his life in ill-health as the sport's paragon, while the handsome professional from Rochester did what most public figures do, particularly professional athletes: refuse to let go and then, when forced to, step aside and revel in the memories of glory days gone by.

Chapter 10

A Has-Been and a Gentleman: 1931–1959

Early in 1931, while golfdom adjusted to life without Bobby Jones, Walter Hagen maintained a competitive schedule on the west coast. By then the "western swing" included a dozen tournaments with more than $75,000 in prize money. Hagen had just turned thirty-eight, was receiving big checks from the L.A. Young Company, and, if he had wanted, could undoubtedly have secured a soft, lucrative position as a club professional; but he showed no signs of slowing down, much less retiring like his amateur counterpart.

Throughout the next decade Sir Walter continued to travel and entertain galleries around the country in weekly open events, although he won few of them. The 1931 season, however, was a relatively good one for Hagen, despite a first-round elimination from the PGA. He finished seventh in the U.S. Open, runner-up in the Western Open, captained the Ryder Cup team to a 9–3 victory, and won the Michigan Open and the Canadian Open. Hagen captured his first Canadian in exciting fashion, defeating Percy Alliss in a play-off. As the *Professional Golfer of America* noted, the victory was a "personal come-back for the winner of many titles, who had been repeatedly consigned to the shelf." H.G. Salsinger, borrowing a phrase that was still fresh, wrote in *Golfers Magazine* that Hagen had finally "completed the cycle" by winning all of the national events. Jack Kofoed of the *New York Evening-Post* was impressed by Sir Walter's style: "I get a kick out of his mannerisms; the assured, theatrical air; the slight tinge of scorn he holds for those who think they can beat the Haig. It's swell. I hope Walter goes on winning golf tournaments for years and years."[1]

Hagen did not do that, but in 1932 he collected one more big event, his fifth Western Open. Gene Sarazen, who had completely revived his own career to become the hottest professional star, was not there, but many other big names were, including Tommy Armour, Olin Dutra, "Lighthorse Harry" Cooper, Ed Dudley, and Tom Creavy, reigning PGA champion. Hagen beat them all, if only barely, finishing one stroke ahead of Dutra. The rest of the 1932 season was less successful. He did win the St. Louis Open but finished third in defending the Canadian Open, tenth in the U.S. Open, and again was eliminated from the PGA in the first round of match play.[2]

Yet two top-ten finishes in the U.S. Open and victories in the Canadian, Western, and St. Louis opens were excellent for a golfer of Hagen's years, and one can easily understand why he found it difficult to exit the arena. The problem, however, as Innis Brown pointed out in the spring of 1932, was that Hagen had almost completely lost his putting touch, often the skill that first leaves a competitive golfer. Brown observed that Sir Walter was taking too much time on the greens, agonizing over putts that once required only a quick look and a bold stroke. Brown found Hagen "stumbling and faltering so badly on the greens that he [Hagen] was actually embarrassed." Hagen tried to rehabilitate his putting by drastically altering his method, ironically adopting one similar to Bobby Jones's, more upright with a narrow stance. Early in his career Jones had used Hagen's stance—low crouch and feet far apart with most of the weight leaning on the front foot—but Jones did not fare well with that putting style, and neither did Hagen with Jones's. Hagen probably needed eyeglasses and his nerves were certainly no longer made of "steel." At any rate, Hagen's putting problems were not related to his stance, regardless of what he told others and himself.[3]

For a fleeting moment in the spring of 1933, it seemed that Sir Walter understood what was happening. The *Chicago Tribune* printed a brief statement from Hagen revealing his "plan to wage a serious campaign to recover his major titles on both sides of the Atlantic, captain the Ryder Cup team to victory in England, and then retire to the business of designing golf clubs and equipment." At first Hagen's plan sounded too ambitious, but a few days later he won his own "Walter Hagen Open," a thirty-six-hole event played in Jacksonville, Florida. Two weeks after that, he won another tournament on the southern swing, the Charleston Open. Having his best winter in years, Hagen seemed ready to go out with irons blazing.[4]

He cooled a bit by the U.S. Open early in June; still, he performed well enough, finishing in fourth place. He next went abroad, where his Ryder Cup team lost narrowly 6.5 to 5.5. The captain did his part, though, winning in the singles and in the foursomes with Sarazen. In the British Open at St. Andrews, Hagen started hot, taking the lead on the first day with a 68. "I just banged them off the tee," Sir Walter told reporters after his round. "I played my irons easily—and my putts dropped. It seemed too easy." Hagen must have felt ten years younger as he maintained the lead through the second round. Then reality set in on the final day; Hagen stumbled to 79–82 and fell into nineteenth place.[5]

Hagen had had enough serious golf for the season, so he spent the rest of the summer in Europe playing in exhibition matches with Denny Shute, the new British Open champion. He could still draw large galleries in the British Isles where "Sir Walter" remained popular, as well as infamous. The first highlight of the tour occurred when Hagen defeated British professional star Henry Cotton in typical, come-from-behind style; the second happened a week later when his 64 set a new record at Inverness. By choosing to stay in Europe, Hagen and Shute passed on the PGA Championship, which brought some criticism from Tommy Armour, who thought Hagen and Shute had a duty to their fellow professionals. Hagen had learned how to deal with such observations. When asked about Armour's comment, he punningly replied, "I'm too busy shooting birdies to grouse with Tommy."[6]

Hagen did not recover any of his lost titles in 1933, and so he apparently felt free to continue competing. In 1934 he fared poorly in all of the major events, including another first-round elimination in the PGA. In August, his former club honored him by staging the "Rochester Centennial Walter Hagen Testimonial Open." Hagen played and finished in a tie for twelfth place.[7]

Hagen gave his last impressive competitive performances in 1935. At forty-two years old, he won the Gasparilla Open in Tampa, finished a remarkable third place in the U.S. Open, and captained the Ryder Cup team to victory. The U.S. Open, held that year at Oakmont, was won by local favorite Sam Parks Jr. The course was as difficult as ever, and Parks took the title with a 299. Hagen posted a 77–76–73–76–302. Essentially, the course leveled the field and provided an experienced but shaky veteran a chance. To his credit, Sir Walter made the most of it and succeeded in capturing the headlines one more time.

Joe Huhn's commentary on Hagen in the *Pittsburgh Press* was illustrative and revealing. After summarizing Hagen's heroic effort, Huhn perpetuated parts of the "Sir Walter" legend, which was growing healthy and strong. "They call Hagen a playboy," Huhn wrote, "and this is what he is. Strict training rules never applied to him. Walter made more money than any other professional golfer in the history of the game, [and] more money was spent by him on clothes than by any other golfer. Hagen was a big-timer, and he does not want to go on playing the small circuit in exhibition matches for small purses."[8]

Yet playing the small circuit for small purses described much of what Hagen had been doing for the past several years. Huhn may have been making a gentle suggestion to Hagen; no doubt he was writing wishfully. To be sure, many fans in the immediate post-Jones era thrilled to see a living legend compete, even if his chances of winning were slim. On the other hand, seasoned observers winced at watching a two-time U.S. Open, four-time British Open, five-time PGA, and five-time Western Open champion make headlines by winning the Gasparilla Open. In retrospect, Hagen's longevity seems impressive, even admirable, but despite his occasional triumphs, it was obvious in 1935 that he was well past his prime. Informed contemporaries found Hagen a somewhat pathetic figure, the quintessential "has-been."

To make matters worse, Hagen had lost his neat, trim figure. That process was hastened by his undisciplined, fast living. In truth, most anecdotes about Hagen's roaring lifestyle date from the 1930s and 1940s, not the 1920s. Huhn's statement that "strict training rules never applied" was wrong; the evidence suggests that Hagen had taken at least adequate care of himself during his prime. Between 1914 and 1929, Hagen tipped the scales from 160 to 180 pounds. Any number in that range was good for him, a man of about six feet. By 1947, though, he would balloon to more than 235 pounds.[9]

Moreover, in the '30s Hagen's tardiness for tee-times and exhibitions became more frequent. Without his old companion Robert Harlow to keep an eye on him, Hagen womanized more than ever, stayed out late, overslept, and began drinking as well as eating too much. His behavior fed the image of the "Merry Haig," a hedonistic throwback to the "Roaring Twenties." Years later sportswriter John Lardner would recall Hagen as the "Rowdy Rebel of the Fairways," and Ted Shane would write that "the giddy 1920s were made for Hagen, and vice versa." Sir Walter got away with a lot more than any later tour professional could imagine because most people seemed willing to laugh off whatever he did as one last antic, and for many in the Depression era, he was undoubtedly a welcome reminder of "simpler, less serious" days. That is not to say that fans forgot how good Hagen once was. Memories of Midlothian in 1914, Brae-Burn in 1919, Sandwich in 1922, and Hoylake in 1924 remained vivid. By 1935, however, they became intertwined with the image of the "Bad Boy."[10]

As so often happens with athletes who do not know when to call it quits, last impressions affect memories, which ultimately affect final evaluations. In Hagen's case, the "Merry Haig" of the thirties overpowered the more serious, well-conditioned Walter Hagen of the late teens and twenties and in the long run, as Al Laney suggested in his memoirs, diminished Hagen's legacy as a competitive golfer. In 1954, Art Stockdale related a favorite anecdote which neatly illustrated the memory of Hagen: "There was the time an official queried Walter about his tardiness in appearing for a tournament. 'Where have you been,' asked the official, 'practicing a few shots?' No,' said Hagen, 'having a few.'"[11]

Hagen finally scaled back his competitive schedule after 1935, focusing mostly on the major events. In 1936, he teamed with Ky Laffoon to win a four-ball event in Toledo (which proved to be his final tournament victory), but he also finished out of the top thirty in the U.S. Open and did not survive into the PGA's match play. Hagen showed up at the PGA without having touched a golf club for weeks. After failing to qualify, he confessed to a reporter: "It used to be that I could lay off two months and be all the better for it, but having got heavier I couldn't do it this time. I never felt right on any shot. If it wasn't one thing, it was another."[12]

He spent nearly all of 1937 and some of 1938 on a world tour with Joe Kirkwood. The old barnstormers took their show abroad one last time, visiting Australia, New Zealand, India, China, and Africa. Along the way, they stopped in Britain, where Hagen led the Ryder Cup team to its second straight victory, boosting the team's overall record to 4–2. For the first time in the competition's history, Hagen was a nonplaying captain of the team, which included young Byron Nelson and Sam Snead. As for the 1937–1938 world tour, it was a fitting way for Hagen and Kirkwood to

cap their careers while thoroughly enjoying themselves. "Going
back into partnership with Hagen seemed like a homecoming.
Together we had eternal youth," Kirkwood recalled.

Kirkwood's autobiography, *Links of Life*, is mostly a string of
tales about that tour; Hagen related some of the same stories in
his autobiography. Apparently, in between their golf exhibitions,
the pair defended themselves against an attacking troop of angry
baboons; Hagen hunted a man-eating tiger; he doggedly pursued
a meeting with "a Zulu king" who was rumored to have 103 wives;
and then he took to eating baboon meat after the chieftain told
him that it enhanced virility. The duo also supposedly raced cam-
els around a pyramid in Egypt, while Hagen adopted a thirty-four-
foot python named "Singo" in Singapore and nearly died of
"black-fly malaria" in India. In possibly the most famous Hagen-
Kirkwood tale of all, one of their 1938 exhibitions brought a temporary cease-fire to the Sino-Japanese War.

Predictably, the pair also gave significant space in their memoirs to their female acquaintances. Hagen even felt experienced
enough to rate the world's women. He discussed the physical virtues of British, Scandinavian, Australian, Indian, Asian, and African females and bragged that he had enjoyed each, but concluded,
"I'll settle for . . . our gorgeous American women." Kirkwood included a description of the topless female caddies in Africa and
the topless women on the island of Bali in the Dutch East Indies.
Bali must have seemed like paradise to Hagen and Kirkwood; the
latter confessed to being badly bitten by "Bali fever." Kirkwood
saw to it that several photographs of the topless natives were published in his autobiography, and Hagen returned with a pile of
such pictures (about all that remains of his memorabilia today).[13]

By the fall of 1938, Hagen was back in the States, where he was
again named captain of the Ryder Cup team. "I considered myself
still an integral part of the golf picture," Hagen remembered. The
PGA's announcement was too optimistic, however, because by then
German nationalism was pulling the world into another great war
that would preclude the 1939 Ryder Cup matches and completely
disrupt the sport of golf. In 1939, Hagen again proclaimed his retirement, although he entered and withdrew from the 1940 U.S.
Open and failed to qualify for the 1942 PGA Championship, suggesting that he still harbored hopes for one more big win.

If the Depression years were subpar for Hagen professionally,
they were little better for him personally. Always something of a

vagabond since leaving his first wife in 1919, Hagen had not yet purchased any property by 1940. The closest that Hagen came to a home was a room at the Book-Cadillac Hotel in Detroit, where Sir Walter "held court," telling stories of the old days and drinking more than his share.

Fortunately, the equipment royalties continued to flow; unfortunately, at least for Hagen, Edna Straus wanted her cut. Hagen had refused to pay his ex-wife the sum awarded to her by the state of California in 1929, and she was determined to collect. Still not legally divorced, the couple came to a settlement of the California ruling in 1931; three years later they modified their agreement, which called for Hagen to pay $250 monthly. But Hagen did not respect that arrangement, either, so lawyers for both parties filed motions and counter motions through 1935 and 1936. Finally, on December 26, 1936, Florida Circuit Court Judge John I. Viney ordered Hagen to pay his wife $7,335 in back alimony, plus interest.

Less than a month later and back at her home near Trenton, New Jersey, Straus-Hagen filed for divorce on grounds of "willful, continued, and obstinate desertion," claiming to be the "world's No. 1 golf widow." In her suit, she requested that she be allowed to keep her golfing husband's surname. En route to California for the launching of his tour with Kirkwood, Hagen stopped at the Robert Treat Hotel in Newark, New Jersey, just long enough to be served final divorce papers. He did not show up in court but told his wife's lawyer that, "he would not, under any circumstances, ever again live" with Edna Hagen. On June 26, 1937, the separation became legal; Edna Hagen neither asked for nor received any further alimony judgment from the court.[14]

The divorce came on the heels of another legal ruling concerning Hagen. On November 12, 1935, Judge William Love of the Supreme Court of Monroe County, New York, dismissed Hagen's suit against the Rochester Red Wings baseball club. The decision was based on the "plaintiff's failure to prosecute the claim." It seemed that Hagen no longer cared about the principle, the money, or whatever it was that had led him to sue the Red Wings.[15]

Hagen may have been relieved to get the divorce from Edna Straus and nonchalant about the Red Wings case, but he was genuinely hurt by another incident during the mid-Depression years. It happened on Saturday evening, July 14, 1934, while Hagen was in St. Paul, Minnesota, for the city's annual open. Having just shot the first two rounds of the tournament, Hagen and his latest manager, Jack Truss, left the Hotel Lowry bound for a dinner at the White Bear Yacht Club. Hagen stopped his automobile at the intersection of Arcade and Fauquier streets and waited for a streetcar to unload. Thinking all was clear, he accelerated his vehicle and, according to Hagen, "Suddenly the boy appeared in front of [my] machine." The lad was six-year-old Lawrence H. Johnson, son of a prominent St. Paul druggist. He was on his way to buy "two cents worth of candy" when Hagen's car struck him. The boy landed in front of an oncoming streetcar but in between the rails so that the streetcar passed directly over him. Yet that near-escape did not matter much, because little Lawrence Johnson died minutes later from various injuries, including a fractured skull.

Crying and "completely unnerved," Hagen was immediately taken into police custody for questioning. He told authorities that he was traveling about twenty-two miles per hour at the moment of impact; the *St. Paul Pioneer-Press* reported that the body was "picked up 80 feet from where he was struck," suggesting that Hagen may have been driving faster. The *Minneapolis Tribune*, however, cited "witnesses" who corroborated Hagen's version— that Hagen's vehicle had stopped for a streetcar and that it was only in second gear when the "boy darted into the street." Following his statement, Hagen was ushered to the county morgue, where he had the awful experience of meeting the boy's father, H. Martin Johnson, who had just identified his son's body. "Mr. Johnson, I don't know what to say," Hagen gasped as he broke down crying again. "I'm terribly, terribly sorry. I have a boy of my own, and I've prayed that nothing would happen to him. I know nothing can ever replace your son, Mr. Johnson, but if there is anything in the world I can do, please tell me. I'm terribly, terribly sorry."

H. Martin Johnson was either a most gracious man or in too much shock to know what to say. Three years earlier he had lost another son in an automobile accident. "I'm terribly sorry too," Johnson replied as the two shook hands. "I feel terribly about the boy, and I'm sorry for you. I guess it was just one of those accidents that couldn't be avoided." That, at least, is how reporters from the *Pioneer-Press* and *Tribune* recorded the exchange. After further questioning, Hagen was released around 11:00 P.M.

Funeral services were held three days later, and on that Tuesday Hagen was again queried by an investigator from the coroner's office. In the meantime, Hagen finished the St. Paul Open in sixth place. The *Pioneer-Press* observed that Hagen played "mechanical golf" and only did that at the insistence of tournament sponsors, who convinced him that he owed it to the fans. Herman Barron, Hagen's partner, remembered that during the last rounds Sir Walter gave no indication of what had happened the previous evening, but in the locker room afterward he "sat down and started crying all over again . . . honest tears."

No charges or other legal action was ever brought, because, as Barron recalled, "there were some connections made, [and] it was Walter Hagen, you know, and it was pretty obvious it wasn't his fault." Actually, by all accounts, everyone seemed satisfied that it was an unavoidable accident, and on Wednesday the *Minneapolis Star* reported that the golfer had been "absolved of blame" for Johnson's death. "I'll never forget it as long as I live," Hagen told a reporter the day after the accident occurred. Joseph Peck, who knew Hagen as well as anyone during the last ten years of his life, noted that the ex-golfer rarely ever drove his automobile, although he was physically able. For obvious reasons Hagen made no mention of the incident in his autobiography.[16]

The fact that Hagen had been spending more time with his own son undoubtedly made the remorse from the Johnson tragedy all the more poignant. Besides his few victories early in the period and the Kirkwood tour, another bright spot in Hagen's life during the Depression was the increased opportunity to be with Walter Jr. Hagen's 1921 divorce from Margaret Johnson had granted his ex-wife custody of Junior until he was fourteen years old. The youth turned fourteen in 1932, and he immediately began to travel with his father. His mother was probably ready for a break, and much more than the stereotypical divorced father, Hagen had the wherewithal to spoil his son, fill his ears with tales of the world beyond Rochester, and rarely, if ever, remain long enough to deal with the consequences. By the late 1920s, Junior was a chip-off-the-old-block, something of a rebel.

Hagen took his son to Britain in the summer of 1933. Junior's presence certainly did not detract from Hagen's golf because it was in 1933 that he jumped out to a lead through two rounds of the British Open. Actually, the trip was a lot of fun; in one newspaper report, almost too idyllic to be true, Hagen was seen pedaling a bicycle along the beach with Junior riding on the handlebars. Hagen remembered that they flew across the English Channel with Douglas Fairbanks Sr. for "some visits to the gay resorts in and around Paris," and that during the return trip aboard the USS

Manhattan, he enjoyed champagne, while Junior and his teenage friends downed "cokes and hot dogs with astonishing rapidity." The most legendary aspect of the sojourn came at its conclusion, when Hagen, who supposedly blew all of his earnings on bubbly, looked to Junior for $25, money the youth had won betting on "deck races."

To be sure, by the 1930s Hagen had a lot of catching up to do with Junior, and it certainly appears that he made herculean efforts. The Hagens were noticed together at numerous tournaments in the period; apparently, Junior traveled with his father quite a bit. In 1926, Hagen wrote that he "planned a college education for [his son] and another profession from the one his daddy took up." Hagen wanted his offspring to have a better start than his own, and his goal was realized when Junior enrolled at the University of Notre Dame. He did not completely avoid his father's profession, however, becoming an accomplished amateur golfer and serving as the captain of the Fighting Irish golf team. Moreover, Junior seemed to respect his father. Of course, what Junior really loved was his father's image; in some ways that was all he knew. As the years passed and the two increased their time together, it became clear that this was one come-from-behind victory that even the great Sir Walter Hagen could not pull off, at least not entirely.[17]

But then young Walter's grandfather had done little better, although it seems that he also made a comeback effort with his own son late in life. Finally warming or at least accommodating to Hagen's athletic career, William Hagen first watched his son compete in 1931; he was on hand, with Junior, at the U.S. Open. Obviously in a good mood at having his son and father along, Hagen organized them for a three-generation photograph. If late in coming, that day must have been a special one for Hagen.

The elder Hagens had about ten years to refurbish their relationship, because in July of 1942 William Hagen died in Rochester, New York. Sir Walter traveled back to his hometown for the funeral and burial at the Brighton cemetery. Seven years later, in October 1949, Louise Hagen passed away at the age of eighty-six.

In the spring of 1941, though, such unhappy moments were still in the future, and Hagen was busy preparing himself to go to the Bahamas for a match to benefit British war relief. There he would meet four of his old friends: Tommy Armour, Gene Sarazen, the Duke of Windsor, and Bobby Jones. For Sir Walter, it would be one more chance to perform and refresh pleasant memories.

Walter Hagen Jr., Walter Hagen, and William Hagen at the
1931 U.S. Open. Courtesy: Country Club of Rochester

Bob Jones Jr. liked to reminisce about the old days too, particularly by the summer of 1942, but he simply did not miss them as much as Hagen. Rather, Jones had been so sick and tired of his glory days in competitive golf that he had brought them to an abrupt end. Nonetheless, as the *Professional Golfer* noted in the summer of 1931, it appeared "that Jones and golf in one form or another are destined to be inseparable," and, for all of his talk about business and the law, Jones himself admitted becoming "deeply involved in enough golf projects to preclude, at least for many years, my taking any serious interest in other activities." So, while Sir Walter struggled during the 1930s with personal tragedy, legal quagmires, and the degeneration of his career, Mr. Jones flourished in retirement, sustaining his image as golf's finest gentleman.[18]

In December of 1930, *Golfers Magazine* had admired Jones for retiring to look out for his "growing family"; at the time of Jones's announcement, his wife was more than seven months pregnant with their third and last child. On January 29, 1931, Mary Jones gave birth to another girl, Mary Ellen. Her arrival was an appropriate beginning to the happiest period in Jones's life. Moreover, a new baby was another good reason for Jones to stop competing, renounce his amateur standing, and cash in on his golf career.[19]

Recognizing his unprecedented market value, Jones quickly decided that he would not rest his family's financial security on the Warner Brothers films alone. For years, manufacturers had dreamed of paying Jones to endorse their products. As of November 1930 he was finally available for professional endorsements, and all kinds of companies scrambled to sign the retired golfer as a spokesman. Yet Jones hardly needed to keep his name before the public, because the films (and eventually his golf tournament) would do that much more effectively than any advertising campaign. So although Jones could have endorsed anything, he limited himself to a few deals that would generally enhance, not dilute, his image. Within days of his movie contract, Jones signed an agreement with the Lambert Pharmacal Company to do a series of broadcasts on the NBC radio network that would supposedly teach the fine points of golf. Soon after, he joined A.G. Spalding & Brothers to design a Bobby Jones line of golf equipment.

Jones's most pressing business concern, however, was the movie contract. Late in February of 1931, Jones and O.B. Keeler journeyed to Hollywood to make the dozen film shorts collectively entitled "How I Play Golf." The work went smoothly, and beginning in mid-April the films were released in two-week intervals, distributed, and shown in movie theaters around the country. Jones was so popular that the studio's big-name performers jockeyed for positions in the ten-minute films, each one of which starred Jones and included a well-known actor or actress and, as the star himself later put it, a "corny" story line. James Cagney, Walter Huston, Frank Craven, and Loretta Young, among others, landed roles. Keeler also made appearances, narrated, and was heavily involved in all aspects of the series' creation.

No expense was spared during production. Director George E. Marshall boasted that three cameras were used so that "no important angle may be lost." "Most of all," said Marshall, "we want to make each picture appear natural and spontaneous, as though

The Jones family in 1932. Bob and Mary are joined by their three children, (l. to r.) Robert Tyre III, Clara Malone, and the youngest, Mary Ellen. Courtesy: Sidney L. Matthew Collection

it was something which might have happened during any afternoon's golf game." One story line, for example, begins in a courtroom with a man who had been struck by a golf ball. Inevitably, the judge asks to have the shot recreated in the courtroom. The attorneys protest that it could be done better on a course, but the judge recoils at such kangaroo tactics until someone mentions that Bobby Jones is practicing at a club nearby. Upon hearing that news, the judge orders everyone to Jones's practice site, where the Atlantan displays his skills, reminding his pupils in his thick Georgian accent that no shot, regardless of how easy it seemed, should be played "haphazuhdly."

Despite their corny plots, the films were a huge success. Jones took them seriously, reportedly working out, trimming down and firming up to 175 pounds. He told reporters that he "never would have consented to make these pictures for silent films, [because] talking pictures give me the opportunity to tell just what passes through my mind when making different shots, something that a spectator could not begin to fathom through the use of subtitles." Fortunately, the star had been blessed with good looks and a pleasant, deep voice, which was accentuated by his southern drawl. Given the general unfamiliarity with "sound" motion picture equipment and Jones's inexperience with it, the retired golfer performed exceptionally well. In his free time, Jones rubbed shoulders with glamorous figures and was the guest of honor at William Wrigley Jr.'s inaugural Catalina Island Amateur Invitational. Still, by early June he was ready to go home. Departing from Hollywood on June 4, Jones declared that he was "definitely out of the movies, as I am out of competitive golf."

He was wrong. "How I Play Golf" was so profitable that Warner Brothers exercised its option to do another six films. Jones could hardly have been disappointed at the chance to make more money, and, besides, by then the entire family could go to California. So in the winter of 1932–1933, Mary, Clara, Bob III, and Mary Ellen spent several months in Hollywood, while Bob Jones filmed a series entitled "How to Break Ninety." The films, which utilized the emerging technology of slow-motion photography, were as successful as the first series, and Jones easily received $250,000 between the two. But lest his fans worried that "Movieland" had gone to his head, one reporter assured them that "Bobby is still Bobby."[20]

When not acting on the links, Jones worked on his radio show. On Wednesday evening, January 15, 1931, the first interview aired

Jones working on the set of his commercially successful instructional
film series. O.B. Keeler types away in the foreground.
Courtesy: Emory University

nationally from Atlanta. Although billed as instructional talks—
one promotional promised "now your radio will help you battle
par"—Jones warned his first audience not to expect "educational
lectures," which he knew would be useless without accompanying
visuals. Instead, the retired golfer spent most of the time reminiscing about famous matches. Yet even in that more relaxed format, listeners detected nervousness in Jones's voice. Afterward,
he admitted being "scared," particularly of that "thing [the micro-
phone] that looks like an electric fan." Keeler, who was by Jones's
side, said that he had "never seen him so nervous, and I've followed Bobby in twenty-seven major tournaments."

The initial installment of Jones's radio talks must have been
awkward. Following a "glowing introduction" by the emcee, Billy
Munday, Jones was supposed to impart "a feast of wisdom [and]
golf lore" through a purely audio medium. Jones may also have
been uneasy with the blatant commercial flavor of the radio spots;
ads promised that the consumer would "find Listerine Shaving

Cream as valuable to your shaving comfort as Bobby's advice is to your game." The series lasted for twenty-six consecutive Wednesdays, running from 8:00 to 8:15 P.M., and, in time, Jones became comfortable enough to produce a respectable show. Nonetheless, his "reminiscences" were no fireside chats. "We did our level best," Jones later wrote, "but I fear it was not too good."[21]

Things went much better at A.G. Spalding & Brothers, where by late 1932 Jones had "purchased a substantial block of stock" and had become a member of the board of directors. The Atlantan's primary contribution was his name and his work as a "living laboratory" for the company's research center in Chicopee, Massachusetts. The first sets of "Robt. T. Jones Jr." matching, steel-shafted woods and irons—along with a copy of "Calamity Jane"—hit both pro shops and retail stores just in time for Christmas 1932. Jones designed the clubs himself with the help of a few other people at Spalding, and, like the instructional films, they were an instant success, so much so that for a few years Spalding had a hard time keeping up with demand. Hagen probably did not agree with him, but Jones could not "resist declaring that these were the first really fine matched sets of irons produced in this country."[22]

Movies, radio shows, and equipment design were not the only commercial projects that Jones worked on in the early thirties, and eventually, they would all be dwarfed by his other interest of the period: the creation of the Augusta National Golf Club and its Annual Invitational Tournament—"the Masters." Jones had decided in the late '20s that he would like to design his own course. "I had always had an ambition, a sort of feeling that I'd like to see some of my ideas incorporated in a golf course," he remarked years later. Jones's grandest dreams came true with the help of Clifford Roberts, a New York financial advisor, and Dr. Alister MacKenzie, the internationally renowned golf architect who designed Cypress Point in northern California.[23]

Of the trio, Roberts was the most powerful force behind the project, not only in the early months but right down to his suicide in 1977. Jones was invaluable, too, providing a name, playing expertise, and the perfect image of southern gentility, while MacKenzie was important only in the early design of the course. In fact, he never saw his project completed; he died unexpectedly on the west coast in 1934. Roberts, who may have met Jones at the 1926 U.S. Amateur, was seemingly not the sort of fellow the Atlantan would have taken to. He was aggressive and ambitious and possessed an uncanny nose for power, as well as sound business sense. Yet Roberts developed a lifelong, businesslike friendship with the retired golfer. MacKenzie, on the other hand, was a more natural partner for Jones. Friends since at least the 1926 British Open, they quickly discovered a common vision of the ideal golf course, one that would provide the "most enjoyment for the greatest number."[24]

Roberts handled the business details and even found Fruitlands, an abandoned 365-acre plantation-turned-tree nursery in Augusta, which, like so much else in the Depression, was for sale at a bottom-dollar price: $70,000. Jones fell in love with the spread immediately, believing that "the land had been lying here for years just waiting for someone to lay a golf course upon it." Jones and Roberts had agreed that their course would be located somewhere in the old Confederacy; for years Augusta had been a favorite winter resort for well-to-do Yankees and was as perfect a location as could be found. The only thing wrong with Augusta was that it was not Atlanta, and some of his hometown fans never forgave him for apparently slighting their city.

It required a lot of skill to raise the capital for the project, particularly given the nation's economy; but Roberts was up to the task, aided by a license to wield the name "Bobby Jones" when entreating prospective investors. Within months he assembled a group of charter members, including Grantland Rice (more for his public relations skills than his money); William Watt, chairman of United Drug Company; and Alfred S. Bourne, whose father had founded the Singer Sewing Machine Company. The entry fee was $5,000, and the objective of membership recruiting was to make the club national but highly exclusive. At an early board meeting, Rice pointed out that many country clubs were governed inefficiently by committee, and he suggested that the best thing for Augusta National would be for the board to vote Roberts and Jones perpetual dictators. Rice's motion carried unanimously.

In mid-1931, Jones and MacKenzie finished the initial design. The $85,000 construction began in the fall, and by January of 1933 the course was ready for club members to play. Jones-Roberts immediately queried the USGA about the possibility of bringing the U.S. Open to Augusta. The USGA said thanks, but no thanks; its event had to be held in June or July, not in April, when Augusta National would be at its most beautiful. So, Jones-Roberts decided to stage their own annual spring invitational. Late March was good not only for the course but also for the event, because that was the time that the nation's sportswriters were heading north from Florida's major league baseball training camps. A stopover in Augusta to cover a golf tournament would be a convenient reprieve from the nation's other pastime.

In spite of all that the project had going for it, Roberts believed that the tournament would be a success only if Jones competed alongside the finest amateurs and professionals. Jones naturally was reluctant, arguing that his entry was unnecessary and that he could best serve as a gracious host. Roberts thought otherwise and convinced Jones that his competitive "comeback" could alone float the tournament. It was one of many disagreements that Roberts won over the years. "I don't think anyone except myself could have prevailed upon him to do it," Roberts recalled.[25]

Since his retirement, sportswriters and golfers occasionally had discussed the possibility of a Jones comeback. Some, like Hagen, predicted that Jones would be unable to resist the thrill of competition. Others, such as sportswriter George Trevor, remembered that Jones had declared he would never play as a professional and believed that such a "highly-principled sportsman" could not reapply for amateur status, particularly since he had cashed in. "There must be some limit in the matter of eating your cake and having it too," Trevor concluded. But if Jones would not play for prize money or as an amateur, he might, as Roberts suggested, simply play as the host of his own tournament.[26]

As for whether or not Jones could still compete, he had played regularly since Merion but usually just in casual rounds with his father, Rice, or Roberts and probably less often than at any point in his life. Occasionally, Jones played charity benefits, such as the match in June 1931 with Mary K. Browne, or the one in New York the following September, in which Jones took on sixty-five fellow lawyers. (Jones played against four on each hole, and anyone who bettered Jones's score on a hole received an autographed certificate saying as much. Jones shot 71, and only five men took certificates home that evening.) Jones regularly proved that he could still go low; in February 1932 he carded a 69 to set a course record at the Augusta Country Club (which literally borders the Augusta National), and in December 1933 he shot 67 in dedicating Atlanta's first municipal course, named after him.[27]

But charity exhibitions and tournament golf were entirely different things, and the so-called comeback would only be meaningful if highly publicized, which in turn meant that the pressure and expectations would be great. Though reluctant, Jones was determined to make his tournament a success, and so late in 1933, under sort of a sports-media microscope, he began serious practice for the inaugural Augusta Invitational. Writers had fun speculating on Jones's chances: could he again defeat all of the money-changing professionals and win his own tournament? Observers immediately noticed that his "smooth and flawless" swing was still intact. "To all outward appearances," one reporter discovered in December 1933, "Jones is as good as ever." He continued to work out at Augusta early in 1934. Grantland Rice wrote an article for *American Golfer* entitled "Bobby Jones Comes Back," which warned professionals that his friend had been averaging around 70 in the three years since Merion. On the other hand, Rice sagely remarked, "no one can say in advance how the nerve strain will affect him, what his mental attitude will be against the keen blades of so many stars, all after his scalp."[28]

Jones maintained his form as the moment of truth approached. On March 3 he shot a remarkable 65 (–7) over Augusta National. Nonetheless, Horton Smith gave the retired golfer "only an 8–1 shot" at winning, saying that "the pace is faster than in the days Jones played. I believe the leading professionals are 25 per cent improved." Smith acknowledged that Jones's mechanical form was as good as ever, but suspected that "the mental strain" and "anxiety" would be too much to overcome. Just three days before the event got underway, Jones feared that his putting would be a problem. "I'm not putting well now. To score in a tournament you must be able to get down an occasional long putt, and I've been unable to do this with consistency. I can drop the short ones, but mostly it is the putts of twenty feet or further that bring the birdies." Did Jones really care about winning or losing? "Yes, I want to win every tournament in which I play." He might have also been thinking, "especially my own inaugural event."[29]

It soon became obvious that Jones had been only partly correct about his putting. He was wrong about the short ones; he could not drop them, either. Jones later wrote that he noticed a "jerk" in his putting stroke early in the first round; one reporter said that he "batted" at the ball. The Atlantan took thirty-five putts, three-putted three greens, and missed "seemingly innumerable putts of four feet." His long game was still very good, though. Jones left himself putts of less than ten feet for eagle on the fourth and 11th holes but missed them so badly that he barely saved birdies. (These are the 13th and second holes, respectively, at Augusta National today—originally the nines were reversed.) His chipping was not good, either. As Jones described it, "I was chopping at the chips." Paul Runyan, Jones's partner that day, thought that Jones appeared to be "worried and to feel the strain considerably." He struggled to a 76 in his first round. Hagen was there, too, posting a 71. When asked about Jones's superb wood play, Sir Walter responded, "Well, the drive is often just one-fifth of a hole. I've been in the rough three times and got three birdies."

Jones improved his overall score on the second day, adding a 74, but he required thirty-eight putts. Despite his two-stroke improvement, it was not a pretty sight to behold. Jones missed eight putts under seven feet—one of eighteen inches and another of sixteen inches—and almost missed three more of two feet, according to Rice. His embarrassment peaked on the 16th (seventh), where 3,000 fans watched him miss the sixteen-incher for birdie. "I was terrible. I was worse today than yesterday," Jones told reporters in the clubhouse afterward. "The minute I reached the green, I had the jitters, blind staggers, and sleeping sickness. I was honestly afraid to walk up to a two-foot putt." Recounting the miss at sixteen, he concluded: "I guess that's the bottom. This thing has become funny instead of tragic. There is just one comfort. I can't get any worse."

In a nostalgic pairing, the type for which the Masters would later become famous, Jones and Hagen played together in the third round. Reportedly, Hagen requested Jones, saying "two rotten putters ought to be coupled anyhow. Maybe we can find inspiration in each other." Fortunately for Jones, they did, and he lowered his score by two more shots, finishing with a par 72. As good as that was, the forty-one-year-old Hagen clipped it by two strokes and kept himself in contention, just five shots behind the leader, Horton Smith. A writer observed "tears in the eyes of many in the gallery as Jones stood on the last green and smiled at Hagen," while one member of the gallery, forgetting himself for a moment, let out a "great rebel yell," which must have mortified the stoic Roberts.

The crowd was in an especially sappy mood that afternoon because it had learned that Jones, for the first time in the event, was using an old copy of Calamity Jane, acquired from his mother's bag. The putter, said one report, "appeared a bit out of place, along with all his other shiny instruments. It was rusty and the shaft was made of wood." The difference for Jones on day three was, in part, Calamity Jane. "Gosh," he said, after reviewing his card, she "must have helped. I sank a few."

Playing with Hagen undoubtedly helped, too. Lester Rice recorded that Hagen "encouraged [Jones] at every turn. With low-voiced words that none other could hear, he cheered him when he holed a putt and softened the pain when he missed one." Moreover, Sir Walter was his old nonchalant self, relieving Jones of the spotlight by playing to the gallery and flashing his old humor. After both scored birdies at the par-3 13th, Hagen exclaimed "Deuces wild!" as they walked to the next tee. "There's life in the old man yet," Sir Walter announced that evening, adding: "Bobby and I always play well together. If Bob and I had only had some of these kids whose nerves are still strong putting for us, we might have had two 67s. Bob's should easily have been a 68 with any luck. He was the old Jones where a real golf shot was involved." As for Jones, he admitted, "I feel better now."

The pairing held together for the final day. Jones dropped a few more putts to finish with another 72; Hagen, meanwhile, blew up to a 77 to tie Jones at 294. "I have no idea of returning to open competition," Jones said, addressing the ever-present rumors. "I hope to have this masters' tournament an annual affair, and I will limit my competition to playing in it for the fun I get out of it." But the Atlantan confessed that he had little "fun" the previous few days, and he seemed happy to have the tournament behind him. Horton Smith won the inaugural event with a 284.[30]

The Masters proved more fun for Jones in later years when the pressure was not so severe. Yet much of the mystery and myth of Mr. Jones had evaporated; everyone now realized what Jones knew all along—that he was mortal and not some golf machine. A few days after the first Masters, Jones said, "There never was anyone invincible in golf, and I don't believe there ever will be." He certainly could not sit idle for months, much less years, pick up his clubs, and win a big tournament. In truth, despite the claims perpetuated by Rice and so many others, Jones had always played much more golf throughout his competitive years than the weekend hacker. Still, faring so poorly in front of so many must have been a hard pill to swallow. The evidence is clear that Jones practiced long hours for the event, took it seriously, and probably nurtured thoughts of winning. "I have to admit that I expected to do better than I had any right to," Jones later wrote. He took the defeat like a gentleman, concluding, "I am sorry I didn't play better, but that is unimportant. I played the best I could, with no excuse to offer, and great golfers set the leading pace."

Undoubtedly, many professionals thought to themselves, "I told you so." Some nearly said as much, including Gene Sarazen, who was in San Juan, Puerto Rico, on an exhibition tour with Joe Kirkwood. When queried about Jones's failed comeback, Sarazen reportedly replied, "I think it would take a year or two for Jones to be up to his old game." But the professional was not certain "whether [Jones's] game would be good enough against the new crop of players who have come up. The newcomers are not afraid of the old big timers . . . ."

Most observers were less brassy in their analysis and agreed with the *Atlanta Constitution*'s Ralph McGill, who wrote, "too many boys in the craft spoke of failure. I can't see where it was a comeback. Comeback from what? Jones wasn't coming back in the sense that he was seeking to regain anything. He had beaten the world. He had everything." McGill could not resist feeding the legend one more time, adding, let us have "no more of this sob stuff. Jones, if he wishes, can spend a few weeks at his game and get it back." Everyone agreed that Jones's 294—an average of 73.5— was not that bad; after all, he finished in a thirteenth-place tie with Hagen and Denny Shute, the reigning British Open champion. Robert Harlow believed that Jones's friends "expected too much of him. As a matter of fact, he did very well indeed." Most professionals, Harlow noted, were probably just relieved that he did not do any better; it would have been an embarrassing "calamity" for them if Jones had won the tournament. Rice affirmed the fact that Jones's fans "had made a mistake" by overestimating his chances to win and then predicted that the "'Masters' Tournament is on its way to become one of the big fixtures in golf."[31]

Rice's prediction, of course, was accurate. In 1935 Sarazen's double-eagle (with Hagen as his playing partner) and subsequent play-off victory over Craig Wood established the tournament's reputation for exciting finishes. It was not until years later, however, that the Masters became a recognized "major," one leg of a professional Grand Slam which also included the U.S. Open, British Open, and PGA Championship. Jones played in the Masters through 1948, the year his health began to decline. In 1935 he finished twenty-sixth. The following spring he set a new noncompetitive course record with a 64 in practice and was quoted at 6 to 1 on the eve of play, but he finished in thirty-third place. In fact, Jones never came close to winning his tournament. In 1935 the press covered his practice rounds and discussed his chances, but not as much as they had in 1934, and each spring, although it still occurred, the Bobby Jones watch included fewer reporters.

Aside from his annual performance in the Masters, Jones continued playing charity exhibitions in the mid-1930s. In the summer of 1936, he traveled to St. Andrews for one of his more sentimental and memorable rounds. The Joneses were abroad with friends, including Grantland Rice, to watch the 1936 Summer Olympics in Berlin. Along the way the party stopped in Scotland, where the Atlanta legend thrilled more than 3,000 by firing a 32–40–72 on the Old Course. Jones had intended to keep the round a secret, but somehow the news got out, and so did the Scots. They had not seen their hero since the 1930 British Open and were feverishly enthusiastic about his visit. Afterward, someone called for Jones to give a speech. "I won't give a speech, but I will sign some more autographs," Jones said as he hurriedly signed whatever was put in front of him. "Golf for me is just fun now. I'll never enter competitive golf again, [but] St. Andrews is still my favorite course." As late as April of 1938, Jones was still squelching rumors about his entering the U.S. Open, while continuing to compete occasionally in charity exhibitions.[32]

The Depression years had been profitable for Jones and not all that bad for golf. Jones had attained financial security for his family, probably beyond what he ever expected. In 1939, the Joneses moved from the house on Northside Drive into a beautiful eighteen-room mansion named "Whitehall," located at 3425 Tuxedo Road in one of Atlanta's most affluent areas. Designed in 1929 by the renowned architect Philip Shutze, Whitehall was a unique structure in that it was in Italian stucco style but made of wood. Soon after moving in, Mary Jones furnished it with European antiques, Waterford chandeliers, and Aubusson rugs. Her husband transformed the garden room into a trophy room and added an indoor gymnasium behind the house. The regular Whitehall staff included a chauffeur, butler, maid, cook, laundress, yardman, night watchman, and, in later years, two nurses. In all, the mansion was the perfect home for a southern gentleman.[33]

Jones was indubitably the statesman of his sport. In 1936, President Franklin D. Roosevelt's New Deal called upon the Atlantan to serve his country as an unofficial advisor to the Works Progress Administration (WPA), which was involved in the construction or refurbishing of 600 municipal golf courses. Jones met with Harry Hopkins, WPA Administrator, and emerged confident about the program: "It will go a long way toward reducing the costs of the game for the average person. That is what is needed to popularize golf." Actually, Jones's sport, which was about to celebrate fifty years in America, was doing quite well.[34]

In 1938, Jones may have read H.B. Martin's article in the *New York Times Magazine* entitled "Golf Has a Birthday." Martin recounted the unseasonably mild February afternoon in 1888 when John Reid and his friends first tried the game in a cow pasture. Martin also discussed the "Apple Tree Gang," the Bounding Billy, Walter Travis's victory in the 1904 British Amateur, and Ouimet's shocking win at Brookline in 1913. He completed his historical summary with the Grand Slam.

If the former Emperor of Golf browsed Martin's piece, he learned that the number of courses in the States had grown to more than 6,000, while the number in Britain was 2,000 and in the rest of the world an estimated 1,000. Approximately one billion dollars was invested in American golf courses, which employed some half-million people, and in 1937 two-thirds of the world's golf equipment was made in the U.S. One conservative estimate in 1931 had put the total number of golf rounds played by Americans at 15 million, compared with 11 million who had turned out to watch major league baseball games that year. Columnists asked, "Ball Bat or Golf Club—What's the Answer?" and "Is Golf Replacing Baseball as Our National Game?" Martin might also have noted that the U.S. had become the premier golf nation in the world, competitively speaking. With their eight British titles combined and involvement in the Ryder and Walker Cup competitions, Hagen and Jones had led the way; actually, Sir Walter and Mr. Jones had done far more to stimulate the rise of American golf than either of them could have appreciated in 1938.[35]

The 1930s were generally good years in Jones's personal life. One exception came on September 23, 1937, when his grandfather died. Yet even in that moment his sadness could not have been too deep, because R.T. Jones of Canton had enjoyed a full life to the age of eighty-seven, outliving most other men of his day. Like Hagen, Jones had more time during the '30s to spend with his family. He taught Bob III how to play golf but did not encourage his son or daughters into competition, foreseeing a nightmare of expectations for them. When she was old enough, Mary Ellen took a few lessons from her father's mentor, Stewart Maiden, but soon concluded "Golf was NOT my game."[36]

Jones had a difficult time relating to young children, and to later generations, he might seem a reserved, distant, even cold patriarch. In that way also, Jones lived life as the traditional southern gentleman; nannies looked after Jones's children just as Camilla had looked after him. "When his children reached the age of eight and had acquired something close to civilized table manners, they were allowed to have dinner with their parents," wrote Richard Miller. As Clara, Bob III, and Mary Ellen grew older, though, their father significantly increased his recreation time with them, often going along to watch Georgia Tech football games on Saturday afternoons, for example. Like granddad R.T., Jones was strict with his children, but he never used corporal punishment and probably spent much more time than his grandfather reasoning and discussing decisions with them. Again, it is easy to see the influence of two generations of social thought on Jones the parent.

Mary Jones saw to it that the children were reared Catholic; they attended parochial schools, such as Christ the King and Sacred Heart. She seemed content to have nannies feed, clothe, and diaper her children. In other words, Mary Jones could be distant, too, and was probably a stricter parent than her husband. Yet Bob and Mary Jones did display affection and approval, providing their children consistency, security, and an old-fashioned sense of propriety.[37]

Thus, by World War II Jones had a good, comfortable life, which he shared with his family and a few close friends. He had completely cashed in on his golf career and had material security that most Americans only dreamed of obtaining. Moreover, the Masters gave him the annual opportunity to keep in touch with his sport, while also becoming one of the most prestigious events on golf's calendar. Each spring Americans were reminded of how the "simon-pure" amateur had once beaten the greedy professionals in the "frivolous, sport-crazed" 1920s, how golf was never "his business," how he had called penalty strokes on himself in the U.S. Open, how gracious he was in victory or defeat, and how he had punctuated his career by winning the Grand Slam. Such memories ensured Jones's image as the finest gentleman athlete ever. So it was in March 1941, as Walter Hagen left the Book-Cadillac

Hotel, that Bob Jones Jr., departed from Whitehall for the Bahamas and one more exhibition with the Haig.

The Hagen-Jones Nassau match was just one of many golf charities conducted during World War II. In fact, a few months later the pair joined forces again. Hagen, as he did each summer early in the war, captained a Ryder Cup squad against an American challenge team. In August of 1941, his squad battled a team of amateurs led by Jones. The amateurs won the series, which was held at the Detroit Golf Club and the event raised about $15,000 for the United Service Organizations (USO). Just as in the Great War, golf did "its bit" for the country, although the sport neither needed nor received the boost from World War II that it got from World War I. In 1942, the USGA canceled the U.S. Open and in its place held the "Hale America Open." Ben Hogan won the event, and more than $20,000 was given to the Allies. Jones entered and finished well behind. Ultimately, golf raised hundreds of thousands of dollars through open events and special exhibitions, such as those played by Bing Crosby and Bob Hope in the spring of 1943.[38]

The Hagen-Jones Nassau benefit, thanks to its notable foursome and referee, may have been the most famous World War II golf event. Sir Walter was a bit giddier than usual when he arrived in the Bahamas to meet Jones, Sarazen, Armour, and the Duke of Windsor, who would serve as the referee. (The Duke had already been the Prince of Wales and, for a time, King Edward VIII.) The stage was perfect, with beautiful weather and women, who were dressed for the conditions and anxious to meet a golf legend. Hagen did not disappoint. Jones-Armour defeated Hagen-Sarazen, but as usual the outcome was overshadowed by Sir Walter's behavior, particularly on the 16th hole.

It was there that Hagen made one of his last highly publicized utterances. As he was preparing to putt, Hagen looked at the Duke, who was standing near the hole, and asked him to pull the pin. "Caddie, take the flag," he said with a smile. Some thought they heard "Eddie, take the flag." Hagen always maintained that it was the former but added that "Eddie" was a "slip which would have

One of Hagen's last big moments–the 1941 Red Cross exhibition in
Nassau, Bahamas. Pictured from left to right: Gene Sarazen,
Dan Walsh, Bob Jones, the Duchess of Windsor,
Walter Hagen, the Duke of Windsor, and Tommy Armour.
Credit: PGA

been so easy for me to make." In either version, it was sassy, irreverent, egalitarian, and thus vintage Sir Walter, who seemed to treat everybody alike, be they humble teenagers or royal aristocracy.

But that was not all. Supposedly, the Duke had been so impressed with Hagen's nonchalance that he inquired of Fred Corcoran about its source. Corcoran related a personal philosophy to the former monarch that Hagen supposedly had told him numerous times before. It went something like this: "Never hurry and don't worry. You're here for a short visit. So don't forget to stop and smell the flowers along the way." That, Corcoran added, was the Hagen creed. As the story goes, the Duke immediately scampered over to the Dutchess, excited to share the profound outlook with his wife.

Whatever the specifics, in the post World War II period no Hagen anecdote would be told more often. Golf writers in the 1950s and 1960s simply could not do a Hagen piece without the lackluster verse, which summarized the hedonistic Haig of the so-called Roaring Twenties. "If there was ever an athlete cut from the same Herculean and incredible mold as Babe Ruth," wrote Arthur Daley in 1950, "that man was Walter Hagen, one of the truly heroic figures of the fabulous Golden Twenties." Daley's statement could have introduced or concluded dozens of columns in the postwar years, even if the "don't worry" lines were not as emblematic of Hagen's life as everyone, including the Haig, wanted them to be.[39]

As it turned out, the Nassau benefit was Sir Walter's final encore, and in the years ahead, except for occasional honors and the publication of his autobiography, Walter Hagen continued to slip into obscurity. Fortunately, his record had been established long ago, and when the PGA announced the inaugural members to its new hall of fame in 1944, Hagen was on the list. Also in the charter group were Jones, Sarazen, and Ouimet. In 1947 Hagen received another honor, being named cocaptain, along with Craig Wood, of the Ryder Cup team.[40]

By 1950 Hagen had relocated from the Book-Cadillac Hotel to the Detroit Athletic Club (DAC). He turned fifty-eight that year and was beginning to reap the consequences of his undisciplined lifestyle. At one point during the summer, Detroit papers reported that doctors had prohibited Hagen from playing any golf. His physical problem was only described as one requiring a "strict diet," which "slimmed him down considerably"; most likely it was related to his heart. Beyond that, Hagen was also bothered by a "leg ailment" that resulted in a brief hospital stay. In September he announced that he planned to be back on the links the following spring, "just as soon as the doctors give me the green light. I feel well enough to go out there and tee off right now—and I'd like to do just that." Hagen added that he was "through with competitive golf"—as if anyone thought otherwise.[41]

Hagen hated to admit it, but he was actually through with golf in any form. In 1953 he left the DAC, finally purchasing his own dwelling, "situated on a knoll facing west on Long Lake near Traverse City, Michigan." For years, stretching well back into his competitive days, Hagen had relaxed in the upper Midwest, especially Northern Michigan. In the late 1940s and early 1950s he had spent time in the city of Cadillac, about forty miles south of Long Lake, where he probably leased a cabin. But the thickly-forested twenty acres outside of Traverse City, including a lakeside cottage, guest-house, and dock, was the first property he ever owned.[42]

Soon after leaving Detroit, Hagen, along with Margaret Seaton Heck, put together *The Walter Hagen Story*. A couple years earlier, in May 1952, Hagen had announced plans to do a book with Robert Harlow and Robert Wise, a friend and DAC member. The book was tentatively entitled *I've Met a Million*. The once-famous duo wrote an initial draft that included extensive information about Hagen's family background and childhood in Rochester. Hagen was anxious to write something that his son and grandson, five-year-old Walter Hagen III, would eventually appreciate. The book was never completed, however, probably because Harlow's health collapsed; he died on November 15, 1954.[43]

So, in 1953 Hagen signed with Heck and sent her the manuscript on which he had been working. Heck told him that while such material "would be of great interest" to his offspring, "it would serve no special purpose" for the general public; in other words, it would not sell. Heck had anticipated a book on the "fabulous Hagen personality," including the "name-dropping" of movie stars and kings, the Kirkwood tour, and so on, as well as any new tales that he could remember. That type of autobiography, she told Hagen, would attract a major commercial publisher.[44]

The final product was just what Simon and Schuster ordered, a well written and entertaining—though disorganized and lengthy—series of the old anecdotes, along with a few precious lines about the man himself. John Lardner reviewed the work for the *New York Times*. He enjoyed reading the "old stories, the gentler, more printable ones," but believed that they failed "to reproduce the whole flavor and dynamism of the old hero." Lardner summarized Sir Walter as a man who "smelled the flowers and picked them too" and "alone revolutionized the social status of professional golfers." Most people seemed more satisfied than Lardner, and the book sold respectably.[45]

The project was not without some hardship. As soon as the book was published, Hagen reportedly ordered 10,000 copies to send to acquaintances around the world, such as Desi Arnaz, Lucille Ball, and William Frawley (Ricky, Lucy, and Fred on the then top-rated television comedy "I Love Lucy"; Hagen had teamed with

Appearing rather portly, Hagen accepts an award in the early 1950s.
Courtesy: PGA

Frawley to win a pro-am event in 1935), Jackie Gleason (star of the "Honeymooners"), Ty Cobb, and President Eisenhower. Hagen apparently thought that because he was the author, or at least because his name was on the dust jacket, he could obtain his copies for nothing. When he refused to pay for the books he had ordered, Simon and Schuster sued him for $17,861. Hagen responded by filing a counter suit for $50,249, charging that his publisher had violated its "agreement by selling copies of the book for less than the price he was charged." The dispute was settled out of court in July 1959, and terms were not disclosed; whatever they were, Hagen must have been relieved to put yet another legal mess behind him.[46]

The royalties rift aside, life on Long Lake was about as good as it could be for a showman without a stage. Hagen lounged in his "Hawaiian shirt—bright with flame gold, and woodsy green" in easy chairs on the dock or aboard his boat, the *Dor-Mee*. He employed a live-in secretary/housekeeper named Doris Brandes, who became like the daughter Hagen never had. She, along with Joseph Peck and a Brittany spaniel named King, comprised Hagen's Long Lake family. Peck was an outdoorsman who lived in neighboring Carlin and worked as a plant inspector. He met Hagen just before the retired golfer moved to Long Lake and introduced him to the finest fishing and hunting spots in the region.

It seems that Hagen knew Brandes from his days at the DAC, and as for King, Peck recalled the day that Hagen received him from a kennel in Kentucky. Hagen had paid handsomely to field train the dog, but on their first day of pheasant hunting, the spaniel flushed a bird and chased it. Hagen was so mad that he almost shot the dog right there. Brandes liked King, though, and convinced Hagen to keep the spaniel. In time, Hagen became so fond of the dog that he insisted the pet be allowed in taverns and restaurants around the state.

During a typical week in the late 1950s, Peck would stop at the Long Lake cottage a couple of evenings, drop off his car, and drive Hagen in his Cadillac to his favorite spot in downtown Traverse City, a tavern called The Little Bohemian's or "Li'l Bo's." There the retired golfer would spend hours shooting pool, playing cards, getting drunk, getting someone else drunk, arguing about this or that, and, of course, relating stories from the glory days. It was not uncommon for Hagen to have a dozen men sitting around him, listening to his stories about Joe Kirkwood or Tommy Armour. Most had heard the tales before but listened and laughed politely in exchange for sponging a drink or something else off the old athlete. Hagen was fully conscious of their motives and did not mind too much. A dozen regulars at Li'l Bo's was a better gallery than none at all. For Sir Walter, it was as though the Westchester-Biltmore, the Pasadena-on-the-Gulf, the Savoy in London, and the DAC had all been reduced to Little Bo's. Occasionally, Hagen drank too much, and at those times not even his inner circle was spared verbal abuse.[47]

Hagen also went on hunting or fishing trips once or twice a month, and Peck always did the driving. Deer, pheasant, and especially duck were the usual game. They often visited Jimmy Robinson's lodge on Lake Manitoba for some prime duck hunting. Robinson's place was a popular spot in the '50s for celebrities. On one occasion Hagen made a bet with a so-called friend that Peck could bag more birds in a day than his "friend." Hagen won the bet by paying his friend's guide to take him to a spot where the canvasbacks "flew one-hundred miles per hour" and paying Peck's guide to take him to a spot where the birds were numerous and slow. Hagen never lost his sense of humor, seizing every opportunity to nail an easy target with a sucker bet, whether it be in hunting or at the billiard table.

Each autumn, Peck drove Hagen to Watertown, South Dakota, a town famous for its pheasant hunting. King, despite his unreliability in the field, always went too. The trio became seasonal fixtures in Watertown and usually stayed for about ten days. Along with his humor, Hagen maintained his impulsive generosity; during one trip, the three stopped at a gun shop in Mankato, Minnesota, where Hagen bought himself an expensive, lightweight Beretta twenty-gauge shotgun and bought his young friend a beautiful twelve-gauge model.

When he was not hunting, fishing, or talking it up at Li'l Bo's, Hagen entertained his Detroit friends and his family—Walter Jr., his wife, Helen, and Walter Hagen III. "Haigie," as Hagen's grandson was nicknamed, was born in 1948 and visited Long Lake a few times each summer, although probably not enough for grandpa. Now and then old friends or competitors, such as Joe Kirkwood, would stop in for a few days. If he had nothing else to do, Hagen would hit brand-new balls into Long Lake with a five-iron or watch a baseball or football game on television while listening to another game on the radio.

In some respects, he was as flamboyant as ever; each year Hagen bought (or probably leased) a new yellow-gold Cadillac. He loved the color and even painted his cottage yellow. To Hagen, everything that was nifty was "solid gold," and a good time was a "hoot." Regular "hoots" and new cars were made possible by the substantial royalties that Hagen still received from Wilson's sale of his "Haig Ultra" equipment line. Wilson had bought out L.A. Young at the end of the war, and the royalty checks grew increasingly larger. In the late 1960s he was drawing approximately $100,000 per year. Yet despite his income and luxurious automobile, Hagen furnished his cottage modestly in a rustic style. One wall displayed only a gun rack with a half-dozen of his favorite weapons; there was nothing in the residence to suggest that its owner had once been a great golfer.[48]

On the whole, by the late 1950s, Hagen's life was comfortable and relaxing—too much so for a man who had fed off the "sweet

A showman without a stage.
Courtesy: Sidney L. Matthew Collection

sounds . . . of the cheers and the applause." In 1956 he wrote: "For me the record books are closed. The cheering galleries? Well, they have mostly gone on their way to follow the new champions around the course." Sadly, while Walter Hagen lounged on the *Dor-Mee* or heckled some local at Li'l Bo's, Bob Jones Jr., was beginning the most painful years of his life.[49]

Jones played several more exhibitions after his match with Hagen in the Bahamas, but for him World War II would mean more than charity benefits. As Jones told one reporter who asked about his game, "I stopped worrying about my golf the day the Germans entered Holland." Following the Japanese attack on Pearl Harbor in December 1941, Jones inquired of his reserve unit commander about possible service. (He had held an Army reserve commission since the spring of 1931.) The officer told him that the best thing he could do was raise money at home; besides his celebrity status, Jones had a wife, three children, and health problems (at that point, a history of varicose veins). Nonetheless, he was determined to do something other than play exhibitions. On June 5, 1942, he was commissioned a captain in the U.S. Army and assigned to the Army's Air Force Fighter Command, which was in charge of air defense over the Atlantic seaboard. A few days later he gave one of his last wartime golf performances, wearing military khakis at the Hale America Open in Chicago.

That summer, the possibility of a German attack on the U.S. seemed quite real. The *American Mercury*, a weekly magazine, carried an article informing Americans that their "high army authorities are convinced that the Nazis will strike. When? Any time. They'll come over. Make no mistake about it." So for several months in Jacksonville, Florida, Jones worked as an Aircraft Warning Service Officer for the southeastern United States. He took his job seriously in the wake of Pearl Harbor, and told his volunteer recruits: "In modern warfare a country's first line of defense is its Aircraft Warning Service. Fighter planes afford the best defense against enemy bombers. Yet the best fighter is at a considerable disadvantage if the surprise of the raid is complete." When the job seemed tedious, monotonous, or even unnecessary, Jones and his command simply recalled their unit's motto, "Tis Better to be Bored than Bombed."

In the summer of 1943, when it had become clear that Germany would not attack the U.S., Jones secured an appointment in the 84th Fighter Wing of the Ninth Tactical Command, which meant a tour overseas. First, though, he proceeded to Harrisburg, Pennsylvania, for two months of boot-camp-style intelligence education. He was trained as a teletype operator and, of all things, a prisoner-of-war interrogator. In England, Jones worked as one of many intelligence officers, helping lay the groundwork for the invasion of Normandy. His unit devised plans to bomb bridges over the Seine River in order to isolate France's northern coast. Moreover, Jones participated in the monumental campaign known as D-Day; although his unit landed the next day after the worst fighting had ended, he still endured hours in a foxhole under sporadic German artillery fire. Jones stayed with the invasion force until, a few months later, news arrived that his father was ill; he then requested and received his discharge.[50]

Jones had spent about a year in Europe and returned to Atlanta on August 25, 1944, looking much trimmer (his weight had dropped to around 155 during the war) but otherwise no worse for his military experience. One reporter asked about his duties, but Jones responded with a smile, "Can't talk about those things, you know." In fact, Jones never spoke much about his days in uniform. During more than two years of military service, he was promoted from captain to major to lieutenant colonel and was awarded the World War II Victory Medal and the Army of Occupation Medal.

Back home, Jones resumed his duties as vice president of A.G. Spalding & Brothers, the job that he had listed as his "main occupation" on his military discharge record. By then his son was a "strapping" seventeen-year-old. Bob III had inherited R.T.'s physique, eventually standing near 6' 4" and weighing 240 pounds. Although he worked hard, the young man could not discover his father's golf ability, except in driving distance. Jones tried to protect his son from the inevitable comparisons to himself, saying in 1947, "Publicity on the kid's golf is embarrassing. He doesn't play that well, and he knows it. He gets undue publicity because he's my son." When asked if his son would play in that year's U.S. Amateur, Jones answered, "He can't leave college [Emory University] to go out to California. We have an amicable understanding about that." A decade later, President Dwight D. Eisenhower showed interest in Jones III's golf prowess. "He is really pretty hot stuff in his back yard," Jones Jr., wrote to the President, "although he has not been able to get his putter working when he tries to qualify for one of the national tournaments. Anyway, I would rather he would stay busy in the Coca-Cola business than to try to be a golf champion. He is doing a very good job and I am very proud of him."[51]

Bob Jones III did qualify three times for the U.S. Amateur but never survived the first round of match play. His last attempt was in 1959; at age thirty-two he was knocked out by a husky youth from Columbus, Ohio, named Jack Nicklaus. When Jones III met Nicklaus on the tee the morning of their round, he told the eighteen-year-old buckeye, "You might be interested in knowing, Jack, that my father was thinking of coming out for this tournament. Then when he found out who I had drawn as my first opponent, he changed his mind. He decided it wasn't worth a trip to Colorado just to watch me play one round."[52]

For a few years after the war, life on Tuxedo Road continued along predictably for Jones. Aside from regular outings with his son or wife, he offered legal advice and attended to his business interests. But in 1948 his life took a drastic, unexpected turn. Since the 1926 British Amateur, Jones had periodically felt pain in his shoulders, back, and neck. He had quietly received treatment from osteopaths and even had several bad teeth removed after being told that they might be poisoning his system. ("Bad teeth" were blamed and pulled for all sorts of muscle and joint ailments in the 1920s and 1930s.) The soreness grew much worse by the spring of 1948 and was accompanied by double-vision, as well as the stubbing of his right foot and insensitivity in his right hand—both the result of locomotor problems; on several occasions he burned his fingers with cigarettes but felt no pain. Swinging a golf club, moreover, brought a "burning feeling" to his left side, and by July he had played his last full round.[53]

On October 30, 1948, Jones underwent the first of two spinal operations designed to cure his symptoms. The seven-hour procedure was conducted at the Emory University Hospital and was immediately declared a success. Doctors removed a bone growth from Jones's spine. They believed that the growth had been caused by some injury during his youth, and Jones began a quick, hopeful rehabilitation. Two weeks later the *Atlanta Constitution* reported that he had walked for the first time since the operation and was expected to make a complete recovery. As for the rumors that he would never again play golf, hospital authorities considered them "completely false."[54]

Unfortunately, this was one time in Jones's life when the rumors were true. The bone growth was not the problem; an extremely rare spinal disorder called "syringomyelia" (not Lou Gehrig's disease) was. Syringomyelia attacks the spinal cord, slowly degenerating the motor and sensory nerves. The results are complete muscle atrophy and loss of coordination; in other words, the body is slowly crippled to nothing. In the process, an attack on the sensory nerve sheath leads to a loss of feeling and eventually a deep, throbbing pain in the neck, shoulders, and arms. The victim's mind is not affected, and, indeed, until his final days Jones would be as lucid as ever. By itself, the disease is not fatal, but victims usually die from a related complication.[55]

No one knew then exactly why, how, or where Jones contracted the disorder. Some logically suggested that it was golf-related because few sports put as much strain on the back and spinal cord. Others speculated that Jones's doctors at Emory had botched the procedure, making his condition worse; but that, experts assured, did not happen. The disorder was not inherited, although it is likely that Jones was born with it; syringomyelia is typically regarded as a congenital disease that does not produce symptoms until adulthood. In 1958 Jones wrote, "I know that my physical condition was not derived in any sense from playing the game, and I doubt that without this playing I should ever have lived to see full maturity."[56]

In the winter of 1949, Jones had not yet been diagnosed; in fact, he and everyone else expected a complete recovery. Within months it became obvious that that would not happen. Jones continued having problems with his right limbs and pain in his shoulder, particularly when he ventured out for a few holes with his wife or a friend. On May 18, 1950, Jones underwent a second operation; the five-hour procedure was done at Boston's Lahey Clinic, world-renowned for its treatment of spinal problems. By then Jones's right side was almost completely paralyzed. He could still walk but only with the use of two canes and a heavy steel leg brace. Publicly, Jones's doctors were cautiously optimistic. In private, they told him that everything had been done, that no mistakes had been made at Emory, and that his body would slowly degenerate. (In 1956 Jones saw another expert from Columbia University but received the same report.)[57]

It must have been frightening and frustrating for Jones to admit that the operations had not solved the problem. Still, in public he kept his chin up, telling one reporter in the fall of 1949, "Now I can stand around the first tee and make a nuisance of myself by giving golfing advice to my friends. And the funny part is they cannot get back at me since I can no longer play." He said that he finally had time for other things, such as learning Spanish or playing bridge, and reminded everyone that he "never did play [golf] as much as it seemed. It was more or less a hobby to me. I used to taper off every fall, and it never occurred to me to take a job as a winter professional." If Jones was perpetuating the myth popularized by Grantland Rice and other sportswriters, he was probably doing it subconsciously; more than ever before, it made Jones and everyone around him feel better to remember that golf had never really been his "business."[58]

While displaying peace and acceptance, Jones was actually feeling confused and anxious. In the early '50s a revealing incident occurred at Whitehall which Jones related to his old friend and golf partner Alexa Stirling. Jones said that he woke up one morning, forgot his condition, and pulled himself out of bed. As soon as he began to move across the room, he fell with his chest and face on the floor. For ten minutes he lay there, pounding his fists and cursing in anguish. "Alexa," he joked, "nobody dared come near me. I would have bitten them." Stirling smiled, recalling the temper that Little Bob had displayed years before in their World War I exhibitions. But when she admired his sense of humor, Jones responded that he was not passive about his condition: "I fight it every day. When it first happened to me I was pretty bitter, and there were times when I didn't want to go on living, [but] I decided I'd just do the very best I could." In time Jones would become famous for another line, "Remember, we play the ball as it lies." Whether he actually spoke the words or not, ultimately that is what Jones had to do—with will, courage, and dignity.[59]

So Jones kept on living. He was determined to stay active, and, although his body withered, his spirit and image grew ever stronger. His golf achievements had already been honored over and over, but there were more accolades to come. In 1944, sportswriters had voted the Grand Slam the "outstanding sports achievement of all time" (Jones received two-and-one-half times the votes of his nearest competitor, Babe Ruth). In 1950, Jones was the overwhelming choice in an Associated Press poll as the outstanding golfer of the first half of the twentieth century. Ben Hogan took second in the balloting, and "the flamboyant Walter Hagen" trailed in third. Hagen agreed, "I would have voted for Jones my-self. He was marvelous." Jones was in impressive company; the same poll ranked Jack Dempsey number one in boxing, Jim Thorpe first in football, George Mikan tops in basketball, and Jesse Owens the best in track and field.[60]

Two years later the PGA made Jones its top amateur of the past fifty years, followed by Evans and Ouimet; Hogan was named top professional, followed by Hagen, Sarazen, and Snead. When asked for his personal fifty-year rankings, Jones immediately said "Hagen, Sarazen, and Armour" because they knew how to win "when the chips were down." He found it difficult to appraise golf-ers he had not competed against but thought that Hogan and Nelson were outstanding. In 1954 the USGA established the "Bob Jones Award," to be given annually for "distinguished sportsman-ship in golf." In 1955, the Atlanta Athletic Club honored Jones on the twenty-fifth anniversary of the Grand Slam. For the rest of his life Jones would receive awards, honors, and testimonial dinners.[61]

Yet Jones did more in the 1950s than sit back and collect hon-ors. He had never been politically active, and if he had voted, he probably cast his ballots for Democrats, as did most white South-erners in the first half of the twentieth century. In 1947, however, Jones met General Dwight D. Eisenhower; by 1951 he was con-vinced that the country needed the general as President. He helped start a "Draft Eisenhower" campaign, and when quizzed about his party affiliations, Jones answered, "I'm just for Eisenhower. But it seems you have to be a Republican to be for Eisenhower." Ike was not only the foremost American hero of World War II but also a man who held the kind of common sense, moderately conserva-tive values on which Jones had been reared.[62]

Conversely, Ike liked Jones, and for that matter, all Augusta National members. "The gang," as Eisenhower referred to club members, were just the sort of self-made, wealthy businessmen with whom the General always seemed most comfortable. So Jones worked hard in 1952, doing what he could to raise financial and political support by serving as treasurer of the Georgia Citizens for Eisenhower. For the first time since the Reconstruction era, much of the southern United States—Texas, Virginia, and Florida—went Republican. Despite Jones's efforts, Georgia remained loyal to the Democrats.[63]

Although Eisenhower easily survived the 1952 campaign, Jones almost did not. In October, while preparing for a fund-raising dinner, Jones suffered a heart attack, the sort of thing that could easily happen to an overactive person afflicted with syringomeylia. He bounced back quickly but with a new appreciation for his limitations.[64]

The day after he crushed Adlai Stevenson of Illinois in the general election, Eisenhower went to Augusta to rest. He and his wife Mamie stayed in Jones's cabin. Then following Eisenhower's inaugural in January 1953, the gang announced that a cabin would be built for the President on the grounds. Eventually, Eisenhower became a dues-paying member, after Roberts-Jones told him that they could not bend the rules to grant an honorary membership, not even for an American hero and President. Throughout his two terms, Eisenhower regularly visited the club for golf, bridge, and relaxation.

Eisenhower and Jones developed a solid friendship during the 1950s. In March 1953 Eisenhower, who did oil paintings in his spare time, presented Jones with a portrait of the "Atlanta Golf Machine" in his prime. On the back of it, Eisenhower wrote, "Bob— from his friend—D. D. E.—1953." At a USGA ceremony a few weeks earlier, a letter from the President lauded Jones for possessing "warmth, unselfishness, superb judgement, nobility of character, [and] unwavering loyalty to principle." His "fame as a golfer is transcended by his inestimable qualities as a human being." Occasionally, Jones would visit the White House; in October 1953 he, Roberts, and Robert Woodruff had dinner there with a large group of the President's friends.[65]

The next year Jones discovered how easy it was to get pulled into the world of Washington politics. He was named in Democratic National Chairman Stephen Mitchell's allegations that the Eisenhower administration had showed favoritism in awarding a government contract to the Southern Company, a utilities operation of which Jones was a director. Eisenhower immediately cleared his friend, while Jones called the charges "utterly ridiculous," adding, "I resent any implication that the President would be subjected to such influence, and I resent the implication that I would be foolish enough to try to bring such influence to bear." The public learned that although Jones was a director of the company, he owned only a small block of stock and was generally inactive in the business. Besides, he was hardly a ripe political target, so the story of Jones's involvement in the "Dixon-Yates Scandal," as it came to be called (named after the chairmen of the utilities companies), gained no traction and died within a few days. In fact, *Newsweek* believed that the accusations against Jones "boomeranged" on the Democrats.[66]

In September of 1955 Jones—along with baseball Hall of Famer Rogers Hornsby, former heavyweight champion Gene Tunney, and several noted physicians and Cabinet members—was appointed to the President's Conference on the Fitness of American Youth. A week later, the President suffered his own heart attack. Jones expressed significant concern, but also said, "I have complete confidence he'll come through." He did, of course, and Jones-Roberts were at Augusta to greet Eisenhower after his reelection in the fall of 1956. In December of 1960 Eisenhower sent Jones a letter saying, "I now demand, as my right, that you, starting January 21 [the day he would leave office], address me by [the] nickname 'Ike.'" That privilege put Jones in select company and underscored their friendship.[67]

Jones's relationship with President Eisenhower contributed to his image as golf's premier gentleman, but his courage and outward good cheer in the face of illness did even more to enhance his stature. The Jones image was solidified, however, by his annual Masters Tournament, which he continued to host. After television came to the tournament in 1956, Americans watched Jones participate in the famous green-jacket ceremony. In sum, Jones, Eisenhower, television, and the Masters all developed symbiotic relationships, which by 1960 made Eisenhower and golf more popular, the Masters a "major" event, and Jones more revered than ever.[68]

When he was not involved with the Masters or politics, Jones tried to relax. Like Walter Hagen, he loved the outdoors; one of his favorite pastimes was quail hunting at Bob Woodruff's Ichauway, a plantation in southern Georgia. For a while after his second operation, Jones was able to shoot, though only with some difficulty. Still, he maintained the hobby until one day when, unable to control his fingers properly, he accidentally fired his weapon. According to Charles Elliott, at that point Jones realized that his hunting days were over.

Fishing was much less hazardous, and Jones went whenever possible. It provided a chance to get out in the fresh air, converse with a friend, and forget his increasing pain. Elliott, a distant cousin, was always his partner. A writer for *Outdoor Life*, Elliott lived near Covington, Georgia, in the area where R.T. had originated more than a century earlier. He was probably Jones's dearest companion in the '50s and early '60s. Until it was no longer practical, Elliott and Jones would spend several days at a time fishing and camping at such places as Altoona Lake near Canton, Blue Ridge Lake along the Georgia-Tennessee-North Carolina border, and nearby St. Clair Lake. Jones's preferred target was large-mouth bass, but he would gladly reel in anything.

For a few years Jones used a regular rod and reel, but when that became too difficult for him, Elliott devised a special rig that only required Jones to squeeze the grip to release the line and squeeze it again to lock it. Elliott even had his eighteen-foot boat equipped with a special seat for Jones's comfort. On one trip, a nervous dockhand looked at Jones and said, "It is amazing that a man in your condition could have been such a great golfer." Jones chuckled and answered, "It wasn't easy." When they had their last outings in the early 1960s, Jones had to be carried to his seat by Elliott and an assistant. The inconvenience did not bother Elliott, who would recall the moments with Jones on Lake St. Clair as some of the most enjoyable of his life.[69]

If the weather or schedule did not permit fishing, Jones played bridge, becoming a very good if not brilliant player. Jones also sustained an interest in fine music; he occasionally ventured into downtown Atlanta for concerts and as late as 1960 served on a committee of the city's Music Festival Association. Beyond those hobbies, he continued to work each day at his law office. There he mostly answered mail and passed along legal advice, particularly related to his substantial financial interests, that included Joroberts, a corporation founded by Jones and Roberts that held investments in several South American Coca-Cola bottling plants. Jones also continued as a vice president at A.G. Spalding & Brothers and was an executive for three other Coca-Cola bottling companies.[70]

Moreover, Jones spent the late 1950s writing another autobiography entitled *Golf Is My Game.* He signed with Doubleday to do the book in 1957 and, with the use of a dictation device, completed the manuscript two years later. Unlike *The Walter Hagen Story* or most other athletes' autobiographical works, *Golf Is My Game* was not ghostwritten. It appeared in the spring of 1960 and became a commercial success, selling more than 35,000 copies, receiving favorable reviews, and bringing more than $50,000 in royalties for Jones. The work was successful in part because it had been years since a book about Bobby Jones had been written. In 1927 Jones and Keeler had collaborated on *Down the Fairway;* in 1931 Keeler had done *The Boy's Life of Bobby Jones;* in 1953, shortly after Keeler's death, Grantland Rice wrote *The Bobby Jones Story* from Keeler's voluminous notes and articles. Essentially, *Golf Is My Game* picks up where *Down the Fairway* concluded. The book provides instructional advice and a detailed summary of the Grand Slam.[71]

Jones ended *Golf Is My Game* with a stirring scene that was still fresh in his memory, his acceptance of the Freedom of the City from St. Andrews, Scotland. In the summer of 1958, the USGA invited Jones to serve as a captain for that fall's inaugural Eisenhower Trophy matches, an amateur international team competition with representatives from twenty-nine different nations. St. Andrews was the logical venue for the event, and Jones readily accepted, eager for an excuse to visit the "auld gray city" one more time. In September, just before leaving for Europe, he opened a second invitation, this one from the town clerk of St. Andrews, asking if he would receive "the Freedom of our City." Jones later confessed that he was not sure what it meant but agreed with little hesitation. In October, Bob, Mary, Bob III, and Mary Ellen Jones arrived in St. Andrews, following an unusually dangerous flight to London. (Their aircraft had lost an engine and had to make an unscheduled landing in Newfoundland.) Jones immediately went to the Old Course, where he slowly and painfully retraced the steps of his British Amateur championship. The next day he met with Jock McIntyre, who had been his caddie at St. Andrews in 1930.[72]

The U.S. squad played well the following week in the Eisenhower Trophy matches but lost on October 13 in a play-off to the Australians. Jones followed his men around the course in a golf cart, hunched over a bit and wearing a scarf and overcoat for protection in the cool Scottish breeze.

The biggest story of the trip, however, had already occurred. On Thursday evening, October 9, Jones accepted the most special award of his life. The ceremony took place in the Younger Auditorium at the University of St. Andrews; the hall seated about 1,700 people and it was packed for Jones. The proceedings began with a prayer, and then Provost Robert Leonard, wearing a crimson robe, gave a brief talk on the history of golf at St. Andrews, highlighting the mutual love between Jones and the city. As the aging golfer listened intently, Leonard recounted Jones's first, ignominious experience on the Old Course and his subsequent triumphs in the 1927 British Open and 1930 British Amateur. The Provost finished by explaining the award; he recited some old lines about

Another cycle complete. Bob Jones receives the
Freedom of the City from St. Andrews.
Courtesy: St. Andrews University

permitting a man "to cart shells, to take divots, and to dry washing upon the first and last fairways of the Old Course," and then urged Jones to be "free to feel at home in St. Andrews as truly as in his own first home of Atlanta."

Jones surprised the crowd by standing to his feet unassisted and slowly moving toward the podium. "He made his way across the stage determined not to give in to his woefully crippled legs," wrote one observer. Deeply inspired by the town's affectionate display, he told its citizens that as an undisciplined young man he had failed to understand the beautiful yet simple complexities of St. Andrews, but "the more I studied the Old Course, the more I loved it . . . so that I came to feel that it was for me the most favorable meeting ground possible for an important contest." Jones spoke eloquently of how true friendship transcended love because it left no room for jealousy, and added, "I salute you as my friends." He talked about the importance of international competition and golf's ability to bridge cultures, and then concluded, "I could take out of my life everything except my experiences at St. Andrews, and I'd still have a rich, full life."[73]

Jones signed the St. Andrews' Freedom Roll, and the crowd gave him three deafening cheers. Just as it seemed the sentimental event was finished, a man in the audience began singing an old Scottish folk tune entitled "Will Ye No Come Back Again?" His voice was hauntingly rich and full, and the crowd joined him in a bittersweet tribute to their "Bobby," who sat in a golf cart smiling back at them, knowing that he never would come back again. Herbert Warren Wind, who witnessed the proceedings, said that the final gesture was so spontaneous and genuine that he found himself moved to tears long after he left the building. Mary Ellen Jones remembered that "people were crying and reaching out to touch him [Jones], and to touch even us, my mother, my brother, and me. . . . I can still feel the tingles in my spine. It was moving." Jones simply called it "the finest thing that ever happened to me."[74]

The ceremony was an appropriate way for Jones to close his active life; another cycle was complete. He never returned to Europe and within a few years would hardly be able to leave Whitehall. The next day the front page of the *Atlanta Constitution* carried pictures of Jones and Benjamin Franklin side by side. Franklin, in 1759, was the only other American to be placed on the Freedom Rolls of St. Andrews.[75]

Chapter 11

Endings: 1960–1971

Whitehall and Li'l Bo's—in many ways, those locales summarize the post-golf lives of Bob Jones Jr., and Walter Hagen. By 1960, each man was spending long hours at his favorite place. While Jones's image as the proper Southern gentleman and golf paragon continued to grow, his body deteriorated and the pain increased. As the *New York Times* put it in January 1960, Jones had "added to his stature as a model of sportsmanship," because "despite a crippling back injury, he had actively worked for the game he loves." Hagen, on the other hand, had developed a relatively comfortable, obscure, and predictable life. He hunted, fished, played cards, shot pool, and always held court. At first glance, neither man would have been taken for once having been among the world's greatest athletes.

Every spring, however, sports fans got a glimpse of Jones at the Masters and were reminded of his outstanding achievements. Beyond that annual rite, other awards and recognitions continued for both men. In January of 1960, Jones was again honored in New York City. The Sports Lodge Banquet celebrated the "Men of the Age"—selected in a nationwide survey—who had defined excellence within their sports: Red Grange in football; Ty Cobb in baseball; Jack Dempsey in boxing; Maurice Richard in ice hockey; Bob Cousy in basketball, and Jones in golf. Two days later, at the National Golf Awards Dinner, Vice President Richard M. Nixon handed Jones another award on the occasion of the thirtieth anniversary of the Grand Slam.

Hagen was not invited to the "Men of the Age" banquet, but in 1961 the Golf Writers Association of America honored him with the first annual Walter Hagen Award, given to the "golfer or official, past or present, who had made the most distinguished contribution to Anglo-American golf." The next year Jones received the Walter Hagen Award, while Hagen picked up the Metropolitan Golf Writers Association's Gold Tee Award for "distinguished achievements in golf." And so the recognitions continued.[1]

In 1963, though, Hagen endured one of the worst periods of his life; "Haigie," his fifteen-year-old grandson, was accidentally shot and killed by a friend. Joseph Peck happened to be at the Long Lake cottage on April 23 when Hagen received the awful news. He remembered that Sir Walter looked as though he would "pass out. He couldn't say anything for a few minutes." Apparently, Haigie and his fourteen-year-old friend had been firing Junior's nine-millimeter automatic pistol in the backyard of his Union Lake, Michigan, home. When they returned to the house, Hagie removed the ammunition clip, and his friend, believing that the weapon was unloaded, picked it up, pointed it at Haigie, and may have pulled the trigger. He told police only that it went off "suddenly" while in his hand. In any case, the single shot remaining in the firing chamber lodged in Haigie's forehead. Oakland County prosecutors immediately ruled the shooting an accident. Peck drove Hagen to Pontiac for a last visit with his only grandchild, who died on April 26, 1963, at Pontiac's General Hospital. A few days later the Hagen family, including Margaret Johnson-Hagen, convened at the Holy Sepulchre Cemetery to lay Walter C. Hagen III to rest.[2]

By 1964 Hagen's own health began to decline. For more than forty years he had smoked excessively. It finally caught up with him when he developed cancer of the larynx. In July of 1965, he traveled with his son to New York for a throat operation. Despite his circumstances, Hagen was as sassy as ever. Golf writer Charles Price, who met the Hagens in New York, recalled that although Sir Walter could "hardly breathe, he managed, in the company of Junior and myself on the way to the hospital, to put away six gin-and-tonics and four steins of beer, smoke a pack of Pall Malls, argue with a bartender, instruct a waiter on the fine art of wrapping sandwiches, forget his mother's maiden name at St. Vincent's registration desk, joke with a priest who had just given the last rites to a patient, shake hands with half a dozen employees, and pinch the bottoms of three different nurses!"[3]

Hagen was unable to give much of an encore on the trip home from St. Vincent's a few months later. He had endured two procedures in New York. On July 15 surgeons performed a tracheotomy

Fred Corcoran and Hagen in 1965.
Courtesy: Sidney L. Matthew Collection

to aid his breathing, and less than two weeks later, on the 27th, they operated again, working hard to remove a malignant tumor from his larynx. Nonetheless, when Fred Corcoran visited Hagen's room soon after the operation, he found the ex-golfer "sitting up, cheerfully watching the Yankees on TV, handsomely groomed as always and wearing an elegant red-silk dressing gown and a beautiful ascot. If I had not known about his illness, I would have imagined that it was nothing more serious than tonsillitis." But it was much more serious, and, despite the doctors' efforts, the cancer spread. In January of 1967, Hagen submitted to a third procedure on his throat at the Munson Medical Center in Traverse City. After each operation Hagen surprised physicians with his feisty rehabilitations, but at seventy-four years, he was in dire physical condition.[4]

In the autumn of 1965, just months after Hagen's return from New York, the *Detroit Free Press* assigned sportswriter Joe Falls his first daily column. Someone mentioned to him that Hagen was living in Traverse City, so Falls obtained Hagen's telephone number and dialed. Doris Brandes answered and told Falls that although Mr. Hagen could not speak into the phone, he would love to visit with the sportswriter at his earliest convenience. The next day, Falls drove up to Traverse City.

Falls found Brandes to be a very pleasant woman, who led him into a large room overlooking the lake. The sportswriter had never met Hagen and, in fact, knew little about him, including the cancer. The man whom Falls met that day was overweight and wore eyeglasses with thick lenses; he could not speak, yet he was standing without a cane or crutches and was grinning broadly at the prospect of reviewing the old days one more time. Falls also noticed that Hagen wore a white bib and, as he continued to do until his death, smoked a cigarette. Then the columnist enjoyed what "might have been the two most marvelous hours of my life," communicating with Hagen, who made noises and gestures which were interpreted by Brandes. As Falls turned to leave, Hagen directed a few more sounds toward his housekeeper. She stopped Falls and asked, "Mr. Hagen would like to know if you'd like to see him hit a golf ball?" "I'd love to." Falls replied. As the sportswriter remembered it, "Both of them smiled. He went to the corner of the room and pulled a club from a golf bag leaning against the wall. He came back to the middle of the room and placed an imaginary ball on the carpet. He took his stance, drew the club back, and swung through the invisible ball. He looked out the picture window and let out a loud whoop, making noises to his housekeeper. 'Oh,' she said, 'Mr. Hagen made a perfect shot—right into the middle of the lake.'" Following the show, Falls left, convinced that Sir Walter was "an entertainer to the very end of his life." Several years later Brandes told Al Watrous that Hagen went through that routine every day, even at the very end when he required assistance.[5]

On August 14, 1967, six months after his third operation, Hagen made one of his final public appearances, attending a dinner in his honor at the Traverse City Golf and Country Club. Organized by members, the Walter Hagen Testimonial was to be a final celebration of Sir Walter's achievements, particularly in the development and rise of professional golf. Many of the big-name professionals were invited, and a few cared enough to make the trip. Arnold Palmer and Cary Middlecoff were there. Also among the 300 present were the aging Al Watrous and Johnny Farrell, PGA President Max Elbin, the mayor of Traverse City, and other local dignitaries. Many who did not attend sent letters. Ben Hogan wrote his "deepest thanks [to Hagen, because] without you, golf would not be what it is today." President Eisenhower, the Duke of Windsor, Michigan U.S. Senator Philip Hart, Bob Hope, Tommy Armour, Byron Nelson, Francis Ouimet, and Jones also sent testimonials. Jones wrote only a few lines but said that he "always enjoyed the many rounds of golf we played together, even when you were giving me a good beating. I still enjoy reminiscing about your performances and our many meetings, both on and off the golf course. I hope you will be aware that such a thing is a truly sincere tribute to you."[6]

The evening's highlight was a short speech by thirty-seven-year-old Arnold Palmer, who earlier that day had impressed the locals by flying into Traverse City on his private jet. Although he had already been challenged by Jack Nicklaus for competitive superiority, Palmer was still the most admired professional golfer in the country. Palmer's appearance in Traverse City was also special because no golfer had been compared to Hagen as much as had the Pennsylvanian. To be sure, Palmer did not resemble the hedonistic Haig, but his unorthodox, combative style, world-famous back-nine charges, and charisma did stir memories of the swashbuckling Sir Walter. (Ironically, the PGA Championship is the only major title that Palmer never won.)

Palmer told the crowd how "thrilled" he had been in 1961 when, after winning his first British Open, he received a long-distance telephone call from Hagen, offering his congratulations. Then he looked at Hagen and concluded, "This meeting could be held in the pro shop if it weren't for all you did to help build the game. Golf is better for Walter Hagen." Palmer's point, if a bit overstated, was absolutely correct and underscored the most significant legacy of Hagen's career: Sir Walter belongs on a short list of athletes, including Babe Ruth, Red Grange, and Jack Dempsey, who in the early twentieth century established modern professional sports. Gene Sarazen had put it differently a few years earlier: "All the professionals who have a chance to go after the big money today should say a silent thanks to Walter each time they stretch a check between their fingers. It was Walter who made professional golf what it is."

The banquet finished in Masters style, with Hagen receiving a blazer and several other gifts. Within a few hours it was over, Palmer and everyone else left, the curtains closed, and the spotlight clicked off again—probably much too quickly for Sir Walter. The local *Record-Eagle* described the dinner as "the biggest thing in golfing that has ever happened in Traverse City."[7]

The following year Hagen received another significant recognition, becoming a member of the Royal and Ancient Golf Club of St. Andrew's, Scotland. Only three other Americans—President Eisenhower, Francis Ouimet, and Bob Jones Jr.—had been so honored. "Though I have not publicly been known for an excess of humility," Hagen wrote club officials, "I assure you at this time it is with just such an emotion that I am pleased to accept your most gracious offer."

That was Sir Walter's last award; by 1969 the aggressive cancer had moved from his throat to his lungs, and he was dying. Hagen languished throughout most of the year, but on September 26 he slipped into a coma. As word of his condition spread, sportswriters across the country began preparing final Hagen commentaries. Many would recall how Hagen toyed with his opponents in match-play; how he showed up late for luncheons and tee times; how he drank and womanized all night and then won play-offs the next day; how he smashed the barriers to professionals at clubhouses in America and abroad; how he made a million dollars playing golf, outdressed everyone, and referred to royals by their first names; and, of course, how he never worried, never hurried, and always took time to smell the flowers along the way. Some recounted his U.S. Open disappointment at Brookline in 1913 and his victories at Midlothian in 1914 and at Brae Burn in 1919; his dismal finish in the British Open in 1920 and his victories in 1922, 1924, 1928, and 1929; and his five PGA Championships, including four consecutive victories from 1924 to 1927. A few noted his five Western Open crowns, three Metropolitan Open titles (consecutively from 1916–1920; the tournament was canceled in 1917 and 1918 because of World War I), and numerous other triumphs on the links, such as the Battle of the Century.

One can only wonder what scenes flashed through Hagen's mind in those final hours. Maybe he recalled some of the old anecdotes as well—his rounds with the Duke of Windsor and so on. After all, Hagen admitted being in awe of wealth and power when he was a working-class caddie at the Country Club of Rochester. As for his golf victories, they may have been just a blur; for Hagen, it might have been enough simply to remember that when golf was played by the likes of "Long Jim" Barnes, Jock Hutchison, Gene Sarazen, Chick Evans, and Bobby Jones, he was once considered the "greatest ever—bar none."

Hagen must have seen images and faces that no one wrote about: sunny days spent chipping golf balls in the meadow along the banks of Allen's Creek; playing games with his sisters during Rochester's long winters in the small, two-story house built by his father, or sledding on the hills near Corbett's Glen; Louise Hagen, his mother; dancing and dinner with Margaret Johnson; the afternoon in 1931 when he, Junior, and William Hagen were photographed together; the birth of his only child and the death of his only grandchild; honeymooning with Edna Straus in 1923 London; globetrotting with Joe Kirkwood; hunting duck on Lake Tulie with Bob Harlow or pheasant with Joe Peck and King in South Dakota; six-year-old Lawrence Johnson; hitting ball after ball into Long Lake with a five-iron, while Doris Brandes admonished him to be careful; his regular court at Li'l Bo's—faces displaying interest, pity, and pleasure while the old athlete reminisced.

Whatever his final images were, they faded away on Monday evening, October 6, 1969. Walter C. Hagen, at seventy-six years, died quietly in his Long Lake cottage. The next day Traverse City friends paid their final respects in a brief prayer meeting conducted by the pastor of the Trinity Lutheran Church. Funeral services were held in Birmingham, Michigan, two days later.[8]

Arnold Palmer flew to Detroit for the funeral to serve as a pallbearer, along with Walter Hagen Jr., PGA Commissioner Joseph Dey, and Al Watrous. Following the service, Hagen's body was carried to the Holy Sepulchre Cemetery and laid alongside Walter Hagen III. Those who attended the reception noticed an easel holding a sign bearing Hagen's Nassau quotation: "You're only here for a short visit. Don't hurry . . . ." The easel was surrounded by flowers and on a table sat a silver bowl containing ice and champagne. The day was beautiful, with a clear, blue sky. That made it easier for the fifty-one-year-old Hagen Jr., to assume his father's role and entertain guests with stories, such as the time that Hagen had once mistakenly cabled his son from Europe with congratulations for his twenty-first birthday on his twentieth.

Fortunately for Junior and his wife, Hagen cleverly had arranged for them to receive the royalties from Wilson's "Hagen Ultra" equipment line long after his death. Hagen also willed his twenty-acre Long Lake estate to Doris Brandes; she was to live there as long as she wanted.[9]

Throughout the next several weeks, sportswriters on both sides of the Atlantic published their obituaries. Most just took their cues from *The Walter Hagen Story* and crafted a string of Sir Walter's shenanigans. No one remembered the thoughts of H.B. Martin, the golf historian and one-time Hagen manager, who years earlier reflected on Hagen's behavior and decided that "If a man hasn't got any faults, it is almost a sure bet that he hasn't any friends. Much has been said about Hagen; some of it is true and a lot of it is just plain gossip." The *London Times* went deeper than many, though. After acknowledging the legion of Hagen anecdotes, the *Times* concluded, "Much less secure is [Hagen's] reputation as a golfer, and the balance should be redressed because even had he never opened his mouth, even if he had dressed for the fairways in sackcloth, he would stand in comparison with the best in the world."[10]

Nearly bedridden himself, Bob Jones Jr., was sad to hear of Hagen's passing, telling a reporter from the *Atlanta Constitution*, "We hate to lose an old friend like Walt, but he was so ill for so long we knew it was inevitable. Naturally, I have fond and interesting memories of Walt, and I know the whole world of golf will pay tribute to him, as I would like to do." The November 1969 issue of *Professional Golfer* included a lengthy series of memories collected from Hagen's former competitors. Bud Harvey, an editor for the magazine, sent Jones a telegram asking him for his "fondest recollection of [Hagen] in the form of favorite anecdote." Jones considered Harvey's request but, as though agreeing with H.B. Martin, figured that the *Professional Golfer* would gather plenty of juicy stories involving showgirls, movie stars, and kings. Hagen, Jones felt, deserved something more, and his response became the introduction for Harvey's piece:

> *"Walter Hagen will always be one of the great names in the world of golf.*
> *He was a colorful and competent competitor and an admirable sportsman.*
> *I am thankful that I had many opportunities to play with him*
> *in championship competition.*
> *I have been asked for an anecdote about Hagen. I knew him so well*
> *and knew so much about him that it is impossible*
> *to select one episode of more interest than others.*
> *I think it is enough to say that his contribution to the game*
> *will always be remembered.*
> *I respected him in life and will revere his memory."*[11]

In some ways the 1960s, like the '50s, would be kinder to Jones than to Hagen. Hardly marginalized, the Atlantan maintained an influential voice in the world of golf. Moreover, Jones did not experience any personal loss on the order of Hagen's grandson's accidental death. On the other hand, syringomyelia continued to exact its toll. To make matters worse, he had to face the period without the support of either O.B. Keeler or his parents. It had been ten years since Keeler died; in July of 1956 Big Bob Jones had passed away; and in January of 1961 his frail but strong-willed mother, Clara Jones, also died. To be sure, Jones had his wife, but by 1962 she was quite weak, stricken by a tumor in her vocal chords. There were also the three children, cousins in Canton, and a handful of friends, such as Charles Elliott, but everyone that Jones had looked to for encouragement and strength was gone.[12]

Nonetheless, Jones endured the last years of his life remarkably well. He stayed active, despite the inconvenience of being barely ambulatory with the aid of two canes. Each weekday around 11:00 A.M., Jones was chauffeured in his tan 1961 Cadillac to his downtown law office at the firm of Jones, Bird, Williams, and Howell. Once in the office, which was almost devoid of golf paraphernalia, Jones handled correspondence and occasionally gave telephone or personal interviews. He communicated with fans, players past and present, reporters, golf writers, Cliff Roberts, and cousin Louis Jones Jr., who oversaw the family's interests in Canton. Sometime between 4:00 and 4:30 P.M., before rush-hour traffic, Jones was helped to his car on Poplar Street and driven back to Whitehall. He would sustain that routine until the final months of his life.[13]

The pain, as Jones described it in 1968, was not great, but he experienced "constant discomfort in all members in all postures." By then he was in a wheelchair and had lost the use of his left arm. The journalist Alistair Cook met Jones in 1965 and was taken aback upon "seeing the extent of his disability, the fine strong hands, twisted like the branches of a cypress, gamely clutching a tumbler or one of his perpetual cigarettes in a holder. His face was more ravaged than I had expected, from the long-endured pain I imagine, but the embarrassment a stranger might feel about this was tempered by the quizzical eyes and the warmth his presence gave off."[14]

Jones eased his pain somewhat by sipping bourbon. Since his competitive days, he had liked to relax with a shot of corn whiskey. Keeler had always indulged heavily, and there is an anecdote or two from Jones's college days that suggest that he occasionally got carried away himself. Because of the way his hands curled and contorted into little more than claws, Jones could not drink from a typical shot glass but only from a mug with a particular handle. He also relied on custom-made fork-holders and cigarette holders, longer and thinner than usual. In 1948, he told his doctors that he drank an average of two to six times per day, in addition to four cups of coffee, two Coca-Colas, and thirty cigarettes. There is no evidence that any of those numbers decreased in his later years; rather, like Hagen, Jones was rarely observed without a drink or a cigarette in hand.[15]

Each April until 1969, he made his appearance for the green-jacket ceremony at Augusta. He looked more drawn, tired, pained, and generally worse every year, but CBS's television commentators said nothing because for so many fans Jones was the highlight. After the 1968 telecast, though, Roberts decided that his old friend looked too bad for the ceremony. Roberts did not have the will to take responsibility for the change, so he (and CBS) allowed Jones to believe that the network had requested his absence. Jones probably considered the decision to be a sound judgment, but he was nonetheless crushed by the poignant reminder of his awful condition.[16]

Jones's removal from the Masters telecast was a culmination of what had been evolving at Augusta National since 1948, when Jones began to show serious effects of syringomyelia. From the club's inception, Roberts had usually had his way, but after 1948 his power at Augusta increased substantially for a number of reasons: Jones became very ill; CBS became ever important, and Roberts handled the network skillfully; and, because of Eisenhower's involvement, the club became a political power-center. Jones humorously acknowledged Roberts's ascendancy in 1965, when the USGA formally reinstated his amateur status. On his application he reported that his present occupation was "assistant" and that his employer was "Clifford Roberts." It was an important point, because while Jones never completely lost influence over Roberts and continued to be the Masters symbol of tradition, amateurism, and sportsmanship, Roberts was primarily responsible for the club and its tournament in the postwar period. Over the years the tendency for some observers would be to credit Jones with what was good about Augusta National and to blame its shortcomings on Roberts. In truth, the New Yorker was ultimately responsible for both.[17]

Bob Jones in 1964. Although ravaged by illness,
he never relinquished his dignity or grace.
Courtesy: Emory University

That is not to say that Jones lost interest in the Masters; rather, he was quite protective of his tournament. For example, in the spring of 1967 Jimmy Demaret, the first three-time winner of the event, made some remarks about the Masters which both Roberts and Jones considered disparaging. The *Houston Post* had Demaret saying that there "was something missing" at the 1967 tournament. He blamed the National's ticket limit for the "lack of enthusiasm" among the crowds and believed that locals had "boycotted" the event as a result. Irked by Demaret's comments, Jones fired off a letter to him in which he pointed out that Demaret was typically referred to in the media as a "three-time Masters champion," suggesting that Demaret's "position of authority in the game is closely related to his performances at Augusta." Although Jones had always thought Demaret a "pretty savvy guy," he was "beginning to doubt, because it makes no sense for you to belittle a tournament from which you have gotten so much mileage on television and in advertising." Jones concluded, "Cliff and I have done everything we could to exalt and glorify the Masters champions. May I suggest to you that it would be in your interest if you should do the same thing?" Demaret returned a conciliatory letter but stopped short of an apology or disavowal of the remarks attributed to him.[18]

Like any hugely successful project, Augusta National became the target of much criticism, mostly because of its exclusiveness and perceived racism. Much of the negativity concerning Augusta stemmed from its setting, an Old South plantation, where black servants and caddies still waited on white elites. Stepping onto the club's grounds was in too many ways like turning back the clock. In the early '60s, when the country embarked on a new era of racial sensitivity, the ambience of Augusta National and the Masters became a problem for many people.[19]

As for Jones, it is impossible to know his precise views on race relations. It seems that he never wrote about or openly discussed his feelings on racial exclusion in golf or in the broader society. That said, he was a traditionalist reared in a racially backward culture, and so it is likely that he harbored the typical paternalistic views of upper-class southern whites. Jones seemed to like President Eisenhower's public positions, including his conservatively moderate race policies, and if he liberalized his views over the years, there is no evidence of it. In fact, in what seems to have been his most egregious behavior, Jones publicly tolerated Roberts-implemented policies at Augusta National and the Masters which were very insensitive and legalistic, if not simply racist.

There is also, however, no evidence of actual race hate from the lives of R.T. Jones, Big Bob Jones, or Bob Jones Jr. On the contrary, they all, particularly Bob Jones Jr., seem to have treated minorities with warmth and respect; from East Lake caddies to his chauffeur, Jones was popular among black people he knew personally. Charles Elliott, who spent long, casual hours fishing and conversing with Jones, recalled never hearing Jones utter any racial, ethnic, or religious slur. That was more than one could have said about most of Jones's fellow countrymen.[20]

In a sense, though, the discussion is unfair; in spite of his superior education, his experience with real estate, the law, and political figures, his writing ability and substantial intellect, Jones acquired his prominence on the links. He was, after all, a thoughtful and highly skilled athlete, not a reincarnation of Thomas Jefferson, as some admirers would have one believe.

Moreover, unlike so many other athletes and celebrities, he refreshingly refrained from offering pretentious social commentary and was modest enough to think that major social problems were outside his area of expertise. In 1955, for example, Jones turned down an appointment by President Eisenhower to serve on the Advisory Committee for the Georgia Republican Party, saying "the reason is singular, namely, that I know that I have not the experience nor the wisdom to be an effective adviser in matters of this kind." He added that, in light of his inexperience, his appointment would seem "an effort to trade on a sports reputation," because people "know me as only a golfer." While admitting that the parallel was not perfect, he reminded Eisenhower of "the amount of stature lost by Charles Lindbergh when he departed from his role as authority in the aeronautical field in order to make [public policy] speeches for the Liberty League." Jones considered Lindbergh at his best when he confined his activities "to the field in which he was obviously entitled to be an authority." Of course, Jones could have relied upon his personal experiences in the New South and used his prestige and golf club to foster progress in race relations; but, given his personality, temperament, and physical condition, such an idea seems unrealistic.[21]

If Jones held his tongue on golf and race, he occasionally commented on other happenings within his sport. In 1968, when the PGA endured an internal war between tournament players and traditional club professionals, Jones reminded everyone of the amateur's contribution to the game and cautioned the circuit professionals against regarding "themselves only as performers whose skills are to be sold to the highest bidder." Jones eventually praised the PGA's decision to establish a commissioner and its selection of Joseph Dey, his good friend and the former executive director of the USGA, as the first man to fill the post. Just weeks before he died, though, Jones confessed his fears that "the game has been too highly commercialized," and that "modern golfers [do not] have the same respect for the game's traditions and the accomplishments of the great players of the past." One of Jones's pet peeves was ghostwritten instructional books, which he characterized as a "fraud that ought to be punished by law." Jones, who wrote *Golf Is My Game, Bobby Jones on Golf, Bobby Jones on the Basic Golf Swing*, and hundreds of instructional columns that appeared under his name, became irritated one day when he "was urged to write [another] book on the basis that Sam Snead had written six." With wry humor, he replied, "I doubt if Snead has ever written a letter."[22]

Predictably, Jones was constantly asked to compare the skills of modern players to those of himself and his contemporaries. He usually refused, consistently holding the position that such comparisons were impossible, and that the best any athlete could do was beat the competition of his day. In 1953, for instance, sportswriters began a debate over the relative skills of Jones and Ben Hogan, who that year had won the U.S. and British Opens and the Masters. When Jones was asked about it, he replied, "How can you make a comparison? I never played against him. We were in two different eras." Yet Jones refused to believe that the players of the 1960s were any better than those of the 1920s. "I never suffered from lack of length," he reminded one interviewer who brought up the driving prowess of Jack Nicklaus. "I could always reach par fives in two, [and] that was with hickory."[23]

Nonetheless, Nicklaus was the contemporary player who impressed Jones the most. The Grand Slam winner once paid the "Golden Bear" his highest compliment, "He plays a game with which I am unfamiliar." Jones closely followed Nicklaus's early career, and despite the generational gap, the two developed a warm friendship. In *The Greatest Game of All*, Nicklaus's 1969 autobiography, the Ohioan referred to Jones as an "idol and friend," while Jones wrote in the foreword, "I think it is completely safe to say that there has not yet been a more effective golfer than Jack Nicklaus." In some ways, Nicklaus was to Jones what Palmer was to Hagen. Because of Nicklaus's technically sound swing, length and accuracy off the tee, perfectionist tendencies, and record in major championship competition, he was compared to Jones more often than was any other player. Nicklaus went on nearly to double Jones's number of major tournament victories and in 1986 won a record-setting sixth Masters title.[24]

When not dispensing golf wisdom, Jones spent time with his wife or a friend at Whitehall. Like Hagen and nearly every other American male in that period, he was fascinated by televised sports and particularly enjoyed watching golf coverage. Jones also gave considerable energy to researching and collecting art objects, especially porcelain vases from Western Europe. He and his wife turned their Tuxedo Road mansion into a virtual museum of Continental antiques. By the summer of 1969, however, the couple had decided that, after thirty years, Whitehall had become an unnecessary expense and a burden to maintain. So that fall Bob and Mary Jones moved into an apartment on Peachtree Road.[25]

They had also moved because Jones's health was rapidly declining. His spinal disorder had led to other physical problems. In March of 1958, six years after his heart attack, Jones suffered what was initially reported as another heart attack and later as a "circulatory collapse" from a severe drop in blood pressure. As of about 1965, he was forced to wear a permanent catheter and had developed respiratory problems, specifically periodic bouts with bronchial asthma. His body was simply shutting down; as atrophy set in, he withered away to ninety pounds.[26]

In 1968, while still able to sit in a wheelchair, he wrote to Dr. Houston Merritt, the Columbia University specialist who had diagnosed his condition in 1956. Jones reminded Merritt that he had once described the illness as "a slowly progressive disease with a relatively good prognosis as far as length of life is concerned." Jones admitted, "I hope you will appreciate that I am saying this with all the good humor of which I am capable, but I am getting pretty fed up with this 'relatively good prognosis.' My life, day and night, is about as nearly miserable as one could imagine." He asked Merritt how he might become more comfortable. The "most important question," Jones wrote, is "based on averages, and perhaps somewhat on conjecture, how much longer am I likely to endure this condition? As a corollary of this, again based on averages, what is the most likely way in which my exit may be achieved?"[27]

Discouraged, sad, and afraid, Jones wanted to know specifically what to expect. Fate, he believed, had determined his introduction to golf, his failures and successes on the course (especially the Grand Slam), and his contraction of syringomyelia. Jones had welcomed the good experiences and had courageously fought the bad ones, but after twenty years the old competitor was tired.

Merritt flew down to Atlanta to visit with Jones and his doctors; it was a kind gesture, but there was nothing more to do. By late 1970 Jones had ceased his regular visits to the office, unable to leave his apartment on Peachtree Road. Within six months he was essentially bed-ridden, except for an hour or two in which he was propped up in an easy chair. Still, he continued answering mail by dictating to his secretary, Jean Marshall; she taped a pen to a tennis ball, which Jones could grip, allowing him to sign his more personal correspondence "Bob." In November he received word that the USGA had completed plans to move its headquarters from New York City to a sleepy spot near Far Hills, New Jersey, and that the new Golf House Museum would memorialize his achievements in a handsome Bobby Jones Room.

Less than a month later, in December 1971, Jones's heart finally collapsed to an aneurysm. When doctors suggested that his life might be extended through transfusions and hospitalization, Bob and Mary Jones refused. In a follow-up letter to Merritt, Ralph Murphy, Jones's Atlanta doctor, confessed amazement at the strength of Jones's heart. "I suppose," he concluded, "it was a tribute to his inner competitive spirit, even though he wanted to go as quickly as possible."[28]

On December 15 Jones, slipping in and out of consciousness, asked his wife to get her pastor. Nominally a lifelong Protestant, Jones decided to convert to his wife's faith. The Reverend John Stapleton of the Cathedral of Christ the King baptized Jones and administered last rites. Some have logically suggested that Jones's eleventh-hour conversion was little more than an effort to please Mary Jones. Charles Elliott and Bob Jones IV were not so sure, arguing that Jones was a spiritually sensitive man and that his declaration of faith was as much for himself as his wife. Jean Marshall told a reporter that Jones "seemed so peaceful after he was baptized. I think it gave him a great deal of comfort." Three days later, on December 18, 1971, Robert T. Jones Jr., died in his sleep at the age of sixty-nine.[29]

The family asked Stapleton to conduct a ten-minute, private graveside ceremony. It occurred on December 21 in a secluded section of Atlanta's Oakland Cemetery amid balmy but otherwise gloomy conditions. Jones's gray metal casket was covered with lilies and snapdragons; the immediate family was there, but no one else. More than one writer noted that it was an ironic exit for a man who had repeatedly been cheered by thousands. Yet for those who knew Jones, it was appropriate. "That's the way Dad wanted it," Robert T. Jones III said. "He didn't want any great fuss."[30]

Throughout the following weeks, the world of golf mourned. Sportswriters, officials, players past and present, corporate executives, and politicians created a flood of eulogies. Arnold Palmer believed that Jones's accomplishments "will live on forever." Although every story on Jones offered readers a description of his career—from his many losses as a club-throwing youth to his thirteen major titles as an impeccably behaved young man—few dwelt on Jones's golf record. Those who did tended to focus on the Grand Slam, but that may not have been the Atlantan's greatest golf achievement. His record in the U.S. Open was astonishing. In eleven starts, he finished out of the top ten only once (eleventh in 1927), and in the nine U.S. Opens from 1922 through 1930, Jones collected four victories and four runner-ups. He simply dominated the tournament for nearly a decade.[31]

Bob Jones Jr., however, had long been recognized as much more than the sum of his golf achievements; he would be remembered for his character, his iron will in the face of physical adversity, and his commitment to family, friends, and sportsmanship. The *New York Times* cited Jones's axiom, "First come my wife and children. Next comes my profession—the law. Finally, and never as a life in itself, comes golf." The *Atlanta Constitution and Journal* noted that "Jones's golf fame [was] transcended by human qualities," while Ben Hogan added, "Jones was a winner. But anyone can be a winner. It was the way he won that made him stand out above all others." Sportswriter and longtime friend Paul Gallico may have put it best: "He was a gentleman, and he loved his friends . . . . He was the best golf player the world has ever known."[32]

From their lineages to their eulogies, Walter Hagen and Bob Jones Jr., had little in common, save a warm, mutual respect and a love of athletic competition. Were it not for golf, their lives most likely would never have intersected, which is precisely why their stories offer insight into sports and American history. Conflicts emerge when these great golfers are taken side by side: materialism versus idealism; pragmatism versus principle; professionalism versus amateurism; and even change versus continuity. Hagen's life went in one direction; Jones's followed another. Yet both men struggled to reconcile the conflicts within their sport and the broader culture. At any rate, one can only hope to understand Hagen by contemplating Jones, and the converse is equally true. But if that does not compel discussion, there will always be Sir Walter's 12 and 11 romp over Mr. Jones in their Battle of the Century.

Notes

Prologue

1. See Stephen R. Lowe, "Change, Continuity, and Golf's Battle of the Century," *Journal of Sport History*, Vol. 26, Num. 3, 521-543, for more detailed coverage of the Hagen–Jones match. Will Grimsley, *Golf: Its History, People, and Events* (Englewood Cliffs, NJ: Prentice-Hall, Inc., 1966), 57–58; Walter Hagen and Margaret Seaton Heck, *The Walter Hagen Story* (New York: Simon and Schuster, 1956), 148–151; "Hagen Overwhelms Bobby Jones," *Professional Golfer*, 6 (March 1926), 24; "The Battle of the Century," *Southern Golfer*, 7 (March 15, 1926), 11; Robert Tyre Jones Jr., *Golf is My Game* (Garden City: Doubleday and Company, Inc., 1960), 96.

2. *New York World*, February 28, 1926; H.B. Martin, "Golf Records Make Interesting Comparison," *Metropolitan Golfer*, 4 (May 1926), 20–21; Gould B. Martin, "Jones No Match for Hagen," *Metropolitan Golfer*, 4 (March 1926), 8; Hagen and Heck, *Walter Hagen Story*, 148.

3. *Sarasota Herald*, March 1, 1926; see also, Hagen, *Walter Hagen Story*, 153–154; Grantland Rice, *The Bobby Jones Story* (Atlanta: Tupper and Love, 1953), 140; and Jones, *Golf Is My Game*, 98. In the last account, Jones recalls that Hagen's ball was not really obstructed by a tree, but was in the middle of the fairway. The *Sarasota Herald* report mentions the tree, however. Also, Hagen's birdie putt was made more difficult by the fact that Jones's missed putt had laid him a stymie (that is, Jones's ball was partially blocking Hagen's path to the hole). Finally, the accounts of the length of Hagen's birdie putt vary from 3 feet to 15 feet. See also O.B. Keeler, "Hagen—Match-Play Master," *American Golfer*, 29 (May 1926), 1; reprinted in Charles Price, *American Golfer* (New York: Random House, 1964), 77–82.

4. First day medal totals: Hagen 71–70–141; Jones, 77–74–151. Most telling, though, was the number of putts required: Hagen used 27 in the morning and 26 in the afternoon to Jones's 31 and 30. Hagen, *Walter Hagen Story*, 154; *Sarasota Herald*, March 1, 1926.

5. *Tampa-St. Petersburg Tribune*, March 8, 1926; *Sarasota Herald*, March 8, 1926; *New York Times*, March 8, 1926, 13; and Hagen, *Walter Hagen Story*,

155. Accounts of the length of Hagen's birdie putt vary from the *Times's* record of forty feet, to Hagen's fifty feet, to the *Herald*'s report of seventy feet. In any case, it was long, and no one, including Hagen himself, expected the putt to fall. Herbert Warren Wind, *The Story of American Golf* (New York: Alfred A. Knopf, 1975), 151.

6. Grimsley, *Golf,* 58; Robert T. Jones Jr., *Down the Fairway* (New York: Blue Ribbon Books, 1927), 148. Rice, *Bobby Jones Story,* 137; Richard Miller, *Triumphant Journey: The Saga of Bobby Jones and the Grand Slam of Golf* (New York: Holt, Rinehart, and Winston, 1980), 161; *New Orleans Times-Picayne,* March 8, 1926; *New York Herald-Tribune,* March 8, 1926. H.B. Martin, *Fifty Years of American Golf* (New York: Dodd, Mead, & Company, 1936), 330; Allison Danzig and Peter Brandwein, *Sports Golden Age: A Closeup of the Fabulous Twenties* (New York: Harper and Row Publishers, 1948), 193.

7. I found the seed for this project in Benjamin Rader, *American Sports: From the Age of Folk Games to the Age of Televised Sports* (Englewood Cliffs: Prentice-Hall, 1996), 194–199.

8. On Hagen and Jones, see Paul Gallico, *The Golden People* (Garden City: Doubleday & Co., Inc., 1965); Grantland Rice, *The Tumult and the Shouting* (New York: A.S. Barnes & Company, 1954); Hagen, *Walter Hagen Story;* Ross Goodner, *Golf's Greatest* (New York: Golf Digest, 1978), 70–79; Wind, *Story of American Golf,* 118–132; George Peper, ed. *Golf in America: The First Hundred Years* (New York: Harry N. Abrams, Inc., Publishers, 1988), 52–61; Bernard Darwin, *Golf Between Two Wars* (London: Chatto and Windus, 1944); Gene Sarazen, *Thirty Years of Championship Golf* (Englewood Cliffs: Prentice-Hall Press, 1950), passim; Al Barkow, *The History of the PGA Tour* (New York: Doubleday, 1989), 17–24, 269; Al Laney, *Following the Leaders* (Classics of Golf reprint, Ailsa, Inc., 1991), 46.

9. Wind, *Story of American Golf,* 119–120; O.B. Keeler, "Showmen of the Game," *American Golfer,* 28 (May 16, 1925), 7; Laney, *Following the Leaders,* 46.

10. For a discussion of Hagen's swing, see Tom Scott and Geoffrey Cousins, *The Golf Immortals* (New York: Hart Publishing Company, Inc., 1969), 43–55; H.B. Martin, *Fifty Years of American Golf,* 325; O.B. Keeler, "Studying the Styles of Champions: Walter Hagen," *American Golfer,* 26 (19 May 1923), 24; *New York Times,* November 13, 1927, XI, 9; September 1, 1929, V, 4.

11. Wind, *Story of American Golf,* 127; interview with Ken Janke (friend of Walter Hagen and executor of Hagen estate), May 14, 1997, Birmingham, Michigan; Hagen and Heck, *Walter Hagen Story,* 176–177, 262; Al Barkow, *History of the PGA Tour,* 19; H.B. Martin, "A Champion in the Making," *Golf Illustrated,* 40 (December 1933), 41.

12. Charles Price, *The World of Golf* (New York: Random House, 1962), 132; Hagen and Heck, *Walter Hagen Story,* 260.

13. J.H. Taylor, *Golf: My Life's Work* (London: Jonathan Cape, LTD, 1943), 212; A.C.M. Croome, "The Other Side of Hagen," *American Golfer,* 29 (September 1926), 26; Martin, *Fifty Years of American Golf,* 324–325; O.B. Keeler, "Studying the Styles of Champions," 24.

14. See Peper, *Golf in America,* 52–60; Herb Graffis, *The PGA: Official History of the Professional Golfers' Association of America* (New York: Thomas Y. Crowell Company, 1975), 167–174 and "The Haig," *Sport,* 27 (June 1959), 88; Al Barkow, *Golf's Golden Grind: The History of the Tour* (New York: Harcourt, Brace, and Jovanovich, 1974), 39–75; *Detroit News,* May 25, 1924; Rice, *Tumult and the Shouting,* 65; "How Hagen and Harlow Hit It Off," *Professional Golfer,* 9 (January 1929), 21.

15. Charles Bartlett, "Walter in Wonderland," *Professional Golfer,* 33 (June 1951), 18; Barkow, *History of the PGA,* 23–24. Rice, "Golf's Bad Boy," 18; Grimsley, *Golf,* 59; Jones, *Golf is My Game,* 97.

16. Grantland Rice, "There's Only One Bobby Jones," *Collier's,* 75 (4 April 1925), 20; E.W.E. Holderness, "Golf's Great Stylist," *American Golfer,* 31 (July 1928); Thomas Uzzell, "A Study of Bobby Jones's Swing," *American Golfer,* 27 (18 October 1924), 8; Martin, *Fifty Years of American Golf,* 361; Scott and Cousins, *The Golf Immortals,* 81–96; Price, *World of Golf,* 174; "In the Locker-Room with Bobby Jones," *Literary Digest,* 105 (5 July 1930), 42.

17. Rice, "There's Only One Bobby Jones," 20. See Jim Barnes's quotation in Martin, *Fifty Years of American Golf,* 357; also, Jerome Travers and James Crowell, *The Fifth Estate: Thirty Years of Golf* (New York: Alfred A. Knopf, 1926), 67; W.E. Woodward, "What Makes Him Click," *American Magazine,* 109 (April 1930), 170.

18. *Philadelphia Inquirer,* September 8, 1916; Rice, "There's Only One Bobby Jones," 20; "In the Locker-Room with Bobby Jones," 42.

19. Francis J. Powers, "Bobby Jones Retires From Competitive Golf," *Golfers Magazine,* 58 (December 1930), 7; Angus Perkerson, "Atlanta, Home of Golf Champions," *Golfers Magazine,* 50 (October 1926), 29; Martin, *Fifty Years of American Golf,* 362. Scholars have done much in recent years to trace the origins of the amateur ethos. Ironically, although amateurism has been usually regarded as an original or pure approach to athletics, in fact one can make a compelling case that professional sports have deeper roots and that the amateurism which Jones and others embodied was actually a fairly recent (late nineteenth century) invention of the Victorian middle and upper classes—an invention that distinguished and protected them from the perceived crass materialism of the working class. For a discussion of the origins of amateurism and its uses, see especially S.W. Pope, *Patriotic Games: Sporting Traditions in the American Imagination, 1876–1926* (New York: Oxford University Press, 1997); also see Donald J. Mrozek, *Sport and American Mentality* (Knoxville, TN: University of Tennessee Press, 1983); Mark Dyreson, *Making the American Team: Sport, Culture, and the Olympic Experience* (Urbana and Chicago: University of Illinois Press, 1998); Rader, *American Sports.*

20. See Stephen R. Lowe, "Demarbleizing Bobby Jones," *Georgia Historical Quarterly* 83 (Winter 1999), 660–682. Bobby Jones, "Not My Business," *Collier's,* 85 (26 April 1930), 13; Powers, "Bobby Jones Retires From Competitive Golf," 7; *New York Times,* November 19, 1930, 26.

21. *New York Times,* July 18, 1926, VIII, 8; Gallico, *Farewell to Sport,* 70; *Atlanta Constitution,* July 11, 1926, November 18, 1930; "The Impredicable

Bobby Jones," *Commonweal,* 12 (23 July 1930), 314; "The Significance of Mr. Jones," *Golf Monthly,* 18 (August 1927), 18.

22. Gallico, *The Golden People,* 280.

23. Charles C. Alexander, *Ty Cobb* (New York: Oxford University Press, 1984); David Owen, *The Making of the Masters: Clifford Roberts, Augusta National, and Golf's Most Prestigious Tournament* (New York: Simon and Schuster, 1999); Steve Eubanks, *Augusta: Home of the Masters Tournament* (Nashville, TN: Rutledge Hill Press, 1997); Curt Sampson, *The Masters: Golf, Money, and Power in Augusta, Georgia* (New York: Villard Press, 1998); Charlie Sifford with James Gullo, *Just Let Me Play: The Story of Charlie Sifford, The First Black PGA Golfer* (New York: British American Publishing, 1992).

24. "Bobby Jones on His Victory," *Golf Monthly,* 20 (June 1930), 314.

25. *New York Times,* July 31, 1927, VIII, 2; Elliott interview.

26. For surveys of 1920s America, see Lynn Dumenil, *The Modern Temper* (New York: Hill and Wang, 1995); Stanley Coben, *Rebellion Against Victorianism: The Impetus for Cultural Change in 1920s America* (New York: Oxford University Press, 1991); Roderick Nash, *The Nervous Generation: American Thought, 1917–1930* (reprint, Chicago: Ivan R. Dee, 1990); Joan Hoff Wilson, ed., *The Twenties: The Critical Issues* (Boston: Little Brown, and Company, 1972); Paula Fass, *The Damned and the Beautiful: American Youth in the Twenties* (New York: Oxford University Press, 1977); Paul A. Carter, *Another Part of the Twenties* (New York: Columbia University Press, 1977); T.J. Jackson Lears, *No Place of Grace* (New York: Pantheon Books, 1981): and William Leuchtenberg, *The Perils of Prosperity, 1914–32* (2nd ed., Chicago: University of Chicago Press, 1993). See also Randy Roberts, *Jack Dempsey: The Manassa Mauler* (Baton Rouge: Louisiana State University Press, 1979) and Roderick Nash, "Sports Heroes of the 1920s," in Steven A. Riess, ed., *Major Problems in American Sport History* (Boston: Houghton Mifflin, 1997), 324–329.

Chapter 1

1. Reid and his friends did engage in a little creativity. They spelled their club's name with an apostrophe, "St. Andrew's," as opposed to the original apostrophe-less St. Andrews, Scotland. The best history of the early sport is still H.B. Martin, *Fifty Years of American Golf* (New York: Dodd, Mead, and Company, 1936); see also, Robert W. Henderson, *Ball, Bat, and Bishop: The Origin of Ball Games* (New York: Rockport Press, Inc., 1947); Herbert Warren Wind, *The Story of American Golf: Its Champions and Championships* (New York: Alfred A. Knopf, 1975); H.B. Martin and A.B. Halliday, *St. Andrew's Golf Club, 1888–1938* (New York: Rogers, Kellogg, Stillson, Inc., 1938); H.S.C. Everard, *A History of the Royal & Ancient Golf Club St. Andrews, 1754–1900* (London: William Blackwood and Sons, 1907); Robert Browning, *A History of Golf: The Royal and Ancient Game* (New York: E.P. Dutton & Company, Inc., 1955); Gene Brown, ed., *The Complete Book of Golf* (New York: Arno Press, 1980); and James P. Lee, *Golf in America: A Practical Manual* (New York: Dodd, Mead & Company, 1895).

2. Garden Smith, *The World of Golf* (London: A.D. Innes & Company, 1898), 253. For a recent history of the country club in America, see James M. Mayo, *The American Country Club: Its Origins and Development* (New Brunswick, NJ: Rutgers University Press, 1998); Richard Moss, "Sport and Social Status: Golf and the Making of the Country Club in the United States, 1882–1920," *International Journal of the History of Sport* 10:1 (1993), 93–100.

3. Quoted in Benjamin Rader, *American Sports: From the Age of Folk Games to the Age of Televised Sports* (Englewood Cliffs, NJ: Prentice-Hall, 1996), 194.

4. Grantland Rice, *The Tumult and the Shouting*, (New York: A.S. Barnes & Company, 1954), 61.

5. In piecing together the origins of Hagen's family, I relied upon materials in the property abstract of the Hagen homestead. For a classic account of the development of Rochester and its surrounding area, see Blake McKelvey, *Rochester: The Water-Power City, 1812–1854* (Cambridge, MA: Harvard University Press, 1945), 163, 334 and *Rochester: The Flower City, 1855–1890* (Cambridge, MA: Harvard University Press, 1949), 7–9, 378–381. See also William N. Hosley, *Special Places: A History of Irondequoit and Allen's Creek Valleys* (Rochester, NY: Water View Publications, 1993), 65.

6. *Rochester Democrat and Chronicle*, September 22, 1913. It seems Monroe County does not have a birth record for Hagen. This information was taken from his baptismal certificate, which includes his full name and date of birth. Years later, after he became famous, Hagen's middle name was widely thought to be "Charles." Hagen put that middle name on a marriage license in 1923, but there is otherwise no legal evidence that it was his name. His baptismal certificate has "Christian." Either Hagen liked the sound of "Walter Charles" more than "Walter Christian" and unofficially changed his name by 1923, or "Charles" was always his legal name, while "Christian" was merely his baptismal name.

7. Walter Hagen and Margaret Seaton Heck, *The Walter Hagen Story* (New York: Simon and Schuster, 1956), 10. Unless otherwise noted, the material I used on Hagen's early life may be found in his autobiography.

8. *Atlanta Constitution*, March 16, 1924.

9. Hagen and Heck, *Walter Hagen Story*, 10–17.

10. See Jim Mandelero and Scott Pitoniak, *Silver Seasons: The Story of the Rochester Red Wings* (Syracuse, NY: Syracuse University Press, 1996).

11. Hagen and Heck, *Walter Hagen Story*, 13–14.

12. Telephone conversation with Alyce Commisso, former Corbett's Glen resident, August 29, 1997; Hagen and Heck, *The Walter Hagen Story*, 42, 287–288.

13. For materials relating to Hagen's baseball career, see O.B. Keeler, "The Hagen Theory of Golf," *American Golfer*, 28 (13 June 1925), 9; Walter Hagen, "Homebred and Foreign Pro Compared," *Golf Illustrated*, 7 (April 1917), 20–21; *Atlanta Constitution*, March 16, 1924; *Los Angeles Times*, December 26, 1928.

14. "Diegel Again Wears the Crown," *Canadian Golfer*, 11 (August 1925), 348; Hagen and Heck, *Walter Hagen Story*, 21.

15. The board minutes of the Country Club of Rochester make no mention of Hagen's hiring, but they do state that Andrew Christy was paid $1,000 in 1910.

16. Interviews with Louis Jones Jr., July 31, 1997, Canton, Georgia and Robert T. Jones IV, October 14, 1997, Atlanta, Georgia; *The Story of A Man, A Town, and A Mill* (Canton Textile Mills, 1949), 9. Louis Jones still has a copy of this brief work, done to commemorate the fiftieth anniversary of the Canton Textile Mills and the life of Robert Tyre Jones, Sr.

17. The murder of William Green Jones is probably the most dramatic episode in the lineages of either Hagen or Jones. William Green Jones's murderer was never apprehended. Interview with Bob Jones IV, October 14, 1997, Atlanta, Georgia.

18. *A Man, A Town, and A Mill,* 4; R.T. Jones, "Christianity as Related to Business," Canton *Cherokee Advance*, October 29, 1920; quoted in Richard Miller, *Triumphant Journey* (New York: Holt, Rinehart, and Winston, 1981), 24.

19. Newspaper clipping, *Atlanta Constitution-Journal,* July 16, 1956, Bobby Jones File, Special Collections Department, Robert W. Woodruff Library, Emory University, Atlanta, Georgia; *St. Paul Pioneer-Press,* July 8, 1930; Keeler, *Boys' Life of Bobby Jones* (New York: Harper and Brothers, 1931), 5.

20. Letter to Mrs. Robert Ingram, February 13, 1970, roll 2, Robert Tyre Jones Jr., Collection, United States Golf Association's Golf House Library, Far Hills, NJ (hereafter "RTJ").

21. Darlene R. Roth and Andy Ambrose, *Metropolitan Frontiers: A Short History of Atlanta* (Atlanta, GA: Longstreet Press, Inc., 1996), 52–53, 62; for a detailed history of Atlanta, see Franklin M. Garrett, *Atlanta and Environs: A Chronicle of Its People and Events,* 2 vols. (Athens, GA: University of Georgia Press, 1969).

22. *Atlanta Constitution,* March 19, 1902; Miller, *Triumphant Journey,* 29; Robert Tyre Jones Jr., *Down the Fairway* (New York: Blue Ribbon Books, 1927), 20; Keeler, *Boys' Life,* 1–2; Keeler, "How Bobby Jones Started," *American Golfer,* 23 (5 June 1920), 4.

23. Letter to Ralph O. Samuel, June 25, 1963, roll 3, RTJ.

24. Letter to Mr. Willard Tomlinson, April 21, 1958, roll 3, RTJ; *Philadelphia Inquirer,* September 8, 1916. For years, golf fans and writers have disputed over the wealth of the Joneses. Did Little Bob come from a "rich" family? Was he born with a silver spoon in his mouth? The answer is yes and no, and it raises an important historical point: not everyone who joined an exclusive athletic or country club in the early twentieth century was super rich, and not every "club" drew from the same socioeconomic pool for its members. The Jones family certainly was not of the old, entrenched elite. The family's history seems to suggest that before R.T., the Joneses were middle class. R.T. Jones, however, significantly elevated his personal material wealth; thus, his heirs were afforded more socioeconomic opportunities. R.P. Jones was at least of the upper middle classes. One way that his class distinguished itself from the lower middle classes and working classes was by joining urban athletic

clubs which brought not only social status but, also very important for R.P., business contacts. So, when Jones's admirers suggest that his amateurism was a financial sacrifice, they are correct, at least to a degree. On the other hand, it is true that the Joneses had the resources and status to join an exclusive club and allow Little Bob to compete as an amateur – proof that the family had much more money than the Hagens of Brighton, NY, for example. It seems fair to conclude that the family of Little Bob Jones was "moderately wealthy" and that today it would be considered upper middle class or, possibly, lower upper class. At any rate, the Joneses illustrate the variations within the "elite" and the "country club" in early twentieth century American society. See Rader, *American Sports;* Mayo, *American Country Club;* Moss, "Sport and Social Status"; Donald J. Mrozek, *Sport and American Mentality, 1888–1910* (Knoxville: University of Tennessee Press, 1983); S.W. Pope, *Patriotic Games: Sporting Traditions in the American Imagination, 1876–1926* (New York: Oxford University Press, 1997).

25. Tomlinson Letter, RTJ.

26. Peper, *Golf in America,* 213; Martin, *Fifty Years of American Golf,* 168–169; Browning, ed., *The Complete Book of Golf,* 129; in addition, Bernard Darwin, *A History of Golf in Great Britain* (London: Cassell & Company, LTD, 1952) also offers a helpful discussion on the evolution of golf equipment.

27. "Golf in America Has Made Great Gains," *New York Times,* August 7, 1910 in Brown, *The Complete Book of Golf,* 8.

Chapter 2

1. Harry Vardon, "What's Wrong With American Golf?" *Everybody's Magazine,* 30 (June 1914), 724; Robert Sommers, *The U.S. Open: Golf's Ultimate Challenge* (New York: Atheneum, 1987), 31; Grantland Rice, *The Tumult and the Shouting* (New York: A.S. Barnes & Company, 1954), 56; for a copy of the USGA's official response to the British press on this matter, see "McDermott's Outburst," *Golf Illustrated* (British), 58 (19 September 1913), 2.

2. "Ouimet's World's Golf Champion," *New York Times,* reprinted in Gene Brown, ed., *The Complete Book of Golf* (New York: Arno Press, 1980), 10.

3. *Rochester Democrat and Chronicle,* September 19, 21, 1913.

4. Walter Hagen and Margaret Seaton Heck, *The Walter Hagen Story* (New York: Simon and Schuster, 1956), 30–32.

5. Henry Leach, "The U.S. Open Championship," *American Golfer,* 10 (October 1913), 583. The Vardon and Ray quotations may be found in Leach's coverage.

6. H.B. Martin, "A Champion in the Making," *Golf Illustrated,* 40 (December 1933), 16; *Rochester Democrat and Herald* and *Union and Advertiser,* September 21, 1913.

7. "Ouimet World's Golf Champion," *Complete Book of Golf,* 9. S.P. Jermain, "Impressions of Ouimet's Victory," *Golfers Magazine,* 23 (October 1913), 281;

the "Thank you, mother" anecdote was related in the coverage of both the
Rochester Democrat and Chronicle and the *New York Times*, September 21, 1913;
Leach, "The U.S. Open Championship," 588; "Tee Shots," *Golf Illustrated* (British) 58 (26 September 1913), 21; see also, Francis Ouimet, *A Game of Golf: A
Book of Reminiscence* (Boston: Houghton Mifflin Company, 1932) and Stephen
Hardy, *How Boston Played* (Northeastern University Press, 1982), 181–185.

8. Stephen Skevington, "Mr. Ouimet's Victory," *Golf Illustrated* (British),
58 (26 September 1913), 31; Leach, "U.S. Open," 573–575.

9. Charles Fountain, *Sportswriter: The Life and Times of Grantland Rice*
(New York: Oxford University Press, 1993), 218; Charles Price, *The World of
Golf* (New York: Random House, 1962), 110; H.B. Martin, *Fifty Years of
American Golf* (New York: Dodd, Mead, and Company, 1936), 250–251.

10. Herbert Graffis, *The PGA: The Official History of the Professional
Golfer's Association of America* (New York: Thomas Y. Crowell Company, 1975),
169; James M. Mayo, *The American Country Club: Its Origins and Development* (New Brunswick, NJ: Rutgers University Press, 1998); Richard Tufts,
The Scottish Invasion (Pinehurst, NC: Pinehurst Publishers, 1962), 91.

11. See *Chicago Daily Tribune*, August 19, 1914; Crafts W. Higgins, "National Open Championship," *Golfers Magazine*, 25 (September 1914), 25;
and Lochinvar, "The Open Championship," *American Golfer*, 11 (September
1914), 986.

12. Charles Bartlett, "Walter in Wonderland," *Professional Golfer*, 33 (May
1951), 17; Chick Evans, "Hail to the Haig," *Golfing*, 7 (May 1939), 7; Graffis,
The PGA, 58.

13. All of this is essentially the opposite of modern conventional wisdom,
which is that wet conditions usually make a course play easier, even if shorter,
as soft greens are more receptive to approach shots and putting is slower.

14. For coverage of the 1914 U.S. Open, I relied on the *Rochester Herald*,
August 22, 1914; Charles Evans Jr., *Chick Evans' Golf Book: The Story of the
Sporting Battles of the Greatest of all Amateur Golfers* (New York: Thomas E.
Wilson & Company, 1921), 207; Lochinvar, "The Open Championship," 981;
Higgins, "National Open Championship," 25–28; and Sol Metzger, "Sir Walter,
Showman," *Collier's*, 88 (25 July 1931), 22; "As They Remember Him," *Professional Golfer*, 50 (November 1969), 9; and "Tee Shots," *Golf Illustrated*
(British), 61 (28 August 1914), 249.

15. *New York Herald*, August 22, 1914; Henry W. Clune, *I Always Liked It
Here: Reminiscences of a Rochesterian* (Rochester, NY: Friends of the University of Rochester Libraries, 1983), 122; *Rochester Democrat and Chronicle*,
August 25–27, 1914.

16. Herbert Reed, "Concerning a Real Champion," *Harper's Weekly*, 60
(22 May 1915), 500–501; see also "Panama-Pacific Tournaments," *Golfers
Magazine*, 27 (June 1915), 53 and San Francisco *Examiner*, April 28, 1915.

17. Baltimore *Sun*, June 16–17, 1915; "Travers Wins National Open Championship," *Golfers Magazine*, 27 (July 1915), 11–17.

18. For coverage of the Massachusetts Open, see *Boston Daily Globe*,
June 31–July 2, 1915; "New England Notes," *American Golfer*, 16 (July 1915),

329–335; "Metropolitan Open Championship," *Golfers Magazine*, 27 (August 1915), 45–46.

19. *Chicago Daily Tribune*, August 18–20, 1915; "Western Open Championship," *Golfers Magazine*, 27 (September 1915), 9–14. For a discussion of A.G. Spalding and the development of the sporting goods industry, see Stephen Hardy, "'Adopted by All the Leading Clubs': Sporting Goods and the Shaping of Leisure, 1800–1900" in Richard Butsch, ed., *For Fun and Profit* (Philadelphia: Temple University Press, 1990), 71–101.

20. H.B. Martin "Professional Golfers Association of America," *Golfers Magazine*, 28 (April 1916), 20–22; Graffis, *The PGA*, 77–99.

21. *St. Paul Pioneer-Press*, June 28, 1916.

22. *New York Herald*, July 12–16, 1916; "The Metropolitan Championship," *American Golfer*, 16 (August 1916), 278–283; *Rochester Democrat and Chronicle*, July 16, 1916.

23. *Milwaukee Sentinel* and *Rochester Democrat and Chronicle*, August 16–20, 1916; H.D. Fargo, "Hagen Wins Western Open," *Golfers Magazine*, 29 (September 1916), 11–15.

24. Notes of the Board Meeting of the Country Club of Rochester, September 20 and October 16, 1916, Rochester Country Club, Rochester, New York.

25. J.G. Davis, "Western Department," *American Golfer*, 16 (September 1916), 387; Herbert Reed, "Afield with a Home-Bred 'Pro'," 30 (October 1916), 44–45.

26. Gene Sarazen with Herbert Warren Wind, *Thirty Years of Championship Golf* (Englewood Cliffs, NJ: Prentice-Hall Press, 1950), 112–113.

27. Robert Tyre Jones Jr., *Down the Fairway* (New York: Blue Ribbon Books, 1927), 39; O.B. Keeler, *The Autobiography of an Average Golfer* (New York: Greenberg Publisher, Inc., 1925), 110–120.

28. Ibid., 42; Quoted in O.B. Keeler, *The Boys' Life of Bobby Jones* (New York: Harper and Brothers, 1931), 58.

29. Quoted in Fountain, *Sportswriter*, 221–222; see Rice, *Tumult and the Shouting*, 74–75.

30. See *Atlanta Constitution*, June 15–20, 1915; "The Southern Championship," *Golfers Magazine*, 27 (August 1915), 54–55; "From the South," *American Golfer*, 14 (July 1915), 273–276; and Jones, *Down the Fairway*, 51.

31. *Atlanta Constitution*, September 12–October 4, 1915; "From the South," *American Golfer*, 15 (January 1916), 222.

32. *Birmingham News*, June 22–25, 1916; *Atlanta Constitution*, June 23–25, July 28–30; 1916; "From the South, " *The American Golfer*, 16 (August 1916), 315.

33. *New York Times*, July 6, 1916, 7; *Atlanta Constitution*, August 1–6, 1916; "Georgia Championships," *Golfers Magazine*, 29 (September 1916), 66.

34. "George Adair," roll 1, The Bobby Jones Collection, Golf House Library, United States Golf Association, Far Hills, NJ.

35. Jones, *Down the Fairway*, 61; O.B. Keeler, "How Bobby Jones Started," *American Golfer*, 23 (5 June 1920), 25.

36. Rice recalled a heated exchange between Jones and Byers; see *Tumult and the Shouting*, 78.

37. For coverage of the 1916 U.S. Amateur, I relied on the *Philadelphia Inquirer*, September 6–10, 1916; *New York Times*, September 5–10, 1916; *Atlanta Constitution*, September 7, 1916; *St. Louis Post*, September 21, 1930; John G. Anderson, "The Amateur Championship," *Golf Illustrated*, 5 (September, 1916), 20; P.C. Pulver, "National Amateur Championship," *Golfers Magazine*, 29 (October 1916), 14; Grantland Rice, "Ace of Clubs," *Collier's*, 86 (27 September 1930), 15; Keeler, *Boys' Life of Bobby Jones*, 75.

Chapter 3

1. "Golf Almost Dead in Great Britain," *Golfers Magazine*, 29 (October 1916), 27.

2. *Rochester Chronicle and Democrat*, January 30, 1917.

3. Walter Hagen and Margaret Seaton Heck, *The Walter Hagen Story* (New York: Simon and Schuster, 1956), 48–49.

4. Birth certificate of Walter C. Hagen Jr., Office of Vital Records, Monroe County, New York.

5. *New York Times*, June 21–23, 1917.

6. *Atlanta Constitution*, June 4–10, 1917.

7. *Chicago Tribune*, July 9–10, 1917; *New York Times*, August 19, 1917, III, 4; The *Times* reported that Jones fared poorly because he was suffering from a digestive ailment. See also Crafts W. Higgins, "Western Amateur Championship," *Golfers Magazine*, 31 (August 1917), 9–14.

8. Charles F. Thompson, "The Reason for the Western Championship," *Golfers Magazine*, 31 (August 1917), 15.

9. Robert Tyre Jones, "'Granny' Was My Friend," Robert Tyre Jones Jr. Collection, roll 2, United States Golf Association's Golf House Library, Far Hills, NJ (hereafter "RTJ"); Grantland Rice, *The Tumult and the Shouting* (New York: A.S. Barnes & Company, 1954), 79; Charles Fountain, *Sportswriter: The Life and Times of Grantland Rice* (New York: Oxford University Press, 1993), 223; Robert T. Jones, *Down the Fairway* (New York: Blue Ribbon Books, 1927), 76.

10. For coverage of the PGA relief matches, see "P.G.A. War Relief Tournament," *Golf Illustrated*, 7 (August 1917), 21–28; "The Professional Golfers' Association Tournament," *American Golfer*, 18 (August 1917), 57–64; *New York Times*, July 27, 1917, 10; August 31, 1917, 9.

11. O.B. Keeler, "How Bobby Jones Started," *American Golfer*, 23 (5 June 1920), 25.

12. J.M. Barnes, "The Western Open Championship," *Golf Illustrated*, 8 (October 1917), 28–31; "The Western Open Championship," *American Golfer*, 18 (October 1917), 198–204.

13. "From the South," *American Golfer*, 20 (May 1918), 674.

14. Henry Clune, *I Always Liked It Here: Reminiscences of a Rochesterian* (Rochester, NY: Friends of the University of Rochester Libraries, 1983), 121–

123 and *The Rochester I Know* (Garden City, NY: Doubleday & Company, Inc., 1972), 355–356.

15. Minutes of the Board, August 9, October 18, 1917; June 5, September 25, 1918, Rochester Country Club, Rochester, New York.

16. *Detroit Free Press,* May 26, 1918; Minutes of the Board, May 15, June 18, 1918, Oakland Hills Country Club, Birmingham, Michigan.

17. Bryon Perry and Kay Healey, *75 Years at Oakland Hills* (Warren, MI: Perry and White, Inc., 1991), 12.

18. Hagen and Heck, *Walter Hagen Story,* 57; Clune, *I Always Liked It Here,* 124.

19. Hagen and Heck, *Walter Hagen Story,* 23; Charles Bartlett, "Walter in Wonderland," *Professional Golfer,* 33 (May 1951), 17; H.B. Martin, "A Champion in the Making," *Golf Illustrated,* 40 (December 1933), 41.

20. Alexa Stirling Fraser, "The Most Unforgettable Character I've Met," article, Bobby Jones File, Special Collections, Robert W. Woodruff Library, Emory University, Atlanta, Georgia (hereafter "BJF"); Robert T. Jones, *Golf Is My Game* (New York: Doubleday and Company, 1960), 94; Jerry Travers and James R. Crowell, *The Fifth Estate: Thirty Years of Golf* (New York: Alfred A. Knopf, 1926), 125; *New York Times,* June 17–August 15, 1918.

21. *New York Times,* September 15–23, 1918.

22. Clifford Roberts, *The Story of the Augusta National Golf Club* (New York: Doubleday & Company, Inc., 1976), 237; "Bob Jones, Class of '22"; "Bob Jones . . . Tech's Most Illustrious Graduate," BJF.

23. Paul Hornung, *Scioto Country Club: 75 Years of History* (Columbus, OH: Scioto Country Club, 1993), 30.

24. *American Golfer,* 20 (October 1918), 131.

25. Charles Evans, *Chick Evans' Golf Book* (New York: Thos. E. Wilson & Co., 1921), 239–273; "What Golf Is Doing in the War," *American Golfer,* 22 (August 1918), 901.

26. R.E. Howard, "War's Effects on Golf: The Problem of Playing Pace," *Golf Illustrated,* 8 (October 1917), 26–27; "The Value of Exhibition Games," Ibid., November 1917, 7–8.

27. Herbert Graffis, *The PGA: The Official History of the Professional Golfer's Association of American* (New York: Thomas Y. Crowell Company, 1975), 91.

28. *New York Times,* March 9, 1919, 19.

29. *Boston Globe,* June 10, 1919.

30. A. Linde Fowler, "National Open Golf Championship," *American Golfer,* 21 (July 1919), 694.

31. Fred Corcoran with Bud Harvey, "The Professional: Walter Hagen," in Robert Trent Jones, ed. *Great Golf Stories* (New York: Galahad Books, 1987), 113.

32. "As They Remember Him," *Professional Golfer,* 50 (November 1969), 9.

33. *New York Herald,* June 13, 1919.

34. This episode is covered in *New York Times,* June 13, 1919, 11; *Boston Globe,* June 13, 1919; *New York Herald,* June 13, 1919; Fowler, "National

Open Championship," 697; see also, Tom Flaherty, *The U.S. Open, 1895–1965* (New York: E.P. Dutton & Co., Inc., 1966) 45–47.

35. Gay Talese, "The Caddie—A Non-Alger Story," in Gene Brown, ed., *The Complete Book of Golf* (New York: Arno Press, 1980), 108; Fowler, "National Open Championship," 698; Hagen and Heck, *Walter Hagen Story*, 59.

36. *New York Herald*, June 13, 1919.

37. Herbert Reed, "Tearing Thru and Out," *Independent*, 99 (26 July 1919), 125.

38. *American Golfer*, 22 (November 1919), 52; *New York Times*, June 24, 1919, 11.

39. *New York Times*, July 14, 1919, 9; "Golf on the Atlantic Seaboard," *American Golfer*, 21 (August 1919), 803–807; New York *Herald*, July 12, 1919.

40. Roberts, *The Story of Augusta National*, 237.

41. *New York Times*, May 6–June 26, 1919; *Atlanta Constitution*, May 8–9, 1919.

42. Letter with newsclipping to RTJ from Frank O. Walsh, April 30, 1962, roll 3, RTJ. Jones later said that the wheelbarrow episode inspired him to learn all of the rules of golf, so that he would never again be caught ignorant about them.

43. O.B. Keeler, *The Autobiography of an Average Golfer* (New York: Greenberg Publisher, Inc., 1925), 209; for complete tournament coverage, including the famous wheelbarrow shot, see *New Orleans Times-Picayne*, June 24–28, 1919 and letter from Frank O. Walsh, RTJ.

44. Hamilton *Spectator* (Ontario), July 24–August 1, 1919; "Records Run Riot," *Canadian Golfer*, 5 (August 1919), 217–221; "Bobby Jones and the Canadian Open," ibid., 16 (March 1931), 813–814.

45. Letter from RTJ to Herbert Warren Wind, September 21, 1971, roll 3, RTJ; Red Hoffman, "The Rise and Fall of Penal Architecture," in Robert Trent Jones, *Great Golf Stories*, 32–35.

46. My coverage of the 1919 U.S. Amateur is based on the Pittsburgh *Press*, August 17–24, 1919; *New York Times*, August 21, 1919, 13; and John G. Anderson, "The Amateur Championship," *American Golfer*, 21 (September 1919), 853–876.

47. *Canton Cherokee Advance* (Georgia), August 29, 1919; *New York Times*, August 26, 1919, 12.

48. *Atlanta Constitution*, September 9–11, 1919; *New York Times*, September 8–11, 1919.

49. Jones, *Down the Fairway*, 136; *Golf Is My Game*, 93.

50. *New York Times*, November 30, 1919, X, 4.

Chapter 4

1. The causal forces involved in modernization—industrialization, urbanization, immigration, social pluralism, and bureacratization, among others—actually began in the late nineteenth century. Lynn Dumenil, *The Modern Temper: American Culture and Society in the 1920s* (New York: Hill and Wang, 1995), among many others listed in endnote #26 of the prologue.

2. *New York Times*, March 1, 1920, 11.

3. Ibid., March 8, 1920, 10–11; "Following the Pros," *Southern Golfer*, 1 (15 March 1920), 14.

4. *New York Times*, March 14–16, 1920; H.B. Martin, "Hagen Wins West Coast Open," *Southern Golfer*, 1 (1 April 1920), 17.

5. *New York Times*, March 31 and May 9, 1920.

6. Walter Hagen and Margaret Seaton Heck, *The Walter Hagen Story* (New York: Simon and Schuster, 1956), 51.

7. Henry Clune, *I Always Liked It Here: Reminiscences of a Rochesterian* (Rochester, NY: Friends of the University of Rochester Libraries, 1983), 125.

8. Interview with Joseph Peck, friend of Walter Hagen, October 16, 1996, Traverse City, Michigan. Stanley Coben, *Rebellion Against Victorianism: The Impetus for Cultural Change in 1920s America* (New York: Oxford University Press, 1991), 3.

9. Grantland Rice, "Hagen, the Homebred," *American Golfer*, 23 (17 April 1920), 19; J.S. Worthington, "Hagen vs. Mitchell," *American Golfer*, 23 (15 May 1920), 9; Hagen and Heck, *Walter Hagen Story*, 62.

10. Quoted in H.B. Martin, *Fifty Years of American Golf* (New York: Dodd, Mead & Company, 1936), 327.

11. Richard Holt, *Sport and the British* (New York: Oxford University Press, 1989), 305; Geoffrey Cousins, *Golf in Britain; A Social History from the Beginnings to the Present Day* (London: Routledge & Keegan Paul, 1975), 134; See also, Charles Bartlett, "Walter in Wonderland," *Professional Golfer*, 33 (June 1951), 18.

12. Quoted in H.B. Martin, *Great Golfers in the Making* (London: John Lane, 1932), 71; *London Observer*, June 27, 1920; *London Times*, June 11, 1920; *New York Times*, June 11, 1920, 15.

13. For coverage of the 1920 British Open, I relied upon the *New York Times*, June 24–July 5, 1920; *London Times*, June 24–July 2, 1920; *London Observer*, June 27–July 4, 1920; and *Golf Illustrated* (British), 69 (2–9 July 1920). In his autobiography, Hagen wrote that he finished fifty-third; contemporary coverage has him in fifty-second place.

14. Quoted in Robert E. Harlow, "A Tale of Two Visits," *American Golfer*, 25 (15 July 1922), 33.

15. Hagen and Heck, *Walter Hagen Story*, 71.

16. *London Times*, July 6–8, 1920; "More New Champions," *Golf Illustrated* (British), 69 (16 July 1920), 543; *Golf Monthly* (British), 10 (August 1920), 22; *American Golfer*, 23 (17 July 1920), 24.

17. *New York Times*, July 27, 1920, 14.

18. In the playoff, Hagen shot 70, Barnes shot 74. *New York Tribune*, July 29–August 1, 1920.

19. *New York Times*, July 27–August 2, 1920.

20. "True Love Stories of Famous People," newspaper clipping in Bobby Jones File, Special Collections, Robert W. Woodruff Library, Emory University, Atlanta, Georgia (hereafter "BJF").

21. *Chattanooga News,* July 8–9, 1920.

22. *Memphis Commercial Appeal,* July 6–17, 1920; *New York Times,* July 15–18, 1920; quoted in Grantland Rice, *The Bobby Jones Story* (Atlanta: Turper and Love, 1953), 28; William E. Woodward, "What Makes Him Click?" *American Magazine,* 109 (April 1930), 171.

23. *Toledo Blade,* August 6, 1920.

24. Ibid., August 11, 1920; Quoted in Martin, *Great Golfers in the Making,* 71; Harry Vardon, *My Golfing Life* (London: Hutchinson & Co., Ltd., 1933), 240.

25. Quoted seemingly everywhere, but in O.B. Keeler, "Memories of Bobby Jones' First National Open," *Golfers Magazine,* 59 (June 1933), 47; Robert Tyre Jones Jr. *Down the Fairway* (New York: Blue Ribbon Books, 1927), 100.

26. *Toledo Blade* and *New York Times,* August 9–14, 1920.

27. Cousins, *Golf in Britain,* 133.

28. *New York Times,* September 23, 1920, 11; October 19, 1920, 13; Hagen and Heck, *Walter Hagen Story,* 81.

29. Jones, *Down the Fairway,* 96; Luke Ross, "I Caddied For Jones When He Threw Clubs," clipping in the Bobby Jones File, Special Collections, Robert W. Woodruff Library, Emory University, Atlanta, Georgia. "Hereafter cited as BJF."

30. For coverage of the 1920 U.S. Amateur, including the yellow jacket incident, see *Atlanta Constitution* and *New York Times,* September 7–12, 1920; also, Jones, *Down the Fairway,* 104–105; Francis Ouimet, *A Game of Golf: A Book of Reminiscence* (Boston: Houghton Mifflin Company, 1932), 103; Charles Blair Macdonald, *Scotland's Gift: Golf* (New York: Charles Scribner's Sons, 1928), 313.

31. "Edgar Wins Southern Open Title," *American Golfer,* 23 (23 October 1920), 32; *Atlanta Constitution,* September 30–October 3, 1920.

32. Max Marston, "Should American Amateurs' Expenses Abroad Be Paid?" *Golf Illustrated,* 15 (April 1921), 14.

33. *New York Times,* May 11, 1921, 14.

34. *London Times,* May 25, 1921; *New York Times,* May 26–30, 1921. Grantland Rice, "The Lion Defends His Lair," *American Golfer,* 24, (18 June 1921), 3; George Greenwood, "The British Amateur Championship," *Golf Illustrated,* 15 (July 1921), 12; "The Attempt at the British Title," *Golfers Magazine,* 38 (June 1921), 17.

35. H.B. Martin, "A Champion in the Making," *Golf Illustrated,* 40 (December 1933), 16.

36. "How Hagen and Harlow Hit It Off," *Professional Golfer of America,* 9 (January 1929), 21; Herbert Graffis, *The PGA: The Official History of the Professional Golfers' Association of America* (New York: Thomas Y. Crowell Company, 1975), 149–150; Hagen and Heck, *Walter Hagen Story,* 81.

37. *Detroit Free Press* and *News* and *New York Times,* May 19, 1921.

38. *New York Times,* May 25, 1921, 14.

39. Jones recalled a 46 on his front nine, while the *London Times* reported a 43 on June 25, 1921. For an even more thorough discussion of this episode,

see Howard Rabinowitz, "Bobby Jones' First Retirement," *Golf Journal*, 46 (May 1993), 31–33.

40. Sidney L. Matthew, *The Life and Times of Bobby Jones* (Chelsea, MI: Sleeping Bear Press, 1995), 120–121; Jones, *Down the Fairway*, 106; Jones, *Golf is My Game* (New York: Doubleday and Company, 1960), 95.

41. *New York Times*, June 21–27, 1921; *London Times*, June 20–27, 1921; "Hutchison Wins British Open Championship," *Golfers Magazine*, 38 (July 1927), 12; R. Endersby Howard, "Impossible They Said But Hutchison Did It," *Golf Illustrated*, 15 (August 1921), 15.

42. *Washington Post*, July 23, 1921; *New York Times*, July 22–23, 1921; Grantland Rice, "Barnes Bucks Destiny," *American Golfer*, 24 (30 July 1921), 4; Hagen and Heck, *Walter Hagen Story*, 166.

43. F.J. Powers, "Who Will Shatter Par at Oakwood?" *Golfers Magazine*, 38 (July 1921), 9; "Hagen Rejoins the Elite," *American Golfer*, 24 (10 September 1921), 13.

44. Grantland Rice, "Correcting Mental Faults," *American Golfer*, 24 (30 July 1921), 19.

45. *Detroit News*, September 9–10, 1921.

46. *New York Times*, September 27–October 2, 1921; J. Lewis Brown, "Pro Title To A Homebred," *Golf Illustrated*, 16 (November 1921), 22; Innis Brown, "Hagen Leads 'Em Home," *American Golfer*, 24 (8 October 1921), 13.

47. *New York Times*, October 3, 1921, 11.

48. Harry Vardon, "Bobby Jones and Other American Amateurs," *Golfers Magazine*, 38 (September 1921), 21.

49. *St. Louis Post-Dispatch*, September 7, 19, 1921; Grantland Rice, "The Siege Gun Gets The Range," *American Golfer*, 24 (8 October 1921), 3.

50. Richard Gordin, "Robert Tyre Jones Jr.: His Life and Contributions to Golf" (Ph.D. dissertation, Ohio State University, 1967), 196.

51. Richard Miller, *Triumphant Journey: The Saga of Bobby Jones and the Grand Slam of Golf* (New York: Holt, Rinehart, and Winston, 1980), 94; *St. Louis Post-Dispatch*, September 23, 1921; Gene Sarazen with Herbert Warren Wind, *Thirty Years of Championship Golf* (New York: Prentice-Hall, 1950), 74; *New York Times*, September 18, 1921, VIII, 3.

52. Kerr Petrie, "The Season's Play Reviewed," *Southern Golfer* (15 December 1921), 7; Miller, *Triumphant Journey*, 95.

53. Grantland Rice, *The Bobby Jones Story* (Atlanta: Tupper and Love, 1953), 59, and *The Tumult and the Shouting* (New York: A.S. Barnes and Company, 1954), 79; Jones, *Golf Is My Game*, 94.

Chapter 5

1. *New York Times*, April 21, 1922, 10. Joe Kirkwood, *Links of Life* (Ronald R. Kirkwood, 1973), 3.

2. Walter Hagen and Margaret Seaton Heck, *The Walter Hagen Story* (New York: Simon and Schuster, 1956), 140–141.

3. *New York Times*, April 21, 1922, 10.

4. Ibid., March 13; May 26, 1922.

5. "Hagen Has a New Shot," *Southern Golfer*, 3 (1 April 1922), 12; Grantland Rice, "Hagen's Conquering Game," *American Golfer*, 25 (15 July 1922), 5; *London Observer*, June 25, 1922.

6. *London Times*, June 21, 1922; *New York Times*, June 23, 1922, 14. Kirkwood finished at 313, alone in nineteenth place. R. Endersby Howard, "A Last-Hole Drama," *Golf Illustrated*, 17 (August 1922), 16; Hagen and Heck, *Walter Hagen Story*, 101; Geoffrey Cousins and Tom Scott, *A Century of Opens* (London: Frederick Muller, 1971), 84–85.

7. Robert Harlow, "A Tale of Two Visits," *American Golfer* (15 July 1922), 6; *London Times*, June 24, 1922; J.H. Taylor, "Walter Hagen the Winner," *Canadian Golfer*, 8 (July 1922), 253; Hagen and Heck, *Walter Hagen Story*, 92.

8. Quoted in "Is Golf Threatening Baseball?" *Literary Digest* (5 August 1922), 59.

9. Jock Hutchison, "America Now the Home of Golf," *Golfers Magazine*, 39 (April 1922), 21; J.H. Taylor, "Walter Hagen's Great Triumph," *Golf Illustrated*, 17 (August 1922), 18.

10. Robert J. Kennedy, "The Westchester-Biltmore Country Club," *Golf Illustrated*, 17 (May 1922), 18; Thorstein Veblen, *Theory of the Leisure Class: An Economic Study of Institutions* (New York, 1899). *New York Times*, July 3, 1922, 11; July 7, 1922, 12.

11. *New York Times*, June 26, 1922, 11; July 2, 1922, 12; July 3, 1922, 11.

12. Richard Miller, *Triumphant Journey* (New York: Holt Rinehart, and Winston, 1981), 132–133; Clifford Roberts, *The Story of the Augusta National Golf Club* (New York: Doubleday and Company, Inc., 1976), 237; letter to Tom Nash, December 8, 1967, roll 2, Robert Tyre Jones Jr. Collection, United States Golf Association Golf House Library, Far Hills, New Jersey (hereafter "RTJ").

13. *New York Times*, March 13, 1922, 12; Robert Tyre Jones Jr., *Down the Fairway* (New York: Blue Ribbon Books, 1927), 119.

14. *Atlanta Constitution*, June 21–25, 1922.

15. Trost quoted in Sidney Matthew, *Life and Times of Bobby Jones* (Chelsea, MI: Sleeping Bear Press, 1995), 54, see also 52–71. Keeler obituary, *New York Times*, October 16, 1950; Robert Tyre Jones Jr., *Golf Is My Game* (New York: Doubleday and Company, 1960), 91; Miller, *Triumphant Journey*, 84–87, 95.

16. *New York Times*, July 2, 1922, 25; July 6, 1922, 14; July 13, 1922, 10.

17. *Chicago Tribune*, July 15–16, 1922; Grantland Rice, "Another Home-Bred Arrives," *American Golfer*, 25 (29 July 1922), 7; *New York Times*, July 19, 1922, 10.

18. *New York Times*, August 6, 1922, 26; August 28, 1922, 8; August 29, 1922, 13; August 30, 1922, 13; R.E. Porter, "Americans Too Strong for the Britons," *Golf Illustrated*, 18 (October 1922), 20–21. The 1921 team competition was considered an "informal" trial; thus, the 1922 competition became regarded as the first official Walker Cup Matches.

19. *Boston Globe*, September 3–10, 1922; *New York Times*, September 4, 1922, 11; September 9, 1922; Innis Brown, "As to Bobby Jones," *American Golfer*, 25 (7 October 1922), 13; Cyril Tolley, *The Modern Golfer* (New York: Alfred A. Knopf, 1924), 205–206.

20. Richard Gordin, "Robert Tyre Jones, Jr.: His Life and Contributions to Golf" (Ph.D. dissertation, Ohio State University, 1967), 69; *New York Times*, October 11, 1922, 16; October 14, 1922, 9; February 10, 1923, 17; February 26, 1923, 11; May 22, 1923, 16; Letter to Mr. Griffith MacLaren Woodley, September 21, 1964, roll 2; letter to Alistair Cooke, October 2, 1968, roll 2, RTJ.

21. *New York Times*, August 24, 1922, 13.

22. Interestingly, *Golfdom* estimated that as late as 1928 some 15% of golfers still teed it up the old-fashioned way. See "Reddys Span 'Nut Notion' to Necessity in Few Years," *Golfdom*, 2 (April 1928), 76–77; William Lowell Jr., "Facts About the Reddy Tee," *Professional Golfer of America*, 9 (August 1928), 21; "How Hagen and Kirkwood Launched the Wooden Tee," *Golf* (September 1973), 34. Lowell, however, was neither the first man nor the first dentist to receive a patent for the golf tee! See Calvin H. Sinnette, *Forbidden Fairways: African Americans and the Game of Golf* (Chelsea, MI: Sleeping Bear Press, 1998), 7–12.

23. Hagen placed eighth in the Southern Open. See *Nashville Banner*, September 28–October 1, 1922; *Detroit News*, August 18–20, 1922.

24. *New York Times*, August 20, 1922, 25; November 20, 1922, 23.

25. Hagen and Heck, *Walter Hagen Story*, 103; Gene Sarazen with Herbert Warren Wind, *Thirty Years of Championship Golf* (Reprint, London: A & C Black, 1990), 92–93; *New York Times*, October 7, 1922, 11; October 8, 1922, 27.

26. *New York Times*, October 25, 1922, 17.

27. Ibid., December 31, 1922, II, 3; "Hicks Rates Hagen Above Sarazen," *Southern Golfer*, 4 (1 February 1923), 34; James Harnett, "An Open Season With The Pros, " *Golf Illustrated*, 18 (January 1923), 24.

28. *San Francisco Chronicle*, January 3–10, 1923; John Hession, "Accuracy in Golf and Shooting," *Southern Golfer*, 4 (15 February 1923), 12.

29. *San Antonio Express*, January 25–29, 1923; Francis G. Trimble, "The Birth of the Texas Open—II," *Golfiana*, 4 (1992), 11–17; H.B. Martin, *Fifty Years of American Golf* (New York: Dodd, Mead, and Company, 1936), 272; Al Barkow, *Golf's Golden Grind: The History of the Tour* (New York: Harcourt Brace Jovanovich, 1974).

30. *New Orleans Times-Picayne*, March 4, 1923.

31. "Hagen Breaks World's Record on Links," *Southern Golfer*, 4 (1 April 1923), 12: *New York Times*, March 18, 1923, II, 1. In his autobiography, Hagen incorrectly recalled making the 62 in the 1921 event.

32. *Atlanta Constitution*, March 24–25, March 29–April 2, 1923; *New York Times*, March 30, 1923, 20; April 1, 1923, 10.

33. *New York Times*, March 25, 1923, II, 2; April 5, 1923, 16; see advertisement in *American Golfer*, 26 (5 May 1923), 3; Hagen and Heck, *Walter Hagen Story*, 110–111; Kirkwood wrote almost nothing of his early Hagen

tours in *Links of Life,* although it is filled with anecdotes from his 1937–1938 Hagen tours.

34. *New York Times,* March 19, April 2, 1923, 16; Innis Brown, "Closing the Winter Campaign," *American Golfer,* 26 (21 April 1923), 13.

35. *New York World,* April 21, 1923; *Rochester Herald,* April 22, 1923; *New York Herald,* April 16, May 1, 1923; *New York World,* May 1, 1923; *New York Times,* April 28, 1923, 13.

36. *New York Times,* May 2, 1923, 17; June 17, 1923, I, Part 2, 2; *London Times,* May 18–June 16, 1923; *London Observer,* June 10–17, 1923; Patterson McNutt, "The Advent of a New Golf Era in Britain," *Golf Illustrated,* 19 (August 1923), 58; George Greenwood, "The Game in Britain," *Golf Illustrated,* 19 (August 1923), 21; Innis Brown, "By the Margin of a Single Stroke," *American Golfer,* 26 (30 June 1923), 3.

37. *New York Times,* June 10, 1923, II, 1; June 12, 1923, 15; June 13, 1923, 14; June 17, 1923, I, Part 2, 2; June 23, 1923, 7; June 26, 1923, 16–18; Robert Harlow, "Treatment of the Professionals Abroad," *American Golfer,* 26 (14 July 1923), 42; Hagen and Heck, *Walter Hagen Story,* 127–128; H.B. Martin, "Hagen and His Critics," *Metropolitan Golfer,* 1 (September 1923), 7.

38. *New York Times,* June 25, 1923, 10; July 12, 1923, 14; July 13, 1923, 11; July 14, 1923, 7; H.B. Martin, "Sidelights of the Championship," *Metropolitan Golfer,* 1 (August 1923), 8.

39. There is some controversy over just when Jones first obtained Calamity Jane and the club's history. It is certain, though, that Jones used the original Calamity Jane only through the 1925 season, after which he replaced it with a copy, Calamity Jame II, custom-made for him by Spalding. For a full discussion, see Sidney L. Matthew, *The History of Bobby Jones' Clubs* (Tallahassee, FL: I.Q. Press, 1992), 3–21.

40. Jones, *Down the Fairway,* 133; O.B. Keeler, "Bobby Jones' Own Story of How He Won," *American Golfer,* 26 (11 August 1923), 7; *Memphis Commercial Appeal,* September 29, 1922.

41. *New York Times,* July 15, 1923, 20; July 16, 1923, 1; Grantland Rice, "The End of the Hike," *American Golfer,* 26 (28 July 1923), 32; Francis Ouimet, *A Game of Golf* (New York: Houghton Mifflin Company, 1932), 139–141; Luke Ross, "I Caddied for Jones When He Threw Clubs," article in Bobby Jones File, Robert W. Woodruff Library, Emory University, Atlanta, Georgia (hereafter cited as "BJF"); Sol Metzger, "On the Rebound," *Collier's,* 87 (13 June 1931), 74.

42. O.B. Keeler, "Bobby Jones' Own Story of How He Won," 26 *American Golfer* (11 August 1923), 44; Jones, *Down the Fairway,* 135.

43. George Greenwood, "The Game in Britain," *Golf Illustrated,* 19 (September 1923), 22; Walter Hagen, "Bobby Jones Hero of Inwood Open," *Metropolitan Golfer,* 1 (August 1923), 7.

44. *Atlanta Constitution,* July 24, 1923; *New York Times,* July 17, 1923, 17; July 18, 1923, 12; Charles Blair MacDonald, *Scotland's Gift: Golf* (New York: Charles Scribner's Sons, 1928), 321.

45. *Chicago Tribune*, September 18–20, 1923; *New York Times*, July 21, 1923, 10; September 16, 1923, I, Part 2, 1.

46. *New York Times*, October 12, 1923, 15; October 28, 1923, I, Part 2, 3; October 29, 1923, 11.

47. William Richardson, "The World's Greatest at Match Play," *Golf Illustrated*, 20 (November 1923), 24; Sidoine X. Jourdan, "The National P.G.A. Championship," *Golfers Magazine*, 42 (November 1923), 12; Grantland Rice; "Match Play Masters," *American Golfer*, 26 (20 October 1923), 9; see also, Sarazen and Wind, *Thirty Years of Championship Golf*, 106–111; Grantland Rice, *The Tumult and the Shouting* (New York: A.S. Barnes & Company, 1954), 69.

48. Memphis *Commercial Appeal*, October 9, 1923; James D. Harnett, "Irrepressible Jock Wins the Western Open," *Golf Illustrated*, 20 (November 1923), 17; Gordon Harkness, "Western Open Championship," *Golfers Magazine*, 42 (November 1923), 21.

49. William White, "The 1923 All-American," *Golfers Magazine*, 42 (December 1923) 10; H.B. Martin, "Looking Back over the Year," *Metropolitan Golfer*, 1 (December 1923), 7; *New York Times*, December 10, 1923, 22.

Chapter 6

1. Walter Hagen, "Motoring to the Southland," *Southern Golfer*, 2 (1 January 1924), 7; "Bear Creek Country Club" and advertisements, *Southern Golfer*, 5 (15 February 1924), 10, 22–23; Walter Hagen and Margaret Seaton Heck, *The Walter Hagen Story* (New York: Simon and Schuster, 1956), 117–120.

2. J. Lewis Brown, "Thrills from the 'Sandhill' Championships," *Golf Illustrated*, 21 (May 1924), 38.

3. Robert Harlow, "The Inside of the Golf Show," *Metropolitan Golfer*, 2 (June 1924), 8; "America's First Golf Show," *Southern Golfer*, 5 (1 March 1924), 13.

4. R. Hay Chapman, "The Miraculous Growth of California Golf," *Golf Illustrated*, 20 (January 24), 23; J. Lewis Brown, "The Growth of American Golf," *Outlook*, 136 (23 April 1924), 688–690; Sol Metzger, "The Rapid Rise of American Golf," *Country Life*, 46 (May 1924), 55–56.

5. Clifford Roberts, *The Story of the Augusta National Golf Club* (New York: Doubleday and Company, 1976), 237; *New York Times*, February 9, 1924, 11; February 15, 1924, 11; *Atlanta Constitution*, March 9, 1924.

6. *Atlanta Constitution*, May 21–22, 1924.

7. *Detroit News*, May 30, June 4–7, 1924; *Atlanta Constitution*, June 3–7, 1924; *New York Times*, June 7, 1924, 8; June 10, 1924, 19; June 15, 1924, 25; J. Lewis Brown, "In the Wake of Walker's Triumph," *Golf Illustrated*, 21 (July 1924), 16.

8. *Atlanta Constitution*, June 18, 1924.

9. *London Times*, June 18–July 12, 1924; *London Observer*, June 22–29, 1924; *New York Times*, June 22–July 12, 1924; Grantland Rice, "Hagen of the Iron Nerve," *Collier's*, 75 (17 January 1925), 14; Walter Hagen, "British Cup

Returns to America," 2 (July 1924), 5; Bernard Darwin, "A Triumph in Courage," *American Golfer,* 27, (26 July 1924), 5; George Greenwood, "Hagen's Melodrama in the British Open," *Golf Illustrated,* 21, (August 1924), 14; "Praise of Walter Hagen," *Professional Golfer of America,* 5 (September 1924), 30; Geoffrey Cousins and Tom Scott, *A Century of Opens* (London: Frederick Muller, 1971), 89.

10. Robert Harlow, "London Papers Praise Hagen," *Metropolitan Golfer,* 2 (August 1924), 9; "Praise of Walter Hagen," *Professional Golfer of America,* 30.

11. *New York Times,* June 30, 1924, 13; John Anderson, "With the Americans at Hoylake," *Golf Illustrated,* 21, (August 1924), 16; Innis Brown, "Hats off to Hagen!" *American Golfer,* 27 (12 July 1924), 11; *Rochester Times-Union,* June 28, 1924; William D. Richardson, "'I Was Lucky,' Says Hagen," *American Golfer,* 27 (9 August 1924), 9; *New York Times,* July 22, 1924, 11.

12. See advertisement in *Golf Illustrated,* 21 (July 1924), 47 and in *Metropolitan Golfer,* 6 (December 1924), 37.

13. *Indianapolis Star,* September 14–22, 1924; *New York Times,* September 21, 1924, IX, 1; William D. Richardson, "Reviving an Old Act," *American Golfer,* 27 (18 October 1924), 17; H.B. NcMeal, "Hagen Wins P.G.A.," *Golfers Magazine,* 44 (October 1924), 22.

14. "Hagen and Sarazen Defeat Amateurs," *Metropolitan Golfer,* 2 (November 1924), 30; "Ask Walter Hagen," ibid., 16.

15. Robert Harlow, "New Florida Golf League Will Help," *Metropolitan Golfer,* 2 (November 1924), 10; "Florida Golf League Will Be Popular," *Southern Golfer,* 6 (December 1924), 32; *New York Times,* December 21, 1924, IX, 5.

16. *Atlanta Constitution,* July 17, July 27, August 8, August 11, August 24, 1924.

17. Jones lost his foursome match on the last hole but won his singles match over Major Charles O. Hezlet, 4 and 3. *New York Times,* September 13, 1924, 19; September 14, 1924, X, 1; September 15, 1924, 25; Gould B. Martin, "America Again Defends the Walker Cup," *Metropolitan Golfer,* 2 (September 1924), 16; Innis Brown, "Battling for the Walker Cup," *American Golfer,* 27 (6 September 1924), 3.

18. *Philadelphia Inquirer,* September 28, 1924; *New York Times,* September 27, 1924, 12; September 28, 1924, IX, 1; September 29, 1924, 13; Luke Ross, "I Caddied for Jones When He Threw Clubs," article in Bobby Jones File, Special Collections, Robert W. Woodruff Library, Emory University, Atlanta, Georgia (hereafter "BJF"); O.B. Keeler, "Checking Back over a Championship," *American Golfer,* 27 (1 November 1924), 3.

19. Jones, *Down the Fairway,* 144; Grantland Rice, "How Bobby Jones Broke Through," *American Golfer,* 27 (18 October 1924), 3.

20. Albert Horning, "Bobby Jones S.A.E. and Golf Champion," *Record,* 44 (December 1924), 355.

21. *New York Times,* November 3, 1924, 23; December 4, 1924, 17; H.B. Martin and Joe Horgan, "How the Golfers are Rated for the Year," *Southern Golfer* (December 1924), 40.

22. Ibid.; James D. Harnett, "Walter Hagen, The Golfer of the Year," *Golf Illustrated* (October 1924), 16.

23. Joe Kelly, "Golf in the Promised Land of Ponce De Leon," *Golf Illustrated*, 22 (January 1925), 14; "Jones and Adair," *Southern Golfer*, 6 (15 February 1925), 40; "About Jones and His Golf" and "Palmetto Dedicated," ibid. (1 March 1925), 12; Grantland Rice, "There's Only One Bobby Jones," *Collier's*, 75 (4 April 1925), 20.

24. *New York Times*, February 28, 1925, 10; March 3, 1925, 17.

25. "Boca Ceiga Course Ready," *Southern Golfer*, 6 (1 January 1925), 34; Robert Harlow, "Pasadena-on-the-Gulf," ibid. (15 January 1925), 24; Hagen and Heck, *Walter Hagen Story*, 125.

26. Robert Harlow, "The Success of the Florida Winter Golf League," *Metropolitan Golfer*, 3 (February 1925), 12; "Florida Winter Golf League Opens," *Southern Golfer*, 6 (1 February 1925), 9; "Florida Winter Golf League," ibid. (15 February 1925), 19; "Winter Golf League Champions," ibid., 12.

27. William Richardson, "Summary of Results of Recent Tournaments," *Golf Illustrated*, 23 (June 1925), 27; "Lost Strayed, or Stolen," *Southern Golfer*, 6 (2 February 1925), 40.

28. *New York Times*, February 2, 1925, 11; February 5, 1925, 15; *Sanford* (Florida) *Herald*, February 6, 1925; "Hagen World's Champion," *Southern Golfer*, 6 (15 February 1925), 36; Hagen and Heck, *Walter Hagen Story*, 124.

29. *Canadian Golfer*, 11 (August 1925), 343; *New York Times*, April 21, 1925, 17; Hagen and Heck, *Walter Hagen Story*, 142–143.

30. Burt Hoxie, "Some Interesting Statistics Compiled at the Open," *Golf Illustrated*, 23 (July 1925), 26; the USGA legalized steel shafted clubs in the spring of 1924.

31. For coverage of the 1925 U.S. Open, I relied upon the following: *Boston Globe*, June 2–6, 1925; *New York Times*, April 12, 1925, X, 5; May 2, 1925, 11; May 11, 1925, 12; June 3–7, 1925; Grantland Rice, "The Miracle of MacFarlane," *American Golfer*, 28 (27 June 1925), 3; William Richardson, "Willie MacFarlane from Aberdeen—and Tuckahoe," *Golf Illustrated*, 23 (July 1925), 27; P.C. Pulver, "The Long Battle for the Open Championship," *Golf Illustrated*, 23 (July 1925), 24; "Ask Walter Hagen," *Metropolitan Golfer*, 3 (July 1925), 24; O.B. Keeler, *The Boys' Life of Bobby Jones* (New York: Harper and Brothers, 1931), 204.

32. Gunn qualified at 154; then he cut his way through V.L. Bradford, 12 and 10 (a come-from-behind victory in which Gunn won an astounding fifteen holes in a row), Jess Sweetser, 10 and 9, and Richard Jones of New York, 5 and 3. For coverage of 1925 U.S. Amateur, see *Atlanta Constitution*, September 5–8, 1925; "Bobby Jones Likes New Plan, *Metropolitan Golfer*, 3 (May 1925), 10; *New York Times*, August 30, 1925, IX, 7; September 3, 1925, 29; Henry Litchfield West, "The Business of Qualifying," *American Golfer*, 29 (November 1925), 6; O.B. Keeler, "The Inside Story of a Golfing Miracle," *American Golfer*, 29 (October 1925), 3; Letter to Ross Goodner, February 19, 1964, roll 2, Robert T. Jones Collection, United States Golf Association's Golf House Library, Far Hills, New Jersey (hereafter "RTJ"). Richard Miller,

Triumphant Journey (New York: Holt, Rinehart, and Winston, 1981), 156 and Sidney Matthew, *Life and Times of Bobby Jones* (Chelsea, MI: Sleeping Bear Press, 1995), 77–78, offer slightly different versions of the Jones-Gunn exchange on the first tee.

33. *Atlanta Constitution,* November 23, 1925.

34. *Brainard* (Minnesota) *Daily Dispatch,* July 13–15, 1925; *Toronto Star,* August 1, 1925; *Canadian Golfer,* 11 (August 1925), 350.

35. For coverage and commentary on the 1925 PGA Championship, see *Chicago Tribune,* September 23, 1925; *New York Times,* September 23, 1925, 19; September 28, 1925, 17; "As They Remember Him," *Professional Golfer,* 50 (November 1969), 8; Innis Brown, "Hagen Extends His Count," *American Golfer,* 29 (November 1925), 14; A.T. Packard, "Walter Hagen Retains P.G.A. Championship," *Golfers Magazine,* 46 (November 1925), 13–15.

Chapter 7

1. Ultimately, the Florida Golf League did resurface in the winter of 1926, but it was scaled down significantly and included neither Jones nor Hagen. See *Southern Golfer,* March 1, 1926, 30; Nan O'Reilly, "Bobby Jones to Play in South," *Professional Golfer of America,* 6 (November 1925), 15; "Bobby to Remain Simon-Pure," *Golfers Magazine,* 46 (December 1925), 19; "Florida Professional League Will Not Function," *Southern Golfer,* 7 (1 January 1926), 16; "Tournament Notes," *Golf Illustrated,* 24 (February 1926), 24.

2. *New York Times,* February 22, 1926, 22.

3. For commentary on the Hagen-Jones rivalry in this period, see "Hagen Again West Coast Winner," *Professional Golfer of America,* 6 (April 1926), 14; "In the Wake of the Winter Season," *American Golfer,* 29 (April 1926), 44; *Atlanta Constitution,* March 23–25, 1926; "Walter and Bobby Have a Wager," *Metropolitan Golfer,* 4 (April 1926), 7; H.B. Martin, "Golf Records Make Interesting Comparison," *Metropolitan Golfer,* 4 (May 1926), 20. Martin's figures include marks from 1920–1925 U.S. Opens, 1920 British Open (only 47 holes, allowing for Jones's pick up), 1923 Western Open, 1925–1926 West Coast Opens.

4. *New York Times,* April 3, 1926, 22; April 16, 1926, 26; April 17, 1926, 13; May 2, 1926, X, 6; May 18, 1926, 23. Although the first official Ryder Cup matches were held in 1927, the *New York Times* did report of a challenge cup donated by S. Ryder in 1926, and the *London Times* referred to the 1926 matches as "The Ryder Cup." See also Bob Bubka and Tom Clavin, *The Ryder Cup: Golf's Greatest Event* (New York: Crown Publishers, 1999).

5. *New York Times,* May 7, 1926, 14; May 10, 1926, 28.

6. For the 1926 British Amateur, see *London Times,* May 26–31, 1926; *New York Times,* May 20–30, 1926; "Walker Cup Team Had Inspiring Departure," *Golf Illustrated,* 25 (June 1926), 25; Chick Evans, "Muirfield—and the Americans," *Golfers Magazine,* 50 (July 1926), 5; "Bobbie Jones and the Amateur," *Golf Monthly,* 17 (July 1926), 16; Sandy Armour, "Sweetser Wins British Amateur," *Golfers Magazine,* 50 (July 1926), 16; *Golf Monthly,* 17 (June 1926), 16; Francis Ouimet, *A Game of Golf* (Boston: Houghton Mifflin Com-

pany, 1932), 161–167; George Pottinger, *Muirfield and the Honourable Company* (London: Scottish Academic Press, 1972), 81.

7. *London Times*, June 1–4, 1926; "America Retains Walker Cup," *Golfers Magazine*, 50 (July 1926), 48; *New York Times*, June 3, 1926, 28; June 4, 1926, 18. Although it was reported that Sweetser had the flu, it was later discovered that he was actually stricken with tuberculosis.

8. Walter Hagen, "Professionals Sail for British Open," *Metropolitan Golfer*, 4 (June 1926), 20; *London Times*, June 5–7, 1926; *London Observer*, June 6, 1926; "Short Putts," *Golfers Magazine*, 50 (July 1926), 38; *New York Times*, May 25, 1926, 30; June 5, 1926, 11; June 6, 1926, X, 1; Robert Harlow, "The Eagle Made the Lion Roar," *Metropolitan Golfer*, 4 (July 1926), 12.

9. For 1926 British Open qualifying, see *London Times*, June 14, 1926; *New York Times*, June 16, 1926, 19; June 17, 1926, 16; June 18, 1926, 17; January 22, 1954, 34; Grantland Rice, "Jones and Hagen in the British Open," *American Golfer*, 29 (June 1926), 5; Henry Longhurst, *Golf* (London: J.M. Dent and Sons LTD., 1937), 123.

10. For Hagen-Mitchell match, see *London Times*, June 19–21, 1926; *New York Times*, June 19, 1926, 7; June 20, 1926, IX, 1; *Golfers Magazine*, 50, (July 1926), 64.

11. Accounts vary as to whether Hagen told his caddie to "tend" the flag or "remove" it. Years later, Hagen recalled having the flag tended, but Darwin's contemporary coverage records that it was removed. For coverage and commentary on the 1926 British Open, see: *London Times*, June 19–25, 1926; Lytham St. Anne's *Express*, June 12, 1958; *New York Times*, June 25, 1926, 15; June 26, 1926, 9; June 27, 1926, IX, 1; Bernard Darwin, "How Jones Won the British Open," *American Golfer*, 29 (August 1926) 12; "More Glory for Bobby Jones," *Professional Golfer of America*, 7 (July 1926), 8; Walter Hagen, "Bobby Jones Puts It Over," *Metropolitan Golfer*, 4 (July 1926), 9; "Again Annexes British Open," *Canadian Golfer*, 12 (July 1926), 222; Gordon Harkness, "The British Open Championship," *Golfers Magazine*, 50 (July 1926), 30; "The American Avalanche," *Golf Monthly*, 17 (July 1926), 14; Geoffrey Cousins and Tom Scott, *A Century of Opens* (London: Frederick Muller, 1971), 94–95; Will Grimley, "Ten Shots that Rocked the World," in Robert Trent Jones, ed., *Great Golf Stories* (New York: Galahad Books, 1987), 219. See also, letters from and to J.K. Wadley, January 8, 1970 and January 21, 1970, roll 3, Robert T. Jones, Jr. Collection, USGA, Golf House Library, Far Hills, New Jersey, (hereafter "RTJ").

12. For some further context on why the British were so enthralled with Jones's amateurism, see Richard Holt, *Sport and the British* (New York: Oxford University Press, 1989). Also, Mark Dyreson, *Making the American Team: Sport, Culture, and the Olympic Experience* (Urbana/Chicago: University of Illinois Press, 1998) offers a discussion of the British critique of America's approach to sport in this period.

13. *New York Times*, June 27, 1926, IX, 1; "Bobby Jones, Amateur," *Outlook*, 143 (21 July 1926), 336; "Bobby Jones and England," *Living Age*, 330 (7 August 1926), 335; Angus Perkerson, "Atlanta, Home of Golf Champions," *Golfers Magazine*, 50 (October 1926), 29.

14. *New York Times,* June 27, 1926, IX, 1; London *Observer,* July 4, 1926; "Bobby Jones, Amateur," 337.

15. *New York Times,* June 27, 1926, 24; "Behind the Scenes," 17 *Golf Monthly,* 16.

16. *New York Times,* June 28, 1926, 16; "Bobby Jones and England," 335; "Bobby Jones, Amateur," 337; "Robert Jones, Esq.," *Independent,* 117 (10 July 1926), 30–31.

17. *New York Times,* July 3, 1926, 10.

18. Ibid., July 5, 1926, 9.

19. *New York Herald,* July 2, 1926; *New York Times,* July 2, 1926, 3; July 3, 1926, 3; July 5, 1926, 8.

20. For 1926 U.S. Open, see *Columbus Dispatch,* July 7–11, 1926; Grantland Rice, "The Lone Stroke of Destiny," *American Golfer,* 29 (August 1926), 5; Jack Hoag, "Bobby the Great," *Golfers Magazine,* 50 (August 1926), 13; Robert T. Jones, *Down the Fairway* (New York: Blue Ribbon Books, 1927), 161; Paul Hornung, *Scioto Country Club: 75 Years of History* (Columbus: Scioto Country Club, 1993), 41; P.C. Pulver, "Bobby Jones A True Champion," *Professional Golfer of America,* 7 (July 1926), 5.

21. *Atlanta Constitution,* July 12, 1926.

22. Hornung, *Scioto Country Club,* 43; "Bobby Jones Confides How He Does It," *Literary Digest,* 16 (31 July 1926), 44; *New York Times,* July 15, 1926, 18; "Bobby Jones Is Interviewed," *Golfers Magazine,* 50 (September 1926), 10.

23. Sarasota *Herald,* August 1, 1926.

24. Interview with Eugene Branch, July 30, 1997, Atlanta, Georgia; Morris Markey, "Bobby Jones," *Harvard-Princeton* (6 November 1926), 11.

25. For coverage of the 1926 U.S. Amateur, I relied upon the following: *Indianapolis Star,* August 29, 1926; *Baltimore Sun,* September 12–19, 1926; *New York Herald,* September 18–19, 1926; William Richardson, "Will 'Bobby' Break the Barrier?" *Golf Illustrated,* 25 (September 1926), 12; *New York Times,* August 19, 1926, 16. Jack Hoag, "Von Elm Scales the Heights," *Golfers Magazine,* 50 (October 1926), 11; Humphrey Fry, "Looking Back at Baltusrol," *American Golfer,* 30 (November 1926), 11. For Jones-Von Elm relationship, see letter from Lester Rice to RTJ, October 20, 1963; letter from RTJ to Lester Rice, October 28, 1963, roll 2, RTJ.

26. *New York Times,* October 28, 1926, 31; Jones, "Down the Fairway," 161; Richard Gordin, "Robert Tyre Jones, Jr.: His Life and Contributions to Golf" (Ph.D. dissertation, Ohio State University, 1967), 93.

27. *New York Herald,* July 20, 1926; "Walter Hagen on the Rampage," *Professional Golfer of America,* 7 (August 1926), 17; Robert Harlow, "Sensational Golf Wins Eastern Open," *Metropolitan Golfer,* 4 (August 1926), 16; *New York Times,* July 21, 1926, 13.

28. *Indianapolis Star,* August 23–29, 1926; Gordon McLean, "Hagen Again Western Open Champion," *Golfers Magazine,* 50 (October 1926), 18.

29. *New York Herald,* September 25–26, 1926; Jack Hoag, "Hagen Is King of Them All," *Golfers Magazine,* 50 (November 1926), 32; P.C. Pulver,

"Hagen An Enduring Champion," *Professional Golfer of America,* 7 (October 1926), 5; Innis Brown, "One Sport Crown Intact," *American Golfer,* 30 (November 1926), 8; *New York Times,* September 26, 1926, X, 5.

30. Larry Engelmann, *The Goddess and the American Girl: The Story of Suzanne Lenglen and Helen Wills* (New York: Oxford University Press, 1988), 269; "Hagen to Play at Vancouver and Victoria," *Metropolitan Golfer,* 4 (November 1926), 28.

31. "How the Country's Stars Rate This Year," *Southern Golfer,* 4 (December 1926), 26; *New York Times,* December 26, IX, 5.

32. *New York Times,* November 22, 1926, 33; November 23, 1926, 28; December 19, 1926, IX, 7; December 27, 1926, 13; January 5, 1927, 17.

33. *Walter C. Hagen vs. Edna C. Hagen,* Superior Court of California, Los Angeles County, January 29, 1929, County Records Center, Los Angeles, California; *Los Angeles Times,* February 1, 1929; Henry Clune, *I Always Liked It Here: Reminiscences of a Rochesterian* (New York: Friends of the University of Rochester Libraries, 1983), 125; Walter Hagen and Margaret Seaton Heck, *The Walter Hagen Story* (New York: Simon and Schuster, 1956), 264.

34. Robert Harlow, "Hagen Defeats Sarazen in Long-Discussed Match," *Southern Golfer,* 8 (1 March 1927), 7; *New York Times,* April 5, 1927, 22; New York *World,* May 27, 1927; *New York Herald,* May 25–29, 1927.

35. *Boston Globe,* June 3–4, 1927; "Americans Defeat British for Ryder Cup," *Golfers Magazine,* 52 (July 1927), 17; P.C. Pulver, "Ryder Cup Stays on This Side," *Professional Golfer of America,* 7 (June 1927), 5; Innis Brown, "Lifting the Ryder Cup," *American Golfer,* 30 (July 1927), 29.

36. Jones's first ace came from an easy four-iron to the 170-yard 11th hole. *New York Times,* February 25, 1927, 17; *Atlanta Constitution,* March 24–29, 1927; O.B. Keeler, "Bobby Shows the Home Folk," *American Golfer,* 30 (May 1927), 17; "Bobby Jones at His Best," *Professional Golfer of America,* 7 (April 1927), 14; "Short Putts," *Golfers Magazine,* 51 (May 1927), 44.

37. *New York Times,* April 1, 1927, 20; April 19, 1927, 32.

38. For coverage of the controversy over Jones's syndicated articles, see *New York Times,* April 21, 1927, 32; April 23, 1927, 12–13; Larry Englemann, *The Goddess and the American Girl.*

39. Jones shot 76–77–79–77–309; Hagen, 77–73–76–81–307, and Armour beat "Lighthorse Harry" Cooper in a playoff to win the 1927 U.S. Open. See *Pittsburgh Press,* June 10–19, 1927; *New York Times,* June 14, 1927, 36; June 18, 1927, 9; Grantland Rice, "Jones Against the Field," *Collier's,* 79 (11 June 1927), 8; "The Victory of Form, Style, and Heart," *American Golfer,* 30 (July 1927), 9; P.C. Pulver, "Professionals Come into Their Own," *Professional Golfer of America,* 8 (July 1927), 5.

40. *New York Times,* June 26, 1927, X, 9.

41. *London Times,* July 2–27, 1927; *London Observer,* July 17, 1927; *New York Times,* July 12, 1927, 19; clippings from *Bulletin,* roll 3, RTJ; O.B. Keeler, "Making Golf History," *American Golfer,* 30 (September 1927), 15; Bernard Darwin, "Bobby Jones' Conquest of St. Andrews," *American Golfer,* 30 (Sep-

tember 1927), 9; "The British Open Championship," *Golf Illustrated* (British), 90 (22 July 1927), 111. Jack Hoag, "Bobby Jones, King of Golfers," *Golfers Magazine*, 52 (August 1927), 13.

42. "The Golfer and the Man," *Golf Illustrated* (British), 90 (22 July 1927), 107; "The Significance of Mr. Jones," *Golf Monthly*, 18 (August 1927), 18; *New York Times*, July 14, 1927, 15; July 18, 1926, VIII, 8.

43. Clair Price, "Jones Discusses Temper in Golf," *New York Times*, July 31, 1927, VIII, 2; July 23, 1927, 9.

44. Ibid., August 26, 1927, 9; *St. Paul Pioneer-Press*, August 16–30, 1927; Grantland Rice, "The Par Wrecker," *American Golfer*, 31 (October 1927), 5; Halford Morlan, "National Amateur Championship," *Golfers Magazine*, 52 (September 1927), 26; William Richardson, "The National Amateur," *Golf Illustrated*, 28 (October 1927), 11.

45. For the Evans-Jones incident, see Chick Evans, "Memories of Bobby Jones' Start," *American Golfer*, 32 (September 1930), 12; *Atlanta Journal*, July 18, 1963; Letter to Joseph C. Dey, Jr., July 22, 1963, roll 1, RTJ; *New York Times*, September 1, 1927, 19.

46. Innis Brown, "Bobby Jones Turns Author," *American Golfer*, 30 (September 1927), 31.

47. "Bobby Jones, Law Student" and "Bobby Now Lawyer," newspaper clippings in Bobby Jones File, Special Collections, Robert W. Woodruff Library, Emory University, Atlanta, Georgia (hereafter BJF).

48. *Atlanta Constitution*, November 19, 1927.

49. *Toronto Star*, August 4–6, 1927; *Boston Globe*, June 28–July 1, 1927; "Farrell Wins Eastern Open," *Metropolitan Golfer*, 5 (July 1927), 12; *New York Times*, June 14, 1927, 39; July 17, 1927, II, 8; *Chicago Tribune*, September 7–10, 1927; Jack Hoag, "Hagen Retains His Title," *Golfers Magazine*, 52 (October 1927), 18.

50. *Dallas Morning News*, November 5, 1927; *Rochester Times-Union*, January 5, 1928; "The Haig Now a Baseball Magnate," *Professional Golfer of America*, 8 (November 1927), 7; Brian A. Bennett, "Rochester, 1928," *National Pastime*, 17 (1997), 50–53; Jim Mandelaro and Scott Pitoniak, *Silver Seasons: The Story of the Rochester Red Wings* (Syracuse: Syracuse University Press, 1996), 20–23; Hagen and Heck, *Walter Hagen Story*, 258–259.

51. For coverage of the 1927 PGA Championship, I relied upon the following: *Dallas Morning News*, November 1–7, 1927; *New York Times*, September 5, 1927, 11; William Richardson, "The Greatest Record in Golf," *American Golfer*, 30 (December 1927), 9; "Amazing Record in the PGA Championship," *Metropolitan Golfer*, 5 (November 1927), 6; Kerr N. Petrie, "The PGA Championship," *Golf Illustrated*, 28 (December 1927), 12; "How the Country's Stars Rate This Year," *Southern Golfer*, 9 (15 December 1927), 26.

Chapter 8

1. Lynn Dumenil, *The Modern Temper* (New York: Hill and Wang, 1995), 303–304; Frederick Lewis Allen, *Only Yesterday* (New York: Harper and Broth-

ers, 1931), 270–289; Walter Hagen and Margaret Seaton Heck, *The Walter Hagen Story* (New York: Simon and Schuster, 1956), 125.

2. Rochester *Times-Union,* January 5, 1928.

3. Hagen and Heck, *Walter Hagen Story,* 88, 187, 242; Robert Harlow, "The Return of Hagen's Ghost," *Esquire,* 28 (May 1945), 42.

4. William Richardson, however, wrote in the *New York Times* that Hagen was guaranteed $2,500 for showing up and that neither man was in danger of losing money. That is corroborated somewhat by Hagen's memory that the winner's take amounted to $3,750, as well as what Bob Harlow wrote in "The Return of Hagen's Ghost," 42. See also *New York Times,* November 19, 1927, 12; March 17, 1928, 13; May 6, 1928, X, 6; Hagen and Heck, *Walter Hagen Story,* 188.

5. *New York Times,* April 20, 1928, 21.

6. Ibid., April 21, 1928, 15; April 26, 1928, 24; April 27, 1928, 21; Harlow, "The Return of Hagen's Ghost," 42.

7. *London Times,* April 25–30, 1928; *Golf Illustrated* (British), 93 (4 May 1928), 117.

8. *London Observer,* April 29, 1928; *London Times,* April 30, 1928; Hagen and Heck, *Walter Hagen Story,* 188–194; Harlow, "The Return of Hagen's Ghost," 42; William Campbell, "Compston vs. Hagen," *Golf Illustrated,* 29 (June 1928), 26; "Britain's Rising Hope," *Golf Monthly,* 19 (May 1928), 17; Francis Ouimet, "Compston's Victory and Hagen's Sportsmanship," *Golfers Magazine,* 53 (June 1928), 28; Robert Harlow, "Compston Slaughters Hagen," *Metropolitan Golfer,* 6 (May 1928), 12.

9. *London Times,* May 8–12, 1928; *New York Times,* May 11, 1928, 19; May 12, 1928, 11; May 13, 1928, Xi, 4; R.J. Tolleson, "Hagen Wins the British Open," *Golfers Magazine,* 53 (June 1928), 22; Innis Brown, "Same Old Hagen," *American Golfer,* 31 (June 1928), 9; William Clarkson, "The British Open," *Golf Illustrated,* 29 (June 1928), 27; "Hagen's Victory Abroad," ibid., 19; Hagen and Heck, *Walter Hagen Story,* 196; Harlow, "The Return of Hagen's Ghost," 42.

10. Charles Bartlett, "Walter in Wonderland," *Professional Golfer,* 33 (June 1951), 18; *New York Times,* May 12, 1928, 11.

11. London *Times,* May 14–28, 1928; *New York Times,* May 29, 1928, 19; "How Hagen and Harlow Hit It Off," *Professional Golfer of America,* 9 (January 1929), 21.

12. *New York Times,* June 9, 1928, 13; Hagen and Heck, *Walter Hagen Story,* 199.

13. *Baltimore Sun,* October 1–6, 1928; E.M. Adams, "Leo Diegel Dethrones King Hagen," *Golfers Magazine,* 54 (November 1928), 18. When the P.G.A. asked Hagen for the Rodman Wanamaker Cup, he could not find it. Supposedly, he had had it for too long and had lost it; another was made for Diegel. See John Lardner, "Rowdy Rebel of the Fairways," *True,* 40 (February, 1959), 91.

14. "How Hagen and Harlow Hit It Off," 21; *New York Times,* October 28, 1928, II, 1.

15. *Boston Globe,* September 11, 1928; Herbert Reed, "Hagen, Hardy Annual," *Outlook,* 149 (23 May 1928), 582; "Canadian Open Championship," *Canadian Golfer,* 14 (August 1928), 320; *New York Times,* August 28, 1928, 21.

16. Robert Harlow, "Walter Hagen, the Artist of Golf," *American Golfer,* 33 (November 1929), 29.

17. *Los Angeles Times,* December 16–31, 1928; *New York Times,* December 23, 1928, X, 6; Hal Sharkey, "Highlights on Western Tournaments," *Golfers Magazine,* 54 (November 1928), 26; Gould B. Martin, "How the Country's Stars Rate This Year," *Metropolitan Golfer,* 6 (December 1928), 26.

18. See Fulton County certificate dated January 3, 1928, admitting Jones to the Georgia bar, roll 1, Robert T. Jones, Jr. Collection, Golf House Library, United States Golf Association, Far Hills, New Jersey (hereafter, "RTJ").

19. *New York Times,* January 5, 1928, 34.

20. For coverage of the $50,000 controversy, see January 8, 1928, XI, 1; "Rob Jones Explains," *Professional Golfer of America,* 8 (February 1928), 20.

21. Richard Miller, *Triumphant Journey: The Saga of Bobby Jones and the Grand Slam of Golf* (New York: Holt Rinehart, and Winston, 1980), 191; interview with Lewis Jones Jr., Canton, Georgia, July 31, 1997.

22. *Washington Post,* April 28–29, 1928; *New York Times,* January 24, 1928, 33; March 7, 1928, 23; March 17, 1928, 10; April 18, 1928, 20; April 29, 1928, XI, 4; April 30, 1928, 16; June 4, 1928, 16.

23. *Chicago Tribune,* June 15–25, 1928; *New York Times,* June 23, 1928; Grantland Rice, "Another Jones or Vardon?" *American Golfer,* 31 (August 1928), 5; George Girard, "Farrell Wins the Open," *Golf Illustrated,* 29 (July 1928), 33. Telephone interview with Thomas Hancock (son of Roland Hancock), October 9, 1997; Darsie L. Darsie, *My Greatest Day in Golf* (New York: A.S. Barnes and Company, 1950), 56.

24. *New York Times,* June 26, 1928, 24.

25. Ibid., August 28, 1928; Grantland Rice, "Making of the Mighty," *Collier's,* 82 (3 November 1928), 17.

26. *Chicago Tribune,* August 30–September 1, 1928; "British Golfing Waterloo," *Golf Monthly,* 19 (October 1928), 17; Walter Hagen, "The Walker Cup Matches," *Golf Illustrated,* 30 (October 1928) 26; E.M. Adams, "America Scores Fifth Victory in Walker Cup Matches," *Golfers Magazine,* 54 (October 1928), 21.

27. *New York Times,* September 6, 1928, 17.

28. *Boston Globe,* September 10–15, 1928; Sol Metzger, "Great Golf Shots," *Country Life,* 60 (September 1931), 49–50; Grantland Rice, "The Cyclonic Bobby Jones," *American Golfer,* 32 (October 1928), 3; Arthur B. Sweet, "Bobby Jones Wins Fourth National Amateur," *Golfers Magazine,* 54 (October 1928), 9; "The Jones Complex on the Golf Links," *Literary Digest,* 99 (6 October 1928), 43–48; *New York Times,* September 17, 1928, 18; September 18, 1928, 27.

29. *Atlanta Constitution,* November 27, 1928.

30. *Atlanta Constitution,* January 6, 1929; O.B. Keeler, "Two Champions Measure Strides," *American Golfer,* 32 (February 1929), 7; Herbert Warren

Wind, *The Story of American Golf,* third edition (New York: Alfred A. Knopf, 1975), 176.

31. *Atlanta Constitution,* May 9, 1929; O.B. Keeler, "The Challenge of Horton Smith," *American Golfer,* 32 (August 1929), 15; interview with Eugene Branch (Jones's former law partner), July 30, 1997, Atlanta, Georgia; *New York Times,* April 3, 1929, 33; May 9, 1929, 22.

32. *New York Times,* June 13, 1929, 23.

33. *New York World,* July 1, 1929; *New York Herald,* June 27–July 1, 1929; *New York Times,* July 1, 1929, 1; June 21, 1929, 38; *Atlanta Constitution,* June 16, 1929; Grantland Rice, "They Can't Stop Jones—Yet," *American Golfer,* 32 (August 1929), 11; Wm. Henry Beers, "The National Open," *Golf Illustrated,* 31 (August 1929), 12; Keeler, "Challenge of Horton Smith," 58; A.W. Tillinghast, "The Open at Winged Foot," *Golf Illustrated,* 31 (June 1929), 42; O.B. Keeler, *The Boys' Life of Bobby Jones* (New York: Harper and Brothers, 1931), 262–267.

34. *Atlanta Constitution,* July 3, 1929.

35. Ibid., July 5–August 15, 1929; Grantland Rice, "The Trial of Lawyer Jones," *Collier's,* 84 (17 August 1929), 10.

36. *San Francisco Chronicle,* August 18–September 1, 1929; "Golf Gossip," *American Golfer,* 33 (October 1929), 53.

37. Jones played solidly, if not brilliantly, in his match with Goodman. Jones began slowly—a cardinal sin in eighteen-hole match play—and, although he squared the contest, he could never take the lead. *San Francisco Chronicle,* September 2, 1929; *New York Times,* September 1, 1929, X, 1; August 31, 1928, 12; O.B. Keeler, "It Was a Great Championship," *American Golfer,* 33 (October 1929), 19; Harold P. Farrington, "The National Amateur Golf Championship," *Golf Illustrated,* 32 (October 1929), 10.

38. Ibid; *New York Times,* September 5–6, 1929; September 9, 1929, 22; E.M. Adams, "Harrison Johnston Replaces Bobby Jones," *Golfers Magazine,* 56 (October 1929), 7; Ring Lardner, "Bobby or Bust," *Collier's,* 84 (21 December 1929), 19; Keeler, *Boys' Life of Bobby Jones,* 270.

39. In a pair of ironies, Jones shot a medal round of 75 to Goodman's 76, and Goodman was eliminated in the second round. Harrison Johnston went on to become the unlikely winner of the 1929 U.S. Amateur. Also, Augusta National fans will recall that Jones's first-round elimination offered him an opportunity to discuss golf course architecture with Dr. Alister MacKenzie, whom he had met well before 1929. See endnote #24 of chapter 10.

40. *San Francisco Chronicle,* September 9, 1929; September 12, 1919.

41. "Is Bobby Jones Losing Interest in Golf?" *Literary Digest,* 102 (21 September 1929), 66–69; *New York Times,* November 7, 1929, 32; November 15, 1929, 24; Miller, *Triumphant Journey,* 151.

42. Allen, *Only Yesterday,* 356.

43. *Los Angeles Times,* February 1, 1929; *Walter C. Hagen vs. Edna C. Hagen,* January 31, 1929, Superior Court, Los Angeles County, California, County Records Center, Los Angeles, California; *New York Times,* September 9, 1929, 15.

44. *New York Times,* January 17, 1929, 3; in 1927 a team of American homebreds had won convincingly on U.S. soil. Interestingly, golf writers have refused to refer to the 1926 matches, in which the American side used some foreign-born players, as the first Ryder Cup contest, despite the *New York Times*'s and *London Times*'s 1926 reports of Samuel Ryder's involvement. Instead, the 1927 matches have become regarded as the inaugural competition. See Bob Bubka and Tom Clavin, *The Ryder Cup: Golf's Greatest Event* (New York: Crown Publishers, 1999).

45. Ibid., January 20, 1929, X, 8. The British also cried "foul" regarding American professionalism of the Olympics in this period. See Mark Dyreson, *Making the American Team: Sport, Culture, and the Olympic Experience* (Urbana/Chicago: University of Illinois Press, 1998), 163–169.

46. *New York Times,* February 3, 1929, X, 2.

47. *Los Angeles Times,* January 10–15, 1929; *Miami Herald,* March 11–24, 1929.

48. For 1929 Ryder Cup, see Hagen and Heck, *Walter Hagen Story,* 211; *London Times,* April 17–29, 1929; *New York Times,* April 10, 1929, 27; April 25, 1929, 25; April 26, 1929, 19; April 27, 1929, 11; April 28, 1929, XI, 1; *London Observer,* April 28, 1929; E.M. Cockell, "At Moortown: A Tale of the Iron," *Golf Illustrated* (British), 47 (3 May 1929), 122; Brownlow Wilson, "Horton Smith—Golf's New Star," *Golf Illustrated,* 32 (November 1929), 16; George Greenwood, "The Ryder Cup Matches," *Golf Illustrated,* 31 (June 1929), 28; Ernest Hargreaves and Jim Gregson, *Caddie in the Golden Age* (London: Partridge Press, 1993), 24.

49. Hargreaves and Gregson, *Caddie in the Golden Age,* 27; *New York Times,* April 29, 1929, 19.

50. Hagen's total for the 1929 British Open was 292. *London Times,* May 7–11, 1929; *New York Times,* May 5, 1929, XI; May 9, 1929, 22; Grantland Rice, "The Battle for the British Open," *American Golfer,* 32 (May 1929), 15; George Girard, "Walter Hagen Again Wins the British Open," *Golf Illustrated,* 31 (June 1929), 30; William Campbell, "The British Open Championship at Muirfield," *Golf Illustrated* (British), 47 (17 May 1929), 180; E.M. Adams, "Hagen Wins Again," *Golfers Magazine,* 55 (June 1929), 60; Al Laney, *Following the Leaders* (Reprint for Classics of Golf, Ailsa, Inc., 1991), 53; Hagen and Heck, *Walter Hagen Story,* 163.

51. *London Observer,* May 12, 1929; *New York Times,* May 11, 1929, 15; Adams, "Hagen Wins Again," 20; "Hagen Again Crowned Golfing King," *Canadian Golfer,* 15 (May 1929), 57; Hargreaves and Gregson, *Caddie in the Golden Age,* 49.

52. Adams, "Hagen Wins Again," 60; Girard, "Walter Hagen Again Wins the British Open," 30; "Bravo! Hagen," *Golf Illustrated* (British), 47 (17 May 1929), 170; P.C. Pulver, "The Man Who Never Is Through," *Professional Golfer of America,* 10 (June 1929), 5; Grantland Rice, "Hagen, the Lion Tamer," 32 *American Golfer* (June 1929), 15; *New York Times,* May 11, 1929, 15.

53. "Hagen and His Game with the Prince of Wales," *Canadian Golfer,* 15 (June 1929), 178; *New York Times,* May 13, 1929, 19; May 16, 1929, 35; May 17, 1929, 30; May 19, 1929, XI, 1; May 18, 1929, 10.

54. Hagen and Heck, *Walter Hagen Story,* 250.

55. "Walter Hagen," *Golf Illustrated* (British) 47 (31 May 1929), 240; Harold Hilton, "Hagen versus Compston at Moor Park," ibid., (7 June 1929), 276.

56. *New York Times,* June 9, 1929, X, 8.

57. "Diegel Again Crowned Canadian Golfing King," *Canadian Golfer,* 15 (August 1929), 303; Margaret Bell, "Short Putts," *Golfers Magazine,* 56 (November 1929), 31; Hagen and Heck, *Walter Hagen Story,* 239.

58. *Los Angeles Times,* December 1–8, 1929; Bell, "Short Putts," 31; "The P.G.A. Championship," *Golf Illustrated,* 32 (January 1930), 13; Hagen and Heck, *Walter Hagen Story,* 239; Herbert W. Wind includes a slightly different version of the Fay Wray fumble in *The Story of American Golf,* 171; my description comes from contemporary *Los Angeles Times* coverage.

59. "Hagen, from Fishing to Golf," *Professional Golfer of America,* 10 (October 1929), 14.

Chapter 9

1. Margaret Bell, "Short Putts," *Golfers Magazine,* 57 (February 1930), 33; P.C. Pulver, "Australian Tour for Hagen," *Professional Golfer of America,* 10, (October 1929), 5; Margaret Bell, "Short Putts," *Golfers Magazine,* 56 (November 1929), 31; ibid., (December 1929), 25; "Editorial Comment," *Professional Golfer of America,* 11 (November 1930), 19; *New York Times,* January 13, 1930, 17; January 24, 1930, 29; February 25, 1930, 33; March 2, 1930, XI, 4.

2. *Seattle Times,* June 22, 1930; *St. Paul Pioneer-Press,* July 10, 1930; Walter Hagen and Margaret Seaton Heck, *The Walter Hagen Story,* (New York: Simon and Schuster, 1956), 243–249; *New York Times,* March 20, 1930, 22; May 31, 1930, 8.

3. See "Match Play" advertisement in *Golf Illustrated,* 57 (April 1930), 61, and "Golf Champions Take to the Screen," *American Golfer,* 33 (April 1930), 37; *Walter Hagen vs. Rochester Red Wing Baseball Club,* January 10, 1936, State Supreme Court, Monroe County, New York; Hagen and Heck, *Walter Hagen Story,* 259.

4. See advertisements in *American Golfer,* 33 (May 1930), 5; (July 1930), 57; (June 1930), 51; *Golfdom,* 4 (January 1930); (April 1930), 45; Janet Seagle, *The Clubmakers* (Far Hills, NJ: United States Golf Association, 1984), 73, 123.

5. "Bob Harlow, Tournament Bureau Manager," *Professional Golfer of America,* 11 (November 1930), 7; Herbert Graffis, *The PGA: The Official History of the Professional Golfers' Association of America* (New York: Thomas Y. Crowell Company, 1975), 148–151.

6. *Seattle Times,* June 22, 1930.

7. *Detroit News,* August 20–24, 1930; *St. Louis Post-Dispatch,* September 19–22, 1930; *Hamilton Spectator* (Ontario), July 28, 1930.

8. Grantland Rice, "Golf's Bad Boy," *Collier's,* 85 (15 February 1930), 18.

9. Bobby Jones, "Not My Business," *Collier's*, 85 (26 April 1930), 15.

10. William E. Woodward, "What Makes Him Click?" *American Magazine*, 109, (April 1930), 36–38; *Atlanta Constitution*, February 19, 1930; Richard Gordin, "Robert Tyre Jones Jr.: His Life and Contributions to Golf," (Ph.D. dissertation: Ohio State University, 1967), 113.

11. Savannah *Morning-News*, February 20–22, 1930; *Atlanta Constitution*, February 19–23, 1930; Robert Tyre Jones Jr., *Golf Is My Game*, (New York: Doubleday & Company, 1960), 108.

12. *Atlanta Journal*, March 10, March 16, 1930; *Atlanta Constitution*, March 16, 1930; O.B. Keeler, "Golf Gossip," *American Golfer*, 33 (April 1930), 23.

13. *Atlanta Constitution*, March 31–April 2, 1930; O.B. Keeler, "Golf Gossip," *American Golfer*, 33 (May 1930), 42; Grantland Rice, "Bobby Jones at the Peak," *American Golfer*, 33 (May 1930), 19 and "Keeping up with Jones," *Collier's*, 85 (24 May 1930), 22; Keeler, "The Battle at Hoylake," *American Golfer*, 33 (August 1930), 54.

14. *Atlanta Constitution*, April 22, April 25, 1930; *New York Times*, April 30, 1930, 21; May 1, 1930, 24; May 7, 1930, 35.

15. *New York Times*, May 14, 1930, 19.

16. *London Times*, May 6–17, 1930; *New York Times*, May 16, 1930, 26.

17. *London Times*, May 20, 1930; *New York Times*, May 19, 1930, 25; May 20, 1930, 34; May 25, 1930, XI, 8; May 26, 1930, 17.

18. In the second round, Jones defeated Sid Roper 3 and 2, and in the third round, he eliminated Cowan Shankland, 5 and 3. *London Times*, May 29, 1930; *New York Times*, May 29, 1930, 15; "Behind the Scenes," *Golf Monthly*, 20 (June 1930), 18; O.B. Keeler, "Bobby Jones Completes the Cycle," *American Golfer*, 33 (July 1930), 12; Letter to Cyril Tolley, October 20, 1958, roll 5, RTJ; Jones, *Golf Is My Game*, 108.

19. Jones crushed Britisher G.O. Watt 7 and 6 in the fifth round. *New York Times*, May 30, 1930, 14. May 31, 1930, 7; *London Times*, May 30, 1930; George Voigt, "The British Amateur," *Golf Journal*, 25 (March 1972), 12–13; Jones, *Golf Is My Game*, 128–129; Gordin, "Robert Tyre Jones Jr.," 125; Richard Miller, *Triumphant Journey: The Saga of Bobby Jones and the Grand Slam of Golf* (New York: Holt, Rinehart and Winston, 1980), 97–108.

20. *London Observer*, June 1, 1930; *London Times*, June 2, 1930; Francis Ouimet, *A Game of Golf: A Book of Reminiscence* (Boston: Houghton Mifflin Company, 1932), 212–230.

21. "Bobby Jones on His Victory," *Golf Monthly*, 20 (June 1930), 29; Herbert W. Wind, "The Grand Slam," in Robert Trent Jones, ed., *Great Golf Stories* (New York: Galahad Books, 1987), 118–126; *New York Times*, June 1, 1930, X, 4; "Mr. 'Bobby' Jones Wins the British Amateur," *Golf Illustrated*, 33 (July 1930), 16.

22. "Tribute to Jones," *Professional Golfer of America*, 11 (April 1931), 23.

23. *New York Times*, June 2, 1930, 17; June 7, 1930.

24. Jones, *Golf Is My Game*, 133.

25. For 1930 British Open, see *London Times*, June 18–21, 1930; *New York Times*, June 12, 1930, 19; June 18, 1930, 19; June 20, 1930, 26; "Inci-

dents of the Open Championship," *Golf Monthly,* 20 (July 1930), 40; John G. Anderson, "British Golf, and American," *American Golfer,* 33 (September 1930), 62; Keeler, "The Battle at Hoylake," 56; Geoffrey Cousins and Tom Scott, *A Century of Opens* (London: Frederick Muller, 1971), 102–104; Miller, *Triumphant Journey,* 108–114.

26. George Greenwood, "Mr. 'Bobby' Jones' Double Event," *Golf Illustrated,* 33 (August 1930), 54; *New York Times,* June 21, 1930, 12.

27. *Golf Monthly,* 20 (July 1930), 60; *New York Times,* June 22, 1930, X, 1; June 28, 1930, 10.

28. *New York Times,* June 28, 1930, 10; June 30, 1930, 15; July 3, 1930, 1; *New York World,* July 3, 1930; Jones, *Golf Is My Game,* 143.

29. *New York Times,* June 28, 1930, 10; *St. Paul Pioneer-Press,* July 4, 1930.

30. For pretournament coverage of the 1930 U.S. Open, I relied upon: *St. Paul Pioneer-Press,* July 7–10, 1930; *New York Times,* June 27, 1930, 18; July 6, 1930, X, 5; July 8, 1930, 20; July 10, 1930, 21; Grantland Rice, "The Open Classic at Interlachen," *American Golfer,* 33 (July 1930), 27.

31. *St. Paul Pioneer-Press,* July 11, 13, 1930; *New York Times,* July 11, 1930, 13.

32. *St. Paul Pioneer-Press,* July 12, 1930; *New York Times,* September 18, 1950, 28; Jones, *Golf Is My Game,* 147; Letter to L.W. Robert, Jr., June 26, 1970, RTJ; Joe Turnesa, "The U.S. Open," *Golf Journal,* 25 (March 1972), 14; *New York Times,* September 5, 1955, 15.

33. Poor Mac Smith, as he had done in the British Open, posted the lowest final round of the event, a 70. *St. Paul Pioneer-Press,* July 13, 1930; *Chicago Tribune,* July 13, 1930; Jones, *Golf Is My Game,* 152; O.B. Keeler, "Jones Writes More History," *American Golfer,* 33 (August 1930), 14; Lincoln Werden, "The U.S. Open at Interlachen," *Golf Illustrated,* 33 (August 1930), 12.

34. George Trevor, "A Very Human Golf Machine," *Outlook and Independent,* 155 (30 July 1930), 502; *St. Paul Pioneer-Press,* July 13, 1930; Grantland Rice, "Last Stop—Merion," *American Golfer,* 33 (August 1930), 11.

35. For coverage of Jones's grand reception, I used the following material: *Atlanta Constitution,* July 15, 1930; "The Coronation of Emperor Jones," *Literary Digest,* 106 (2 August 1930), 32; *New York Times,* July 15, 1930, 17.

36. "Flyer Stops Train Before Flaming Span," newsclipping in BJF; Jones, *Golf Is My Game,* 154; Jones places the deadly East Lake storm in the summer of 1930, but it appears he related the same story to Paul Gallico in October 1929, so he must have recalled the date incorrectly in *Golf Is My Game.* See Paul Gallico, "Jones of Jonesville, Georgia," *Liberty* (26 October 1929), 52.

37. *Atlanta Constitution,* September 15–16, 1930; *Philadelphia Inquirer,* September 17, 1930.

38. Grantland Rice, "Ace of Clubs," *Collier's,* 86 (27 September 1930), 15; "From Merion to Merion," *American Golfer,* 33 (September 1930), 13.

39. *New York Times,* September 18, 1930, 36; September 19, 1930, 30; *Philadelphia Inquirer,* September 20, 1930; Jess Sweetser, "The U.S. Amateur," *Golf Journal,* 25 (March 1972), 16.

40. For coverage of the 1930 U.S. Amateur, see *Philadelphia Inquirer,* September 24–28, 1930; *Atlanta Constitution,* September 29, 1930; New York *Times,* September 26, 1930, 18; *New York Herald-Tribune,* September 28, 1930; "The U.S. Amateur Championship," *Golf Illustrated,* 34 (November 1930), 10; Grantland Rice, "Untrod Ground," *American Golfer,* 34 (November 1930), 7; Warren Brown, "That One Man Quartet," *Golfers Magazine,* 58 (November 1930), 21.

41. *Philadelphia Inquirer,* September 28, 1930; *New York Times,* September 28, 1930, X, 1; "And Now Bobby Jones Plans to Golf for Pleasure," *Literary Digest,* 107, (11 October 1930), 42; Keeler, "Jones Writes More History," 14 and "Speaking of Retiring," *American Golfer,* 34 (November 1930), 12.

42. *Atlanta Constitution,* November 18, 1930; Jones, *Golf Is My Game,* 173; *New York Herald-Tribune,* November 18, 1930; George Sargent, "Sargent Explains Movie Innovation," *Professional Golfer of America,* 11 (October 1930), 12; Francis J. Powers, "Bobby Jones Retires From Competitive Golf," *Golfers Magazine,* 58 (December 1930), 7; Sidney Matthew, *The Life and Times of Bobby Jones* (Chelsea, MI: Sleeping Bear Press, 1995), 200.

43. *Philadelphia Inquirer,* September 23, 1930; Jones, *Golf Is My Game,* 171–172.

44. *Philadelphia Inquirer,* September 30, 1930; *Atlanta Constitution,* September 28–30, 1930; *New York Times,* September 28, 1930, X, 1; September 30, 1930, 31.

45. *London Observer,* November 23, 1930; *New York Times,* October 1, 1930, 33; George Trevor, "'The Rest' versus Jones," *Outlook and Independent,* 155 (16 July 1930), 420.

46. "Amateur or Professional?" *Golf Monthly,* 20 (December 1930), 17.

47. *New York Times,* November 18, 1930, 24; *New York Herald-Tribune,* September 28, 1930.

48. *London Times,* November 18–19, 1930; *London Observer,* November 23, 1930.

49. Francis J. Powers, "Bobby Jones Retires from Competitive Golf," *Golfers Magazine,* 58 (December 1930), 7; *New York Times,* November 19, 1930.

50. "Will Bobby Jones Come Back?" *Literary Digest,* 107 (6 December 1930), 43–48.

Chapter 10

1. Hamilton *Spectator* (Ontario), July 10–15, 1931; *Detroit News,* July 9–15, 1931; "Walter Hagen Wins at Last," *Canadian Golfer,* 17 (July 1931), 219; "Another Victory for Battling 'Sir' Walter," *Literary Digest* 110 (1 August 1931), 36; "The Haig Came Back," *Professional Golfer of America* 12 (August 1931), 20; H.G. Salsinger, "Completing the Cycle," *Golfers Magazine,* 60 (August 1931), 5.

2. "The Haig Landed His Championship," *Professional Golfer of America*, 13 (August 1932), 10; *New York Times*, July 3, 1932, III, 3; October 10, 1932, 22.

3. Innis Brown, "When Hagen's Putting Touch Failed," *American Golfer*, 35 (March 1932), 12.

4. *Chicago Tribune*, March 8, 1933; *Jacksonville Times-Union*, March 11–12, 1933; "Hagen Decides to Show 'Em at Charleston," *Professional Golfer of America*, 13 (May 1933), 19. Hagen did not accept the prize money for winning his own event. Al Barkow's "player biographies" in *The History of the PGA Tour* (New York: Doubleday, 1989), lists the Tournament of the Gardens Open as another victory for Hagen in 1933.

5. *New York Times*, July 6, 1933, 17.

6. *Golf Illustrated* (British), July 28–August 25, 1933; *New York Times*, June 27, 1933, 20; June 28, 1933, 25; July 30, 1933, III, 1; August 5, 1933, 14.

7. *Rochester Chronicle and Democrat* and *Times-Union*, August 6–11, 1934.

8. *Tampa Tribune*, February 21–25, 1935; Pittsburgh *Press*, June 10, 1935.

9. Vincent Flaherty, "The Hagen Guy," *Sportfolio* (September 1947), 115.

10. John Lardner, "The Haig: Rowdy Rebel of the Fairways," *True*, 40 (February 1959), 54; Ted Shane, "The Fabulous Haig, Prince of Golf," *Reader's Digest*, 61 (October 1952), 41.

11. Art Stockdale, "Hagen Was Good to the Last Shot," *Sport* (April 1954), 24.

12. *New York Times*, November 18, 1936, 33.

13. Joe Kirkwood and Barbara Fey, *Links of Life* (Ronald R. Kirkwood, 1973), 26; Walter Hagen and Margaret Seaton Heck, *The Walter Hagen Story* (New York: Simon and Schuster, 1956), 261; 296–318; interview with Ken Janke, family friend and executor of Hagen's estate, May 14, 1997, Birmingham, Michigan.

14. *Edna C. Hagen vs. Walter Hagen*, November 25, 1936, Sixth Circuit Court of Florida, Pinellas County, Florida; *New York Times*, December 27, 1936, 32; March 30, 1937, 9; June 26, 1937, 13; *Hagen vs. Hagen*, January 27, 1937, Superior Court of New Jersey, County of Essex, New Jersey.

15. *Walter Hagen vs. Rochester Red Wing Baseball Club, Inc.*, November 12, 1935, New York State Supreme Court, Monroe County, New York.

16. In researching this tragic event in Hagen's life, I took material from the following: *St. Paul Pioneer-Press* and *Minneapolis Tribune*, July 15, 1934; *Minneapolis Star*, July 16–18, 1934; Al Barkow, *Golf's Golden Grind: The History of the Tour* (NY: Harcourt, Brace, Jovanovich, 1974), 120–121; interview with Joseph Peck, friend of Walter Hagen, October 16, 1997, Traverse City, Michigan.

17. For Hagen and his son, see Walter Hagen, "Pros and Their Sons," *Metropolitan Golfer*, 4 (September 1926), 18; *New York Times*, July 5, 1933, 14; Hagen and Heck, *Walter Hagen Story*, 224–225.

18. "Jones Joins Spalding," *Professional Golfer of America*, 12 (July 1931), 22; Robert Tyre Jones, Jr., *Golf Is My Game* (New York: Doubleday & Company, 1960), 193.

19. Francis J. Powers, "Bobby Jones Retires from Competitive Golf," *Golfers Magazine,* 58 (December 1930), 7.

20. For Jones's Hollywood experience, I used the following: "Bobby Jones Upsets Hollywood," *Literary Digest,* 109 (18 April 1931), 44–45; O.B. Keeler, "The Camera Takes the Place of the Gallery for Bobby Jones," *Golfers Magazine,* 59 (May 1931), 11; "Honor Bobby Jones," ibid., 59 (May 1959), 61; Robert A. Blodgett, "The King Tees Up for the Movies," ibid., 59 (February 1931), 10; "How Bobby Will Make Movies," "Bobby Jones Quits Movies Forever, Starts Home," "The Joneses Off for the Coast," and "Bobby Jones Signs Long Film Contract," newspaper clippings in the Bobby Jones File, Special Collections, Robert W. Woodruff Library, Emory University, Atlanta Georgia (hereafter "BJF"). *New York Times,* March 5, 1933, IX, 4; Richard Gordin, "Robert Tyre Jones, Jr.: His Life and Contributions to Golf" (Ph.D. dissertation, Ohio State University, 1967), 150.

21. For Jones's radio interviews, see *New York Times,* January 15, 1931, 27; advertisement in *American Golfer,* 34 (February 1931); Jones, *Golf Is My Game,* 175.

22. Advertisement in *Professional Golfer of America,* 12 (December 1931), 9. See also Sidney Matthew, *The History of Bobby Jones' Clubs* (Tallahassee, FL: I.Q. Press, 1992), 43–47.

23. Jones, *Golf Is My Game,* 192–200; Gordin, "Robert Tyre Jones, Jr.," 153–162; the story of Augusta National and the Masters has been told over and over again, most recently in David Owen, *The Making of the Masters: Clifford Roberts, Augusta National, and Golf's Most Prestigious Tournament* (New York: Simon and Schuster, 1999); Steve Eubanks, *Augusta: Home of the Masters Tournament* (Nashville, TN: Rutledge Hill Press, 1997) and Curt Sampson, *The Masters: Money, Power, and Golf in Augusta, Georgia* (New York: Villard Press, 1998). See also Charles Price, *A Golf Story: Bobby Jones, Augusta National, and the Masters Tournament* (New York: Atheneum, 1986); Clifford Roberts, *The Story of the Augusta National Golf Club* (New York: Doubleday & Company, Inc., 1976).

24. Ibid; Jones, *Golf Is My Game,* 195. For years it has been assumed and written that Jones first met MacKenzie in California after his early elimination from the 1929 U.S. Amateur. The Jones/MacKenzie relationship actually goes back to at least 1926. See Sidney L. Matthew, 'Birth of Bobby's Dream Course,' *Links* 12 (April 1999), 54.

25. *Augusta Chronicle,* April 3, 1966; also quoted in Gordin, "Robert Tyre Jones, Jr.," 157.

26. George Trevor, "Will Bobby Jones Come Back?" *Outlook,* 157 (11 February 1931), 227.

27. *New York Times,* June 30, 1931, 31; September 22, 1931; February 19, 1932, 25; *Atlanta Constitution,* February 8, 1948.

28. Grantland Rice, "Bobby Jones Comes Back," *American Golfer,* 37 (March 1934), 7; *New York Times,* December 19, 1933, 29.

29. *Atlanta Constitution,* March 22, 1934; *New York Times,* March 4, 1934, III, 8; March 13, 1934, 28; March 20, 1934, 28.

30. For coverage of Jones's first Masters, I relied on the following: *Atlanta Constitution*, March 24–28, 1934; *New York Times*, March 23, 1934, 30; March 24, 1934, 11; March 25, 1934, III, 2; March 26, 1934, 24; Lester Rice, "Bobby Jones Loses at Golf, But Wins Affections of Rivals," *Literary Digest*, 117, (7 April 1934), 42; Jones, *Golf Is My Game*, 197. Apparently Jones occasionally uttered the term "Masters" early on, despite what he wrote in *Golf Is My Game* about being reluctant to use the "presumptuous" label.

31. For additional commentary on Jones's performance, including the Sarazen quotation, see *New York Times*, March 29, 1934, 31; Robert Harlow, "A Distinct Advance for Pro Golf," *Professional Golfer of America*, 14 (April 1934), 8; Grantland Rice, "The Masters' Fixture," *American Golfer*, 37 (May 1934), 23; Gordin, "Robert Tyre Jones, Jr.," 158.

32. *London Times*, July 28, 1936; *New York Times*, July 28, 1936, 14; April 7, 1938, 28; Grantland Rice, *The Tumult and the Shouting* (New York: A.S. Barnes & Company, 1954), 86–87.

33. "Bobby Jones' Home Site of Decorator Show House No. 8," newspaper clipping in BJF; Richard Miller, *Triumphant Journey: The Saga of Bobby Jones and the Grand Slam of Golf* (New York: Holt, Rinehart, and Winston, 1980), 215.

34. *New York Times*, April 28, 1936, 1; May 1, 1936, 29; May 3, 1936, IV, 8.

35. H.B. Martin, "Golf Celebrates a Fiftieth Birthday," *New York Times Magazine*, February 20, 1938; "Ball Bat or Golf Club—What's the Answer?" *Literary Digest*, 111 (26 December 1931), 33.

36. *New York Times*, September 24, 1937, 21; Furman Bisher, *The Masters: Augusta Revisited* (Birmingham, AL: Oxmoor House, Inc., 1976), 30.

37. Interview with Robert Tyre Jones IV, October 14, 1997, Atlanta, Georgia. See Miller, *Triumphant Journey*, 214–215 and Bisher, *The Masters*, 29. Miller's book is particularly strong on the Jones family.

38. "Hale," not "Hail." Hale was the name of the man who suggested the fund-raising event. O.B. Keeler, "Golf for the Nation's Sake," *Esquire* (June 1942), 26; Herbert B. Graffis, *The PGA: The Official History of the Professional Golfers' Association of America* (New York: Thomas Crowell Company, 1975), 220–248; Charles Price, *A Golf Story*, 108; *New York Times*, August 24, 1941, V, 1; August 25, 1941, 20; June 16, 1942, 29; June 19–20, 1942, 29; June 20, 1942, 19.

39. For material on the Nassau benefit, see *New York Times*, September 5, 1950, 34; Hagen and Heck, *Walter Hagen Story*, 288–289; *New York Times*, April 8, 1941; Fred Corcoran, *Unplayable Lies* (New York: Duell, Sloan and Pearce, 1965), 76–77.

40. *New York Times*, May 26, 1942, 29; May 27, 1942, 30; April 9, 1941, 36; October 9, 1947, 33; January 3, 1949, 15.

41. *Detroit News* and *Free-Press*, September 6, 1950; *New York Times*, October 7, 1969, 47.

42. *Detroit News* and *Free Press*, October 6–7, 1969; Hagen and Heck, *Walter Hagen Story*, 322.

43. *Detroit News* and *Free-Press*, May 8, 1952; *New York Times*, March 27, 1966, V, 6; Contracts between Walter Hagen and Robert Wise, May 26, 1952, and May 18, 1953; Ernest Fuller, a friend of the Hagen family and one-time neighbor of Walter Jr., allowed me to examine a thin file of what might be called the "Hagen Papers," which are in his possession; interview with Ernest Fuller, November 26, 1997, Detroit, Michigan.

44. Letter from Margaret Seaton Heck to Walter Hagen, October 10, 1953; interview with Ernest Fuller, November 26, 1997, Detroit, Michigan.

45. *New York Times*, May 20, 1956, VII, 6.

46. Letters from Ty Cobb, June 18, 1960, from Desi Arnaz, May 11, 1959, and telegram from Jackie Gleason, February 17, 1959, to Walter Hagen; interview with Ernest Fuller, November 26, 1997, Detroit, Michigan; letter to Walter Hagen, July 31, 1956; Papers of Dwight D. Eisenhower, Eisenhower Presidential Library, Abilene, Kansas (hereafter "DDE"); *New York Times*, July 11, 1959, 17.

47. Unless otherwise noted, I relied on my interview with Joseph Peck, October 16, 1997, Traverse City, Michigan, for much of the information relating to Hagen's days in Traverse City.

48. Letter from L.B. Icely to Hagen, September 9, 1944, interview with Fuller; letter from Herb Graffis to Robert T. Jones, Jr., October 8, 1968, roll 4, RTJ.

49. Hagen and Heck, *Walter Hagen Story*, 323.

50. Rolls 5 and 6 of the Robert Tyre Jones Jr., Collection contains dozens of military records, orders, etc., that allow one to track his military service to Europe, Golf House Library, United States Golf Association, Far Hills, New Jersey. Specifically, see "Separation Qualification Record" and "Honorable Discharge," roll 5, RTJ; "Bobby Jones Welcomed Home after War Service in Europe" and "Bobby Jones Warns Atlanta to Prepare Against Bombing," newspaper clippings in BJF; Miller, *Triumphant Journey*, 218–220; Price, *A Golf Story*, 107–113; Gordin, "Robert Tyre Jones, Jr.," 164–167; *New York Times*, June 7, 1940, 28.

51. "Separation Qualification Record," roll 5, RTJ; "Son's Publicity Frets Jones," newspaper clipping in BJF; *New York Times*, March 16, 1952, VI, 36; letter from Robert Tyre Jones Jr., August 14, 1956, DDE.

52. Jack Nicklaus with Herbert Warren Wind, *The Greatest Game of All: My Life in Golf* (New York: Simon and Schuster, 1969), 19; Miller, *Triumphant Journey*, 216.

53. Miller, *Triumphant Journey*, 22–48. Much of my material for Jones's illness comes from Miller's book, which has done the best job to date treating the subject. See also, Roberts, *Augusta National Golf Club*, 115–117 and Gordin, "Robert Tyre Jones Jr.," 167–170.

54. Ibid.; *Atlanta Constitution*, November 12, 1948; *New York Times*, November 11, 1948, 42; November 18, 1948, 40.

55. Miller, *Triumphant Journey*, 226. Lou Gehrig's disease leads to the destruction of the nerves themselves, including the brain. Syringomyelia limits itself to an attack on the nerve sheath, or the covering of the nerve, which is why the victim does not lose his mental faculties. Eventually, the nerves are

exposed, leading to a constant, throbbing pain. See John A. Anson, Edward C. Benzel, and Issam A. Awad, eds., *Syringomyelia and the Chiari Malformations* (Park Ridge, IL: American Association of Neurological Surgeons, 1997).

56. Ibid.; Roberts, *Augusta National*, 116–117; Gordin, "Robert Tyre Jones, Jr.," 167–168; Jones, *Golf Is My Game*, 17.

57. Roberts, *Augusta National*, 117; *Boston Globe*, May 19, 1950; *Atlanta Constitution*, October 11, 1952; *New York Times*, May 19, 1950, 36; May 20, 1950, 10; May 25, 1950, 43; October 11, 1952, 25; October 27, 1952, 32; Miller, *Triumphant Journey*, 225–226.

58. *New York Times*, October 19, 1949, 44; March 1952, VI, 36.

59. Alexa Stirling Fraser, "The Most Unforgettable Character I've Ever Met," article, BJF; Al Laney, "He Does Not Live in the Past but in the Present of Golf," *Golf Journal*, 25 (March 1972), 6.

60. *New York Times*, October 7, 1969, 47.

61. Ibid., February 8, 1944, 18; February 2, 1950; March 16, 1952, V, 5; September 21, 1952, V, 7; January 24, 1954, V, 1; September 29, 1955, 42.

62. Ibid., October 31, 1951, 18.

63. Ibid.; Eubanks, *Augusta*, 66–67; Price, *A Golf Story*, 115–116; "Bobby Jones Treasurer of Ga. Citizens for Ike," newspaper clipping, BJF.

64. *Atlanta Journal*, October 14, 1952.

65. *New York Times*, February 2, 1953, V, 2; March 1, 1953, 1. There are approximately four hundred pieces of correspondence between Jones and Eisenhower; most of it is located at the Eisenhower Library in Abilene, Kansas, and the rest belongs to the USGA's Golf House Library in Far Hills, NJ The letters generally deal with birthday wishes, health concerns, golf tips, and bridge games. Eisenhower was never as close to Jones as he was to Roberts and several other club members, but the correspondence reveals a considerable degree of familiarity.

66. The Dixon-Yates Scandal, though, lasted much longer, leading to a Senate investigation and demanding the Eisenhower administration's attention. For coverage of this and other aspects of the Eisenhower presidency, see Chester J. Pach, *The Presidency of Dwight D. Eisenhower* (Lawrence, KS: University of Kansas Press, 1991); Stephen Ambrose, *Eisenhower*, vol. 2, *The President* (New York: Simon and Schuster, 1984). For Jones's involvement with the Dixon-Yates affair, see *Atlanta Constitution*, August 17, 1954; *New York Times*, October 27, 1953, 32; "Boomerang: Dixon-Yates Scandal," *Newsweek*, 44 (30 August 1954), 20, and *Time*, 64 (30 August 1954), 12; "People of the Week," *U.S. News and World Report*, 37 (27 August 1954), 14.

67. *New York Times*, September 18, 1955, 71; September 27, 1955, 26; Atlanta *Constitution*, November 27, 1956; letter from Eisenhower to Jones, December 26, 1960, roll 1, RTJ (emphasis in original).

68. Owen, *Making of the Masters*; Eubanks, *Augusta*; Sampson, *The Masters*.

69. Interview with Charles Elliott, July 31, 1997, Covington, Georgia; Charles Elliott, "Another Grand Slam for Bobby Jones," *Outdoor Life*, 114 (December 1954), 34–35; *Atlanta Constitution*, December 21, 1971.

70. See summary of Jones's business positions compiled for tax purposes, roll 4, RTJ.

71. Letter from Jackson P. Dick to Jones, December 12, 1960, roll 1, RTJ; Miller, *Triumphant Journey*, 231; Price, *A Golf Story*, 119; New York *Times*, November 20, 1960, VII, 10; Jones, *Golf Is My Game*, passim.

72. Letter from Neil C.H. MacKenzie to Jones, September 11, 1958, roll 5, RTJ; *New York Times*, June 19, 1958, 43; October 4, 1958, 16; Bisher, *The Masters*, 30; "Bobby Jones, Old Caddy Reunited at St. Andrews," newspaper clipping in BJF.

73. Gordin, "Robert Tyre Jones Jr.," 173; *New York Times*, October 14, 1958, 47 "News of the Week," *Golf Illustrated* (British), 159 (25 September 1958); "Scott's Corner" and "Australia Win After Playoff," *Golf Illustrated* (British), 159 (16 October, 1958), 588–589.

74. *London Times*, October 10, 1958; Bisher, *The Masters*, 30–31; Herbert W. Wind, "Will Ye No' Come Back Again," *Sports Illustrated*, 9 (27 October 1958), 64.

75. *Atlanta Constitution*, October 10, 1958.

Chapter 11

1. *New York Times*, January 25, 1960, 33; January 27, 1960, 37; Traverse City *Record-Eagle*, January 23, 1962; Rochester *Democrat and Chronicle*, July 25, 1961.

2. Death certificate for Walter C. Hagen III, May 7, 1963, Oakland County, Michigan Department of Health; *Detroit News* and *Free Press*, April 24–28, 1963; interview with Ernest Fuller, November 26, 1997, Detroit, Michigan, and Joseph Peck, October 16, 1997, Traverse City, Michigan.

3. Letter from Charles Price, July 15, 1965, roll 6, Robert Tyre Jones Jr. Collection, Golf House Library, United States Golf Association, Far Hills, New Jersey (hereafter "RTJ").

4. Fred Corcoran, "Unforgettable Walter Hagen," *Reader's Digest*, 100 (April 1972), 107; *New York Times*, July 16, 1965, 23; July 28, 1965, 13; January 28, 1967, 28; *Traverse City Record-Eagle*, July 28, 1965; January 19, 1967.

5. *Detroit News*, June 9, 1996; October 10, 1969.

6. Letter to Traverse City Golf and Country Club, July 21, 1967, roll 2, RTJ; *Traverse City Record-Eagle*, August 15, 1967; *New York Times*, August 15, 1967, 47.

7. *Traverse City Record-Eagle*, August 15, 1967; *Detroit News*, October 6, 1969; John Lardner, "Rowdy Rebel of the Fairways," *True*, 40 (February 1959), 54; Gene Sarazen with Herbert Warren Wind, *Thirty Years of Championship Golf* (London: A & C Black, 1950), 111.

8. Certificate of Death, Walter C. Hagen, October 6, 1969, Grand Traverse County, Michigan Department of Health; Traverse City *Record-Eagle*, October 6, 1969.

9. For Hagen funeral, see: Ibid., *Detroit News* and *Free Press*, October 10, 1969; Ted Shane, "The Fabulous Haig, Prince of Golf," *Reader's Digest*, 61 (October 1952), 44.

10. H.B. Martin, "A Champion in the Making," *Golf Illustrated*, 40 (December 1933), 41; *London Times*, October 7, 1969.

11. Telegram from Bud Harvey, October 6, 1969, roll 2, RTJ; "As They Remember Him," *Professional Golfer*, 50 (November 1969), 6; *Atlanta Constitution*, October 7, 1969.

12. Letter to William C. Caye, February 27, 1962, roll 1 and letter to Charles Yates, February 7, 1962, roll 3, RTJ.

13. Letter to Police Chief Herbert T. Jenkins, May 13, 1965, roll 1; letter to Officer Hoyt Duncan, April 5, 1965, roll 1; letter to Edward Dewey, March 3, 1958, roll 1, RTJ.

14. Quoted in Steve Eubanks, *Augusta: Home of the Masters Tournament* (Nashville, TN: Rutledge Hill Press, 1997), 105. For another reflection on Jones's final years, see Charles Price, "The Last Days of Bobby Jones," *Golf Digest*, 42 (April 1991), 184–188.

15. Letter to Dr. Houston Merritt, September 10, 1968, roll 4; letter to F.H.R. Baraldi, August 20, 1963, roll 1; letter from Georgia Warm Springs Foundation, September 15, 1958, roll 1; letter to Rueben W. Askanase, August 19, 1965, roll 1; medical summary compiled by Richard Wilson, M.D., September 21, 1948, roll 4, RTJ.

16. Eubanks, *Augusta: Home of the Masters Tournament*, 104–105; Sampson, *The Masters: Golf, Money, and Power in Augusta, Georgia* (Villard Press, 1998). David Owen's *The Making of the Masters: Clifford Roberts, Augusta National, and Golf's Most Prestigious Tournament* (New York: Simon and Schuster, 1999) argues that Roberts was not responsible for Jones's removal from the televised ceremony.

17. Ibid., especially Owen, *Making of the Masters;* Jones's application for reinstatement to amateur status, roll 3, RTJ.

18. Letter to Jimmy Demaret, April 25, 1967 and from Demaret, May 4, 1967, roll 1, RTJ.

19. For opposing treatments of this topic—and others—see on one side, Eubanks, *Augusta* and Sampson, *The Masters* and, on the reverse side, Owen, *The Making of the Masters*.

20. Indeed, Elliott claims to have never discussed race relations with Jones. Interview with Charles Elliott, July 31, 1997, Covington, Georgia. For allegations of racism at the Masters, see Charlie Sifford and James Gullo, *Just Let Me Play: The Story of Charlie Sifford, The First Black PGA Golfer* (New York: British American Publishing, 1992).

21. Letter from Robert Tyre Jones Jr., June 15, 1955, Papers of Dwight D. Eisenhower, Eisenhower Presidential Library, Abilene, Kansas (hereafter "DDE").

22. *Bobby Jones on Golf* (1966) and *Bobby Jones on the Basic Golf Swing* (1969) were both instructional works and essentially collections of articles written by Jones years before. See press release to the *Golf Journal*, November 3, 1968 and letter to Joseph Dey, January 29, 1969, roll 2, RTJ; Herbert B. Graffis, *The PGA: The Official History of the Professional Golfers' Association of America* (New York: Thomas Y. Crowell Company, 1975), 439–458;

letter to Bill Clark, September 22, 1971, roll 1, RTJ; letter to Bob Allison, October 9, 1962, roll 1, RTJ.

23. *London Times*, April 7, 1968; *Atlanta Constitution and Journal*, December 19, 1971.

24. Letters to Charles Nicklaus, November 17, 1961 and June 25, 1962, roll 2; letter to Chet Smith, May 11, 1962, roll 3, RTJ; Jack Nicklaus with Herbert W. Wind, *The Greatest Game of All: My Life in Golf* (New York: Simon and Schuster, 1969), 9, 13.

25. Letter to the Office of the City Clerk, Atlanta, September 10, 1969, roll 3, RTJ.

26. *Atlanta Constitution*, March 30, 1958, March 31, 1958; letter to Houston Merritt, September 10, 1968, roll 4, RTJ.

27. Letter to Merritt, RTJ.

28. Letter to Houston Merritt from Ralph Murphy, January 19, 1972, roll 4; letter from Frank Hannigan, November 18, 1971, roll 3, RTJ; Sidney Matthew, *The History of Bobby Jones' Clubs* (Tallahassee, FL: I.Q. Press, 1992), 70.

29. Interview with Elliott, July 31, 1997 and Robert T. Jones IV, October 14, 1997, Atlanta, Georgia; *Atlanta Constitution and Journal*, December 19–20, 1971. Jones also made reference to prayer in a letter to President Eisenhower; see letter from Robert Tyre Jones, Jr., June 15, 1955, DDE.

30. *Atlanta Constitution and Journal*, December 21, 1971.

31. *New York Times*, December 19, 1971, V, 7.

32. *New York Times*, December 19, 1971, 60; *Atlanta Constitution and Journal*, December 19, 1971; *Augusta Chronicle*, December 20, 1971. For a good collection of personal reflections on Jones, see J. Edmund Welch, "Robert Tyre (Bobby) Jones Jr.: His Victories Over Golf and Physical Afflictions," a paper presented at the 1985 annual conference of the North American Society for Sport History and located in the Bobby Jones File, Special Collections, Robert W. Woodruff Library, Emory University, Atlanta, Georgia.

Index